WISH YOU WERE HERE

WISH

INSIDE PINK FLOYD'S

YOU

MUSICAL MILESTONE

WERE

Will Romano

HERE

Backbeat
Books

GUILFORD, CONNECTICUT

Published by Backbeat Books
An imprint of The Rowman & Littlefield Publishing Group, Inc.
4501 Forbes Blvd., Ste. 200, Lanham, MD 20706
www.rowman.com

Distributed by NATIONAL BOOK NETWORK

Copyright © 2020 by Will Romano

Design and composition by Michael Kellner

Library of Congress Cataloging-in-Publication Data available

ISBN 978-1-61713-684-9 (paperback)
ISBN 978-1-4930-5076-5 (e-book)

♾™ The paper used in this publication meets the minimum requirements of
American National Standard for Information Sciences—Permanence of Paper for
Printed Library Materials, ANSI/NISO Z39.48-1992

This book is dedicated to my wife, Sharon, for her encouragement, understanding, strength, and assistance in this project, as well as to my three furry kids—Gilligan, Maggie, and Molly.

CONTENTS

ACKNOWLEDGMENTS

Many individuals helped along the way in completing this project. I want to thank as many people as I can here. I've listed their names in no particular order.

John Beekman at the New Jersey Room (Jersey City Free Public Library), Boston Public Library system, staff at the Los Angeles Public Library, Center for Local and Global History at the Cleveland Public Library, Cully Sommers (Librarian II, Music, Arts, and Literature Department), Detroit Public Library, Hillsborough County Florida Public Library, Vancouver Public Library Information Services, Charlotte A. Kolczynski and the staff of the Arts Department—Music (Boston Public Library), Meg Gers (Periodicals Department, Enoch Pratt Free Library), Nassau County Police Department (Records Division), Jacqline Barnes, Amy Sparks, James Devitt (Director, Public Affairs at New York University), Perry Genovesi (Librarian II, Music Department Parkway Central, Free Library of Philadelphia), Alex Hernandez (Reference Librarian, Denver Central Library), The Ivan Allen Jr. Reference Department at the Atlanta-Fulton Public Library, Andy Kettle, Michael Mazur for his encouragement, Tony Romano for his interest, Ola Torjas at the Swedish Film Institute, the research staff at the Joel D. Valdez Main Library (Pima County, Arizona), staff at the San Diego Public Library, Kelly Walsh, Timothy R. Williams of the Carnegie Library of Pittsburgh, San Francisco Public Library.

For their candor and/or assistance: Dr. Drew Thompson, Jonathan Deull, Christopher Case, Debi Doss, Michael Chaves, Tom Duncan, Simon Francis of Simon Francis Mastering, James Boss, Junior Publicist at Reybee, Inc.

A special thanks to those who agreed to speak or correspond with me for this project, including production icon Alan Parsons, Floyd recording engineer Brian Humphries, bucket-list interview and Hipgnosis cofounder Aubrey Powell ("Po"), former Floyd comanager Peter Jenner, Roger Waters and Floyd collaborator Ron Geesin, Nigel Lesmoir-Gordon for the conscious-raising conversation, Jenny Spires for her conscientious responses, Stephen Pyle for decades of great work and memories of Syd, Martyn Ware of Heaven 17 and Human League fame, Justin Furstenfeld of Blue October, Marco Bellone of Cuneo-based Pink Floyd tribute act Eclysse (as well as his mates and band manager, Renato D'Herin), Cyrille Verdeaux of French progressive rock band Clearlight, Eric "Eroc" Sosinski (Pink Floyd tribute band Wish You Were Here), Warr guitarist Trey Gunn (Security Project, ex-King Crimson), and the great Mike Howlett for his thoughts on Nick Mason and Gong.

Other interviews were conducted with producer Joe Boyd, the lovely and talented Venetta Fields of the Blackberries, glass player Igor Sklyarov, Mono Lake Committee's Communications Director Arya Degenhardt, producer Michael Goldswagger, artist/illustrator Mike McInnerney (the Who), filmmaker Michael Meschke, classical cellist and composer Haflidi Hallgrimsson, former Harvest promotional exec Stuart Watson, legendary producer Shel Talmy, guitarist Parker Griggs of Radio Moscow, photographer Howard Bartrop, Principal Edwards Magic Theatre's Root Cartwright, actress and Pink Floyd support vocalist Durga McBroom, Brit Floyd's Damian Darlington, guitarist Steve Boltz, filmmaker/documentarian Peter Clifton, graphic designer Pearce Marchbank, illustrator Joe Petagno, recording artist and songwriter David Courtney, Unicorn's Pat Martin, former DJ and current radio reporter Jeff Baugh, educator and author George Dennis O'Brien, Kick Horns's Tim Sanders and Simon Clarke, former Hipgnosis retoucher Richard Manning, Eddie Prévost of AMM, Didier Malherbe (formerly of Gong), Pat Boone, Joshua White (of the Joshua Light Show), Neil Rice, and laser Man Jay Heck.

I'm also indebted to the late Soft Machine bassist Hugh Hopper, the Alan Parsons Project's Eric Woolfson (RIP), Supertramp saxophonist John Helliwell, filmmaker Anthony Stern, singer Jody Ashworth (formerly of Trans-Siberian Orchestra), drummer John "Twink" Alder for past interviews, and Richard Evans.

I would like to thank my brother, Michael, without whom I would hardly have listened to some of the more conceptual rockers—and would not have seen Pink Floyd in 1988. Whenever I hear the songs "Run Like Hell" and David Gilmour's "Short and Sweet," my mind immediately conjures an image of Mike's Fender Telecaster, a wall of guitar amps, a digital delay unit, and myself behind the drum kit, trying to keep up . . .

A special thanks to publisher John Cerullo (sorry, John), Clare Cerullo, Barbara Claire, Jessica Kastner, Bernadette Malavarca for her patience, the always-exceptional Marybeth Keating, Steve Thompson, and all at Backbeat and Rowman & Littlefield for helping me make this work possible.

1975: MACHINES, MADNESS, AND MARTYRS

It's strange and somewhat surprising how the United States presidency of Gerald Ford has been reevaluated in the last few decades. Some of Ford's critics, and those who would be given to ridicule, finger-pointing, knee-jerk reactions to political rivals, and outright derision for his pardon of President Richard Nixon have conceded the unique challenges he faced while in office.

History tends to forget sordid details and paints our collective memory with a broad brush. A Gallup poll from 2006 revealed that Ford held a respectable job approval rating of 60 percent, with surprisingly low negatives, and his favorability had risen considerably from when he left office. All this despite the fact that Ford's political fumbles and actual physical tumbles became fodder for skits by Johnny Carson and Chevy Chase of *Saturday Night Live*. Not bad for someone who was never elected to or served a full term in the highest office in the land.

Beyond being underappreciated in their time by critics, Pink Ford, too, received more than they bargained for when they first entered public life. And, like Ford, Floyd also stumbled before national audiences, at least according to reviews by music scribes reporting in the mid-1970s.

What's sometimes overlooked is that both the former occupant of the Oval Office and iconic progressive rock musicians exhibited a certain grace in the face of relative adversity, personal or otherwise. It only stands to reason, then, that Floyd's contemporaneous effort, 1975's *Wish You Were Here* (*WYWH*), deserves a second look and perhaps a reevaluation.

Floyd, arguably one of the greatest rock bands in history, nibbling on the edges of progressive rock, psychedelia, blues rock, and pop, skillfully fused all of these styles into palatable and profound records, often framed by their overarching lyrical architecture.

WYWH sounds nearly as soulful and accessible as any mid-'70s Top 40 entry and yet just as futuristic as the countless (and sometimes best forgotten) efforts recorded by Floyd's so-called prog rock fellow travelers.

Most music fans are aware of 1973's *The Dark Side of the Moon*, a strangely moving thematic song cycle exploring various aspects of life that drive humankind mad, and 1979's *The Wall*, the unavoidable result of former lead vocalist/lyricist and bassist Roger Waters's festering isolationism and the band's overdriving, interstellar ambition.

In the minds of many, *WYWH* will always play second fiddle to these records yet is named as being among Floyd's best, if not their best album. Even members of the band have cited it as such, although large swaths of the public are still in the dark about it. Case in point: When Atlantic Records artist Ed Sheeran joined Nick Mason, Genesis's Mike Rutherford, and The Feeling's Richard Jones for a rendition of "Wish You Were Here" at the closing ceremonies of the 2012 Olympics in London, many of the British singer-songwriter's fans hadn't realized it was a Floyd song he was performing.

Few would deny that the Floyd musical juggernaut and success of *The Dark Side of the Moon* were solidified by *WYWH*, however. According to the Recording Industry Association of America (RIAA), *Dark Side* has sold over fifteen million copies in the US, with estimates of forty to fifty million copies purchased worldwide. And these astronomical figures were tallied prior to Floyd making their music available via Apple's iTunes.

By comparison, sales tracking numbers kept by the RIAA surprisingly reveal that *WYWH* has sold over six million copies in the US alone. (The last time the record was certified was in May 1997.) John Edginton's 2012 documentary on *Wish You Were Here* estimates the album has moved over nineteen million copies worldwide.

We must urge caution, though. The recording industry itself has explained its difficulty in tracking album sales occurring prior to 1980. The official tally, as history has shown, rarely tells the whole story anyway. *WYWH* is a masterpiece in its own right, and its success undoubtedly contributes and expands upon a Pink Floyd Paradox: despite its stratospheric revenues, Floyd is still perceived as fighting the good fight. And fight they did.

Back in the mid-1970s, Floyd was nearly knocked out by an overbearing industry and the unreasonable expectations of breathing the rarified air of rock stardom. Having a No. 1 record and making cash registers ring in various countries across the world far exceeded even the teenage dreams of the band members. What should have been Floyd's ticket to freedom became one of the biggest obstacles to the band's survival, imposing creative lethargy, if not out-and-out musical paralysis.

Waters went so far as to pronounce Floyd all but dead after *Dark Side*. On some level he was correct—at least initially. Dissolving the band unit was discussed, and there was talk of each member going his separate way. Floyd was breaking apart, and perhaps symbolically, both of the band's namesakes, Pink Anderson and Floyd Council died in the mid-1970s. (Anderson on October 12, 1974, in South Carolina and Council on May 9, 1976, in North Carolina.)

Delaying the inevitable, Floyd initially returned to an old experimental idea, titled *Household Objects*, only to abandon it. Unfocused and unmotivated, Floyd turned up in the studio, albeit piecemeal and oftentimes tardy, present physically but absent mentally for a variety of recording sessions.

Had the guys succumbed to inefficiency and buckled to the seductive power of leisure and boredom, we wouldn't be talking about *Wish You Were Here* and perhaps not even Pink Floyd. Lucky for us, and them, Floyd looked inwardly to produce a conceptual, self-referential album mortared by overarching concepts such as absence, madness, self-delusion, and the perils of the music business.

On a personal level, both Waters and drummer Nick Mason were weathering stormy marriages, the turmoil of which was translated into the kinds of vitriol that was spilled into Floyd's often dour and acerbic poetry. Nonetheless, *WYWH* was created in the spirit of camaraderie. Four souls waged war against a rigged and cruel, often inhuman, system, better known in Floydlandia as "The Machine," while also paying tribute to a fallen hero and victim of the industry—the musical Rosetta Stone and bedrock of the band's very existence, guitarist/lead vocalist/lyricist Roger "Syd" Barrett.

Absence, withdrawing from life, is a coping mechanism, Waters theorized, and Syd represented the most extreme example of absence in modern life, inspiring the mammoth centerpiece of the album and grand salutation, "Shine On You Crazy Diamond." The classic title track has been interpreted in many ways, including as an ode to crazy diamond/flawed musical wizard Barrett. Guitarist/vocalist David Gilmour has said that he can't sing "Wish You Were Here" without his mind travelling to Barrett and his once-great presence—and the *absence* of that presence. For Waters it was something of a personal rallying cry: Never Give Up. Don't retreat from the world.

The country-ish twang and emotional depth of the song stand diametrically opposite to the colder, more menacing and mechanical studio-created throb of "Welcome to the Machine." Where "Wish You Were Here" seems like a revelation, the cynicism of ". . . Machine" and "Have a Cigar," the lead off track on the original side 2, threatens to make this one of Floyd's darkest records.

WYWH is not summarily dragged down by the weight of Floyd's psychological baggage, however. Instead, quite paradoxically, the band manages in five tracks (four if you count "Shine On . . ." as one entry) a balance of relative sparseness with expansive self-indulgency, reverence with fragility, bitterness, and despair.

Failing to see how *WYWH* could achieve its full potential, artistically and commercially, *absent* a connecting theme, Waters steered *WYWH* away from being a collection of songs with no common thread, eschewing Gilmour-favored tracks that would eventually appear on the 1977 studio effort *Animals* under the titles "Dogs" and "Sheep."

It was also Waters's idea to split the twenty-six-minute "Shine On You Crazy Diamond" into two large multisectional chunks, of similar duration, cocooning the record in coherency and roundness. As a result, nearly every song on *WYWH* feels connected to overarching lyrical subject matters, as well as the band's collective past. You'd be hard-pressed to make that claim about another Floyd studio record up to that point. *Dark Side* awoke a universal consciousness in fans across the globe, yes, but *WYWH* was as personal as Floyd had ever gotten circa 1975.

As the 1970s wore on, Floyd's albums became less and less about the band and more and more about Waters's singular vision. The misanthropic album *Animals*, from 1977, is shaped by its broad Orwellian generalizations about the human condition. Although *WYWH* offers a glimpse at the venom and bile Waters had been building up inside him, toxins that would eventually poison the band toward him, the lanky bassist/vocalist dominated the creative proceedings from roughly 1976 through to the early 1980s, and his ascendancy to the Floyd musical throne would leave one hapless keyboardist on the battlefield and the others in the dust, lost in the fog of war.

WYWH is, then, a contradiction. It's a consummation of all that made Floyd's music great and, dare we say, glorious, while also being a reliable time capsule: a snapshot freezing the beginning stages of a slo-mo implo destined to rip apart the band.

$$\equiv$$

Throughout 1974 and early 1975, Floyd wondered who, where, and what they were—as a unit and as individuals. Quite simply, it was a band without a country, trying to produce an album of equal or better quality comparative to *Dark Side*, a record that had "trapped us creatively," Gilmour said.

The 1960s underground music ethos did, to a degree, guide Floyd, as they'd spent years wandering the recording industry wilderness performing experimental music before their albums achieved gold and platinum status. But by the mid-1970s, the darlings of the psychedelic London music scene had evolved (devolved?) into a huge cog in the pop music "Machine," a two-billion-dollar industry, estimated *Variety* in January 1975.

Punk's ascendancy and the "kill your idols" aesthetic were on the cusp of breaking into the collective consciousness. Critics, who once exalted the shamanic characteristics of rock stars, launched full-frontal assaults on mainstream music icons and their tendencies toward overindulgent lifestyles and recording projects.

The rock era fostered plenty of chance taking, record making, and record breaking, not to mention nearly continuous sold-out shows, but platinum and gold records were met with cynicism by a press growing disillusioned and bored with the status quo. It was fashionable to target Floyd for its mammoth appeal, as much as it was fair game to call them relics of a different age.

Ushered in by allies in the media, punk would shock the world and attempt to eradicate all before it. But what some critics pegged as antiquated, fans viewed as timelessness. Indeed. Although the band's success likely fueled press attacks, never let it be said that the band had completely forgotten their roots.

It's clear that as Floyd were scaling the heights of fame, the band owed a great debt of gratitude to their fallen former bandleader. For one thing, elements of madness inherent to Floyd's classic lyrics and beloved music not only alluded to Syd but were inspired and dedicated to him.

In a relatively short period of time, Syd became the object of a cult of personality, with a legion of devotees, including David Bowie, Marc Bolan, musicians populating the progressive rock subworld known as the Canterbury Scene, and other trendsetters and ravers of London's underground music and arts worlds in the 1960s.

Post-Syd, some critics viewed the band as faceless and longed for the band's less choreographed, and freer, psychedelic days. Barrett was a fountain of far-out ideas, authored the band's first pop hit, and was chief songwriter for Floyd's debut, *The Piper at the Gates of Dawn*, and his experimental approach provided a musical blueprint for the rest of the band's songwriters to follow. "They all knew how much they owed to him," former Floyd comanager Peter Jenner told me.

The myths and legends surrounding him grew exponentially after Syd's unceremonious exit. Syd's unfortunate deterioration and enigmatic persona provided creative fodder for Floyd, casting a long shadow across their fifty-year history and elevating him to the status of band martyr.

The press, as it often does, speculated on Syd's mental condition, which seemed to underscore how little we understood, and still understand, about mental illness. Even Syd's sister, Rosemary Breen, claimed Barrett saw life differently from most, perhaps hinting at eccentricity. It's difficult to say what Barrett may or may not have been dealing with, although according to some sources, he did eventually check into hospitals at different points in his life.

There were those who had wondered if Syd had some form of "psychotic break," triggered by events dating back to the mid-1960s and prior to his infamous LSD use. Depending on what friends you kept, any inside info you may have had access to, and music papers you'd read, Syd was either suffering from schizophrenia, the victim of self-inflicted "bad trips," someone who despised the machinations of fame, or was plagued by all of the above. Reasons for Barrett's mental decline are likely many and are still being debated today.

The answers as to why Barrett exited from Floyd and who benefited become murkier with the passage of time. I will go out on a limb and say that the Floyds felt incredibly guilty about what was (and was not) done to help Syd, and how these unfortunate events unfolded as the last glowing embers of the Summer of Love crumbled.

Many young artists, even during the heady peace-and-love days of the 1960s, harbored secret ambitions of conquering the world through rock stardom. In climbing the ladder of fame, some are more willing than others to absorb personal losses in human cost and suffering, bargaining with "The Machine," until such time as the mental and emotional tolls can be properly counted and paid. In the end, unprecedented success in the music industry is oftentimes equivalent with creating your own prison cell, or, in the words of the title track of *Wish You Were Here*, "a lead role in a cage."

Barrett's distaste and disinterest in rock celebrity may have been proven prophetic. The international triumph of *Dark Side* made icons of Pink Floyd but mired the band in complacency and a locked them in a cellar of personal torment. Fame, Waters concluded, was nothing to aspire to. With his socialist sympathies stirred, Waters, more than perhaps any of his bandmates, was deeply conflicted about his newfound solvency.

"We've learned that piling up material goods cannot fill the emptiness of lives which have no confidence or purpose," US President Jimmy Carter said in 1979. Waters could have easily spoken these same words, and virtually did during an interview conducted by friend and writer Nick Sedgwick in 1975. Referring to the whole of the 1970s as a "baleful decade," Waters went on to say that the populace was living "very mournful days."

If Floyd appeared lost, then the rest of the Western world did, too. Nothing, it seemed, could fill the void. *Wish You Were Here*, intentionally or inadvertently, reflected this general societal malaise and absence of accountability and direction—as much as it was shaped by its times.

First of all, in the mid-1970s, we experienced the painful and dramatic final spasms of the Vietnam War and had come to the realization that we were powerless to stop forces that were never truly under our control in the first place.

Moreover, in December 1974, noted British author and journalist Anthony Sampson identified a dulling of the senses as a prelude to talks of US President Richard Nixon's possible impeachment, the undertaking of the unthinkable. We needed to be administered a "deliberate anesthesia" to calm fears of nationwide and global calamity.

The misery index in the US soared in the mid-1970s and continued into the Jimmy Carter presidency. A toxic societal stew brewed, for what Carter later deemed a decade-long "malaise," sounding the alarm that the country had been "confronted with a moral and a spiritual crisis," permeating our everyday lives and high-stakes politics on both sides of the Atlantic.

In the UK things were perhaps more dire, as the people were hapless victims of years of bad public and economic policy. The "gloom industry," the *Times* noted in September 1975, was rapidly growing. This after the publication, in January, had predicted a more positive future.

Some historians have noted a dire and perplexing situation that had rotted the British socioeconomic fabric from within—a perfect storm of seemingly bottomless unemployment, slow economic growth, and stratospheric inflation, otherwise known as "stagflation," a term that had actually been used a decade earlier by a conservative Parliament member.

By January 1975, the rate of inflation in the UK was nearly a whopping 20 percent, public spending was astronomical at 60 percent of the Gross Domestic Product, and since early summer, unemployment had been tracked in the seven-figure range. All signs pointed to catastrophe, as the public had lost trust in the government's ability and willingness to draft policy to right the ship.

Because OPEC oil prices skyrocketed, Britain was vulnerable to the possibility of strikes by coal workers, who'd already walked off the job in 1972 and threatened to do so again in 1974. These were no mere idle words: when the coal workers *did* strike that year, it sent the country into a tailspin, causing the British government to cut commercial use of electricity to only three days per week, enacting the infamous Three Day Order. A political standoff ensued, in which Prime Minister Edward Heath fenced with the National Union of Mineworkers.

A deal was eventually struck, but Heath's political career suffered fatal wounds for, as conservatives viewed it, caving to the exorbitant demands of labor. A similar game of political chicken was played in the US a year later, when the "woke" mayor and governor of New York visited Washington to ask President Gerald Ford for a bailout for the City That Never Sleeps. When Ford refused, it inspired the New York *Daily News* tabloid/sensationalist headline from October 30, 1975: "Ford To City: Drop Dead." In actuality Ford never uttered those words, and he would eventually reverse his thinking on the matter. Through an act of Congress, he would help get New York City up and limping again. "Too timorous to cut social services, too poor to pay for them, both governments face the same dilemma," wrote William Saffire for the *New York Times*, comparing New York's predicament with the mishandling of the British economy.

In early 1975, famed CBS Evening News reporter Eric Sevareid remarked that Great Britain was "sleepwalking into social revolution." The London *Times* called for a revolution in the spirit of the nation."

Author Mark Garnett, in his book *From Anger to Apathy: The Story of Politics, Society and Popular Culture in Britain Since 1975*, outlines a growing apathy among the British public toward political corruption, holding government representatives accountable, and unchecked greed of the collective upper classes generally perceived as the power elites. Even the creeping paranoia of Communist revolution, possibly even takeover, loomed in the minds of a hyperactive and supersensitive minority that had witnessed gains for Marxism in Southeast Asia or had imagined scenarios for Britain similar to the fall of the Weimar Republic in Germany. By contrast, the public may also have been moved to "endemic incivility" by mass media, which tends, Garnett theorizes, to emphasize the negative.

Circa 1975, senseless death, waste, famine, crime, rampant unemployment, and poverty were no more horrific than they'd ever been. With increasingly regularity, however, we were becoming desensitized and willing to bargain for our core principles in order to gain a measure of comfortable numbness. Anything to make the pain just go away.

This was reflected in some of our sedate popular music. Soft or AM rock provided not only a soundtrack and spiritual salve for an ailing country, but also an opiate for a Western world poised to fade into incoherency and willful unconsciousness. No one seemed to care much for the losses we racked up, sleepwalking as we were through the post-counterculture mist of broken promises and unfulfilled social change. This hippie hangover was medicated with names as varied as Seals and Crofts, America, Bread, and country-pop and folkies like James Taylor and John Denver.

Some leaders acknowledged we needed revitalization. Pope Paul VI declared a "Jubilee," calling on hundreds of millions of faithful to recognize 1975 as "a year of special public observation," ironically urging "abstention from normal work." in a world absent in many ways. An "internal renewal," designed for individuals who had "lost the certainty of truth," must be imminent.

As if we hadn't been bombarded enough with startling revelations, 1975 also marked the public airing of a famous case involving governmental LSD testing in November

1953. Frank Olson, a civilian biochemist stationed at Fort Detrick, Maryland, was somehow involved in the covert CIA-run interrogation program Project Artichoke, partly established to ascertain how US assets and captured spies could handle hostile interrogation under the influence of a hallucinogen such as LSD—erroneously believed to have been a kind of "truth serum."

Although the six-part Netflix series *Wormwood* postulates something slightly different, the official story has Olson consuming a glass of liqueur, unaware it had been laced with LSD. The doctor then suffers "severe psychosis and delusions" before flinging himself from the tenth floor of the Statler Hotel in Manhattan, New York.

Much of the details of the CIA's secret testing came to light due to the Rockefeller Commission and United States Senate Select Committee to Study Governmental Operations with Respect to Intelligence Activities, headed by Senator Frank Church, just as the Olson story surfaced in Seymour Hersh's July 10, 1975, article for the *New York Times*. In an unprecedented move by the executive branch of the United States government, Ford issued a personal apology in the Oval Office to the Olson family, essentially acknowledging the intelligence community's culpability in this matter. (In 1976, the Olsons agreed to a financial settlement of $750,000 for years of covert intelligence community deceit.) In succeeding decades, Olson has become a kind of hero/martyr to some who stand up against the maleficence and secrecy of the intelligence community.

As the specter of Frank Olson manifested itself, the byproduct of governmental culpability and hallucinogenic experimentation gone amuck, so too Floyd's supposed acid casualty had reemerged, live and "in the fleshy." A portly and paunchy Syd entered EMI Studios at Abbey Road on June 5, 1975, just as the band was finishing *WYWH*. Syd's presence shocked and saddened the band. In short, they were rocked to their very foundations as the tremors of unresolved band business could no longer be sustained.

If the mid-1970s were a time of reckoning—politically, socially and economically—perhaps it was only logical that Floyd would come, literally, face to face with its past. This reflective focus explains perhaps why *WYWH* bears the noxious scent of the singer-songwriter movement so prominent in the 1970s, in which private thoughts and personal observations garnered mass appeal. For a Capital Radio broadcast from 1977, Waters explained that some of the lyrics on the later *Animals* weren't "the direct expression of my feelings, as the lyrics on *WYWH* were."

Listening to the record, we're given to a form of psychogeometry—receiving impressions of the band's emotional depth and pent-up rage and the universality of their messages. *WYWH* is chilling, even deflating at moments, but the record also achieves equilibrium by diluting heaps of lyrical bitterness with an ounce of lyrical sarcasm; sobering, but also simmering with a heady stew of psychedelia and prog rock percolating just under its AOR surface.

The Dark Side of the Moon may have been more commercially viable, and *The Wall* the unavoidable upheaval bursting forth from the tectonic shifts of Waters's emotional core, but *WYWH* nonetheless is a more concentrated, celebratory, and arguably collaborative effort. The musical abilities and attributes of each individual member demonstrated on *WYWH* are self-referential and unassailable.

The commanding presence of keyboardist Rick Wright alone makes this a unique and valuable record. In addition, the Floyd recording and touring unit of Gilmour, Mason, Waters, and Wright—with extended personnel saxophonist Dick Parry and the support vocalists, the Blackberries—had been together for a couple of years by the mid-1970s. There was a kind of stability in the ranks with the band operating, arguably, on all cylinders.

WYWH is a "band record" in every sense of the phrase. The Floyd themselves seem to agree. In a 1987 interview with *Q*, Waters explained that Floyd was "not a band, and had not been a band in accord for a long time. Not since 1975, when we made *Wish You Were Here*."

The album's track cycle loops through Floyd's musical and historic odyssey and circles back to Barrett. No doubt Barrett was hardwired into the musical circuitry of Floyd's other conceptual efforts, but by the mid-1970s Floyd had publicly acknowledged the gravity of Barrett's creative vision, and the band's reason to be. *Cash Box* magazine, in its review of the record, went as far as to say Floyd was "treading the level of their origin" and dubbed *WYWH* a form of Floydian "reincarnation." Put simply, *Wish You Were Here* is the *story* of Pink Floyd told throughout its song cycle.

≡

In August 1988, when Pink Floyd pulled into the Nassau Veterans Memorial Coliseum for a string of concerts they'd staged to support the Roger Waters-less studio album *A Momentary Lapse of Reason*, a packed crowd filled the huge arena waiting for a band that had staged a comeback only one year earlier. Most fans were keenly aware that this was a different Pink Floyd, one that had resurrected itself without cofounder Waters. When Waters walked away from the band in the mid-1980s, he assumed there was no Floyd without him. Gilmour and drummer Mason thought otherwise, and after a very public airing of their grievances a ruling came down: Gilmour and Mason were free to tour under the Floyd banner.

With keyboardist Wright relegated to free agent for the comeback tour, the new-look Pinks constructed a visual and musical spectacle, later issuing audio and video releases, both titled *Delicate Sound of Thunder*, documenting their stretch at the Coliseum in 1988. A bluish-black cloud shrouded the stage as equipment and gear lights flared like constellations in the night sky. Images of a lone oarsman were projected onto a large, circular upstage screen illuminating an otherwise dark arena, accompanied by the music of the instrumental track "Signs Of Life," the first song on *A Momentary Lapse of Reason*, first conceived as a track for Gilmour's 1978 self-titled solo debut.

Soon the low hum of synths, something resembling glass clinking, and bluesy Indian music-flavored guitar work morphs into "Shine On You Crazy Diamond," a song that implored Syd to maintain his great creative light and slice through shadows, real and imagined. As the rousing first few moments of "Shine On" receded, the classic crystalline four-note guitar riff reverberated throughout the hall, piercing the seductive darkness like a projectile of light. It's a seminal point in the show, and in this writer's own experience it has been paralleled by few musical moments during the entirety of the 1980s. Quite simply, it was riveting and the hairs on the back of my neck stood up.

Despite the theatrical absurdity and brilliance of Floyd's 1988 Coliseum concert series—blinding white lights, dancing lasers, a floating and exploding hospital bed, and a flying inflatable pig packing (for legal purposes) one monstrous scrotum sack—it's been those four notes I've chased ever since.

Shrewdly Gilmour chose a song from *WYWH* to reconnect with the music and reintroduce fans to the band—after Floyd had pressed the pause button for a few years. No doubt this was an attempt, a fairly successful one in my view, to link Floyd's foundational years spearheaded by cofounder Syd Barrett with this New Machine. (Syd always seemed to pop up when members of Pink Floyd needed him most.)

Then again, the band suspected there was something magical about the sequence too, no doubt years prior to 1988. During a band rehearsal in 1974, guitarist Gilmour played a soulful, slightly eerie, and mournful series of notes that made Waters prick up his ears and ask, "What's that?" Gilmour found these four notes on the fretboard, but hadn't thought much about their deeper meaning. Waters' imagination was fired, however, and the sequence came to represent the sadness and irreversible course of Syd's saga and plight.

The four-note "Syd Sequence," if you will, was the basis for "Shine On." The glacial pace of the song reflects the slow-motion, all-encompassing societal crises in the mid-1970s, as well as the medicinally zonked nature of the times in which it was first conceived.

Following *Wish You Were Here*, Floyd took a sharp turn into much harsher, darker sonic territory with 1977's *Animals* and descended into deeper psychological meltdown with 1979's *The Wall*, the band's ultimate monument to paranoia and self-absorbed catatonia. There are those who would say our world traveled along a very similar trajectory. Racked with unsustainable overseas military conflicts, governmental scandals, political assassination attempts, and a near-total erosion of the public trust, we were reeling and directionless, reaching for the autopilot button.

Maybe that's why *WYWH* means so much to so many. Floyd was afflicted by the same ills we all were but emerged victorious with a band statement counter to the era's external dissonance. Unlikely messengers in uncertain times, Floyd stormed through a gauntlet of personal turmoil, flagging ambition, constant distractions, critical excoriation, and the wreckage of their shifting saga to claim a real crazy diamond, one hell of a sonic gem—perhaps the greatest progressive rock record of the mid-1970s.

By re-examining the band's history and the popular culture of the era, we might endeavor to arrive at fresh conclusions regarding Floyd and its important, great work. Revisiting *WYWH* is more than just a stroll down memory lane, however: understanding

Floyd's journey will help us to comprehend the wider implications and impact of the band's music and progressive rock in general in the 1970s, and perhaps offer lessons for us in the twenty-first century.

WYWH might be Floyd's greatest work, but the band didn't walk away unscathed. As the world seemed to descend into the depths of lunacy, so too the shadow of madness trailed Pink Floyd, and shaped it, not only throughout the mid-1970s but from its earliest days.

WISH YOU WERE HERE

CHAPTER 1

CROSSFIRE OF CHILDHOOD
AND STARDOM

Cambridge. Steeped in traditions of academia and scientific inquiry with a history of creative free thought, mid-twentieth century youth daydreamed and envisioned a wider world beyond the banks of the River Cam.

Prior to Pink Floyd's success in the London underground scene, Cambridge was not only the home of three of the five main characters of the band's storied saga, but also the dream factory fueling the band's musical ambitions. The Floyd boys were enlightened by the magnificence of the River Cam in their beloved Cambridge and the multitude of natural noises of the environment, presenting a kind of wilderness of sonic wonders to be found in the forest of the mind and an idyllic Cambridge childhood.

The wordless opening moments of "Shine On"—pure textural thickness submerging the listener—manifests Floyd's present, past, and a host of possible futures, which teem with a seemingly endless stream of ideas, sounds and life.

On a spiritual level Floyd was never very far from the sea. In later years, guitarist/vocalist David Gilmour docked his floating studio barge on the banks of the River Thames to record portions of 1987's *A Momentary Lapse of Reason*. In the song "Sorrow," Gilmour's lyrics, written prior to the music, presents the river as a friend, an all-seeing eye, and a harbinger of apocalyptic decline and personal loss.

"The river is a very, very common theme," Gilmour told *Musician* magazine in 1992. "Rivers are a very symbolic, attractive way of expressing all sorts of things."

=

Eric Fletcher Waters was a second lieutenant in the C company of the Eighth Battalion of the Royal Fusiliers when the Germans mowed the men down and forced the Allied armies back into the sea. As a Christian, Eric was a conscientious objector to WWII until he joined the British Communist Party. He felt he could no longer sit by as fascists were attempting to storm the world. This decision, this change of heart—and mind—sealed his fate.

Roger Waters, born on September 6, 1943, arrived within a week of his father's army commission. Shaped by forces that he could not possibly begin to understand, Roger, it would seem, was a hostage to fate. The die was cast and he'd spend much of his adult life attempting to understand his past, his father, and his family.

Eric Waters, aged thirty, died during the Battle of Anzio in WWII on February 18, 1944, a months-long campaign claiming forty-thousand-plus casualties. It's believed that by the time he was three years old, Roger sensed some form of familial deficiency. Instinctively, he knew someone or *something* was absent from his life, and he asked questions regarding is father's whereabouts.

Mary Waters was a strong woman who believed in leftist causes and instilled a certain pattern of political thought in young Roger. "My mother taught for many years at the Cambridge primary school where Roger Waters's mother was the deputy head," says Tim Sanders, member of the Kick Horns, who appear on David Gilmour's 1984 solo album *About Face.* "She was formidable, a tough, old-fashioned socialist, widowed by the war, but a woman of great strength and kindness."

Nearby, Roger Barrett, later known to millions as "Syd." was born January 6, 1946, and grew up on Hills Road, Cherry Hinton. Roger's father, Max, a pathologist and an amateur singer and painter, was the father of five children, including Roger, Alan, Rosemary, Donald and Ruth.

Max was a member of the Cambridge Philharmonic Society and installed a piano in the house, which brought the family together and had a profound impact on Roger Barrett. Supportive of his son's interest in music, Max bought the young Roger a banjo and later a guitar, when the younger Barrett pleaded to have one. By the time Barrett was fifteen, however, signs of trouble in the young artist's future were already manifesting themselves. Max died of cancer in December 1961, and some have said this one incident devastated the younger Barrett.

Graphic designer Storm Thorgerson, another member of the Cambridge set and cofounder of the design firm Hipgnosis, which would go on to design many of Pink Floyd's iconic album covers, suspected that Max's death was one of the first major psychological blows Syd was dealt.

Barrett lost an encouraging presence in his life, but various family members and the atmosphere in Cambridge provided support he'd lean on throughout his life. By the early and mid-1960s, a bourgeoning art and hip social scene had sprung up in Cambridge, propelled by avant-garde modern jazz, spiritual transcendence offered through Eastern mysticism, and the escape from reality induced via certain illicit substances.

"Cambridge with all its magnificent buildings, and the beauty of the city, and the artistic and academic atmosphere was a suitable place for this counterculture to flourish," says Nigel Lesmoir-Gordon, a Cambridge native and long-time friend of the band. "I never felt any pressure from my parents—my father wasn't there anyway. My mother let me do what I wanted . . . I was able to flower there. Cambridge, London, Oxford,

Liverpool, and Edinburgh. There were these little clusters. . . . They were places where this flowering could take place."

"The mental presence of those brilliant minds, all of whom had a real individuality, really encouraged eccentricity," filmmaker Anthony Stern, another Cambridge native, told me in 2008. "It's like how people describe life before the First World War. Vienna in 1900 was the height of civilization, really."

As a young person, or any person in Cambridge, the corpus of the culture seemed to encourage innovative thinking and individuality. There's a kind of tradition of creative, innovative and scientific thought in Cambridge that most surely impacted the youth in the 1960s. Just ten years earlier, in a lab at the University of Cambridge, Francis Crick and American James Watson discovered the structure of the basic building blocks of life—DNA.

"Cambridge [is] a place of intense academic study and learning and creativity," filmmaker Anthony Stern once told me. "It is probably true to say that there are more geniuses per square mile in Cambridge than almost any place in the English-speaking world. . . . When you walk down the streets in Cambridge you hear the voices of Byron, Keats, Shelley, Wordsworth, Isaac Newton, and more contemporary twentieth-century writers. . . . My parents were literary critics. . . . [Syd's] father was very much an academic, and he was surrounded by the same milieu of English literary eccentricity. My best friend's great grandfather was Charles Darwin, for example."

The English tradition of holding nature in sacred reverence was stitched into the fabric of Cambridgian life. This awe of nature no doubt impacted budding artists around the city. "I have no doubt that Syd experienced, as I say, the quality of beauty in Cambridge," said Stern. "But Cambridge, the sound of the bells and the architecture, the Medieval stones—they just emanated a sense of tranquility and peace. Also a sense of snobbery. For heaven's sake it's not all good, because there is a sense of fear and awe of not being able to come up to expectations. That creates the alienation of the young Syd and the young Anthony Stern and others too. I've actually isolated this little phenomenon and called it 'Cambridge Syndrome.'"

"Anthony Stern's observations of that period . . . do contain some truth, which ties in with the 'Art School Phenomenon,'" says Stephen Pyle, Cambridge native, internationally renowned sculptor, and former Syd Barrett bandmate. "Also, Cambridge had a unique dynamic, triggered by a wary distance between the 'town' and the 'university,' which on occasions led to violence."

"We couldn't avoid being influenced by all that was going on around us in Cambridge, even if by a simple process of osmosis, it happened," says Jenny Spires, band friend and former love interest of Syd Barrett. "Most of the people I have an affinity with are from this 'huge body of culture' Ant speaks about. It's inspiring. A strange phenomenon; it stretches down through the ages ad infinitum. There is no end stop. It's ongoing."

No doubt some who grew up in Cambridge felt the weight of centuries of so-called progress and scientific investigation, while others recount slightly different formative experiences. As with so many in the Floyd saga, Lesmoir-Gordon grew up absent a father or father figure. "My dad was in the army intelligence corps, and I was born in 1943," says Lesmoir-Gordon. "At the end of the war, he had started an affair with another woman, and my mother wouldn't tolerate it and sued for divorce. I was brought up by my mom. That was wonderful actually. She was into Bill Haley and liked rock 'n' roll. Gave me a lot of freedom."

Future members of Floyd benefited from the academic and creative atmosphere of Cambridge. Barrett, Waters, and the later Floyd David Gilmour all attended Homerton school for art. Gilmour went to Perse, as did other well-known Cambridge figures such as Anthony Stern. By the time he was in his mid teens, Barrett was playing with local bands. Syd joined Geoff Mott and the Mottoes, along with Nobby Clarke, bassist Tony Santi, drummer Clive Welham (later of the Ramblers) and singer Mottlow/Motlow, later of the Boston Crabs.

As a way for Barrett to cope with the death of his father, his mother allowed rehearsals to occur on Sundays in her home, which was now being rented out. Roger's widowed mother, mainly for the cash, rented out her home too, and although the Barrett family wasn't in the same financial predicament, a parade of tenants lived at 183 Hill Road.

Barrett was drawn to Chuck Berry, Bo Diddley, Pete Seeger, the Shadows, and later the Beatles and Stones, and Clive Welham described Barrett as being enamored of humor of Peter Sellers and Spike Milligan. It's been reported that Barrett would fall over laughing at *The Goon Show*. In one report he was caught singing an early twentieth-century Tin Pan Alley song, "Shine," which later appeared in the classic 1946 movie *Casablanca*.

"When I started playing at fourteen, fifteen, I was playing the British version of Dixieland jazz, requiring fairly lazy drumming," says Stephen Pyle.

> Trad jazz and popular music records did not usually celebrate the rhythm section. I moved quickly on to listening to modern jazz records for which drummers were stars. My earliest heroes were Art Blakey, Philly Jo Jones, and the best and most arrogant of the lot, Buddy Rich. This leads us to a strange serendipitous cross-Atlantic phenomena: the arrival of Chicago Blues 45 rpm records as I recall on the Pye label. All across the country, aspirant musicians were listening to Delta blues artists who migrated to Chicago, such as Howlin' Wolf and Muddy Waters. On from them, we discovered older Delta blues artists as well as Bo Diddley and Chuck Berry—five years after Buddy Holly had plundered their songs. This attention was happening all over the country, from Eric Burdon in Newcastle and Van Morrison in Dublin, to Eric Clapton, Keith Richards, and many others in London, and a few in Liverpool.

As Nigel Lesmoir-Gordon alluded to, there was something about Cambridge, however, that seemed to be a step ahead of most of the country. Music and musicians seemed to flourish there. "This was with no radio plays, no press coverage," says Pyle.

How was this possible? Why? In cities like Cambridge bands were forming like some sort of epidemic, basically copying the hit parade, normally three guitars, a drummer, and a singer. The most adept of these being able to copy both US and UK hits. In approximately 1961, I and a singer-pianist called Alan Barnes formed an electric blues band called Hollerin' Blues, and we enjoyed a modest success around the pubs and clubs, including the sergeant's messes [mess halls] at a couple of US air bases—a good source for cigarettes and Levi jeans. We became Those Without, before Barrett joined.

Cambridge was buzzing and Barrett enjoyed the nightlife, getting in with the hip crowd. In fact, Barrett was feeling his oats; he took a nickname, which can be traced back to a drummer named Sid Barrett who appeared regularly at a Cambridge nightclub.

Barrett became more serious about music and eventually joined Those Without, but on bass guitar. "I think it was a Hofner, on which he was quite adept," Pyle remembers.

He later changed to lead on another Hofner. We considered ourselves to be purer blues than the other bands around, including Jokers Wild, who were far superior musically, as they could sing harmony and covered Four Seasons hits as well as Wilson Pickett and a broad range of popular music. We played on a number of occasions the Victoria Ballroom, a dance hall within a cinema, for which Jokers Wild was the resident band. The Blue Horizon Club was launched in a room at the Guildhall one starry night with Those Without as the only attraction. It was an absolute fiasco. We had friends joining us onstage, and played a very mixed bill badly. The club closed that night and never opened again.

Barrett possessed a range of interests and influences. Pyle describes his later experiences with Barrett, attending an art class with him in the 1960s. "The Art Foundation course that Syd and I attended for two years was at The Cambridge College of Arts and Technology, which also taught skills to trade apprentices, like signwriting, lettering, technical drawing, printmaking, which is considered a fine art," says Pyle.

"Life Drawing" should really be titled, "Drawing from a live model," as it merely involves drawing a naked person, always female in the 1960s. I recall Syd on one occasion having to leave the class as he was becoming uncontrollably aroused. In addition we studied "Still Life" drawing and painting, sculpting and mold making, and casting, which was very relevant to my later career. Also there was History of Art, taught by the flamboyant Jasper Rose, an eccentric Cambridge academic with whom Syd became quite good friends.

Born in the Midlands, just outside Birmingham, not far from England's manufacturing and engineering nerve center, future Floyd drummer Nick Mason was weaned on automobiles in Britain's Motor City.

Mason could have been anything he'd liked, it seemed, having been born into a well-to-do family. Born January 27, 1945, Mason grew up in Devonshire Hill, a wealthy neighborhood in Hampstead. Mason's father, Bill, was a motorcar documentarian for Shell Oil and a racecar driver. He also collected vintage cars. Much like his father Bill, a filmmaker, Mason nurtured a taste for classic automobiles and was in awe of fast cars—machines, which would occupy much of his time and thoughts in later decades.

The family later moved to London where Mason tried his hand at music, playing hunt-and-peck at the piano keyboard first, until he was given a drum kit and discovered his love of the rhythm and rock 'n' roll of Bill Haley and Elvis Presley. He made the jump from a school band, in which he played Dixieland jazz, to rock 'n' roll with a band of local friends, called the Hotrods. Mason watched English and American bebop drummers in London and was influenced by them, and he idolized Chico Hamilton after seeing the 1959 film *Jazz on a Summer's Day*.

Although wooed by jazz as a teen, he enrolled in architectural studies at Regent Street Polytechnic and began study in 1962. Eventually the pull of music was too strong to ignore and he believed pursuing a career path as a professional architect was futile.

Mason hooked up with Regent Street Poly guitarist Clive Metcalfe, Regent Street Poly singer Keith Noble, Keith's vocalist sister Sheilagh, and later Roger Waters, and they began jamming together as the Sigma 6.

=

Rick Wright was born on July 28, 1943, in Hatch End, Middlesex, and he didn't have any clear career direction at his young age other than secretly holding the belief that he'd like to be musician, having fallen in love with jazz.

Wright's father was chief biochemist at Unigate Dairies—so reported the *Financial Times*—and young Rick may have felt pressure, for a time, to please his family and forsake music. This would not be the case. Instead of his passion for music waning, he learned several instruments, including trombone and piano, and eschewed pop music for jazz.

A guidance counselor at his high school unwittingly gave him good career advice—go into the field of architecture—although not for the reasons he may have believed. At Regent Street Polytechnic, Waters met Nick Mason and future Floyd keyboardist Wright, both of whom were studying architecture and living together in Highgate.

Wright disliked Regent and eventually failed there, only to enroll in London College of Music. This fateful decision changed the course of his life. The story goes that Wright joined Sigma 6, which soon morphed into the Abdabs (a.k.a. Screaming Abdabs and Architectural Abdabs). The band went through several permutations regarding their name: Tea Set, Meggadeaths, Architectural Abdads, and Spectrum Five.

The Sigma 6 was a group in transition: it wasn't long before Keith Noble and his sister exited, as did Metcalfe. Cambridge guitarist Bob Klose, of Blues Anonymous, joined, as did vocalists Chris Dennis and Wright's love interest, Juliette Gale, another

Poly student who'd go on to marry the future Floyd keys man. Juliette did not stay long, however.

Syd and Klose remained friends, despite Klose enrolling in Regent Street Polytechnic and Barrett at Camberwell Art. Because Klose's musical skills were more accomplished relative to the others, he was made lead guitarist. Waters was "demoted" to rhythm guitar and finally bass.

Waters, Mason, and Wright had varying degrees of seriousness to their studies, until their feelings about architecture and higher education in general ran the spectrum of sour—from disgust to utter boredom. Music became their vocation. Wright, for his part, was expanding his musical horizons by listening to contemporary composers such as Karlheinz Stockhausen and his electronic experimentations.

Waters moved into Mason's apartment in Highgate. The apartment's landlord, Mike Leonard, was a Hornsey College of Art and Regent Street Poly teacher, whose interests ran to mixed media—combining light and sound. The future members of the Floyd, then known as Leonard's Lodgers, had discussed the idea of using an enormous upstage screen to project films and slides and such. The concept, one thinks, was to immerse the audience in sound and image.

"They were lodging in Mike's house while they were both attending Hornsey Art School—that is, Syd and Roger," Anthony Stern said. "Mike Leonard . . . was experimenting with light machines for projection purposes. They were gadgets with revolving plates with perforated holes and very powerful projected light behind them and series of electric motors that made different items go in front of this projection and a diffusing screen in front of it. . . . It projected silhouettes in color onto a surface, onto a screen."

Chris Dennis left for the service and Barrett emerged as the front man and singer/guitarist for the band, now called the Tea Set. The lineup was Klose, Barrett, Mason, Waters, and Wright.

The Tea Set recorded in late 1964 and began playing live in early 1965, earning a residency at London's Count Down Club, at Palace Gate. Syd began writing original songs, and it's been suggested that the future Floyd song "Bike" was among the material he penned at this time.

When it was revealed that there was another band running around with the moniker the Tea Set, the name the Pink Floyd Sound, a mash up of the names of Piedmont Bluesmen Floyd Council and Pink Anderson, which Barrett had been ruminating over, was suggested. The guys ran with it.

The Pink Floyd Sound and Jokers Wild often shared a bill; for one show, an up-and-coming songwriter Paul Simon was sandwiched in between the two bands in what was known as the "cabaret" slot. The show was significant not only because a young Paul Simon was on the bill, but also because Gilmour joined the four-piece Tea Set.

By the mid-1960s, artistic approaches to popular music were changing rapidly. Let's remember the world that we are exploring. Many musicians across a few genres were experimenting with or had been using feedback—from electrified blues players to pop and harder rock bands, such as the Kinks and the Who. Syd had been tooling around with guitar-amp feedback and echo boxes earlier with his buddy guitarist David Gilmour, and this style and approach clashed with the more traditional jazz man Klose.

Klose was one of the few natural players, perhaps the greatest and most technically adept player in the band. His exit, it has been cited, was one reason why the Floyd tilted toward the avant-garde and shifted away from blues and R&B numbers, which required a greater concentration of traditional musicianship.

This caused considerable dissention within the ranks. Klose, already feeling pressure to focus on his studies, never wanted to explore this amorphous sound. He eventually decided to drop out of the band, and in 1965 he left. Syd had seized the reins, but it was an uneasy ascendency. Barrett knew his technical limitations as a vocalist, even as a guitar player, and wanted to bring in his friend David Gilmour (born March 8, 1946), who'd earned the enigmatic nickname "Fred," to shoulder some of the musical burdens. Barrett would later accompany "Fred" to San Tropez, France, where they were supposedly arrested for allegedly busking illegally, or performing on the street without a music license.

In Barrett's personal letters to love interest Libby Gausden, he seemed to be suggesting that Gilmour could assume the vocals duties for the band, then called the Spectrum Five, in the mid-1960s. If this was, indeed, the case, Barrett proved himself to be prophetic in his proclamations and inclinations. It's a circumstance with which Floyd fans have become acquainted.

Barrett went back to Cambridge for the holidays in late 1965, and this brought new perspectives. After an acid trip at future playwright David Gale's parents' house, a friend of Barrett, Paul Charrier, supposedly had a revelation about spiritualism, Indian mysticism, and meditation, and found himself in Delhi within a few short weeks to learn more about the Sant Mat sect.

Charrier returned from the subcontinent in sheer exuberance. Seeing how evangelical he was about Sant Mat, some in the Cambridge set, including Barrett, were more than a little intrigued. Keeping an open mind, Barrett accompanied friends to a lecture in London that Maharaj Charan Singh, also known as the Master, was giving.

It may have been a rare occasion that Syd had decided to follow the crowd—and it was at his own peril. After hearing the Master's talk of love, Barrett supposedly asked to be initiated in the sect. Singh Ji demanded abstinence from alcohol, drugs, and meat, as well as sexual promiscuity, which on the surface would seem to disqualify Barrett from the get-go. This makes one wonder why Syd was interested in the first place, other than perhaps that his hip Cambridge friends seemed to find enlightenment and religion.

Barrett seemed fascinated, anyway, but some say he was rebuffed by the guru. Storm Thorgerson had always explained that this rejection by Maharaj Charan Singh was psychologically damaging to the young Syd, and inched him closer to isolationism and a full withdrawal from the greater world.

It was believed that the Master saw something within Barrett that did not make him a great candidate for the spiritual life and failed to initiate the budding rock star. Some say it was Barrett's youth or something more deeply connected to the core of Barrett's character. Lesmoir-Gordon questions the legend surrounding these events, and suspects that the entire sordid tale may have just been hyped, largely misunderstood, or framed incorrectly. "All the master said to him was, 'Finish your study,'" says Lesmoir-Gordon. "He didn't say, 'No, you can't [follow me]. You're no good.' He just said, 'Think about it. Read a few more books.' The Master never really rejected anyone. I don't think it cut very deep but, of course, I don't know for sure."

"The master had nothing to do with Syd's mental health issues," adds Spires. "If the Master had accepted him, he wouldn't have stayed at this point. That's just how Syd was. And that's probably what the Master knew. He told him to finish his studies before he applied for initiation."

For some the spiritual path became a way of life. "Syd was interested then, because several other close friends followed the Master, and he thought he wanted to," says Spires. "On the other hand, several others of our friends didn't choose to."

"When the master said you have to be a vegetarian, I was hot for it," Lesmoir-Gordon says. "One day [wife] Jenny and I said, 'No more meat, fish, or eggs.' I haven't had any of those since 1968. My children were brought up like that and are vegetarians to this day. There are all sorts of reasons for being a vegetarian: Karma, health . . ."

≡

Perhaps the Master was correct. Barrett may not have ever had the drive to remain a devotee, because it was the school system—and the contacts he had already made within it—that would pave his true life path. The rise of progressive music in Britain and the formation of Floyd had as much to do with Cambridge, musicians wanting to record hit singles, and Britain's legendary art-school phenomenon.

Pete Townshend, John Lennon, Eric Clapton, and Keith Richards, just to name a few, all attended some form of art school, igniting interests in visual arts, art, architecture, and of course, music. This experimentation, which was virtually state sanctioned, then spilled over into other areas of British life.

"I think the post-war generation, we were one of the early generations that didn't have to do national service, which was one of the first concrete manifestations of being out of the war," says Peter Jenner, who'd go on to comanage Floyd.

"The highly developed English art and design school system was a product of Victorian ideas about training for industry," says Mike McInnerney.

By the late '50s, all art colleges were monotechnics with a high degree of autonomy setting up foundation courses to filter and prepare the best talents for study and awarding their own national diploma. The British government, recognizing the importance of creative industries for the economy, commissioned the Coldstream Report on art college education in 1960, which led to the setting up of university degree equivalent awards for painting, sculpture, and design. This had the effect of swelling art-school entrants with grammar-school backgrounds at the expense of working-class students, as well as a shift from commercial art to the new profession of graphic design.

"The art school experience encouraged creative curiosity, inventiveness, a desire to communicate and take risks," continues McInnerney.

For rock musicians it would intensify interests in stagecraft, create links between sonic and visual expression, as well as a desire to experiment with the latest technology in the recording studio. According to Brian Eno of Roxy Music, art-school-trained rock musicians were comfortable in recording studios using technical developments to "paint with sound," unlike students trained at music school whose focus was solely on performance. A new generation of rock and pop musicians, artists, and designers articulated the look, mood, and poetry of a youth culture that developed into a social force. I remember clearly during the '60s how helpful musicians could be at getting the message out, funding campaigns, supporting groups, and stimulating an expanding commercial scene driven by young entrepreneurs.

The government grant offered the most creative and outside-the-box thinkers to go to school, get educated, and have money in their pockets to do so.

I was so lucky to be the age I was at an art school in London in the 1960s," says graphic designer Pearce Marchbank, a friend of Nick Mason for decades. "*International Times* was next door and then there was *Oz* magazine, which later went to trial [for indecency]. We had full grants then because of the Labor government. They paid our tuition and gave us a living grant as well. We didn't have to worry about money. It was brilliant. It did spawn rock music in this country. Almost every art school had its band. A lot of them become well known. The Floyd were the band of the Regent Street Polytechnic. They weren't an art school but it was an architectural school. It is not far away from it.

By 1965–1966, the Cambridge circle of friends was exploring life outside the city and coming into its own. "There was a time when we all went to London," says Lesmoir-Gordon. "Some went to art school, some to film school, and the whole Cambridge set moved to London."

"Nigel had been very much involved in poetry readings and 'happenings' in Cambridge," says Spires. "He and Jenny were at the Albert Hall in 1965 for the poetry readings when the Beat poets, Ginsberg, Corso, and Ferlinghetti, read—*Wholly Communion*, filmed by Peter Whitehead. They were friends of Nigel and Jenny, the original 'Beautiful People' of the scene in London."

It was in this burgeoning art scene in London that Barrett would become a legend and a martyr. The Cambridge set became bolder and more adventurous, wanting to explore new sensations, new sounds, new methods of thought, and new substances. It wasn't long before LSD (lysergic acid diethylamide) emerged as substance-sustenance in their lives.

Those who grew up in the shadow of the mushroom cloud prophesized and viewed psychedelic drugs as being a tool of intervention—healing and enlightening a sick planet, torn from wars and injustice. LSD offered a wormhole in the space-time continuum. By taking LSD, we, as a people, had the power to shift consciousness, opinions, lives. The progressive rock band Nektar suggested this, a few years later in the early 1970s, with their album *A Tab in the Ocean*.

Given the enormous power of psychedelic drugs and hallucinogens, and their ability to rearrange consciousness, these substances were deemed otherworldly, imbued with divine power. The very phrase "psychedelic," coined by Dr. Humphry Osmond, who provided the necessary dosage of mescaline to Aldous Huxley for him to complete *The Doors of Perception*, can be translated as "clear mind."

In psychotherapy and shamanic ritual use of the hallucinogen, there had been, if not set guidelines, then a setting and hallucinogenic arc that users experienced while under the influence of mind-altering drugs. As the potent substance became widely disbursed among the general population, anything resembling a template process was increasingly abandoned, assuming LSD takers were even aware of such a thing.

Individuals did call upon more experienced friends or even medical professionals to guide them through their journeys, and there were handbooks of sorts, namely Aldous Huxley's *The Doors of Perception* and *Island*; *The Psychedelic Experience: A Manual based on the* Tibetan Book of the Dead, cowritten by American ambassador for LSD and former Harvard professor Timothy Leary, Ralph Metzner, and Richard Alpert (a.k.a. Ram Dass); and *Psychedelic Prayers After the Tao Te Ching*, also by Leary, offered initially as a limited-edition hardcover book through the League for Spiritual Discovery and advertised in counterculture literature such as the *IT*. But taking too many cues from or following anything written to the letter could hamper self-discovery and enlightenment. Leary believed the drug a sacred sacrament, a basic right of every human being—a kind of spiritual manifest destiny—to take the drug and see the world from a different perspective. To know God.

LSD use was, for a time in the UK, the focus of a kind of cultish ritual. A need for consciousness expansion not only led to a religious-like devotion to the drug, but also encouraged some LSD zealots to seek out Eastern philosophy, even fuse ancient mysticism and its practices with LSD use.

"I've experimented myself with psychedelic states of mind, and it can show you things you wouldn't have seen otherwise," says Parker Griggs of the neopsychedelic rock band Radio Moscow, a fan of Syd Barrett–era Floyd. "I like the psychedelic point of view and state of mind that offers something that we have never really been able to totally figure out. One of the main reasons I experimented too was because those psychedelic albums were made for the experience."

Many users knew that the origins of the drug lay in a lab in Europe in the first half of the twentieth century, but the impact and effect of these psychedelics substances made a mystic of even the most casual of users. Some have credited British psychiatrist Dr. Ronnie Sandison with first introducing LSD to the UK in the early 1950s, although many still recognize what a pivotal historical figure Sandoz chemist Dr. Albert Hofmann was to the entire underground movement.

Maybe. There are other tales told too. The story goes that a chemistry student from Cambridge was on a research grant in America and returned to the Isle of Albion with the secret ingredients for LSD, helping to kick off a revolution.

Some have even claimed that Brit Michael Hollingshead was part of a transatlantic network of operatives infusing certain communities with LSD. This (likely) false narrative has been elevated to urban legend, with little evidentiary support. Hollingshead, whose antics and public persona mirrored that of Leary's own psychedelic shtick, was dubbed "the man who turned on the world," a moniker which served as the title of his 1973 book. He's also credited with facilitating Leary's first LSD experience.

Hollingshead, wrote Andy Roberts in *Albion Dreaming*, believed LSD could crack the "existential malaise" of the modern world and cure the "sickness of insensitiveness and ignorance" dubbed "normality" and "mental health."

However LSD was introduced to Britain, and whoever was responsible for its appearance, may have been of little consequence for the transplanted Cambridge set. 101 Cromwell Road, a bohemian destination at which members of Floyd would hang out or perform, was one of a few centers for hallucinogen experimentation, which sprouted in different London enclaves by the mid-1960s. Along with Bill Barlow, Lesmoir-Gordon set up shop for those wandering souls making the transition from straight life to enlightenment through substances, and/or from Cambridge to London.

"101 was where the acid was distributed," says Lesmoir-Gordon. "The acid came from Hofmann's lab in Switzerland, via Timothy Leary. . . . People were coming around, and there would be Beatles, the Stones, Donovan, PJ Proby; there'd be Allen Ginsberg, Burroughs, John Esam [writer/counterculture figure]. 101 was a kind of subculture center."

"In the summer of 1966 I was seventeen when I moved to London," says Spires. "My school was just round the corner from 101 Cromwell Road, in Gloucester Road. I first went to the house with a boyfriend, who had a loft bed there. He was [art dealer] Robert Fraser's assistant, and Robert had a studio opposite. The beautiful grand Georgian houses on Cromwell Road were later demolished to make way for the London Air Terminal. 101 was a six-story building. The upper floors were split into four large flats.

"Nigel and Jenny Lesmoir-Gordon lived on the grand second floor with ceiling-to-floor windows and a balcony at the front," Spires continues.

> The rooms were vast. Nigel was at film school, and Storm and Po [Aubrey Powell] later followed him. He and Jenny shared the flat with other friends from Cambridge; it was a place where poets, writers, musicians, and artists gathered. 101 wasn't exactly

a place to "hang out" and "get high"; that was incidental to the place as people visited. But I believe this happened a couple of years later when people turned up, hung out, and never left. . . . The original characters had moved on [by then].

Word—and product—spread through the underground arts movement or counter-culture. Wild theories circulated and still cloister in certain segments of society as to why LSD and other hallucinogens seemed to catch on so quickly.

"Because LSD has permeated all levels of society," wrote Andy Roberts in his book *Albion Dreaming: A Popular History of LSD in Britain*, "it has become fashionable to spec-ulate that a conspiracy lies at the core of worldwide LSD story. The arc of this conspiracy stretches from the belief the drug was created as part of an unspecified sinister plot, to belief that the CIA introduced LSD to post-war youth in order to dilute the desire for political and social change."

The idea of drug use became so common, so pervasive, that it was just assumed that when a musician was performing onstage and thinking out of the box, he or she was using LSD. AMM's Eddie Prévost admits that he never dabbled in hallucinogenic substances, but that didn't stop observers thinking he did.

"The following abbreviated tale may amuse you," says Prévost.

> During the late 1960s, AMM performed in a Berlin church during a very cold winter. We were situated on the altar space, which was made of marble. During our performance and as part of my desire to appreciate the environment, I took off my shoes and socks just to how feel how cold it really was. I played in this condition for some time. Some months later in London, I was waiting to meet a musician friend who had just finished a concert, and among the other people there were two Americans who I did not know and who had not recognized or noticed me, talking about the AMM concert in Berlin. They deduced that my behavior and perhaps that of my colleagues indicated that we were on some drug high.

Syd eventually moved to 2 Earlham Street, still a student at Camberwell, and hooked up with uprooted Cambridge natives Susie Gawler-Wright and boyfriend Peter Wynne Willson, lighting director at the New Theatre with a very priestly pedigree, whose great uncle was the bishop of Bath and Wells. Also living there was Jean-Simone Kaminsky, publisher of pornographic novels.

"At this time Duggie Fields and Rog Waters lived on the top floors with some other architectural students from the London Poly," says Spires.

> I knew Rog from the Stanhope Garden days, but had only recently met Duggie, who was at the Chelsea Art School. A couple of times the Floyd rehearsed upstairs in the kitchen, and some of the people in the flat were smoking dope, but there was nothing unusual about this for me, having grown up in Cambridge and with Syd.

At this time he was living with his girlfriend Lindsay Corner at Earlham Street off Cambridge Circus, and occasionally, I would run into them here and Syd would invite me to gigs.

=

In March 1966, the Pink Floyd quartet, known previously and variously as Sigma 6, the Abdabs, Spectrum Five, the Tea Set, and the Pink Floyd Blues Band, performed at the Spontaneous Underground, a "happening," one of many known to the era hosted by the Marquee club, which was steadily becoming the epicenter of the burgeoning and innovative rock scene in London—an important link between free expression, artistic creativity, psychedelic drug use, and live underground rock music.

It was here, it's been reported, that soon-to-be Floyd comanager Peter Jenner saw the band. Jenner, a professor at the London School of Economics, appreciated "New Orleans jazz," Jenner says, "and then shortly after, I got into Duke Ellington and Count Basie and Charlie Parker. I was a terrific jazz fan."

Jenner attended shows by jazz artists when they swung through London but also spent time in Pekin, Illinois, with future business partner and Floyd comanager Andrew King. Being fairly close to Chicago, Jenner made his way into the jazz and blues clubs of the Windy City's South Side and the cultural and musical exchange known as Maxwell Street. "As jazz became more and more indigestible and difficult to enjoy," Jenner says, he found that "blues became more and more attractive."

Floyd was still doing covers, but their "blues" were expanded by squeals of guitar feedback and instrumental avant-garde noodling. Wright, with his continuing interest in electronic composers, explored the sonic textures of the organ.

The story Jenner has always told is that when he saw or heard Floyd for the first time, he couldn't figure out what instrument was making what noise. "Instead of being wailing guitar solos, there was this wall of noise," Jenner says. "I knew about Stockhausen and John Cage and thought this was far out."

Pink Floyd eventually hooked up with Jenner, whose eventual partner Andrew King was a refugee of the British Airways company. Flush with cash, King was looking to infuse capital into a musical venture when King and Jenner came upon Floyd. Jenner and King had designs on signing the band to their DNA Records, but nothin' doin'. The band wasn't interested, except to have a bona fide manager, which they sorely needed. A deal was struck and Blackhill Enterprises was formed as a six-way partnership. Blackhill was the name of a farmhouse owned by Jenner and King.

Jenner and King also ran DNA Productions, a label established to promote pop avant-garde bands. One of their signings, AMM, improvised using sonic effects generated through standard instruments and found objects, such as transistor radios.

"I was much more familiar with John Hopkins, 'Hoppy,' and Ron Atkins than the other members of DNA," admits Eddie Prévost, percussionist with AMM. "But obviously, we became aware of Jenner's involvement with Pink Floyd. My impressions of them all are difficult to distinguish from many of the other people in the London scene of that time. DNA though, were certainly 'producing' 'movers' of the avant-garde."

AMM used transistor radios in their live performances, household items Floyd would employ for *WYWH* and in live performances for *Animals*. Waters also tuned into radio stations for his *Radio K.A.O.S.* tour. Pink Floyd, periodically, would use radio in their recorded songs and live performances, through the mid- and late 1970s. For some time afterward, a number of artists, such as David First (Notekillers), whose father was an electrical engineer, explored radio waves through the technique of heterodyning—mixing two radio signals to create a third.

"As you can hear on our first LP, *AMMMUSIC*, there are some surreal interjections pulled in quite spontaneously from the mass of sound on the airwaves," says Prévost. "My guess is this had the effect of surprising contrast with the sounds we were making."

Cellist and pianist Cornelius Cardew, who'd studied at the Royal Academy of Music, was a disciple of John Cage, but by 1974 was a politically active member of the Communist party. He was largely critical of the so-called iconic figures of the avant-garde in his book *Stockhausen Serves Imperialism*. Cage later said, in effect, that Cardew's commitment to social change had little impact, as far as he could see, on the status quo and may have been detrimental to his musical output.

The 1960s held promise for Cardew, however. He joined AMM in the mid-1960s, attracted to their informal compositional structures. AMM's guitarist, Keith Rowe, ran ball bearings up and down the fretboard of his electric guitar, sending strange and wonderful signals through the pickups, creating animal or mammalian cries—a technique Barrett and later David Gilmour would popularize.

"I certainly did turn Syd on to [AMM] and he did see Keith Rowe playing," Jenner says. "Keith was an extraordinary guitar player and undoubtedly we lifted stuff off of Keith Rowe; Syd did. I reinforced that. He was certainly the person I saw who rode ball bearings up and down the fretboard."

Promoting or turning Floyd into another AMM would not be a viable commercial option, however. Jenner worked out that the only way he could make money with DNA was to have a hit record. "That was the only way you could cover the cost of one day in the studio," says Jenner. "But we were an avant-garde label, so we needed an avant-garde pop artist."

Floyd continued to perform through 1966, and Barrett was becoming very popular among his circle of friends. Blossoming documentarian Nigel Lesmoir-Gordon filmed Barrett for a movie erroneously titled *Syd's First Trip*, partly at Gog Magog Hills. Archaeologist and occultist T. C. Lethbridge is often associated with this site, as he made extraordinary claims to having discovered ancient chalk figures that have not been sufficiently proven or even disproven to this day.

"I was in film school and I had the . . . loan of an 8mm Bolex camera," says Lesmoir-Gordon.

I filmed everything all the time. Never bothered with anything like focus or anything. I went back to Cambridge one weekend with Jenny and took some acid down there and we went out to the chalk pit—Gog Magog Hills. It wasn't Syd's first trip. It wasn't. That is pure fantasy. Jenny [Gordon, wife] says that she had . . . the idea to make a film with Syd. I don't know why we chose Syd, because he wasn't a rock star or anything much, but for some reason I focused on him.

Syd's First Trip was unedited, raw, spontaneous, but has become a kind of iconic entry in the Barrett cannon. "Literally. I sold it to the Pink Floyd when I was poor. I don't own it anymore. It is an extraordinary record. If you look at Syd, he has short hair, wearing a blue raincoat, it's all before the psychedelic thing kicked in. . . . That was 1966."

Syd was younger than Nigel and Jenny, but they both knew that he possessed a certain spark. "We had a lot of respect for him, because he seemed to be something special," says Lesmoir-Gordon.

He was a guitarist, a painter, a poet, and there was something magnetic about him, and he became part of our group, whose key players were myself, David Gale, David Henderson, Andrew Rawlinson, Jenny, a couple of other girls, Roger Waters on the periphery. David Gilmour was younger, and I didn't really know David that well then.

Floyd seemed to be at the center of a cultural vortex. In 1966, the pivotal London Free School (LFS) was established, supervised by Peter Jenner, Andrew King, John "Hoppy" Hopkins (who earned a degree in physics from Cambridge), Michael X (radical Michael de Freitas, a.k.a. Michael Abdul Malik, leader of a Black Power commune, later convicted of murder and executed by hanging in spring 1975), and others, like Elektra Records producer Joe Boyd, and John Michell, author of esoteric and investigative works on archaeo-astronomy.

"At the time I met John 'Hoppy' Hopkins, I was art editing the magazine *People and Politics* for George Clark, a founder member of CND," says Mike McInnerney.

George was organizing local community action groups and established the first tenant associations in Notting Hill, along with Rhaunie Laslett, in order to fight for tenant rights and improve poor living conditions created by slum landlords. Together with Hoppy they established the London Free School in the basement of 26 Powis Terrace.

LFS offered an alternative education, a hot-button debate in Britain at the time, and later, in 1968, students at Hornsey College of Art staged demonstrations over funding and curriculum, kicking off protests countrywide. Believing that formal education can only give one a piece of the ultimate truth, the LFS's mission was to expand knowledge and have different walks of society—the elite and working class—rub elbows and intermingle.

LFS was anti-educational system, a flag Floyd waved with varying degrees of intensity and purpose throughout the 1970s and culminating in 1979's *The Wall*.

"The school aimed to offer education through lectures, discussion groups, further training and education night classes in subjects essential to daily life and work including housing problems, race relations, mental health and law as well as apprenticeships, music, art and literature classes," says McInnerney, who'd later design the cover of the Who's enduring rock opera *Tommy*. "Plans for the school were genuine and ambitious, but a developing counterculture and urgent local politics shifted the focus of some of those involved."

LFS would sponsor the Notting Hill Carnival, a revival of an early twentieth-century festival. Trinidadian Claudia Jones resurrected the festival and infused it with Caribbean culture, not only as a celebration of diversity but in response to race riots and racial division in London.

"Notting Hill, in the early sixties, was a divided community split along lines of wealth, class, race, and poverty—a situation familiar in most urban centers of major cities but more pronounced in Notting Hill," says McInnerney.

> Ladbroke Grove, which ran north to south like a spine through the area, mirrored the divisions precisely from the well-heeled area of Holland Park at its southern end to the slum housing of North Kensington and Kensal Green at its northern end. These marginal northern wards with their overcrowded properties and cheap furnished and unfurnished rentals had absorbed waves of immigrants over many years including an influx of Jamaica immigrants in the late '50s. These new residents mixing with a poor white working class, impoverished bohemians, and the ebb and flow of itinerant outsiders produced a dynamic social mix, creating both community tensions as well as cross-cultural possibilities.

Jones, a member of the Communist party, died in 1964, and by 1966, Hoppy, Michael X (a political radical and strong man for Polish real estate kingpin Peter Rachman), Rhaunie Laslett (who envisioned the revival of the festival), and others associated with the LFS took up the cause. Notting Hill Fayre/Carnival, promoted by the London Free School, was set up to protest the lack of public access to supposed public property. There was light push back from the cops, who threw a couple people in the slammer, including a man in a gorilla suit.

"The London Free School helped create an alternative press, the Notting Hill Carnival, and concerts at All Saints Church Hall, which first introduced Pink Floyd and the psychedelic sound to a developing counterculture," says McInnerney. "Hoppy was at the center of these activities operating out of his apartment in Queensway."

Although in years past it has been noteworthy as much for its peaceful gatherings as its incidents of physical altercations, the Notting Hill Carnival draws a million people a year, according to some estimates, and it is easily among one of the world's largest street festivals. The Floyd's participation in the Carnival eventually led to concerts at All Saints Church Hall in Powis Gardens. Floyd played the Countdown and All Saint's Hall and, of course, later on in 1966 the UFO, which regularly hosted late night/early morning raves from 10:30 p.m. to 4 a.m. More about this in a moment.

≡

Floyd didn't play very many shows in the first half of 1966, and of those, the majority were at the Spontaneous Underground at the Marquee club in London. But on October 15, Floyd and psychedelic art-rock band Soft Machine, slimmed down to a quarter, appeared at the Roundhouse at a fundraiser for the new *International Times*, an underground counterculture paper patterned upon, among others, New York's *The Village Voice*.

Appearing in solidarity with the *IT* was less about connecting to or creating a trend than measuring Floyd's rise within the underground and acceptance by the counterculture. Paul McCartney, dressed in Middle Eastern garb; director Michelangelo Antonioni, then working on *Blow Up*; and other hipsters of the music, fashion, and film worlds, even a palm reader, were there for the festivities.

Floyd was given more money than the Softs, largely because they had a working light show. However, the Soft Machine delivered a driver and motorcycle, equipped with contact mikes to add to the madness of their brand of psychedelic pop-rock. When the Floyd took the stage, the driver took girls in the venue for a spin on the streets surrounding the Roundhouse.

At Essex University in March 1966, Pink Floyd had established themselves as a multimedia act, and many consider this to be Ground Zero for their light-and-sound stage production. Because of their willingness to fuse music or sound, dance or physical movements, lighting and other media into one experience, nightclub goers were more connected to themselves, each other, the spirit of the times, and the impetus for Floyd's art.

The Floyd and their management, not to mention the innovative tech types around them, had only heard about the excitement being generated in San Francisco rock venues and New York by the likes of the Velvet Underground, a band Jenner initially attempted to manage until he was told by John Cale that one Andy Warhol had everything covered in the management department. Working in the dark helped Floyd develop a unique spin on the sound-and-light multimedia shows being seen on at least two continents at the time.

But lighting designers didn't so much learn to walk but crawl in the dark recesses of the UFO club. The lighting and general aura of the events at UFO were patterned upon some of the psychedelic clubs in San Francisco and New York, although most of the organizers and operators had not spent much time in America, or even flown overseas at all.

Jenner and the Floyd seized the day and even introduced a custom-made lighting system into the tech for the band's shows, which were further developed principally early on by Joe Gannon, the band's young lighting director; Russell Page; Wynne Willson; and Gawler-Wright. Unusual for the time was the concept of having lighting looks designed by a dedicated, traveling lighting operator.

Liquid chemical and ink slides, a projector, heating agent (Jenner has been quoted as using a blowtorch), renovated theatre lighting gear, and a keypad controller for the spotlights turned Floyd's front-of-house lighting station into an impressive, if somewhat low tech, visual command center.

Floyd's slide projections were beamed upon a screen behind the stage and onto their bodies, as lights played in sync with drum patterns. *IT* reported on the "Rave-Up" in their October 31, 1966, issue, estimating a total of twenty-five hundred people had attended. "Darkness, only flashing lights," the newspaper read. "People in masks, girls half-naked . . . . Pot smoke."

The *IT* described Floyd as having done "weird things to the feel of the event with their scary feedback sounds, slide projections playing on their skin (drops of paint run riot on the slides to produce outer space/prehistoric texture on the skin), the spotlights flashing on them in time with a drum beat."

Drug taking erased imaginary barriers separating the crowd and the musicians. Through the sheer power and allure of the music and the potency of hallucinogenic agents, artist and observer were drawn together, communicating through telepathic means, to create a new kind of experience, a new kind of organism through multimedia. "Interstellar Overdrive" was apparently too much for the infrastructure systems of the building: it's been reported that the power cut out during the song, bringing an end to the night.

"There was that narrow entrance for an unpleasant start," the *IT* read. "That communal toilet that ended up in flood. A giant jelly made in a bath for the party was unfortunately run over by a bicycle."

"I wasn't at any of the London Free School gigs, which seemed to set the ball rolling for the Floyd with their newfound light shows, with Pete Wynne Willson, but I was at the Launch of *IT* at the Roundhouse, when the Floyd and Soft Machine played," Spires says. "Ostensibly, it was the first real gathering of the tribes since the Albert Hall poetry readings, and was packed."

Some believe it was at this show that Syd had used ball bearings and a Zippo lighter on the strings of his guitar. "I couldn't tell you if this was the first gig where Syd used a Zippo or ball bearings, however," says Spires.

> I had seen him play slide guitar before in the days when he played the blues and I was with him. But from the huge collapsed jelly in the middle of the Roundhouse, to the motorbike Soft Machine revved up and the incredible rumble of "Astronomy Domine," it felt like something very special was happening in London. From this time, I was pretty much going to Floyd gigs again and was at the launch of UFO, which Hoppy and Joe Boyd started, the Electric Garden, and Middle Earth.

Norman Evans, writing for *IT* issue December 12–25, 1966, caught Pink Floyd at London Free School's sound/light workshop and explained that Barrett "provided a huge range of sounds with new equipment, from throttled shrieks to mellow feedback roars."

A second benefit concert at the Roundhouse was given to raise awareness and give aid to what we today know as Zimbabwe, dubbed "Psychodelphia Versus Ian Smith" in December 1966. Smith was the prime minister of Rhodesia, which had seceded from the British Southern Rhodesia, creating tensions between the white minority and black nationalists that stretched into the next decade. Floyd returned to the Roundhouse in early 1967, playing third fiddle to the Who and the Move. Floyd played another benefit in mid-December, "You're Joking?" and made an appearance at the Royal Albert Hall.

When it appeared that the *IT* was not going to continue on a profitable basis, Joe Boyd and Hopkins sought another club to rent and found the Blarney Pub, and they ran all-night raves in the Irish drinking establishment as the Unlimited Freak Out club, or "UFO" club, which regularly hosted Floyd and screened films by Kenneth Anger and Andy Warhol.

The December 23, 1966, gig at UFO is remembered fondly. Originally UFO had debuted as Night Tripper presented by UFO, featuring Floyd. Along with Soft Machine, the Purple Gang, Tomorrow, and the Crazy World of Arthur Brown, Floyd had played there regularly. Floyd was, for all intents and purposes, the house band at UFO, mirroring their American cousins Big Brother and the Holding Company at the Avalon Ballroom in San Fran. Grateful Dead and Jefferson Airplane are sometimes thrown into the same bin as Floyd. Yes, both the San Francisco scene and Britain's London underground nurtured a mixed-media approach to live-rock music events, but what Floyd was doing was far more abstract and impressionistic.

Experimentation of all kinds happened at UFO—musical, chemical, and technical. Lighting designers, such as Soft Machine's Mark Boyle, honed their craft there, and Floyd's big noise was the hottest draw at the venue—maybe in the entire London hippie underground.

Lighting designer Peter Wynne Willson strategically placed light fixtures for maximum effect. Each member of the Floyd was paired with quad lighting throwing beams on him, all in service to casting large, amorphous shadows on the screen behind the band. When these shadows overlapped, they'd produce a different lighting look altogether—what Wynne Willson once told author Nicholas Schaffner were "colored shadows."

"I saw Pink Floyd a handful of times in the '60s and '70s, including with Cream and Hendrix in Spalding for Barbeque 67, one of the first rock festivals in the U.K.," says Neil Rice, veteran light show designer, operator of The Odd Light Show, and former owner of Optikinetics Ltd, formed in 1970 and known for its mechanized "effects" projectors and rotating effects cassettes, or wheels. "On the occasions that I saw the Floyd indoors, I was most impressed by the flashing colored lights that were positioned around the foot of Nick Mason's drum kit. These shone up through the kit and cast dramatic shadows on the screen behind. I later learned from Peter Wynne Willson that these were spotlights, with high-speed color wheels in front of them, being switched sequentially, known as Daleks, a reference to Dr. Who."

"By the time they played at All Saints Hall [for their Sound Light Workshops] they were using slides and projectors to cast images in time to the music onto the band, a basic set up by Joel and Toni Brown who had arrived from Timothy Leary's psychedelic center in Millbrook, New York," says McInnerney.

> This created a harsher, more strobe-like trance effect for anyone on acid, unlike the easy, floating, unwinding, fluid effects of liquid slides used in later Sound and Light Workshop performances. By then Peter Wynne Willson and girlfriend Susie Gawler-Wright had become Pink Floyd's light operators. Peter had access to theatrical lighting equipment that he adapted for the band, painting blank slides with colored ink to become, through the effects of heating and cooling, kinetic liquid slides that would swirl and bubble and become a key aesthetic of the movement. Later on I painted Susie Gawler-Wright with psychedelic patterns for the free-speech cover of the post-bust emergency issue of *IT* number 11 [April 21–28, 1967], published a week before the 14 Hour Technicolor Dream event at Alexandra Palace.

"Peter started sandwiching chemicals between two layers of glass," Anthony Stern recounted to me. "When they got heated up by the heat of the projection bulb, you got some very unusual explosions of visual energy, similar to that which is experienced when taking LSD."

"U.S. liquid light shows employed overhead projectors with glass clock faces used as bowls for the liquids," says Neil Rice. "In essence, we Brits worked with small vertical glass slides, with colored liquids held between them by capillary attraction, relying on the heat of the projector to boil them. The U.S. [light show designers] worked with horizontal liquids manipulated manually, blown by fan, or straw in the mouth, and even sometimes dangerous and pungent chemical reactions."

A theory holds that the success of British psychedelia was its ability to mine repressed, forgotten, or otherwise psychological aspects of listeners' youth and help them revert to childhood. It seems to be embedded in the DNA of British psychedelia. Indeed. The title of the band's debut, *The Piper at the Gates of Dawn*, was taken from a children's novel, *The Wind in the Willows*.

"It's like toyland," Anthony Stern told me.

> LSD definitely takes you back to childhood. It reminds you of your childhood. I remember that experience of looking at things like I was three or four years old— having that sense of nonjudgmental vision. That is a little bit of what stayed with Syd the rest of his life, I think. The critical faculties just disintegrate and therefore you stop making sense.

Dr. Robin Carhart-Harris, at the Department of Medicine at the Imperial College of London, explained that "the LSD state resembles the state our brains were in when we were infants: free and unconstrained." John Harris, in his book *The Dark Side of the Moon: The Making of the Pink Floyd Masterpiece*, commented that the band's "aesthetic identity" was established through not only their improvisational jams and extended tracks, but also Barrett's lyrics "that somehow fused the hallucinatory mindset of psychedelia with the ghosts of his childhood."

The visionary visuals that marked Floyd's early live performances aided and enhanced this psychological and developmental process.

Mike McInnerney was one of many influenced by Floyd's music and light shows, who forged an aesthetic mixture of liquid psychedelia, cosmic bubbles, and almost mandala-like designs meant to communicate the actual experience of taking a hallucinogen. McInnerney would become the art editor of *International Times* and created the poster for the 14 Hour Technicolor Dream as well as the logo for Jenner's and King's DNA record label.

"Designs that explored a visual language expressing personal experiences of psychotropic drugs offered a different visual world to the entrenched angular aesthetics of Swiss-modernist design taught at college," McInnerney tells me.

> Observations made during long evenings at the UFO club influenced this aesthetic, watching Mark Boyle light shows for bands such as Pink Floyd and Soft Machine, watching people floating around in a world of their own blowing bubbles. I cultivated an interest in soft, fluid, poured, melting, liquid, abstract forms that were beginning to influence new materials and new ways of making sculpture at the time, as seen in the work of Barry Flanagan, David Medalla, and Claus Oldenburg.

Being consumed by the psychedelic projections beamed onto themselves, Floyd was absorbed into the fabric of the show, foreshadowing the band's 1970s formula for touring success. By the mid-1970s, Floyd had given up the pretense of becoming well-known personalities and, in fact, courted an aura of mystery. In the band's semi-privacy, EMI developed marketing gold.

For the Capital Radio Floyd interview series, which aired in December 1976 and early 1977, Mason once described the projections and lights as working off a "control board, rather like a piano, so that they can be used very rhythmically. And then there are sort of effect lights that are usually colored slides or wet slides, which are slides with some sort of liquids on them so that you get some movement."

Bandleader and Cream lyricist Pete Brown told Schaffner that Syd was "a creature of the imagination," who he estimated "appeared to exist and live in those light shows." Author Jenny Fabian went as far as to theorize that Floyd were some kind of tulpa—a physical manifestation created out of pure thought. The sights, the elongated jams and improvisations, created something from nothing, as if deities. For some this is what Floyd and specifically Barrett would become—to the band's and Syd's dismay.

≡

When Syd flopped with his girlfriend Lindsay Korner at Peter Wynne Willson and girl-friend Susie Gawler-Wright's apartment in Earlham Street, he began writing material that would end up on the band's debut album, *The Piper at the Gates of Dawn*.

The two couples played the board game Go, sparking Syd's interest in the *I Ching* and inspiring the song "Chapter 24," which would appear on *Piper*. "Lucifer Sam," originally titled "Percy the Ratcatcher," the subject of a proposed short film, was written partially about someone close to Syd. Spires is said to be Jenny, the witch, Syd refers to in the song. Syd couches his lyrics in the occult, a subject for which he had a budding interest as a teenager in Cambridge, when Seamus O'Connell's mother helped introduce young Syd to the mystical wonders of the Tarot.

"When Syd and Lindsay lived at Earlham Street, they had a cat Syd called 'Rover,'" says Spires.

> It was apparently part Burmese, very sleek and beautiful. By November '66, I was living at Earlham Street too, and the touchy-feely cat was everywhere. I had recently met the filmmaker Peter Whitehead and suggested he use the Floyd for the soundtrack of his film *Tonite Let's All Make Love in London*. He agreed, spoke to Pete Jenner, and booked Sound Techniques in Chelsea for the 12th January '67; a studio he often used when making pop videos for *Top of the Pops*. Syd was really happy about doing this. He knew Peter from Cambridge but had lost touch. It remains some of the best footage of the Floyd and Syd that there is from the time.[1]

"By Christmas of '66, Lindsay and I moved into a flat in Maida Vale briefly," Spires continues.

> Over the holiday, we both went home to Cambridge. On Boxing Day, Syd rang to say he was coming to collect me, because he wanted to play me a song they were going to record for their first single in the new year, and he brought Rover the cat with him. He told my mum, "The cat loves Jenny, and his name is Rover Angelica." Then we drove over to his mum's, and he played me an acoustic "Arnold Layne," about the dire consequences faced by a guy who stole underwear from washing lines. . . .

The term "Jennifer Gentle" came directly from conversations or correspondences Syd

---

1. Whitehead flipped the bill for the session and filmed Floyd performing "Interstellar Overdrive." Both the Snapper Music EP *London '66–'67* and See for Miles release *Tonite Let's All Make Love in London . . . Plus* includes this extended track, which differs from the version recorded later and released on *Piper*. The latter contains footage of Floyd performing the song. The freeform improvisational piece "Nick's Boogie," recorded at the same time at Sound Techniques studio and produced by Joe Boyd, is powered by Mason's tribal tom pattern.

had with Spires. "Syd had been writing to me from the time we met in December '64, when he was at Camberwell and I was still at school," says Spires.

> We wrote letters back then, because we had no phones. I had been to several early Floyd gigs with him; the last, before I moved to London, was the Spontaneous Underground at the Marquee in January '66. After this he wrote and said he had looked for me at the weekend, and waited for me so we could talk, because I was so "gentle" and always listened. I still have the letter. Like most teenagers, we had several ongoing conversations about the world and its ways, but that is how I became Gentle Jennifer.

By April 1967, another fundraiser—called the 14 Hour Technicolor Dream—was staged at the Alexandra Palace, one-time home of BBC Television. Since its first issue, the *IT* had been the victim of police investigations, in which personal and business effects were confiscated in a raid in March 1967.

Yoko Ono, Tomorrow, the Soft Machine, the Move, the Crazy World of Arthur Brown, Alex Harvey, future Floyd collaborator Ron Geesin, the Pretty Things, the Purple Gang, Sam Gopal, Alexis Korner, and others performed across two simultaneous stages—a virtual blueprint for outdoor music festivals for decades to come. It was a celebration of all things hippie. Even a cottage industry cropped up: temporary head shops were opened to facilitate hippie commerce, enhancing the main musical attractions.

"The Alexandra Palace was almost like a palace on the hill, where the flower children could meet and play," says Purple Gang's Chris Joe Beard.

> It was huge, before the Great Hall burned down years later. [14 Hour Technicolor Dream] was a coming together of the tribes and made a huge statement that the event was for *International Times* and editor "Hoppy" Hopkins, who were both deemed to be on the wrong side of the establishment and the law at the time. Money was required and it was a benefit; the bands played free. They even hired a Helter Skelter and it stood to the right of the stage we had played. I sat on the top and saw John Lennon arrive to give his presence and support for Yoko who was doing a "happening" below.

The Purple Gang's song "Granny Takes a Trip" was embraced by the counterculture, and yet much of the material on the band's Transatlantic recording debut, *Strikes*, bears a passing connection to Americana, roots, old-timey, blues, and folk music. Perhaps separating psychedelia from roots music is a mistake. This sliding through of musical styles was part and parcel of the acid-tinged high holy days of 1967 underground Britain.

If it can rightly be said that the 1960s are loosely tethered to the 1920s, then the decades of the 1970s and 1930s/1940s mirror one anothe, as well, as both eras were shaped by crippling economic conditions and foreign wars.

History cycles in forty-year increments, it seems. With each tilling of the fertile cultural soil, popular society benefits from fresh perspectives and a casting off of traditional thought. *IT* was part of the 1960s version of this cultural phenomena, clueing in the scene makers and giving them the lowdown on upcoming events, all the while fighting against the churning currents of their chief competitors and, one might say, rivals, the mainstream press.

"I cannot fully explain why the so-called counterculture took to us on the strength of one song," explains guitarist Chris Joe Beard.

> But our full act was seen around town and in some University Halls. . . . We quickly ditched the 1920s gear for the London look and it was noticed. Jimi Hendrix opted for an eighteenth-century Hussar's jacket, probably found down the Kings Road in Chelsea. Maybe on Carnaby Street? The Pre-Raphaelite look was in evidence, and of course Afro was very cool. Mods were always hanging around the UFO door and appeared at the entrance to the Technicolor Dream, curious to know what the freaks were up to and to see if they could stop it spreading. The '60s are known for the Carnaby Street mods look and the Kings Road look typified by Granny Takes a Trip boutique was favored by the UFO crowd plus musicians.

For some, Floyd's performance at the 14 Hour Technicolor Dream was the pinnacle of the London underground music movement—and the height of LSD use in the epicenter of cultural activity at the time. The bands were on hallucinogens, the people in attendance had dropped acid, and this communal experience was heightened by the searing orange glow of the rising sun at dawn as Floyd commenced their performance.

"The 14 Hour Technicolor Dream was on 29th April '67, six months after the launch of *IT*," says Spires.

> It was organised by Barry Miles of Indica Books and Gallery, Dave Howson and Mike McInnerney, as a fundraiser for Hoppy when he was busted. The Floyd arrived very late from a gig in Amsterdam the evening before. They played as the dawn broke over the park at Alexandra Palace—a beautiful, lyrical experience.

"The huge hall was filled with noise, and I can still recall the smells, the dusty floor-boards, the dope and incense," recalls Chris Joe Beard.

> I wandered around until dawn and joined a meditation group, sat on the floor passing joints round until Pink Floyd arrived very late, and very pissed off. . . . The dawn shafts of light shot across the dusty void and glinted back at us from the round "reflectors" Syd had stuck to his guitar.

Multimedia events would be the wave of the future, and it started its build in the heady days of the 1960s. "There was a very complex integrated—mish-mash, if you like—of musical genres and disparate art forms all working in the arena," says AMM's Prévost.

"As the 1970s progressed and rock music in particular became more profitable, these crossover meetings occurred less and less."

≡

Back on Earlham Road, and within a limited amount of time, Barrett had written most of the songs that would appear on *Piper* as well as material later released under Syd's own name. The music just seemed to flow out of him as if Syd had been extraordinarily or supernaturally incentivized—the complete opposite of how he would be perceived just a few short years later.

June Child, later Mrs. Marc Bolan, said that Barrett was something of a "blinkered horse," focused on writing to the exclusion of nearly everything else but science fiction, Eastern mysticism, and his girlfriend. Perhaps, but Barrett knew a good thing when he heard it. Legend has it that Jenner had heard Love's version of Burt Bacharach's "My Little Red Book" and hipped Syd to it. Jenner, who admits he is not a musician, had to hum the song—out of tune—to Barrett. When the guitarist thought he'd picked up on the vibe, composing the song's riff, it was not Love at all, but something else entirely and transformed itself into the live staple and Floyd epic "Interstellar Overdrive."

"I go around to Syd and I say I heard this great song by Love," Jenner relates.

> I begin the sing it to him, and Syd then proceeds to play it. Who wrote that song? Is it Love who I had heard? Was it my misinterpretation of Love, which I am sure I misinterpreted it and got the notes wrong? Was it Syd, who took my thing and turned it into something that can be played on the guitar, which ends up being "Interstellar Overdrive"?

These are long-term mysteries that we will not answer here, except to say that by 1967, something was in the air in Britain that assisted young, creative minds in progressing their art. And Floyd was, indeed, evolving at an alarming rate. In January at Thompson's Recording Studio, a version of "Interstellar Overdrive" was cut, as was "Let's Roll Another One," written years earlier and retitled "Candy and a Currant Bun" to please the cultural and moral monitors at the BBC.

"I'll tell you a seismic shift for me . . . was hearing . . . a very early version of Pink Floyd's 'Interstellar Overdrive,'" Stern told me in 2008.

> I think it was recorded in November '66. . . . That is a track that I came to use in a film I made called *San Francisco*, which came out in 1968. . . . Somewhere between '66 and '68 [there] was a huge development of psychedelic music. The sound of "Interstellar Overdrive"—it was quite earth shattering. It was the first record I had ever heard that wasn't two-and-a-half minutes long, and it was a rolling improvisational piece.

Stern and Barrett were planning a film, tentatively titled *The Rose Tinted Monocle*, inspired by the work of engineer and architect Richard Buckminster Fuller, who had just designed a twenty-story-high biosphere, constructed of a series of interconnecting triangle shapes and resembling a magical yantra, for the 1967 World's Fair in Montreal, Quebec, Canada. It never came to pass.

Floyd continued to innovate onstage, however. Barrett talked about creating a "painted sound"—swirling feedback, the use of film projections—to enhance the band's live performances and turn them into multimedia psychedelic spectacles. Syd used a Zippo lighter for a slide effect, and the band's experimentations, sonic jams, or freakouts stretched songs such as "Astronomy Domine" and "Interstellar Overdrive" by a half hour or more.

As the weeks passed, it became evident that the star of the show—and the band—was Barrett. Some observers were put off by Nick Mason, perhaps because of a sense of aloofness, which may have been misread insecurity. And Wright was often derided, sometimes by members of the band, for falling back on the same ideas. Rick's organ bit, "Rick's Turkish Delight," was as much a description of the Eastern-tinged organ riff he'd inject into any particular jam or recorded song as it was a good-natured ribbing about Wright's seeming propensity for playing the same or similar riffs anywhere and everywhere to fill a gap with a somewhat simplistic, almost vacuous, and commercialistic sonic texture. All of this aside, it was time for the band to get serious. They needed to approach record labels at, what they assumed, was the height of their popularity.

Initially, management wanted to take Floyd over to Polydor, but after consulting booking agent Bryan Morrison, Jenner and King rejected this and waited for the really big money. The trouble was that EMI wanted to make sure they had a band that could generate a reasonable ROI before sinking cash into the band. One way to convince EMI to loosen the purse strings was through the appearance of a demo, which could be issued as a single.

At Sound Techniques Studios, with Joe Boyd producing, Floyd cut "Arnold Layne." As alluded to earlier, the song is fairly simple, if a bit twisted: A fellow named Arnold secrets ladies underwear from washing lines to slip them on under his own clothes. He's caught and sentenced to hard labor on a chain gang.

The song not only spoke to the private fetishes of a buttoned-down culture, but also to the absurdity (i.e., men in drag) so instrumental in English comedy. In addition, the line "takes two to know" might hint at hypocrisy or dirty little secrets kept by the very same authorities that clamped down on Arnold's kinky so-called crimes. "Pink Floyd deal with eccentricity a lot, and English eccentricity is part of their modus operandi," says Purple Gang's Chris Joe Beard.

Given Boyd's relationship to the band and his history as the cofounder of the UFO club, it was a *fait accompli* that he'd produce the band's first recordings. In his book *White Bicycles*, Boyd said he'd played a demo of Floyd for Elektra founder Jac Holzman, but the label curiously rejected it. "Jac just didn't get it, I guess," Boyd now says. "It was kind of a strange sound to hear for the first time without the benefit of seeing the light show."

There was a point when Boyd, who'd found success in England with the freaky or psychedelic folky act the Incredible String Band, may have wanted to sign Floyd to his own Witchseason label, but management, perhaps due to financial or other concerns, moved away from this option.

Beecher Stevens came to EMI in 1967 and headed their A&R division. After hearing Floyd, all the pieces appeared to be in place. He signed Pink Floyd. Stevens will likely always be remembered for having passed up signing the Beatles to Decca. Perhaps with this in mind, he offered Floyd, one of the leaders of the burgeoning psychedelic scene in London—one the boys at the label perhaps did not really understand anyway— five thousand pounds as an advance. "The band proposed 'Arnold,' and Jenner and I agreed," says Boyd. "I don't recall any other suggestions."

What made the song so special? Boyd worked closely with Sound Techniques owners John Wood and Geoff Frost, solidifying a working relationship with the former. When Boyd and Wood recorded "Arnold Layne," the band was set up in the studio with very little separation. The band was arranged in a circle around Mason's kit, and the engineers battled reflections. Sound bounced everywhere in the room, and the eventually the studio needed dampening to achieve something less than an astronomically boomy drum sound.

What really transported Floyd's music into what is recognized as psychedelia has as much to do with the production as the songwriting. Effects applied to the drum kit for the band's debut single "Arnold Layne" are reminiscent of Tomorrow's underground anthem "My White Bicycle." "My White Bicycle" contains reverse audio, and there is a similar slap-back effect on the snare or the click of a drumstick tapping the snare's metallic rim. "I don't know for sure, but I think it was John Wood's tape delay," Boyd says.

"Arnold Layne" was released as a single with "Candy and a Currant Bun." Depending on what area of the world you lived in, you might have bought the single in 1967 with "Arnold Layne," "Candy," and "Interstellar Overdrive." It was issued in the UK on the Columbia label. Cream's lyricist Pete Brown praised the song as the first English single that dealt with things English—English fetishes—rather than follow the American lead in music.

Pirate radio Radio London banned the song, perhaps less for its content than the band's cult-figure status or simply payola. Barrett scoffed at the decision, saying most people like to cross dress and we should "face up to reality" that this was the case. Radio Caroline did play it a bit, but the hoopla surrounding Radio London's refusal to spin "Arnold Layne" may simply be attributed to the fact that EMI had not greased enough wheels to garner airplay.

"It was only when we realized that to get airplay on the 'pirate' radio stations/ships, you had to pay did we wake up to the fact that we were in a serious business environment," says Beard of Purple Gang, whose "Granny Takes a Trip," also produced by Joe Boyd, was itself banned.

Pirate Radio fees were doable for niche companies like Transatlantic Records and others who were of the underground, or near to it. This meant you got to hear stuff that was different from music the "suits" were dictating. The smaller labels seemed to be run by younger people with new ideas but smaller wallets. Of course an act can be talented enough to build up a big following, but even Brian Epstein bought in copies of "Love Me Do," and Peter Jenner has admitted the same for "Arnold Layne." And if you think about some of the dross that made it big?

"Arnold Layne" went on to become a Top 20 British hit in the spring of 1967. The creepy promotional film short shot for "Arnold Layne" showcases the boys in female masks, walking single file on the beach at East Wittering, Sussex, exercising in those masks, and carrying around a disembodied mannequin—all in service to putting the poor bugger back together. Arnold Layne, presumably the gentlemanly dummy being escorted around the beach, one piece at a time, is dressed in female clothes.

Floyd went from strength to strength and continued to impress in live settings. Promoted by Christopher Hunt, the multimedia event Games for May at Queen Elizabeth Hall—a venue ordinarily reserved for avant-garde or classical music—employed Floyd's four-way audio system, a concept hatched by Floyd and producer Norman Smith during recording sessions at Abbey Road.

Historically identified as nothing short of the first surround-sound concert, Games for May featured four-way system's speakers, aligned in a circular array, intended to immerse the listener in sound from the four corners of a venue. Placement of speakers near the back of a venue, dedicated to prerecorded sound effects, became a Floyd audio standard, virtually predating the headphones-induced listening experience record buyers would come to know throughout the 1970s.

Bernard Speight designed a system for the Floyd to achieve maximum volume and coverage. Through a dual joystick-operated controller dubbed the Azimuth Coordinator, sound could be directed to whichever quadrant the user wanted. Wright—who helped Floyd achieve, among other things, wild keyboard splashes across a room—handled the device. It was the first occurrence of Floyd using the controller in a live setting.

Oftentimes sound, from footsteps to reverse cymbal crashes, bird calls, and maniacal guffaws, traveled throughout the club thanks to prerecorded effects committed to four-track tape played via an analog Revox machine. The band improvised, jammed on "Interstellar Overdrive" and "Pow R. Toc H.," and even wrote a new song for the occasion, appropriately titled "Games For May," later to appear retitled as "See Emily Play," as Floyd's second single. The band rehearsed it in Andrew King's apartment house—Syd's then-temporary home.

"Emily" was based on a real person, Emily Tacita Young, despite Barrett's explanation that the idea came to him when meditating or sleeping in the woods. Emily, the teenaged daughter of Labor MP Lord Kennet, was a UFO regular and often danced to the psychedelic sounds of the underground alongside her school friend, Anjelica Houston.

It was easy to become lost in self-revelry as Floyd was cloaked in projections—amoebic-like images percolated over and undulated across the physical frames of the band members, as if the very fabric of space and time had been stretched. A dash of performance art was on the agenda, too, as Mason sawed wood in proximity to a microphone, creating a constant barrage of white noise. Waters, famously, chucked potatoes at a gong, Syd assaulted the fretboard of his guitar with a ruler, and Wright manned the bubble-maker machine.

Floyd crew members tossed flowers to audiences—perhaps in the hopes of creating a sense of togetherness, harmony, and peace. In reality, the stunt got Floyd banned from the hall, because the flower residue and bubbles left a mess in their wake. If that weren't enough, someone swiped the Azimuth Coordinator. But the band wasn't without a control box for long: they had another one built. The second box had dual-joystick controls to manipulate the Farfisa organ and recorded sound effects. May 1970 *Record World* explains that "'wrap-around sound' is exactly the vehicle Pink Floyd has needed all along to best convey their highly electric, highly galactic journeys."

Not everyone was *totally* impressed. Antony Thorncroft, writing for the *Financial Times*, concluded that audio and visual didn't always make a synchronous marriage. In the main, the music was underdeveloped, and "instead of using a scalpel on the imagination the Floyd were relying on the electric drill."

This write-up would become the template for critical reaction to the band's live performances. . . .

=

With the success of "Arnold Layne," EMI was convinced they could underwrite an entire record with Floyd. By giving the green light to the band, EMI set wheels in motion that would, in some ways, travel farther than they ever imagined.

Mysteriously, Joe Boyd did not receive a call to produce the follow-up single. EMI was notorious for clinging to their in-house engineers, and frowned upon freelance producers or recording engineers commandeering their control rooms. EMI's guy was the aforementioned producer Norman Smith, a veteran of Abbey Road, having worked with the Beatles, but was apprehensive about recording Floyd. This was his big break as a producer, yes, but the band was nothing like any he'd worked with.

Smith was also a bit confused about how Floyd, prior to the release of "Arnold Layne," had gained a following without airplay or a single. Would they take to an establishment producer? Smith was charged with achieving nearly two distinct goals: make Floyd conform to policies of EMI's business structure, and ensure they received some form of radio airplay.

EMI changed producers, but the thought was that they needed to achieve a sound similar to "Arnold Layne." It turned out they couldn't do this at Abbey Road. At least not so easily. Boyd no doubt took delight in knowing that Floyd ended up recording at Sound Techniques to achieve a sonic texture similar to "Arnold Layne."

"See Emily Play" emerged with subdued glow, Barrett's voice restrained. It feels as if Smith was suppressing a kind of looniness that almost threatens to break free of its production restraints.

A lot went into the recording of the track. In 2007, *EQ* magazine quoted Smith as having recorded piano on "See Emily Play" at half speed. When played back at full strength, it gave the track a richer, more colorful sonic signature—if not a slightly zany fairgrounds quality. As he had done for the Beatles, Smith mixed timpani with Waters's bass tracks for a further ballsy, brassy, bottom-end punch. Barrett dragged a Zippo lighter across his Danelectro guitar to achieve the scratching noises at the song's opening, and may have sent his signal through the Binson.

"For me, a great unsung person in the Floyd saga, and for Syd, was Norman Smith," Jenner says, "who helped not convert, but took the ramblings and turned them into very concise three- or four-minute songs. . . . Everybody had enormous respect for him, because he worked with the Beatles—and the Beatles were god-like."

"Emily" was a hit in Britain, soaring within the Top 10, making it a bigger smash than "Arnold." Floyd had established itself as a psychedelic pop band.

=

It was no secret that Syd was taking more than his share of LSD. From what I can gather, he may have been behaving erratically, but his friends and associates failed to see any trouble signs.

David Gilmour, who had briefly returned to England to purchase audio equipment to replace a stolen microphone, was gigging in France with his band Flowers and was invited by Syd to check out the band working on "See Emily Play" at Sound Techniques. Expecting to feel a twinge of jealousy, Gilmour was instead quite concerned for his friend. He remarked at how Syd seemed to have changed. He wasn't himself. He was distant, with a thousand-yard stare. This story is bolstered by Joe Boyd's famous account of Barrett blanking when the label owner and producer said hello to him at the UFO.

Barrett's condition may have been a symptom of the spirit of the age. For all the retrospective rose-colored views we hold in the West about the Summer of Love, the cracks in the foundation supporting the ideals of the London underground were already visible. The operators of the UFO club had gained cultural status thanks to the success of the all-night "happenings," and this certainly ruffled the feathers of the local authorities. Tensions were flared when the 14 Hour Technicolor Dream was staged at Alexandra Palace as a protest to police crackdowns on hippies and cannabis users.

For law enforcement, UFO became ground zero for the lawlessness of the hippie movement—free love, psychedelic drugs, blaringly loud rock music. "The messages being sent out via the [*IT*] and street meets were causing the establishment to cast a suspicious eye over what was happening," says the Purple Gang's Chris Joe Beard. "Cannabis was demanded on tap and the home secretary to be arrested. Gay rights and racial issues were highlighted. LSD was talked about openly, and of course, there was condemnation of the Vietnam War."

After the crackdown at UFO, Hoppy wound up in jail on a drug possession charge. The fact is, Hoppy had been harassed, or "warned," to tone down the excitement at his live events. Invariably, Hoppy would not yield. Slowly, air was being let out of the balloon, perhaps in hopes of deflating the entire underground movement.

"Hoppy was the pivotal figure of the counterculture in Britain—but London-based," Chris Joe Beard says of Hoppy, who recorded barrelhouse-style honky-tonk piano with the Purple Gang for their song "Bootleg Whiskey."

> He was once a scientist, but was also a brilliant organizer, idealist, leader, revolution- ary—also a good photographer. It might be an overstatement to say the removal of Hoppy fatally damaged the underground in itself, but the sinking of the pirate ships played its part. The daughter of a high-ranking politician and aristo overdosed in UFO, and the club was in trouble as well. Weekend hippies and society kids began to get in there, and it seems the atmosphere was evaporating rapidly.

Hoppy was sent to jail within days of the release of the Beatles's groundbreaking pop art-rock record *Sgt. Pepper's Lonely Hearts Club Band*—the moment we tradition- ally have celebrated as the height of the Summer of Love, when the underground went mainstream.

Realistically, *Sgt. Pepper's* was ushered into homes across the nation and the world just as one of the most pivotal counterculture leaders was headed for Wormwood Scrubs. Rock stars were running for cover from crackdowns by the fuzz. It was obvious that something had changed: the psychedelic merry-go-round that was 1967 was wheezing in collapse. Overpolicing, something Floyd would become intimate with in the coming years, was one thing. But some might reason that the UFO club, a possible microcosm of the larger hippie movement in the 1960s, was a ticking time bomb: a dream factory that threatened the status quo. The blossoming psychedelic movement, Julian Palacios wrote in *Lost in the Woods: Syd Barrett and the Pink Floyd*, "seemed to be withering slightly."

By the second-half of 1967, the detrimental effects of the hippie lifestyle were already apparent. Some thought they'd found God in small tabs of paper, others in the psyche- delic meanderings of the music that filled the air throughout the year and the Summer of Love.

As human beings susceptible to addiction, we seem to be hardwired to chase the next high, needing each trip to be more intense than the last. Toss in enterprising chemists and entrepreneurs exacerbating the ills of a half-baked "free society" running off the rails, and you have a recipe for disaster. It seemed the psychedelic summer was over before it began: like sand castles swept away with the first incoming tide.

=

It's the stuff of legend that Floyd had been recording in a neighboring studio in EMI Abbey Road to the Fab Four when they were completing *Sgt. Pepper's Lonely Hearts Club Band*. In his book *Pink Floyd: The Early Years*, operator of the Indica bookstore Barry Miles rightly takes credit for inviting Paul McCartney down to the UFO club to see Floyd and gently nudging him to pop in to see the young band's sessions for *The Piper at the Gates of Dawn*. As it happens, three quarters of the Beatles—Paul, George, and Ringo—stopped by to say hello.

It's long been known that Syd was not altogether happy with the sessions at Abbey Road for *Piper*, and as Smith told *EQ* magazine, he would finish a take, listen to it on playback, pay attention to the producer's suggestions on how a guitar track could improve, and have another go. Then he'd proceed to play the track the same way. Every time. The process was a bit frustrating: Syd believed his art was being tweaked, and Smith wanted to make what he believed was a good record without losing control of the sessions.

Despite some friction in the creative process, Smith, recording engineer Peter Bown, tape op Jeff Jarrat, and the band tracked wonderful sounds, including songs that are now considered staples of the British psychedelic movement. One could even be forgiven for thinking a track such as "Astronomy Domine" is quintessential British psychedelic "space rock." Peter Jenner's voice, sent through a megaphone, was recorded multiple times to create a disorienting echoing effect. Jenner rattles off the names of planets in our solar system, astrological signs, as well as other presumably astronomical items in a stream-of-consciousness rant, difficult to decipher even upon multiple listens. Wright's beeping Farfisa organ notes could pass for extraterrestrial transmissions, like the SETI "Wow! signal" allegedly detected a decade later in an Ohio observatory.

"Astronomy Domine" has been interpreted as a blow-by-blow account of Syd's early acid trip, one in which he fixated on a plum and orange and transformed them into two planets of our solar system. Barrett thumbed through a book on astronomy for inspiration, and a quick perusal of the lyrics might garner a comparison to Holst's *Planets* suite. It's travelogue as cosmic boomerang: we ricochet off celestial bodies while being hurled through our solar system, tethered to a spiraling satellite via a planetary sized bungee cord.

By contrast, the lyrics also seem to discuss the frightening aspects of one's own topographical psychic landscape. The demonic descending tones drag us down into a Venusian underworld of vibrant magenta and crimson, a rugged terrain contoured by fear, isolation, paranoia, and perhaps also awe and wonder. Rhythmic pulse is as important as chordal framework here. Notes flair and cascade over a 12/8 pulse. The incessant rhythmic drive is somewhat unnerving as it rarely, if ever, lets up.

The following track, "Lucifer Sam," slinks with the velocity of a spy movie theme song. The sleek main guitar riff is somewhat derivative of surf music, but its added textures and timbres, such as maracas and bowed bass lines, don't as much transform the song into an ethnic or "world music" entry as something paradoxically resembling sci-fi film music.

"Lucifer Sam is just a song about 'cats': a 'hip' cat, a 'ship's' cat, and how they hang out together," says Spires. "It's a play on that. I think the alliteration makes it seem mysterious.

It's such a tight composition and the Floyd play it brilliantly. I have been asked if I mind being called a witch, but it was the 'Season of the Witch,' a new age was dawning. The air was full of mystery and witchcraft. . . . I took it as a compliment."

Feudalistic fairy tale–like settings and fictional characters are entangled with psychedelic or synesthesian imagery in "Matilda Mother." A child's plea for storytelling time to continue might be a good metaphor for the LSD experience. The song is lyrically inspired by nineteenth- and twentieth-century historian, Christian scholar, and children's author Hilaire Belloc and his book *Cautionary Tales for Children*. "Matilda Mother" is awash of mid- and late-1960s counterculture influences—everything from Marvel Comics titles to Aleister Crowley, occult literature, and the Middle Earth fantasyland of J. R. R. Tolkien. Musically, "Matilda Mother" is no less magical. Wright sings lead, and his infamous "Turkish delight" organ transports us to some exotic land; Waters's succinct bass lines are airy, but if sped up might have just as easily been at home on a contemporary soul recording.

Mouth effects mark "Flaming" as well as "Pow R. Toc H.," revealing not only a sense of innocence in the songwriting, but also the absurd. The former is practically a blueprint for psychedelia: what sounds like someone blowing through the top of an empty beer bottle, a fascination with nature, impossible acid-induced fantastical imagery, cracking bells conjuring tasseled-footed faeries frolicking on the moor, and an amalgamated style positioned somewhere between forest-dweller folk and madrigal.

Written solely by Waters, "Take Up Thy Stethoscope and Walk" offers glimpses of some of the lyrical ideas Floyd would pursue in the 1970s, including the transmutation or alchemical process of turning lead into gold. A rare religious reference to Jesus and the crucifixion lends the entire affair a whiff of death and resurrection.

It's thoroughly a studio creation, but the middle section feels as though it had been spontaneously composed. The spewed vocal quips ("doctor, doctor"), Waters's loping bass line, and Wright's organ make for an uneven, menacing beast.

The bleeping and *blurping* noises of "Interstellar Overdrive," a nine-plus minute improvisational track, was recorded in February 1967 and is powered by the hot-rodded guitar lick and shadow-bass line opening the track. Barrett's guitar is simply cranking on "Interstellar Overdrive." The unusual rhythmic bleeping (at approximately 2:20) may actually be bass-fret flicking. Wild panning effects near the 8:40 mark have all the momentum and sonic power of wind gusts. One could argue that Floyd was setting a fresh, if not new, precedent in pop music.

"Interstellar Overdrive" creeps, crawls, beeps, rattles, floats, ebbs and flows, and skitters along, operating on the basis of something wildly different from traditional pop-song format. It's likely not coincidence that one of Syd's favorite jazz artists, John Coltrane, released a record titled *Interstellar Space*. Syd would listen to Frank Zappa and the Mothers of Invention's *Freak-Out* and John Coltrane's *Om* while tripping on acid.

In both cases, Coltrane the jazzer and Floyd the improvising electric rock band, the artistic mission, if you like, was to explore both inner and outer cosmos, and underscore the golden thread that connects, well, everything. For Coltrane it was the spiritual "Om" in his increasingly avant-garde music, and for Floyd it became (at different moments in time) the melodic, rhythmic, and sonic drone, or northern, anti-blues moan.

Waters was always skeptical of outsiders bestowing the crown of space-rock kings upon Floyd and, indeed, Barrett. Then again, even if references to celestial bodies and sci-fi characters did not exist in "Astronomy Domine," the cinematic parade of sounds in "Interstellar Overdrive," despite being devoid of Barrett lyrics, seemed to hint at futuristic machinery and electronics. In fact, since sound, not words, is the active agent, the instrumental retains a measure of purity, unabated by verbal language, which communicates something infinitely deeper and universally resonant, like cosmic bells ringing in the chasm of space.

Anthony Stern once told me that there was a connection—or, in his terms, "crossover point" —between the sonic exploration Floyd was embarking upon in the mid- and late 1960s and some of the sound effects heard on science fiction programs in Britain during Barrett's (and Stern's) youth, such as *Journey Into Space*. "Syd would have watched those shows," Stern told me. "I didn't know him then, but those sound effects come from a general obsession and interest in science fiction."

"Chapter 24" was written when Syd was under the influence of *I Ching*, an ancient Chinese text, which has been used for prophecy/prognostication, divination, and a practical guide for living. The *I Ching* contains sixty-four signs, or chapters, and is said to be a "tool assisting the observation and understanding of the anatomy of events," writes Thomas Cleary in his 2005 translation of the text. Some users and observers have believed the *I Ching* to be a method by which one can align oneself with the "celestial mechanism" or the order of the heavens. Based on the concept of balance, or yin and yang, the *I Ching* exists to help humanity deal with change.

Barrett appears to reference the eternity of the soul and also talks about movement in six stages, with the seventh completing a spiritual cycle. In ancient alchemical teachings, the number seven refers to the transformational stages a base metal must experience in its evolutionary development towards achieving perfection—gold.

For centuries mystics and sages understood that primitive alchemy, practiced at the bottom of the crucible, was an all-too-literal translation of the transmogrification of the imperfect self into soulful enlightenment. Artists had long explored mapping the soul through musical composition, and Floyd was no exception.

Eastern flourishes, which breeze through the Floyd catalog, are subtly present here, from the splashes Mason draws from his cymbals to the hypnotic minimalistic electric piano riff, which acts as sonic webbing for the verses. The droning Farfisa fits perfectly with the lyrical thrust of the song, tracking the path of the fiery ball at the horizon line, evoking the hazy glows of either sunset or sunrise—or both simultaneously.

"Scarecrow" clippity-clops along to the sound of woodblocks being struck in waltz time. Barrett's vivid, childlike imagery communicates eerie, even prophetic, concepts. The poor straw fellow remains motionless, likely outliving his usefulness. Although this has been discussed in the past by other observers, it might be worth repeating that Barrett specifically references a scarecrow standing in a *field of barley*. We can't overlook the importance of ergot's link with hallucinogens. It's a haunting song that could have easily been written a hundred years ago—if not a hundred years on from its actual historical era.

Still, one can't escape the feeling that "Scarecrow" contains personal observation and reflection. When Barrett wrote "now he's resigned to his fate," one wonders if Barrett is psychologically projecting. Was this an early and very public self-diagnosis?

The closing song on the American release, the inimitable "Bike," began life in the studio in May 1967. It's doubtful that the image of a bicycle was meant to funnel into LSD iconography, but it may have crossed Syd's mind. Dr. Albert Hofmann, a chemist working for the Switzerland-based Sandoz, synthesized ergot into LSD in 1938. By 1943 Hofmann accidentally dosed himself with the hallucinogen and it changed his life, in more ways than one. Three days later, on April 19, 1943, on what is today known among LSD enthusiasts the world over as "Bicycle Day," Hofmann intentionally downed .25 milligrams of LSD-25, hopped on his bicycle, and went on what some have called mankind's first acid trip.

"Bike" may be attempting to capture the exhilaration experienced when one takes a psychotropic drug. Its ambling vocal lines spill across bars and wreak havoc on the song's sense of balance, as time signatures shift between common time and 6/4, and 4/4 and 5/4. The freeing aspect of this song is something like releasing your hands from the handlebars as speeding downhill.

Barrett's voice appears in both channels as piano and electric guitar underpins the melody and possibly organ bass pedals. Author John Cavanaugh hears a harmonium and oscillator in the mix as well. The glassy tones of the piano (beginning at approximately 0:48) streak through the verses, jumping with references to a mouse named Gerald and making time with a girl in a room full of ringing and musical clocks.

During the mid-section of the song, beginning at 1:56, the Abbey Road audio library contributed sound effects, including cranking gears and ticking time machines. Looped voices that could easily be mistaken for duck quacks, or calls, cycle as the song fades—a cacophony reminiscent of the second ending of "A Day in the Life" from *Sgt. Pepper's*, etched into its runoff groove.

Piper was released in August 1967, forever establishing the legend, myth, and cracked reality of Syd Barrett, and ringing in sympathy with *Sgt. Pepper's*, if not vying for the Top Psychedelic Album of the 1960s slot.

≡

As the British Underground was breaking apart, so too, within nine months or so, the Haight had devolved from an acid-fueled Utopian Dream to a den of thieves, junkies, and small-time creeps and criminals. Where acid once flowed freely, by the fall of 1967, speed was the drug of the day.

"A movement like the one in San Francisco usually doesn't last very long—probably eighteen months to two years," Quicksilver Messenger Service's Gary Duncan once told me. "But the repercussions last decades."

Once illicit substances, those made illegal by the year 1967 in the UK, infiltrated and perverted the underground, it ultimately undermined the counterculture's resistance against convention. There's no getting around this: illegal activity mixed with outspokenness for social change can be a dangerous concoction—poison to the elites—and because of its increasing visibility, the youth movement garnered plenty of unwanted attention.

The *News of the World* erroneously referred to Floyd as social deviants (ironic that this was the name of Mick Farren's musical crew) and called out Mick Jagger for his excessive drug intake, when the target was actually Brian Jones. Jagger sued the *News of the World*, and the paper went to war with the psychedelic drug scene. The crackdown on the UFO club was just one harbinger of an anticlimactic denouement of the British underground or hippie scene centered around drugs.

Confusion was everywhere. The utopia that some promised had not emerged. Even some of the underground's leading lights were beginning to dim. Maybe Syd's impending "drop out" was a larger protest. He was rejecting a system that he didn't want to be a part of.

Syd perhaps could see a bit farther down the road than any of the other members of the band. So much so that even getting started on the path to pop stardom meant betraying his principles. Or worse: being made a circus performer, in some clownish and Dada-esque imitation of life. The trouble was that the band, and even Syd, had pop-star ambitions. It would be difficult for anyone to deny this completely. Syd liked the attention he garnered from being an underground cult hero.

When *Top of the Pops* came calling, largely due to Smith's influence, Barrett was far from amused he would be miming to "See Emily Play" for the cameras. He was a live musician, even more than a studio hound, and the thought of practicing in Abbey Road Studio One to a playback of the song was too much for Syd to handle. He and the band survived the first *Top of the Pops* appearance, but the following week, when Barrett refused to play, was the last straw for Smith.

Maybe there was a measure of self-sabotage responsible for Syd not wanting, or being able, to handle some of the rigors of the road and the long slog to rock royalty. Combine this with his natural tendency to be a performance artist, and this psychological cocktail was bound to be destructive of any notion he could have had toward pretentiousness.

=

The cocktail of pressure to produce hit songs for an impatient record company, stretching the limits of the brain with LSD, and a heavy gigging was slowly unraveling Barrett—and by association Floyd.

With EMI banging down the door for another single, Andrew King and Peter Jenner kept the label at bay, saying Barrett needed a little rest and time to clear his head to deliver another hit record to EMI. Blackhill sent Barrett to Formentera, with hippie doctor Sam Hutt and family in tow, optimistic he'd snap out of it and improve his mental health. Wright and Juliette also accompanied while Waters was in nearby Ibiza with Judy, just a hop, skip, and jump away.

At a show in late July 1967, at the Alexandra Palace for the "International Love-in," Barrett was backstage and seemingly incapable of moving of his own freewill. Immobile, speechless, and positively catatonic, Barrett was simply unable or unwilling to perform.

Acting quickly, Waters and the future Mrs. Bolan roped an electric guitar around Syd's neck and practically dragged the underground idol onto the deck to perform. It was a momentary and pyrrhic victory: Once on stage, Syd stood motionless, not playing his guitar at all. When it appeared as though he would finally fret a few notes or play a chord, his instrument failed to ring out. His hands, his body, weren't coordinated and willed not to work.

Syd's bout of staring at the Alexandra Palace had some thinking he'd gone full zombie. It appears some have confused Syd's blank countenance during the July performance at the Ally Pally with the 14 Hour Technicolor Dream a few months earlier. Whichever you believe, frozen Barrett could not produce a note. At the end of the band's performance, Bryan Morrison's employee, June Bolan, grabbed the money from venue managers and raced the band out of there. *Melody Maker's* famous headline, "Pink Floyd Flake Out," summed it all up nicely.

Incredibly, the band still managed to record together. "Set the Controls" and "Scream Thy Last Scream" were tracked in August 1967. Some sources say that Mason uses his bare hands to play during "Set the Controls for the Heart of the Sun." This may be the case, but Mason referenced jazz drummer and bandleader Chico Hamilton and his performance at the Newport Jazz Festival 1958, captured for the highly influential film *Jazz on a Summer's Day* released the following year.

Hamilton is actually shown at Newport playing with mallets, not his hands. The soft if somewhat uniform drumbeats, both in the Hamilton Quintet's "Blue Sands" and Floyd's "Set the Controls," might be constructed of alternating sticking patterns involving double and single strokes. Either way, they both have a classic timpani quality that foreshadows the use of this orchestral instrument on *WYWH*.

"Set the Controls" and "Scream Thy Last Scream" were intended to be opposite sides of a single, but they were shot down by EMI for not being commercial enough.

The band was losing their grip. They had not scored with a hit since the spring, and Syd seemed more and more introspective and distant. "Apples and Oranges" and Wright's "Paintbox" were earmarked for the band's next single while the band was on tour with Jimi Hendrix, but it fizzled out. Waters complained that the production is what sunk "Apples and Oranges." Perhaps.

In October in De Lane Lea, Floyd started recording "Vegetable Man," and later that month "Jugband Blues," with Norman Smith, both written by Barrett. "Scream Thy Last Scream" is loony and maddening, but also comical, including the "chipmunk" voices shadowing Barrett's lead vocals. Proto-punky "Vegetable Man" doesn't hold back in its naked psychological assessment of its author.

"Songs that Floyd suppressed," says Jenner, "are great songs in terms of people listening to them and reading the lyrics, 'Scream Thy Last Scream' and 'Vegetable Man'"

> I think those are great songs in terms of people listening to them and reading the lyrics and thinking, "Fucking hell." If you want to be a psychiatrist, you should be forced to listen to those songs quite often. "Vegetable Man" was written in my house and . . . it was a description of who [Barrett] was and where he was. He is referring to himself when he says, "Vegetable Man, where are you?" He is saying "I have become a vegetable." Scary.

The American tour of late summer 1967 was, in some ways, a blur of drugs, alcohol, sunshine, women, music, Capitol Records chauffeurs, tourist traps, and making friends with Alice Cooper and his band. Floyd played the Fillmore West and also the Winterland, sharing the bill with Janis Joplin and Big Brother and the Holding Company.

Syd seemed to descend further into his own world. He was detuning his guitars onstage, making for adventurous but impossible music for his bandmates to follow. At the Cheetah Club Syd blanked, causing Roger and Rick to think quickly and handle the vocals.

Waters has told the story of Barrett allowing a cigarette to burn down to nothing, oblivious to the charred stick disappearing in between his fingers. Waters intimates that it must have singed Barrett but Syd didn't seem to care about—or *feel*—the pain. It was this image, and others like it, that would inspire the Pink character of *The Wall* and his life review, feeling increasingly numb by the hour.

Floyd were booked for key television appearances in November 1967: one with the *Pat Boone Show* and another with Dick Clark's *American Bandstand*. It's believed that Floyd, or Barrett, appeared on the *Perry Como Show* or the *Perry Como Kraft Music Hall*, but this, to my knowledge, never came to pass. By fall 1967, Como was making limited television appearances, although he did have a holiday special that aired in late November, featuring Jefferson Airplane and Sérgio Mendes.

Barrett ran through rehearsals just fine for the *Pat Boone Show*, but when it was time for the live broadcast, Syd froze.

I contacted Pat Boone by email to ask him about the Barrett appearance, hoping to get the former TV host's reaction to Syd's possible deteriorating mental health. Evidently, the question or context in which it was asked was unclear, and the exchange seemed to devolve. Boone's reply to my email was priceless and perhaps more illuminating than if he had answered the question straight off: "I was quite surprised to hear from you about Pink Floyd," Boone wrote. "Anybody reading that [sentence] cold, including me, would assume you mean that Syd Barrett was already slipping away mentally, as exemplified by his booking the group on the Pat Boone syndicated TV show."

Of course, the mere act of booking oneself on the *Pat Boone Show* should not, in and of itself, constitute mental illness. But there were plenty of other indicators of Barrett's strange behavior reaching unprecedented levels. One Barrett story has practically passed into legend: On the same day as the live Boone broadcast, Floyd had played two shows at the Cheetah Club in Santa Monica. Backstage, Barrett poured in his hair a concoction of Brylcreem with crushed Mandrax pills, presumably because he did not care for the perm a hairstylist had given him a few days earlier.

When Barrett and the band took the stage, some members of the audience were appalled by Barrett's appearance. He looked liked one of the villains in *Raiders of the Lost Ark*—his face appeared to be melting before their eyes.

The following day Floyd lip synched "Apples and Oranges" on Dick Clark's *American Bandstand* and then agreed to a brief interview after the "performance." Clark attempted to ask Floyd a series of questions. As Clark soon found out, they were not a chatty bunch.

The pretend performance is atrocious but there have been other examples of bands doing similar things. Floyd was *not* unique in this way, even if it's abundantly clear that they were not actually playing live. Perhaps this is what bothered Barrett? Maybe he felt foolish lip synching?

After their West Coast tour and a date on the continent, the band signed on for more British dates in November and December, supporting Jimi Hendrix. Syd was a fan of The Jimi Hendrix Experience's *Are You Experienced?* but there doesn't appear to have been much interaction between the two. Irony of ironies: Syd had shared dates with one of his idols but his grip on reality was slipping away.

It's generally accepted that Nick Mason was a fan of Keith Emerson's band, the Nice, and their guitarist Davy O'List was recruited to temporarily replace Syd. My research indicates that O'List subbed for Syd on only one show. The schedule was a bit grueling and the band had barely twenty minutes to perform every night—for weeks.

Off the road Syd didn't appear to be doing much better. Another incident has passed into Pink Floyd legend. Lesmoir-Gordon, wife Jenny, and several others were at a cottage at Blackhill Farm in Herefordshire, owned by the King family, just as the band was disintegrating in the fall of 1967.

"We were coming back from this trip to Wales. Stash De Rola, a.k.a. Prince Stanislaus Klossowski de Rola, was a friend of ours, and he used to hang out at 101," says Lesmoir-Gordon. "He said that Peter Jenner had a house, a cottage, in the Black Mountains and we could go down there for a week or so. Jenny, myself, Stash and a girl called Gaye, Syd, and I don't know if it was Lindsay [Corner/Korner, former girlfriend]. I can't remember. Five or six of us."

There were some memorable moments. "One day we took a trip and Syd took a trip balancing on a wine bottle with his hands pressed up to the beam of the cottage," says Lesmoir-Gordon.

Reflecting on Syd's behavior, Lesmoir-Gordon now claims that Barrett was already far gone, but the group was not equipped to deal with mental illness, let alone recognize signs of it in Syd. "We had no experience," says Lesmoir-Gordon. "We just thought he was an eccentric poet."

What happened next, however, baffled them. "One morning we got up and he got a shit on the doorstep," says Lesmoir-Gordon. "He was really losing it then. Often we thought he was just being nonconformist in the conformist situation of a band."

"It is a form of rebellion to not conform, to not play to what other people's expected game is," Anthony Stern once told me. "That can come from all sorts of historical family background, resentments, anger, sadness, disappointments. When his father died Syd felt so deserted and may have felt that 'What is the point in succeeding if your father isn't even there to give you any praise?'"

What role his father's death actually played in Syd's seeming mental absence or withdrawal we'll never truly know. Syd may have been dealing with emotional and psychological demons, on top of the pressures to produce a hit single—something he apparently despised doing. These things aren't mutually exclusive. If anything the stress of the music industry may have hampered Barrett's ability to cope and caused his constant need for escape.

LOSING THAT LIGHT IN YOUR EYES

Was Syd losing it or was he being obstinate? With increasing regularity, Floyd could no longer answer this question and, whatever the true reason, believed Syd was, on some level, sabotaging their attempts to have a career in music. A sense of creeping paranoia rose within the ranks: the idea that someone in the band being a poison pill was fraying what was left of their nerves.

It's no secret that Roger was ambitious. Long before Syd left, Waters came into the possession of a Chrysler Plymouth Powerglide and decided to load the car up and take a trip to Greece. Roger and his girlfriend Judy, Lesmoir-Gordon and his girlfriend Jenny, and Rick Wright went to the Isle of Patmos. Waters supposedly had his first acid trip there, and he made honest assessments concerning his life path. "Jenny said to Roger in the early days: 'Roger what do you want?'" says Lesmoir-Gordon. "Roger said, 'I want to be rich and famous.' He did. That is what he wanted."

Around Christmastime 1967 the band seriously offered Cambridge guitarist David Gilmour the job as the fifth member of the Pink Floyd, presumably as the backup singer and guitarist, second to Syd, on a European tour in early 1968. Gilmour seemed uniquely suited to slip into Barrett's place. He had traveled through France with Syd, traded guitar licks with him, and even shared some of the same tastes in guitar effects. Gilmour could also approximate Syd's sound and style to a "T."

Gilmour—born March 6, 1946, at 109 Grantchester Meadows, near the River Cam and the walk and bicycle path locals refers to as the Grantchester Grind—received a single, "Rock Around the Clock," when he was young, only to see it demolished when an au pair sat on it. Another influential early musical figure for Gilmour was Pete Seeger, whose folk style may be detected in songs such as "Fat Old Sun" and the socially conscious "Murder," from 1984's *About Face*.

After graduating from separate high schools, both Syd and Gilmour went to the Cambridge College of Arts and Technology. Although they adored Chuck Berry and the Beach Boys, the popularity of British bands the Beatles and the Stones had inspired them to forms bands.

Gilmour joined the Newcomers and performed with the Ramblers until some of the members went on to form Jokers Wild, featuring Clive Welham, guitarist John Gordon, bassist Tony Santi, and multi-instrumentalist (sax, keys, guitar) John Altham.

Jokers Wild played Frankie Lymon and Chuck Berry, and came to the attention of Jonathan King, whose "Everybody Has Gone to the Moon" was a hit in the UK and who would later produce Genesis. Through his business contacts with Decca, it was decided that Sam and Dave's "You Don't Know What I Know" b/w Otis Redding's "That's How Strong My Love Is" should be recorded as a single. Before anything could come of the single, pirate radio dug up the original Sam and Dave and, well, that spelled the end to Jokers Wild, even if their popularity in Cambridge insulated them from career missteps.

Gilmour was a reasonably mature young man. The story goes that Gilmour's father, Doug, a doctor and a geneticist, and David's mother Sylvia, a teacher and film editor, moved to Greenwich Village, New York City, where the academic worked as a lecturer for New York University (NYU). After Doug was lured to New York, David was living in an apartment in Mill Road.

I checked with NYU to verify that a Doug Gilmour actually worked there in the 1960s, and found some intriguing information. With the help of a public affairs professional at NYU, a Douglas G. Gilmour, born June 15, 1921, was found to be a senior researcher in psychiatry at the university's School of Medicine between the years 1965 and 1971. This time frame generally matches up with what has been typically reported. It's likely Doug had been in America and returned home to Cambridge. Years later, with wife Sylvia, he arrived in New York where he accepted a job at NYU.

It's been reported that Doug took a job in the early 1960s in America. If he had, it may not have been at NYU, as far as I can tell. Interestingly, the Douglas G. Gilmour I was looking for held a PhD from a Cambridge university (NYU records were unclear on which one) and was a research professor of microbiology at NYU's School of Medicine between 1976 and 1982. David Gilmour's dad supposedly attended Homerton College at the University of Cambridge and later lectured there.

One thing everyone seems to agree on is the relative freedom David enjoyed as a teen. He seemed to make his own decisions and even travel, years before he was officially an adult. In a 1992 interview with Nicky Horne of the BBC, Gilmour related that in 1966 he hooked up with a band who'd been offered a job in the south of Spain. After returning to the UK, the band was invited back to Europe, this time France, and the band stayed in the country for a few months.

By January 1967, Gilmour and the band moved to Paris and gigged around the country. Resources were scant. There was very little to eat and not much money. By the time Gilmour had made his way up to northern France in 1967, he'd fallen under the spell of *Sgt. Pepper's*.

Names such as Polanski, Kubrick, Antonioni, Medak, and Forman have floated around the Floyd universe for years, and it was assumed that Roger or Nick were the first Floyds to have made inroads into movie work. They did, but as it happens, it was Gilmour who perhaps struck first in the film business. While in France, Gilmour cut a couple of tracks, "Do You Want To Marry Me?" and "I Must Tell You Why," for the movie *A Cœur Joie* (*Two Weeks in September*, starring Brigette Bardot), with French film soundtrack composer Michael Magne (*Gigot*).

Gilmour was having little success otherwise, however. When many so-called hippies in London, San Francisco, and New York were "freaking out" on acid and promoting free love, Gilmour was eking out an existence as the proverbial Englishman in Paris, procuring a taste for the culture—if not a life on the streets. Gilmour and gang had little to lift their spirits, aside from hearing the psychedelic sounds of London wafting over the Channel. Gilmour supposedly heard *The Piper at the Gates of Dawn* and was a tad bit green with envy at his friend's success.

By this point Jokers Wild, which had transitioned into Bullitt, had suddenly transformed its moniker once again, into Flowers. Changing their marketing language may have improved self-image, or simply kept them in step with a rapidly mutating culture, but offered very little in the way of revenue. Living hand to mouth tested a young Gilmour's resolve. At their lowest point, financially and spiritually, Gilmour found himself in a hospital recovering from malnutrition and infectious disease.

Before the road could extinguish Gilmour's spirits and claim another aspiring musician, the up-and-coming guitarist left France and headed back to England. Bassist Rick Wills and drummer Willie Wilson went back to Cambridge, and Gilmour, refusing to surrender his dream, embarked on a new chapter of his life in London.

Visiting Floyd in the studio and then seeing the band at the Royal College of Art convinced Gilmour that something was amiss with his friend's band. Depending on who is recounting, Syd was either not playing or ruining the band's overall stage sound. It was after this gig that Nick Mason approached Gilmour about augmenting Floyd's personnel. It seemed like a logical choice. Gilmour was from Cambridge and, after all, had taught Syd Stones licks and experimented with slide guitar, acoustics, and echo boxes—all approaches and gadgets favored by Syd.

"I was the one who . . . rang him up in Cambridge and said, 'Can you get down to Brighton? The Pink Floyd need a guitarist,'" Lesmoir-Gordon says. "David has said that . . . it was Nigel who did it. . . . I was closer to Syd, and David was a bit younger. Roger and David were on the periphery of the Cambridge set. But you'd see them down by the river and the coffee bars, but I never really connected with Roger or David then."

Gilmour's first show was, presumably, the band's performance at the Dome on December 2, 1967. It's unclear if Syd was present for the entire show. The band may have been a five-man lineup for part of the set.

What Syd may have thought about all of this remains a mystery, but there is some evidence to indicate he clearly was not thrilled by the events that had transpired. The rest of the band, however—meaning the core three of Mason, Waters, and Wright—were somewhat relieved to have Syd's guitar and vocalist friend, an experienced player, there to back up their increasingly unreliable leader.

Gilmour admitted he felt like an outsider for a while, even though he knew Syd since he was fifteen. There would be moments Syd would shoot daggers at Gilmour. "There was a long period of time when I was not really sure what I was around to do, and played sort of back-up guitar," Gilmour told Chris Welch in 1973. "Following someone like Syd Barrett into the band was a strange experience. At first I felt I had to change a lot, and it was a paranoid experience. After all, Syd was a living legend, and I had started off playing basic rock music—Beach Boys, Bo Diddley, and 'The Midnight Hour.'"

When the band set up in a rehearsal space in a West London school, they attempted to work through a new track that Barrett was toying with, titled "Have You Got It Yet?" It was nothing less than hours-long head fakes perpetrated by master performance artist Barrett.

In attempting to teach the band his new song, Barrett continually changed his creation every time they took a pass at learning it. Barrett never played the song twice the same way. It took hours of monotonous incoherence for the joke to sink in. Whether this was done to piss off the band members, who were so clearly dissatisfied by Syd's performances, or proof of Barrett's deteriorating mental condition, is anyone's guess.

"He didn't like the music business or what it was," says Jenner. "If I want to make music and you want me to develop a career, there is a conflict, which is difficult to resolve and it needs to be resolved. . . . I want to make music because I want to make music, and you want me to make music because it's for my career. You want me to go down to write another hit song. I want to write another song."

"When Syd didn't want to behave himself when they were doing a TV program called *Top of the Pops*, the others didn't get it," Stern told me. "They said, 'We came all of this way, worked so hard. What do you mean you don't want to do it?' He totally didn't want to do it."

Barrett's drug intake may have made him more sensitive or paranoid and less willing to go along for the ride. "[Barrett] wasn't motivated by the usual things that concern eighteen- or nineteen-year-old boys," Stern said. "He wasn't after conquering the world. He was out to play the best music that was inside of him. He was already a kind of wise guy in the sense that he looked inwards rather than outwards."

=

By January 1968, Floyd were faced with the earthshattering realization that a founding member of the band, someone who was the de facto leader of the group, was likely never coming back. Syd's bandmates in Floyd were determined to go on, however. Waters even spoke to management about Syd and demanded they figure out a way for the band to move forward—with or without Syd.

The idea went up: maybe Syd could become a Brian Wilson–type character, someone who would not travel with the band on the road but write songs. This notion quickly ran aground the more unpredictable Syd became. Ironically, one of Syd's ideas was to introduce a saxophonist, a banjo picker, and female singers into the Pink Floyd musical universe. Unbelievably, it was dismissed as being too far out for the band. The use of backing singers and saxophonist would, of course, help contribute to the greatness of *The Dark Side of the Moon*, long after Syd had left the band. It should be noted that Syd's brother Alan was a saxophonist, and this may have helped instill certain artistic instincts in his younger brother, who picked up the ukulele.

The fact is, Floyd had been dealing with Syd troubles for months. Just prior to the release of *Piper*, when Syd did not turn up for a BBC Radio One broadcast recording scheduled for late July, may have sealed Syd's fate. He walked up the block, out of earshot of the band. They tried to flag him down in time to save their slot and ultimately had to cancel their appearance, absent one renegade bandleader. A couple of days later, an unpredictable Syd turned up, a potential threat to the band's longevity.

Travelling to a gig at the University of Southampton, passing the vicinity of Barrett's apartment house, the question emerged: "Shall we pick up Syd?" A response came rapidly: "Why bother?"

Syd may not have known what was happening inside the band—or why he was no longer being collected for the band's shows. He still retained the Floyd's itinerary, however, and despite the band writing him off, continued to show up at gigs. That is until one day he stopped trying to play onstage, or even watch from the audience—and simply vanished.

By spring 1968 Syd was officially gone, and Gilmour was fully installed as guitarist and vocalist. The six-way partnership Blackhill Enterprises had been dissolved, and Floyd was now under the watchful eyes of manager Bryan Morrison.

Jenner and King would no longer look after their affairs but, believing Syd was the true creative force behind the success of the band, backed the troubled leader under the naïve assumption they could manage him. None of the other members seemed to be prolific songwriters, and King and Jenner weren't very familiar with Gilmour and the depth of his talents. "Roger said, 'You can't see it without Syd, can you?'" Jenner says. "I really couldn't."

If Floyd were like most bands, this would have been the end of the story. Syd Barrett would have snapped out of his funk and become a major star, and the rest of the band would have forever been tied to the Summer of Love—little more, perhaps, than a novelty.

After Jenner and King exited, a fellow by the name of Steve O'Rourke, who was working for the Bryan Morrison Agency, was assigned Floyd. For all intents and purposes, O'Rourke would be the band's manager, helping to usher in their greatest triumphs and bear witness to some of their most crushing self-inflicted blows. Over time, Floyd would come to appreciate O'Rourke's negotiation skills and professionalism. Stories have passed into legend about O'Rourke's honesty, the lengths to which he'd go to seal a deal, and his insistence on running every decision, great and small, by the Floyd for their approval.

"Bryan Morrison reassured them and told them to keep going," Jenner says. "I'm sure they were a bit worried about whether they could go on paying their rent. Bryan Morrison said they could—but not if they did not turn up for gigs. I doubt he said exactly that, but that was the reality."

And Barrett? No one could see it coming. Even Wright, who, it was said, Syd admired, felt it best to stay with the band. "We all feel guilty," says Lesmoir-Gordon. "Obvious the Floyd feel guilty. We didn't help [Syd]. We didn't know what to do."

Even today, there is open debate as to what exactly was troubling Syd. Was he schizophrenic? An acid casualty? Both? "I hardly knew what the word schizophrenia meant," says Lesmoir-Gordon. "We used to call it manic depression. . . . The thing is, you have to remember that we were born in the Second World War. We grew up in a reactionary world where the survivors of that war were trying to put everything back together again."

Mason called the band's lack of real concern "completely callous" and once compared Barrett's Floyd fate with the aftermath of Bob Welch's exit from Fleetwood Mac. The Barrett family was not vocal about Floyd's decision to nudge Barrett out of the band he'd founded, but seemed to operate under the veil of muted disapproval. If Syd thought he was undermined, he didn't appear to hold a long-term grudge against his former mates.

"Syd never said anything negative to me about the band," claims Jenny Spires.

> He loved it all. He was really good friends with Roger Waters and looked up to Rick. It was always affable among them all. When the cracks began to show in Syd, they were all much shaken and feeling the pressure—Syd was the main writer and instigator of their sound. When whatever happened to Syd in July '67, it wasn't from him taking too much acid as a lot of people thought. He was suffering from a combination of things including nervous exhaustion, but that didn't explain everything, as we know. He was definitely wired. I hadn't seen much of him, so I was confused by the stare and demeanour. The others did what they could, asked David Gilmour to support Syd onstage. He knew Dave well and wasn't intimidated by him. It's true that just before this, he seemed disaffected and said he didn't want to be a "pop star," because he saw the band going that way. . . . He was always ironic about it."

Floyd was left holding the bag, however. Rick Sanders, in his bio on Pink Floyd, indicated that "after the split with Syd, the main trouble was that they had no sense of direction at all—a malaise that continued to afflict the group, on and off, up to the present day."

More changes were afoot. Peter Wynne Willson either quit or was given his walking papers, perhaps due to the business arrangement he had with the band. It may have been too expensive to keep him on, and instead Floyd elevated his sometimes-replacement, John Marsh, to handle the lighting. June Bolan was out, too, and with that, Syd's best friends were gone.

LEAVING SPACE FOR MADNESS

The transition from Syd-era Floyd to post-Barrett wasn't as painful as it could have been, however. The band kept Barrett's tunes in their sets, with Gilmour covering his friend's vocals and guitar parts. As the band had done with Syd, they'd improvised on a nightly basis, an approach that would become a cornerstone of their early post-Barrett aesthetic.

Being somewhat faceless worked to Floyd's advantage. The benefit of hiding behind the visual projections is that most people, even if they had heard or heard of Pink Floyd, might not associate one member of the band with the name. Pink Floyd was a sound—a collective—and not necessarily the vision of just one man. Or so it would be for the next few years anyway.

The first free Hyde Park show in June 1968, organized by Blackhill, featuring an eclectic and bluesy Jethro Tull, Marc Bolan's Tyrannosaurus Rex, and experimental folkie Roy Harper, was a turning point for the band. Floyd gave a strong performance and proved it could weather the fallout from the nuclear option of pushing Syd's exit from the band.

Floyd was clawing their way back. In the studio, Norman Smith, the man the band owed so much of its success, was bowled over by the band's new sound and the group's autonomy. Smith didn't so much butt heads with Floyd as become completely confused by the direction of the record they were making, eventually titled *A Saucerful of Secrets*.

Floyd's music seemed to blur the lines between the real and surreal. "Corporal Clegg," on the surface, appears to speak about military metals and service members' sacrifice. But did Clegg actually win these honors and face the horrors of war, or did he simply imagine he did? The lyrics state that he acquired medals of different colors at the zoo, and won them in a dream. Is he even a corporal? The song doesn't seem to answer this, and by its end it has devolved into kazoo looniness (is it kazlooney?), courtesy of Gilmour and Mason.

The true highlight of the record is "Set the Controls for the Heart of the Sun," which plods along with an unnerving, near-Indian-music-style drone, and is spurred on by the low, controlled rumbling of Mason's mallet melee. It remains vaguely hallucinatory, yet manages to steer clear of hippie-chic cliché.

All the earmarks of Floyd's and Waters's later work seem to be present here: a subtext that incorporates insanity, death, and possibly a poetic allusion to sexual consummation—an act which some might argue is procured through a mixture of ego loss, lunacy, and personal destruction. There's even a reference to "the wall."

Lyrically inspired by ancient Chinese poetry (and its title lifted from the mind of Michael Moorcock), "Set the Controls" had been termed as suicidal psychedelic/schizophrenic sci-fi. While it's true that some of these images could be interpreted as pure hallucinatory fantasy, taken literally, they may speak to the cosmic connectedness a mesmerized observer experiences in a process of self-realization.

For years my tendency was to tag this piece as an offshoot of the same familial branch of Floyd's evolutionary tree as "Interstellar Overdrive." It may, in spirit anyway, be closer to "Echoes." We're journeying with the speaker through a crescent of time, the very moment between the darkness of night and the appearance of the first rays of dawn, where both exist. This is Floyd yin and yang at its finest: a paradoxical and transitional musical/lyrical world that shaped the band's recordings throughout the next decade—and beyond.

"A Saucerful of Secrets" was, it was later revealed, composed of four movements: "Something Else," "Syncopated Pandemonium," "Storm Signal," and "Celestial Voices." Miles, writing for the *International Times* in the issue dated July 26–August 8, 1968, was disappointed in the title track, calling it "too long, too boring and totally uninventive," which stands in stark contrast to opener "Let There Be More Light."

Rick Wright's "Remember a Day" recalls the days of youth in which we attempted to "catch the sun." Barrett recorded slide guitar on the track, which reportedly was recorded during the *Piper* sessions, and Norman Smith played drums.

"Jugband Blues," Barrett's major contribution to *A Saucerful of Secrets*, was recorded prior to the *Saucerful* sessions. Its largely acoustic structure unravels and escalates to a sonic maelstrom, thanks, in large part, to the frenzied free-form style the orchestra was directed to play. The horns sound drunken, and when the song suddenly cuts out, it's like the aural equivalent of a psychotic break. The resounding, albeit slowly fading, finale hints at the majestic sublimity of a classical recital.

"Jugband Blues" does have its precedents. The middle section and crescendo does recall "A Day in the Life." As the final "proper song" on *Sgt. Pepper's*, "A Day in the Life" rests outside the bracketed *Sgt. Pepper's* "narrative" and is, strangely, a microcosm of the entire record. "Jugband Blues" similarly stands outside most of the material on *A Saucerful*, largely due to the quirkiness of Barrett's writing style.

Norman Smith recollected that the idea of putting orchestration on "Jugband" was more or less his. In a conversation with Syd, the concept morphed into Floyd using a Salvation Army Band at Syd's request. Syd said he had an idea of what he wanted, and guided by Syd's missive, Smith did not bother writing any musical notation.

Smith and production crew tracked down a Salvation Army band, which according to some reports were stationed on the street not too far from the studio, and scheduled an evening session at De Lane Lea studios. The plan was for Syd to, if not conduct in the traditional sense, at least interact with the brass band and explain what he was hearing in his head so they could translate this into a recorded performance.

Barrett was an hour late, and when he eventually arrived, to a waiting Smith and packed studio, was a bit overwhelmed. When Smith asked Syd for direction, Syd shrugged his shoulders and said he wasn't sure what the band should play.

Miffed, Smith reminded Barrett of their conversation and the producer shot back, "How would you like them to play?"

"Let them play anything," said Barrett, as he was leaving for the door.

Smith regrouped, got everyone on the same page, and took control of the situation. He didn't want people walking out—as a founding member of the Floyd had just done. Instead, on the fly, he jotted down a few basic chords of the song and then allowed the brass band to experiment within those parameters.

The result is a surprisingly drunken uproar, a rip in the musical fabric—but that's its beauty. Whether Barrett ever really had an idea—probably not—about exactly what he wanted, he knew enough to leave space for madness.

But what does the song mean? When Barrett sings, "I'm most obliged to you for making it clear that I'm not here," perhaps he's really thanking the band for relieving him of the stress and the burden of being a rock star. Maybe that's what he wanted? If Syd was indeed losing his mind, apparently he was still a sentient enough being to recognize, with clarity, what was happening to him and still create compelling art.

To his credit, Norman Smith may not have understood the goal of the boys' music, but he introduced them to the joys of the studio and recording ideas on their own. In essence, Smith saw fit to give Floyd some space—even if he was confused by their direction.

In subsequent years, the band would conclude that *A Saucerful* was a major stepping-stone toward self-production and wrangling creative control from the label or even prospective producers and engineers. This was a milestone in and of itself, and a bridge leading toward productions such as *The Dark Side of the Moon* and *WYWH*.

In a lot of ways *A Saucerful of Secrets* was the beginning of Pink Floyd. The album cover by Hipgnosis was the result of superimposed images, including the stations of the zodiac, our solar system, and bottles of potion.

Prior to working on Floyd album covers, the rag-tag design company that would become Hipgnosis designed book covers. Po indicated to author Mark Blake that the phrase Hipgnosis was written in pen outside the door of their/Barrett's Egerton Court apartment house.

Secrets was released in July 1968 to an ever-turbulent world. The previous month, US Presidential candidate Robert F. Kennedy was assassinated by Sirhan Sirhan, perhaps due to RFK's support of Israel during the 1967 Six-Day War. At Sirhan's 1969 trial, the defense team argues that the alleged assassin was a so-called "Manchurian Candidate"— subdued by self-hypnosis and victim of the surveillance and intelligence community's controversial mind-control experiments. Many political pundits thought RFK could have won the Democratic Party's nomination for President of the United States in 1968 and eventually a temporary residence at the White House.

By the close of the year, the single "Point Me at the Sky" b/w "Careful with That Axe, Eugene" was released but promptly flopped. Floyd was beginning to understand they were not made, without Syd, to be a singles band. In fact, most of *A Saucerful* went against this grain.

Eventually "Eugene," in its extended live form, became one of the iconic or flagship Floyd songs, emblematic of their musical daring and willingness to challenge their audiences. Perhaps too droning and mesmerizing to be considered completely deranged, "Eugene" is buoyed by a two-beat bass line bump, loony atmospheric scatting, doubling guitar squawks, the *shooshing* sibilance and squeaking squalls of vocal effects, and Waters's deliciously bloodcurdling scream. It's clear that something is "off" about the song, on more than one level. The darkness within the track is palpable, unavoidable, and undeniable.

The post-Barrett band wasn't generally perceived to be criminally violent or clinically insane, yet this relatively frightening track is either evidence of genius mimicry or undiagnosed and deeply rooted emotional disturbance. In 1968 Floyd may not have been capable or willing to hold a mirror up to themselves, although this ripping off of the mask reveals subconscious truths about the collective human psyche.

SEEKING HELP?

Syd had moved out of Richmond and had taken up at Egerton Court with his girlfriend Lindsay Korner. Storm Thorgerson, Aubrey Powell, and David Gale also resided there. David Gale, Storm, Barrett and others were experimenting with LSD—some say morning glory, a plant whose flower had hallucinogenic qualities when ingested. Supposedly, as recounted by others, Gale, Barrett, and fellow trippers took hallucinogens in Gale's parents' house while they were out of the country.

It's difficult to pinpoint the exact date or whether the incident happened—or was imagined to have happened in the heady days of the late 1960s. Legend had it that Barrett was urged to go see psychiatrist R. D. Laing—or was made to go. It was at this much-confused moment in diagnosing and caring for mental health that the Barrett-less Floyd was moving away from their sci-fi public predilections and embracing notions of insanity.

In the US, in the mid-twentieth century, a social autopsy was performed regarding the release of psychiatric patients from state hospitals, second-guessing the policies enacted by the government and those in the mental health profession, who relied too heavily on community clinics and drugs to address issues facing patients. In addition, the costs involved in running hospitals and caring for those with mental health issues were beginning to reach critical mass.

In the US, it led to a grand reevaluation championed by Congress's Joint Commission on Mental Illness and Health, established in 1955, in which fewer patients were being admitted, and in increasing numbers, more and more patients were being released—in some cases with no place to live but the street.

Squalid living conditions and abusive treatment of patients in state mental institutions had long been a matter of public outcry, but the pendulum had swung back too far in the opposite direction. The Community Mental Health Act, legislation passed by Congress in 1963, only accelerated the problem.

The UK had been dealing with this issue even earlier. It's true that the mental health sectors in both the US and the UK were in serious need of reform, due to patient neglect and abuse. But was the decision to continue deinstitutionalization policies the correct remedy?

Funding, the shifting notions of sanity and insanity, psychologist David Rosenhan's experiment from 1973 exposing flaws in mental health diagnosis—all contributed to a re-examination in care. A new hands-off approach to the mentally ill had created more freedoms, perhaps, but more problems. Government and society, in general, seemed to slink away from the growing problem on both sides of the Atlantic. As a result, society as a whole has had to deal with rampant homelessness and perhaps an epidemic of violence that's still not being properly addressed.

Community clinics, particularly in the US, began administering tranquilizers, keeping those with existing conditions in their chemically imbalanced state. Yet what LSD was to some hippies—a panacea drug to open doors of the mind—tranquilizers were to psychiatrists during roughly the same era.

Certain drugs *did* help individuals stay out of hospitals, but budgets dictated that institutions de-staff and ultimately shut. This, coupled with the false assumption that local clinics could quite possibly eradicate mental health problems, only doomed the policy shift and fostered chaos.

So-called anti-psychiatrist R. D. Laing advocated for the use of hallucinogenic drugs over tranquilizers for therapeutic purposes. He would essentially trip with his patients, although he'd ingest a smaller dose of the hallucinogen. Like so much of the counter-culture, Laing's radical theories and antiestablishment stance manifested itself in his theories challenging orthodox views on madness.

"What we were doing with the hippie thing was what [Laing] was doing with psychology," says Jenner. "Miles was doing with the papers and . . . Laing was doing with shrinking and we were doing with the music."

A peripheral character at the Notting Hill Free School, Laing eventually was spotted around the London underground rubbing elbows with some of the most active minds of the counterculture. "[Laing] seemed to be thinking that insanity might be a very subjective idea; that perhaps madness might give people some kind of greater insight," Roger Waters told author John Harris.

No record has come to light to illuminate what transpired at their meeting—if there even was one. It is a tantalizing thought, however, to think that Laing could probe Syd's psyche and discuss the death of his father, LSD use, and the obvious breakdown of the Pink Floyd unit.

Andrew Rawlinson, Waters's friend from Cambridge, explained in Tim Willis's Barrett biography *Madcap* that Syd was aware of Laing and his theories. The details are fuzzy, but Floyd lore hints at a meeting between Laing and Barrett.

Several reports seem to fit two or three vague templates: 1) Accompanied by Waters, Barrett sat motionless during the car ride over to Laing's office; he approached the doors of the building but refused to go in; 2) Aubrey Powell and flat mate David Gale hailed a cab to take a receptive Barrett to Laing, but Syd never left his apartment; 3) Syd briefly visited with Laing, only once, and did not become a regular patient.

"My memory on all that is a bit shaky," says Jenner. "I think [Barrett] did actually go and see [Laing] but it never got any further than that. It wasn't like he became his doctor. He did go to see him, though."

"In 1968, a close friend of Syd's arranged an appointment for him with the psychologist R. D. Laing," Spires counters,

> but when they got there he refused to go in, and no one was going to force him. Laing wouldn't have seen him under those conditions. I was aware of Laing, because the buzz was he was turned on and had a new approach to psychotherapy. He was rather strange. I am not sure I would have wanted to see him if I had a choice either.

In any case, there may have been little Laing could have actually done for Syd. There have been reports, for years, of Barrett being locked behind closed doors in his own apartment and prone to violent tendencies. He also began walking the streets, seemingly aimlessly, in no rush to go home.

Some in the media, even the proponents of LSD, were questioning its potency and the safety of using the drug. Others were staunchly defiant, regardless of the human cost. The January 16–29, 1967, issue of the *International Times*, edited by Tom McGrath, explored the impact of the usage of LSD in British culture with a front-page opinion piece, telling readers that "a man's religious beliefs are untouchable: if he happens to use a drug to reach his vision, he should be left unmolested by the Law and those so many doctor gentlemen so anxious to label others 'insane.'"

Not only did this editorial show deference to Laing's notions of madness, but Laing's image even appears next to the published piece. It also highlighted what many young people believed about LSD and hallucinogens: they are powerful, yes, but necessary for society to take that next great evolutionary step, to free one's mind and achieve a "divine vision" or, perhaps most practically, operate as a mechanism or tool for psychoanalysis.

This theory was met with disapproval from some surprising quarters of the scientific community. "LSD is . . . the most inappropriate means imaginable for curing a depressive state. It is dangerous to take LSD in a disturbed, unhappy frame of mind, or in a state of fear. The probability that the experiment will end in a psychic breakdown is then quite high," Albert Hofmann wrote in *LSD, My Problem Child*.

"Among persons with unstable personality structures, tending to psychotic reactions, LSD experimentation ought to be completely avoided," Hofmann continued. "Here an LSD shock, by releasing a latent psychosis, can produce a lasting mental injury."

Did LSD unlock a latent psychosis in Syd? And if he were taking too much of the hallucinogen, was it all voluntary? Although for years some within the Floyd universe maintained that Syd could have been fed LSD without his knowledge, prior to moving to the less-frantic confines of Egerton Court, certainly most of his trips were undertaken with his full awareness. Spiking someone's drink wasn't unheard of in the 1960s, but this behavior ran counter to hippie etiquette. Ironically, this thinking may have led many to be more vulnerable than they had previously thought.

What has never been sufficiently answered is the question of how much the LSD use contributed to Syd's deteriorating mental state. Citing medical research, author and underground pioneer Barry Miles speculates in *Pink Floyd: The Early Years* that a deficiency in adrenaline metabolism in the brain could help form a chemical compound, such as adrenochrome, with similar side effects to mescaline "and therefore psychosis." Miles further posits that it may have been Floyd's own lighting show, the projections onto their bodies, the images beamed directly into their eyes, that could have triggered a chemical chain reaction inside Syd's brain.

It is impossible to know really, and however this chemical process began, the implication is whatever altered Syd's brain, it made his psychological and emotional conditions virtually incurable through mere holidays in the Mediterranean.

The counterculture sought total freedom, but its search for personal liberation led to unintended consequences, what we might call "bad trips." "A bad trip is usually symptom of something," Cambridge filmmaker Anthony Stern once told me. "In other words you're getting these symptoms that make you very frightened, indeed." What level, if any and for any extended amount of time, Syd experienced paranoia via a "bad trip" is another variable in the Barrett story. Barrett appeared to be chasing something altogether different through LSD.

"[Syd] also became greedy for the experience," Stern told me. "I know for a fact at Earlham Street in Soho, in the mid- to late '60s, he was taking acid virtually every day, according to people who had lived with him, so he was trying to get there and stay there. A bit like a guru or someone . . . who forces himself to stay in this high level of *Samadhi*, I think it's called: a highly evolved state."

Did Syd take LSD as a way of not only expanding his mind, but as a means of improving himself? Maybe we have been looking at this all wrong. Did Syd believe his mind was operating differently from others of his generation, but wanted to change this and, quite paradoxically, conform? In other words, stop the madness.

Syd's slow descent into the dark side of the counterculture's obsessions may have revealed inner truths but perhaps also deep-seated fears. Said Stern, the body and psyche are not equipped for such a journey, and instead of trekking through the broken wreckage of a psyche one begins to self-destruct. "I think it's fair to say that his mind would have been destroyed one way or another fairly soon," Stern told me. "If it hadn't been LSD then it may have been [something else]."

On LSD, it seems, the mind attempts to understand itself. This feeling of "the other," a second presence and fellow traveler with you, could be the mind attempting to split and analyze itself at the death of the ego. Some have described Syd as just that: a kind of "other." Syd's sensitivity to the world around him may have turned the psychic spigot permanently to the "on" position. What does someone do when too much information, too many sensations, filter through the brain? Oftentimes the antidote is to break down and shut out the world.

In *Trouser Press*, February 1978, Jerry Shirley, drummer on some of Barrett's solo material, said that "Syd is alive but he doesn't exist anymore."

BARRETT'S BACK?

Syd apparently wasn't rolling over and giving up altogether on music. Because Syd appeared to be motivated to record in the studio, Jenner attempted to reach him.

Floyd's rising popularity gave Malcolm Jones pause, and his new label, EMI's subsidiary Harvest, presented an opportunity to capitalize on Barrett's growing notoriety. Jones was convinced that Barrett's public and private persona could be rehabilitated and benefit all parties involved. When Jones heard "Terrapin" and "Clowns and Jugglers," which would later be retitled "Octopus" after a fairgrounds ride (Syd's own "Helter Skelter"), this was the clincher.

"Every summer the fair arrives in Cambridge," says Jenny Spires. "It unpacks from huge lorries on to the tufted grassland of Midsummer Common, next to the river. It was a crazy, heady time for us when the fair came. Originally it marked the twelfth-century feast of Etheldreda, but by the time we were teenagers, it was a large travelling fair of rides with flashing neon lights and loud rock 'n' roll showcasing Dodgem cars, shooting galleries, a Helter Skelter, the Haunted Tower and the fabulous Octopus ride.

"Syd recreates the madness and high spirits of the fair in 'Octopus'," Spires continues.

> The excitement beyond words . . . "Trip to heave and ho, up down, to and fro, you have no word." Then later he compares this to the quiet of the wood he loved, "Isn't it good to be lost in the wood?" And well, yes, "Lost in the Woods" has come to mean it's great being out there, "far out," lost in the woods, away from it all, but it's only half the story. The loud music and flashing lights are attracting him. Kind of Romantic, but he uses the song to describe how he is torn between these two worlds—the madcap on the border between these two extremes.

Even if Barrett didn't produce a bona fide chart-topping hit, a record of new Syd material could do modestly well, keeping money rolling into the coffers and Barrett on the road. But opening the door to the possibilities of bringing Syd into the studio was a risky prospect—an opportunity for greatness but also the possibility that hours and days of hard work would run horribly off course.

Jones may have initially been elated by the potential and premise of the project, but his enthusiasm waned as the sessions became increasingly hopeless—and endless. The recording process was so drawn out, in fact, that Jones nearly pulled the plug on the whole damn thing.

As it turns out there was some salvageable material from all those sessions, thanks largely to Barrett's ex-bandmates, who would handle the production duties. The pressure was on to complete the album and attempt to shut Syd off from outside distractions.

"Things would come to his brain and he couldn't recycle and put them into a shape," Jenner says.

> I think he was getting a series of flashbacks and flash-forwards, inspirations, and then, *blip*, it's gone. My analogy, which I still use in dealing with Syd, was like spotting a trolley bus, an electronic trolley bus, in my youth. We used to have some big fogs in London in the 1950s and I remember waiting for the bus—but you couldn't hear it coming. It was silent. Then suddenly there would be some light and the bus would come out of the fog. Then it would go back into the fog. You couldn't see it before or after but in the event that you caught it or it stopped you knew there was a trolley bus. You'd have these tunes or things that would come and then they would disappear back into the fog.

Constant and different takes, overdubs galore . . . and the clock was running down. Jones called a meeting and demanded the record needed to be finished—and very soon— or the entire misadventure would be *shitcanned*. Bringing on Waters and Gilmour as producers was a stroke of genius.

There's been some speculation that the rawness and realness of these tracks, the abandoned starts, the mumbling and swallowed words between takes, made it to the final mix deliberately as a marketing angle. Where songs on *Piper* were infused with a kaleidoscopic array of sonic textures and colors, the paintings presented on *The Madcap Laughs* seem to work in grays, browns, and shades of black.

Indeed. When one listens to these songs it paints a picture; you feel as though Syd is standing in front of you as he plays. That kind of intimacy is immediately identifiable and memorable, perhaps as much as the songs themselves. Gilmour, Waters, and Jones were not only building breathtaking tracks and offering snapshots of the absolute state of Syd's mind, but creating a mystique around Syd that continues to this day.

"If It's In You" begins with a false start followed by heartbreakingly strained vocals— which nearly all musicians have experienced at one point or another in the studio. "If It's In You" presents Syd at his most vulnerable, with false starts and verbal exchanges with his recording session overlords, as he explains that he's working out how to approach a tricky ascending-descending vocal line while simultaneously straining to stretch the word "thinking" into what could be two dozen syllables, and strumming acoustic guitar, even as tape rolls.

Syd asks for the tape to be cut (and it does sound as if there is an edit here, in deference to him). The session picks up, again, Syd clears his throat and, with some trepidation and a stutter or two here and there, nails the vocals and guitar playing in the take saved for prosperity.

In "Cold Look" we hear the madcap mumbling, strumming his acoustic guitar with one hand while leafing through his crib sheets with the other. Did these details remain in the final versions purely for the level of intimacy they represent? And why did a major work, like "Opel," only see the light of day nearly two decades later? "Perhaps we were trying to show what Syd was really like, but perhaps we were trying to punish him," Waters was quoted as saying in Willis's Syd bio, *Madcap*.

If a punishment was in order, as Waters suggested, couldn't the opposite be true, too? Did Syd really want to be in the studio? Did Syd feel guilty about the past but showed up in the studio because he believed his former bandmembers wanted him to succeed—and didn't want to let them down?

Interestingly, at any given moment, the project benefited from a total of at least three former and current members of the band working on these tracks. Whatever motivation animated the major players in this drama, this was (at times) Floyd virtually unplugged, unadorned and dysfunctional—a semi-group effort of sorts. It's been reported that Gilmour in particular handled much of the instrumentation for the songs that appear on Syd's first solo record.

Whatever the marketing strategy, Gilmour and Waters had to drag Syd across the finish line to complete the recordings. "I don't know where all that stuff with Dave and Roger and Syd came from, or what they did in the studio," Jenner says. "I think they invented most of it. [laughs] I don't know. Then, again, Syd certainly did have lots of songs in his songbook before he left the band—or the band left him."

However they materialized, Barrett did, indeed, appear to have a wealth of material. "Octopus," originally titled "Clowns and Jugglers," was cut in July 1968 and features members of Soft Machine, who finished the track in May of the following year. A version of the song, appearing on *The Madcap Laughs*, features David Gilmour on drums, who extracted an album title from the lyrics of "Octopus."

Strange and disconnected thoughts filled the conversation in the studio when Soft Machine's drummer Robert Wyatt, bassist Hugh Hopper, and keyboardist Mike Ratledge were set to track their instruments. The Softs were stunned when, after Wyatt began asking questions about the tracks, Barrett provided odd and disjointed responses.

A typical exchange went something like this:

Wyatt: "What key are we in?"

Barrett: "Oh, yeah."

Despite, or perhaps because of the amorphous nature of the communication between the musicians, "Octopus" is one of Barrett's most successful tracks: Ratledge contributes his signature otherworldly sonic radiance along with customary organ blurps, Wyatt maneuvers a rhythmic pattern resembling a shuffle-march, and Hopper provides bottom-end sludge.

And because Jenner managed former Soft guitarist Kevin Ayers, Barrett allegedly recorded with him too. However, the version of "Singing a Song in the Morning" featuring Syd has never been officially released as far as I know.

"Here I Go" seems cheerful and lighthearted, but a closer examination reveals layers of metaphors that seem difficult to ignore, perhaps like much in the Barrett solo catalog. The story Syd tells is of a boy who fancies a girl who actually doesn't like his songs. The object of the boy's affection to him: "a big band is better than you." The narrator eventually hits it off with the girl's sister, someone who appreciates the boy's (Syd's?) songs, and the two appear to live happily ever after.

What was Syd getting at with his lyrics? Was this a metaphor for Floyd? The record business at large? Or was the girl someone he actually knew and dated? Was this his fantasy of a "normal" life with a girl? Someone who could accept him for all his qualities and personal faults?

The Purple Gang was set to cover "Here I Go" after being handed a tape of the song. "It was a small tape, 8 ips I think," says Chris Joe Beard. "He had handed it to Joe Boyd in the studio, Sound Techniques Old Church St. Chelsea, to give to us, as he had heard 'Granny Takes a Trip' and loved it. He thought 'Here I Go' might do for a single follow-up for us."

Beard admits he struggled with chords of the song at first, and was faced with another dilemma: the Purple Gang's label didn't want the band to cover anyone else's songs. "I put the tape in my guitar case and took it back to our digs with Boyd at 90 Westbourne Terrace, Bayswater," says Beard. "Later we asked Nat Joseph, head of Transatlantic Records, if we could learn it and record it, but he strictly forbade me. He insisted all our songs should be home grown and kept 'in house.' They didn't want to pay other publishers. So we didn't do it."

Syd himself would see his material shelved. Some material would be re-recorded, and the twenty-minute experimental jazz-rock excursion titled "Ramadan" (sometimes appears with an "h") went unreleased at the time and featured the sound of a cranked motorcycle around 7:37 into the song as well as percussion courtesy of friend Steve Peregrin Took.

Took, who swiped his stage name from J. R. R. Tolkien's literary fantasy world, was a founding member of Tyrannosaurus Rex (also T. Rex), formed in 1967 and spearheaded by guitarist and tastemaker Marc Bolan, a Barrett devotee. It's been reported that Took also made social appearances with Barrett.

Either through scientific calculation or sheer default, the batch of songs that would emerge from Barrett's early solo sessions, and the subsequent ones in which many of these songs were completed, present a fragile, raw, and semi-acoustic artist. The relatively sparse nature of some of the material of the Barrett solo songs was intended to show Syd's true artistry. Barrett's seemingly offbeat vocal pacing and his strumming were more in line with folk-rock contemporaries than the underground psychedelic and art-rock worlds from whence Barrett came.

"Dark Globe," the first stirrings of which were tracked in late July 1969, invokes pathos, fantasy, and absence. It's a song, *Rolling Stone* magazine reported in 1987, that Waters continued to sing in the tub for decades after it was recorded. With his voice cracking, Barrett strains to sing above his strummed guitar, spinning fanciful lyrics that fuse his personality with nature.

Barrett paints images of a "pussy willow," "poppy birds," and "a person with an 'Eskimo chain' that has 'tattooed my brain.'" We can't escape the notion that Barrett may have used the word *Eskimo* as a reference to his girlfriend of Inuit heritage, Iggy, or as a way of stressing the connection in the British psyche between poppies and youth, war, burial, death, and remembrance. Well, anymore than we can escape poppies' link to opium. Barrett's identity is in there, somewhere, but he appears to have flown on or blown away with the summer breeze when he sings: "Won't you miss me? Wouldn't you miss me at all?"

Based on the James Joyce poem of the same title, "Golden Hair" from Syd's solo debut *The Madcap Laughs* is one of Barrett's most memorable solo recordings and was recorded in June 1969. "When I was working with Syd, the song that really got me was 'Golden Hair,'" Jenner says. "I find it really upsetting. Every now and again there would be these glimpses of the Syd that I had known and then they would disappear . . . into the fog, again."

1969

Billed as *The Massed Gadgets of Auximenes—More Furious Madness from Pink Floyd*, the band's Royal Festival Hall show of April 1969 is remembered secondly for the panned sound effects pumped through the venue's quad system.

It's foremost recalled for the addition of performance art to the act, provided by former art student Peter Dockley, who ran around the venue in a monster costume and a gas mask, scaring some of the audience members. Some swear it was a gorilla costume and one report holds that Dockley sat down next to a young girl and sent her screaming out of the hall.

None of this was meant as a distraction, although it did "enhance" the live event. The musical score featured two large works: *The Man* and *The Journey*. The dual pieces were conceptually linked, a bit like the Moody Blues' 1967 LP *Days of Future Passed*, meant to portray a day in the life of an ordinary person. An orchestral version of a kind called *The Final Lunacy* was staged in London at the Royal Albert Hall in June 1969.

Sections of these songs surfaced as material on the *More* soundtrack, *Relics* compilation, and as studio material for the double album *Ummagumma*. Mason indicated that some of sounds created for the show were repurposed for either "Alan's Psychedelic Breakfast" from 1970's *Atom Heart Mother*, or the abandoned *Household Objects*. "The Man" also contained parts of concepts Floyd developed further. "Nightmare," for instance, boasts ticking clocks and ringing alarm bells and spoken-word audio, the substance of which was the basis for the schoolteacher's pudding-and-meat screed from *The Wall*.

Floyd synthesized some of its earliest performance arts ideas and funneled them into their recent creations. A wooden table was hammered and sawed onstage for "Work," just in time for the road crew to place cups of tea on it. The sound of machinery on prerecorded audiotapes could be seen as a precursor of the throbbing robotics of "Welcome to the Machine" and, perhaps more importantly, a transistor radio was tuned on stage and the frequency was sent out to the audience via PA, foreshadowing the car-radio intro to "Wish You Were Here."

A rail ride from Paddington station, London, to Paris partly inspired the entire project. Graffiti scrawled on a wall leading into a train tunnel read something like: "Get up, go to work, come home, go to bed," repeated several times, right up to the point the wall met the edge of the tunnel. Waters thought this was inspired genius: it was a representation of a life of the workingman, until he enters a dark tunnel, which could be interpreted as death, one supposes.

In May 1969, an announcement was made that the following month, EMI was going to issue progressive material via a new imprint, the Harvest label—the company's first new label since 1962. Harvest was scheduled to release four LPs and two singles. Shirley and Dolly Collins, Edgar Broughton Band, Deep Purple (who had previously been on Parlophone), and Pete Brown. Floyd, Third Ear Band, and the Pretty Things were coming up behind them. Double-fold sleeves meant higher retail prices—by 25 cents.

For the time being, Floyd was hard at work in Marble Arch in London at Pye with recording engineer Brian Humphries on the soundtrack for the film *More*, using a stop watch to time their cues. Floyd were known for projections accompanying their music, but soundtrack work was a whole different kettle of fish.

More was filmed in Ibiza, trendy as a vacation spot for the Cambridge set in the 1960s, and the virtual capital of the electronic dance culture in the twenty-first century—a bawdy beacon of EDM hedonism for Europe and the world.

Directed by Barbet Schroeder, *More* is a hippie adventure turned nightmare—a perfect parable for the ever-shifting cultural climate of the late 1960s. The main character attempts to kick heroin by using LSD, but when the purported cure has no effect, our hero falls back into addiction. A cautionary tale about the excesses of the counterculture if there ever was one, *More* quite eerily is positioned in a very strange and unnerving chapter in popular history.

Some memorable moments of the soundtrack include the Hendrix-ian "The Nile Song" and "Green Is the Colour," with the same kind of scatting that we'd later hear in "Wish You Were Here." It should be noted that Waters-penned, Gilmour-vocalized "Cymbaline" tackled the pressures involved in maintaining balance when living in a pop band, from intelligently rhyming lyrics to staying a step ahead of vulture-like competitors, who wait for the successful and confident to falter and fall off the high wire to peck their eyes out.

Despite the delightful and almost ghostly melody, the song plods along with the certainty and darkness of a funerary dirge. Maybe the message we should receive is that working in the music business is a kind of death, a hell that lays claims to the soul?

Although it had been issued earlier in the year for the UK market, Floyd's soundtrack for *More* was released in the US on August 9, 1969—the very same day the Manson Family brutalized and murdered five people at Roman Polanski's Beverly Hills home, 10050 Cielo Drive, including the director's pregnant wife, actress Sharon Tate. It wasn't until a few years later that Floyd got to know Polanski, a bit, through ballet director Roland Petit in the early 1970s. For Manson, Tate and Polanski were symbolic of an establishment that needed to be eradicated, and one that rejected him.

More seems to reflect a growing sense, a perception in mainstream consciousness, about the times: the Summer of Love had breezed through, leaving a chill in the air, while the Manson murders helped to further erode the Hippie Dream and bring it to a screeching halt. The Rolling Stones concert at Altamont later in the year sealed fate and dampened any hope for a utopian society.

The last vestiges of psychedelia and a fertile, radical counterculture were slowly drying up. It may have been the dawning of the Age of Aquarius, but we were entering into a strange new phase of this so-called global enlightenment. And if Manson was not indicative of your average hippie, if he can rightly be called a "hippie" at all, then he certainly was the embodiment of the counterculture's dark impulses run amok.

It was both timely and perhaps prophetic that Floyd would begin to pull back somewhat from their psychedelic tendencies, circa 1970, and start anew with something resembling a more symphonic approach. Perhaps unwittingly, Floyd was reflecting the jagged schism in the larger culture. On the one hand, some had philosophized that the Manson murders and Altamont were the spiritual end of the 1960s. On the other, on the East Coast, the Woodstock festival would be viewed by historians as the culmination of the hippie movement.

"Woodstock was an affirmation and, at the same time, the culmination of the free-spirited hippie movement which had spawned so much creative, positive energy," says Jenny Spires, who happened to be travelling through America in 1969 and went to the three-day festival of music, love, and peace. "The fact that there were tailbacks for miles, it rained, and people were totally exposed to the elements didn't seem to dampen those spirits."

The detrimental effects of the hippie lifestyle, including rampant drug taking, the communal life, and free love, led to emotional and physical abandonment, the breakdown of the family, ever-widening racial divides, crime, drug abuse, and disease—to name only a few of the plagues that were visited upon mid-twentieth-century society.

HARVEST RISES

The double album *Ummagumma*, the first Floyd record to appear on EMI's new subsidiary label Harvest, is composed of live tracks and studio material. Predating works such as Soft Machine's *Third* and Emerson, Lake & Palmer's *Works*, *Ummagumma* was culled from recent live shows and carved out a spot for each member to shine individually.

Gilmour's tri-panel "The Narrow Way" provides what might be the most disturbing and accessible of the entire compositional-based experiment. Wright's austere "Sysyphus" is told in four movements, much like a traditional classical symphony, and Mason's "Grand Vizier's Garden Party" is constructed of tape manipulation, possibly treated percussion, and loops. It's really a deconstructed drum solo that skirts the more cliché and purely technically acrobatic aspects of this time-honored percussive workout. Mason's former wife Lindy contributed the flute we hear in the track.

Waters's work is the most amusing. A fly flutters about at the opening of the folk-laden "Grantchester Meadows," clearly buzzing out a melody of some sort, until it's swatted away. A *splat!* announces the opening of "Several Species of Small Furry Animals Gathered Together in a Cave and Grooving with a Pict."

Waters's faux Scottish accent, an almost incomprehensible language, sounds partially like gibberish mixed with English—sharing a kinship with the work of Ron Geesin and foreshadowing moments of *The Wall.* This writer believes the song concludes with the line, "and the wind cried Mary," referencing "The Wind Cries Mary" from the Jimi Hendrix Experience's debut *Are You Experienced?*

The front cover appears to be some variation of the Droste effect, but the back cover image, conceived by Mason, is just as intriguing. Guitars and amplifiers are arranged in a mirrored alignment, a single-dot gong rests atop the Floyd tour bus, like the pyramidal all-seeing eye of Ra, and roadies Pete Watts and Alan Styles are recessed into the gear and situated behind a pair of timpani. In the foreground, drumming implements are fanned out on the pavement. The rhythm of the road.

THE HIPPIE DREAMS CRASHES, FALLS TO EARTH

In the summer of 1969, the Apollo Moon landing captivated the world—a peak moment in our shared history for which Floyd provided the soundtrack during the BBC's broadcast of the historic event. By 1970, some say the world had changed. Among other things, the Beatles had just broken up, more body bags emerged from the bellies of military aircraft (thirty-six thousand Americans had died in Vietnam at the close of 1969), and the denouement of the '60s, the cluster fuck known as Altamont, shocked a nation.

In England a pall had also set in. Acid ran roughshod over a generation of counterculture *dimensionauts*, leaving users bereft and zombified, or worse. After a return from their spiritual sojourn to India, Lesmoir-Gordon says he felt something had changed about London, and England in general.

"What happened in 1970 with Brian and Janis [Joplin] and Jimi, and all those people died, the fucking light went out," says Lesmoir-Gordon. "I don't know what happened. Rubbish piled up in Royal Avenue. We had rubbish collection strikes, power outages. . . . Daisy, my daughter, was born in 1970, and you know . . . 'Nige, I missed the party.'"

As Western society was ambling out of the middle decades of the twentieth century, we had not only taken onboard certain tendencies toward consumerism and conformity, but also extremism, violence, and hopelessness. Radicalism gained force, yes, but so did complacency and a need to return to a kind of "normalcy." In short, people were getting on with their lives.

The relative passivism of the 1960s was no more, and cities across the globe were headed toward a kind of reckoning—politically, economically, socially, and philosophically. What did it all mean?

CHAPTER 2

DAFT COW

In late February 1970, Syd Barrett, along with drummer Jerry Shirley and Gilmour, performed on *The John Peel Show* on BBC 1, presenting songs "Terrapin," "Gigolo Aunt," "Effervescing Elephant," "Baby Lemonade," and "Two a Kind"—a selection of semi-acoustic renditions of songs (mostly) from Barrett's solo records.

In June, at Extravaganza 70, a music and fashion festival, Syd, along with Shirley on drums and Gilmour on bass, played a quick set at the Olympia, which included the song "Octopus," before Barrett thanked the crowd and whisked himself offstage. Barrett's show of appreciation and brief set was met with intermittent clapping from a confused crowd.

Barrett's appearances onstage may have been fleeting, but his recorded music seemed built to last. Barrett's self-titled second album exists in a wider sonic spectrum of instrumentation and vocal overdubs relative to *Madcap*. Gilmour's lusher electrified production, one would think, could have been a boon to this project, positioning Barrett's visions in a more psychedelic setting. More often than not, however, it neutralizes the sparse beauty of Barrett's writing approach, rendering the album somewhat tame. But some songs *do* manage to capture a bit of Barrett's playfulness and utter kookiness, including the drunken "Maisie," "Wolfpack," the tuba-tastic "Effervescing Elephant," and "Rats," the most disorienting and creatively successful track on the record, marked by what feels like sliding time signatures and Guthrie/Dylan/Lennon lyrical streams of consciousness.

The ballad "Wined and Dined" is supposedly inspired by the tumultuous on-again/off-again relationships Barrett kept with model Gayla (or Gala) Pinion, one of a few serious girlfriends he kept in his life. "It is Obvious," which credits Gilmour with second organ, features Wright's keyboard runs reminiscent of what we hear in "Alan's Psychedelic Breakfast" from *Atom Heart Mother*.

"Birdie Hop," initial tracks for which were cut in June 1970, is said to be inspired by Hoppy. (The song was later released on the EMI/Capitol/Harvest rarities and outtakes compilation *Opel*, from 1988.) Julian Palacios hypothesizes in his book *Lost in the Woods* that the "flies" referred to in the lyrics are not only metaphors for disease, disintegration, and death, but the Flies, Floyd's nemesis when the band was a fixture of the London music underground.

Considered a very early British punk band, The Flies (not to be confused with the '70s punk band the Flys) shouted "Sellout" at the Floyd from the side of the stage at the Roundhouse in April 1967. Not to be churlish, but with a penchant for cover songs and the overt pop-y nature of some of the Flies' psychedelic output, the band had little room to talk (or scream) about Floyd.

Recorded in the summer of 1970, but not included on *Barrett*, were a few outstanding tracks, "Dolly Rocker," "Let's Split," "Word Song," and the long-sought-after demo, the farcical "Bob Dylan Blues," which surfaced on an EMI/Harvest collection released in the early twenty-first century, titled *The Best of Syd Barrett: Wouldn't You Miss Me?*

≡

Barrett was behaving more erratically, shutting himself up in his room in the apartment he shared with painter Duggie Fields. Even as an endless string of acquaintances, would-be lovers, star-struck fans, and fair-weather friends regularly visited, Barrett remained something of a hermit. When Barrett ventured outside his cave, increasingly, he abandoned his London flat for Cambridge, leaving Fields to clean up any potential and uncomfortable personal messes having arisen from his interactions with God knows who.

If the problem of Syd's "friends" had been brewing for some time, surely other private storms had been developing as well. Syd had reportedly been violent on occasion with Gala, causing the couple to break up. Clearly a passion burned, and it's likely love existed between them—once. But the relationship may have been symbiotic as much as romantic. A vulnerable Barrett needed stability, which the gainfully employed Gala provided, and the aspiring model may have desired the status of savior and succor, attempting to coax the cult figure away from the edge through an endless supply of second chances.

The excitement of the English capitol, Swingin' London of just a few years earlier, now held no fascination for Syd. Once the musical prince of the underground music scene, Barrett had been reduced to a noncommunicative phantom, a shut-in trying to escape from his self-imposed prison sentence.

The decision was made to leave London altogether, with Gala, and return to Syd's mother's basement in Cambridge, where they both could live unmolested and in relative calm. Despite the security of his mum's house, Barrett let his imagination get the best of him and began spying on Gala at her work, believing she was having an affair with an old flame. There was no evidence she was unfaithful.

If "Wined and Dined" was truly inspired by Pinion, it's fascinating that, in the song, Barrett refers to love in the past tense. Stranger still, Barrett wanted to marry Pinion. Syd supposedly had the ring picked out, and he and Gala were engaged in October 1970.

Early autumn may have been the pinnacle of their time together. In the coming days and weeks, Barrett's propensity for physical altercations was not lessened by the appearance of an engagement ring.

However, Gala simply couldn't take the violence, and tired of playing the role of the resilient one, she escaped the basement—and trekked back to her parents in Ely. Perhaps sensing that he was about to be dumped, Barrett attempted to save face by writing a "Dear Jane" letter to Gala. Within hours of mailing it Syd regretted his rash decision and penned another note, this one asking for forgiveness. Unsure of her next move, Gala left, again, this time for Jerry Shirley's rural home in Essex.

After speaking on the phone and hashing out their concerns about where the relationship stood, the embattled couple agreed to meet at a neutral location. The plan was to head back to Shirley's to listen to each other, discuss their situation, and reconcile. The conversation took a turn for the worse when Barrett accused Gala of cheating on him—this time with Shirley.

Muttering something about Shirley being a *just a drummer*, traditionally the lowest lifeform in the rock band pecking order, Syd spiraled out of control, causing more than a scene back at Shirley's farm and doing irreparable damage to what was left of the nearly salvageable romantic partnership.

Gala wanted out. She was done. The courtship was over.

ATOM HEART MOTHER

In retrospect, the filmmaker was probably, the entire time, looking for something like "Careful with That Axe, Eugene," if not that exact track. Director Michelangelo Antonioni, without communicating such, whisked Floyd away to Italy for weeks in Rome, urging them to burn the midnight oil to create music that pleased him.

The more music Floyd threw at Antonioni, the more he rejected. Ultimately, Antonioni reasoned that Floyd's music was too overwhelming for the screen—it was stealing the director's thunder, and possibly detracting from the visual impact of the film. Finally, Antonioni chose to use a few tracks by Floyd, including a version of "Careful with That Axe, Eugene," itself based on an earlier songs such as "Murderistic Woman" and "Keep Smiling."

The erstwhile "Eugene," listed on the *Zabriskie Point* soundtrack as "Come in Number 51, Your Time Is Up," was used for the home-detonation scene of the film. The Carefree, Arizona, mansion demolished in the movie is merely a replica of what was used in the rest of the film. The desert home upon which it was patterned was part of the same studio complex used by Orson Welles for the fabled *The Other Side of the Wind*.

Other Floyd tracks include the somewhat country-and-western-fried "Crumbling Land," boasting acoustic guitar picking, timpani blasts, and blanketing organ. The effects-laden audio mash-up, "Heart Beat, Pig Meat," contains wordless vocalizing, heavy breathing, and a repetitive heartbeat pulse, which could be compressed, looped audio of Mason playing kit drums with his hands or sticks.

Despite the band's exasperation, something golden did come of the time the band spent in Italy trying to please and unsatisfied filmmaker. As most fans are aware, the track "The Violent Sequence" was repurposed for "Us and Them."

After their frustrating interactions with Antonioni, it was back on the road where the band were piecing together their next great song, dubbed "The Amazing Pudding." They had toyed with the idea of recording a symphony orchestra, having once shared a stage with the Royal Philharmonic at the Albert Hall. Floyd had envisioned a tour of the UK in March 1968 with a one-hundred-piece orchestra and choir, but this never came to pass. Pity. It seemed to be the spirit of the age: the Beatles used strings in their music in the 1960s, and others, such as the Nice, Deep Purple, the Moody Blues, Uriah Heep, and even Yes, augmented their rock sounds with orchestral bigness during the late 1960s and early 1970s.

Still on a country and (heavily) western kick, Gilmour came up with the main riff and believed the chords of the emergent song were reminiscent of the theme for *The Magnificent Seven*, something he had titled, "Theme from an Imaginary Western."

The foundation of what was known then as "The Amazing Pudding" was cemented with the rhythm section—bass and drums. Much of this work, however, was rearranged or discarded. Some, even members of the band, thought this work all amounted to very little.

That's when word came down from EMI that tape edits were not to be attempted on "The Amazing Pudding" or "Epic." This meant the band had to do the backing tracks all the way through. All of what would amount to twenty-three-plus minutes. Floyd had hit another brick wall: their envisioned orchestral rock track needed something, but they were exhausted and didn't know where to turn.

Enter Scottish experimental composer Ron Geesin, who would be introduced to the Floyd universe via a go-between, Sam Cutler, the onetime Grateful Dead comanager and tour manager for the Stones through their appearance at Altamont. Geesin had just finished working on the track "With A Smile Up His Nose They Entered," for Pete Townshend's tribute to spiritual guru Meher Baba, *Happy Birthday*. The piece was slated to feature Lindy Rutter (Mason's then-wife), but circumstances prevented it.

After Floyd handed tapes to Geesin, in the hopes he could overlay something dramatic onto the music, the composer got to work. Stripped to his underwear, sweating in his Ladbroke Grove flat in the heat of the spring of 1970, Geesin composed the piece he titled "Epic," guided by little or no input from the band members. When he completed it, the opening horn/symphonic section harked back to Jerome Moross's Western movie theme for *The Big Country*, at least according to Rick Sanders's Floyd book from the 1970s. In this writer's opinion, it might also recall the sweeping melodies of Dvorak's *Symphony No. 9* or "New World Symphony."

Regardless of what has been written or said about "Epic," Geesin correctly clocked a moving force inside Floyd's music when he discussed a pervasive, if somewhat metaphoric, "subterranean drone" mixed with the sound of "extra-terrestrial" craft. The paradox of this alchemical wedding of the cosmic and underground became a hallmark of progressive rock for the next decade.

This "drone" was given life, partially, through Floyd's own tape-based experimentation and the band's mash-up of different sounds and moods was originally meant to be a drum solo. Both Mason and Waters curated sound effects for the piece, such as explosions, a motorcycle vrooming, or a horse whinnying. The sound collage, beginning at 17:55 or so, not only points to "Echoes" but also the later *Dark Side* introduction, "Speak to Me." In this case the collage is a recap and not a preview, but the effect is the same: shrouding the work in a cinematic sonic fog. This electronic madness ends with the spoken phrase: "Silence in the studio!"

One could argue that the maniacal cackling heard in the title piece of *A Raise of Eyebrows*, Geesin's 1967 LP for the Transatlantic label, as well as "We're All Going to Liverpool," "A Female!" "A World of Too Much Sound," "Freedom For Four Voices and Me," and the vocal narration of "Positives," were tape-based forerunners to Floyd's material produced from the late 1960s onward. Geesin even plays a banjo in "Certainly Random," an instrument Syd had wanted to introduce into the Floyd.

"Nick Mason has certainly mentioned my influence on them of magnetic tape manipulation," says Geesin. "I learned from Roger the importance of 'now': to consider the 'when' of any event; to consider the leaving of space, silence, not to manically bundle everything in, which I still do."

Geesin describes his process of tape-based looping:

I did use some tape loops, generally, but more sound loops—and sometimes both, synchronously. In 1967, I devised a system of running a large spool of tape between two tape machines and had an assembly made by a Royal College of Art engineer: an extendable arm between the two machines that could be accurately adjusted and set to vary the distance between the record head on the first machine and the playback head on the second. By running the tape in this arrangement, I fed the audio material appearing at the playback head back into the mixer so that it went back onto the tape at the record head.

"By injecting rhythmic material, a forever metamorphosing 'round' can be created—but one mistake means start again," Geesin continues.

By injecting constantly random material, a "vast vista of organised noise" can be created, although one needs an extra length of delay—minimum of 25 seconds, otherwise the listening brain will detect even slight repetition. Although I could never say I invented this technique, I certainly used it to best effect. After I had used it a lot, probably too much, I read an article by Robert Fripp in which he described his version of the process. . . . Both Pete Townshend and Pink Floyd tried it, from my instruction, but couldn't get on with the necessary and somewhat mechanical accuracy of live input to achieve a meaningful work.

While Floyd provided plenty of elements of "the other," there were still traditional sounds that needed to be added to the mix. For instance, Geesin had written a lead part for cello and invited Icelandic classical musician and composer Hafliði Hallgrímsson to perform the beautiful string melody for "The Amazing Pudding."

The cellist had a bit of history with Geesin, who had called him "out of the blue," says Hallgrímsson, who was a member of the Haydn String Trio and playing with the Monteverdi and the London Bach orchestras.

> I have no idea where Ron Geesin got my phone number. I liked Ron very much and found him very interesting to talk to. He got in touch with me again, later, and asked me if I would be willing to record at the Abbey Road, for a Pink Floyd album. I was only faintly familiar with the name of the group, and I decided to use the opportunity to find out how pop groups worked.

Hallgrímsson heard the piece cold, thought the music "attractive" and "was handed earphones," Hallgrímsson reports.

> This was a new experiment for me. As I needed to hear myself, I covered my right ear with that side of the earphones, but placed the other in front of my left ear. It all happened quickly and when asked what I wanted for a fee, I said, "60 pounds sterling," and left the studio to walk to the next tube station.

Not all of the session work for "Epic" would be so efficient. For one thing, Geesin thought he could handle conducting the orchestra assembled at Abbey Road when uncooperative operatives and detailed musical scores, flared tempers, and some inexperience created a perfect storm of near-session killing toxicity.

Geesin got on with some of the string players, but the horn section proved more taxing. Disagreements devolved nearly into actual physical violence before it all settled down, and choirmaster John Alldis galloped in and saved the day, conducting for the session.

Other strange occurrences were manifesting around the studio for the recording of *Atom Heart Mother*. There's so much lore and mythology surrounding Syd's appearance during the *WYWH* sessions that it's suffocated any spark of a discussion of previous Barrett sightings at Abbey Road in the 1970s.

Syd was, after all, also recording his second album in Abbey Road in the summer of 1970, around about the same time Floyd were working on *Atom Heart Mother*. Syd, apparently, dropped in on the band. He was quiet, motionless, observed his former bandmates and then silently exited. Geesin intimates that Syd wandered around, not saying much. Despite his unassuming manner and near-invisibility, Geesin referred to Syd as a "Jesus figure."

According to the authors of *Crazy Diamond*, Waters had also spotted Barrett outside the studio—perhaps in summer 1970 when he was shopping at Harrods. Like so many aspects of the Syd saga, the time frame for this encounter is a bit hazy. *The Mirror* quotes Waters as saying it occurred somewhere around 1977.

Strangely, when Barrett recognized his former mate, he dropped the bag he was holding to the floor and rushed for the exit without stopping to say hello. When Waters approached the mysterious package, the lanky bass player opened the bag and discovered nothing but pounds of sweets.

≡

Other songs were populating *AHM*. Wright's "Summer '68" reflects upon a casual sexual encounter and regrets it. Gilmour's wispy and dreamy "Fat Old Sun" pops up in the guitarist's live set from time to time, and Waters' confessional folkie "If" is a pre-*WYWH* and *Dark Side* stab at understanding himself, the immutable laws governing his behavior, and the nature of madness.

There's nothing particularly psychedelic about the first few minutes of the closer, "Alan's Psychedelic Breakfast," but its sound effects do create vivid visuals: chewing, a dripping faucet, a man muttering to himself and chortling, washing up, the repeated sound of a match being struck, popping bacon frying in the pan . . . "Alan" is Alan Styles, one of the band's roadies at the time, the star attraction of a piece largely created by Mason.

The drip, drip, drip of the runny faucet at the end of Alan's "psychedelic" morning ritual closes the record. Well, sorta. An endless drip was built into the original LP's run-off groove for the UK pressing. The droplets fall in what appears to be a repetitive rhythm, similar to the cyclical heartbeat pattern that commences *and* closes *The Dark Side of the Moon*.

If "Alan's Psychedelic Breakfast" is "psychedelic" at all, it's in the way it could induce an altered state of consciousness, similar to the Beatles's "A Day in the Life" does—or, at least, in the way it attempts to recreate a drug-taking experience.

≡

It's no secret that by 1970, Hipgnosis were persona non grata at EMI. Showing up with a picture of a cow for intended use on an LP album cover—and nothing else—no band name, no album title, forced the executives to think Storm and Po were both daft. Waters loved it. As someone self-referential as he, undercutting the band's image, poking fun at the Floyd, was perfect for this adventure.

Seemingly, an image of a diver plunging into water would have been welcomed with open arms by EMI, but it was ultimately rejected. This image was picked up, however, in the *WYWH* era, and a similar cover concept may have been recycled for Def Leppard's *High 'n' Dry* from 1981.

As far as this writer can tell, the album had yet to be named. On June 27, at the Bath

Festival of Blues and Progressive Music, Floyd premiered "The Amazing Pudding." Historically Floyd was billed as playing June 27, but the band did not take the stage until the early hours of Sunday, June 28. Floyd staged "Atom Heart Mother" in all its brassy ballsy-ness, tinkling-ride cymbal stickiness, and echoing guitar reverb and Hammond organ glow.

In mid-July, Floyd entertained twenty thousand people in Hyde Park, appearing on the bill with Kevin Ayers and the Whole World, Roy Harper, Edgar Broughton Band, and Third Ear Band. Famously, a tape recording of an infant crying was played during a moment of relative quiet, shocking the crowd.

The "caveman"-like choral grunts of what would ultimately be titled "Atom Heart Mother" recall *Tubular Bells*, but Floyd's piece predates any similar vocal heard in Mike Oldfield's masterwork. Interestingly enough, Oldfield was a bassist in Kevin Ayers and the Whole Word, which appeared at Hyde Park in 1970. Although the caveman bit was not as pronounced as it would be on record, its strange phrasing, despite available sheet music, seemed to take members of the choir by surprise.

The as-yet-untitled piece was performed live for John Peel's Sunday show, and reportedly it was Geesin who directed the Floyd crew to a newspaper in the control room. Waters took the title from one of two *Evening Standard* articles, published July 1970, on a fifty-something-year-old woman who underwent surgery to implant a nuclear-powered pacemaker in her body.

The piece would eventually be tagged with the title "Atom Heart Mother." It's why we see such arbitrary and nonsensical phrases as "Funky Dung," "Breast Milky," and "Mother Fore" for each of the song's movements.

Floyd were not altogether pleased with the results, however. The record had been rushed, largely due to scheduling recording sessions in-between tours. The orchestral and choral aspects of the music were not a direction Mason, particularly, wanted to venture too far into. Mason wasn't alone: Gilmour thought that layering the orchestra and choir on top of band's bed tracks was a mistake, and went as far as to call the record "a load of rubbish." Perhaps the record would have been better, Gilmour mused, if the band and orchestra/choir's tracked in one go. By the same token, Geesin regretted not being given proper credit for his input.

Geesin's relationship with Waters eventually disintegrated, although this had more to do with extraneous matters of politics and disagreements than the *AHM* sessions. "We had moved apart by 1973, in some ways regrettably in my view then," Geesin says.

Somehow, *Atom Heart Mother*—cow and all—reached No. 1 in the UK and helped Floyd emerge from their psychedelic rock beginnings into a full-fledged progressive rock act with classical leanings. "Our direction has always been erratic, and I think we've managed to fool most of the people most of the time," Mason told *Disc and Music Echo* in 1970.

Piecing together a suite such as *Atom Heart Mother* may not have been as fulfilling as Floyd, or anyone else, initially envisioned, but the band members were reaching high points in their personal life. Mason and Wright became fathers and bought residences around London. Gilmour gravitated toward Essex, and Waters moved to Islington.

In 1970, around the time of *Atom Heart Mother*, Floyd achieved what Nick Mason called "financial independence." Floyd had toured America from April through early June, and while gigging was still costly and put the band as a whole in the red, Floyd had paid their debts. Royalties were just enough to cover costs, even if not much more.

=

During the months of July and August, as the "Atom Heart Mother" suite was being mixed, Geesin had been working on music for the broadcast documentary *The Body*, and needed melody in the music being scored for the film.

"The producers said that there needed to be some songs," Geesin says.

> I suggested Roger and the film producers "recruited." Remember that our work was initially for the feature film *The Body*. Later, the album *Music from The Body* was constructed for EMI Harvest [released in fall 1970]. The film "project" was in no way influenced or directed by our input, only enhanced. For the album, we made the opening pieces for each side, "Our Song" and "Body Transport," as celebrations of working together and nothing to do with the film. Roger remade all his songs because the film versions were, in his opinion, too rough. . . . "Give Birth to a Smile" [featuring Pink Floyd] was remade at Island Studios.

Using a click track and a razor blade, Geesin stuck together snippets of body sounds—mostly Ron's but some Roger's—to make a cluster of rhythmic chatter. Geesin admits that it was Waters who wanted to connect much of the musical tissue of the project into a free-flowing garment. The individual pieces attempt to tell a story, even if an overt one never truly surfaced.

Atom Heart Mother was released in October, and the band was on the road, again, from late September through October 1970. By early January, Floyd were back in the studio for work on their next album, later titled *Meddle*. Not satisfied with the technical options available to them at Abbey Road, Floyd decided to branch out and seek other recording spaces to fulfill their needs. George Martin's new AIR Studios, as well as Morgan Studios, fit the bill, for a time. Command Studios were employed for some recording and sessions involving a quadrophonic mix of the album.

It's important to understand that Floyd were gigging throughout the recording process, which stretched across months. Europe, Japan, and Australia dates were scheduled for July and August, and Floyd even performed "Atom Heart Mother" in Switzerland at Montreux. North America was next, and Floyd trekked through the Heartland, East Coast, Pacific Northwest and Canada in October and November.

It was such a compartmentalized existence: write, record, gig, rinse, and repeat. Floyd spent a few days at a time getting on tape any idea that popped into their minds. If the author understands this correctly, different members of the band worked alone for a time, putting down snippets of songs, until the other members added their contributions to that particular piece of music.

By Gilmour's estimation there were "hundreds" of song ideas that were whittled down to thirty-six different bits. It was from these Frankenstein-like parts that a new epic track would be built. Mason admitted to *Record Mirror* in February 1971 that Floyd was approaching the production of *Meddle* differently than they had in the past—by pursuing ideas rather than simply laying down tracks.

Although ultimately titled "Echoes," it was known variously throughout pre-production and the album's recording sessions as "Nothing, Parts 1–24," "Looking Through the Knotholes in Granny's Wooden Leg," and later "The Return of the Son of Nothing," which was also the working title of the new album.

Floyd played this forerunner to "Echoes" at the University of East Anglia and later the outdoor venue Crystal Palace Garden Party bowl with Faces, Mountain, and Quiver in May 1971.

Rain clouds and a torrential downpour did little to put a damper on the band's set, which featured fireworks and a large inflatable sea creature, later dubbed an octopus. It rose from the lake at the front of the stage as Floyd closed their set with "A Saucerful of Secrets." It's also the show in which, it was said, vibrations from the music shortened the lifespan of the fish in the pond. Over the years some have believed this story to be slightly less than true, but Mason confirmed it in his book *Inside Out*.

The first wisps of the piece, tinkered with in Abbey Road in early 1971, revealed only the faintest shadow of what the final work would be. Then something significant occurred. The band had been mucking around in Abbey Road when Wright touched his piano, quite offhandedly, in a rehearsal. Upon playback Wright's piano notes were transformed into *twinks*—something resembling underwater-sonar-like pings of a submarine—sent through a Leslie speaker cabinet and a Binson echo unit. Soon all the pieces clicked together, having been edited to make coherent sense. The band had erected a twenty-minute-plus musical monster, stunning the studio help and all in attendance. "Echoes" would claim the entire second side of the LP.

It was a strange beast, however. Gilmour's honey-glazed and Wright's ghostly vocals harmonize; a funky jam propels the track and is buttressed by backwards audio and effects, such as tape-delay echoes. Cross fades help to tie everything together. Wright's pings were left in the final mix, because Floyd could never perfectly replicate those sounds at Air Studios. Gilmour's guitar is unleashed.

At approximately 7:25, the feedback and whammy-bar vibrato transforms Gilmour's steady-handed, blues-centric, six-string musical messages into what could be classed as heavy metal. With Mason and bassist Waters holding down the funky fort and Wright's (likely) overdubbed organ runs, Gilmour's showcase threatens to break out into total chaos. In this case, it's a tempest in a teapot—controlled madness—the hallmark of a band in transition from cultish psychedelic music to a more commercial progressive rock.

The whale or seagull cries (starting at 11:25) are a kind of tribute. Jimi Hendrix had passed on as the band was recording the track, and it seems as though Gilmour's sonic squalls, whale calls, or seagull cries, however you'd like to describe them, are some kind of tribute, capturing anguished, primordial fear of birth and death. Of course, seagull-like cries can be heard in at least one other earlier song, "Embryo," but with "Echoes," Floyd leaves behind a two-dimensional audio world and embraces true theatre of the mind.

This sonic metamorphosis not only helps enhance the evolutionary and immersive or aquatic themes in Waters's lyrics, but also introduces the next phase in the developmental stages of Gilmour's initial ideas. True, the musical setting devolves or breaks down in this section, but this serves to highlight the animalistic, the *primal* thematic threads sprouting from the very root of the song's theme and purpose.

It seems counterintuitive at first blush, but what we're witnessing is growth: these evocative sounds are conveyances for psychological regression—a trip through our collective homo sapiens past, getting us closer to some kind of universal truth. Waters likened "Echoes" to a tone poems, traditionally categorized as being based on a literary work (though a composer could use a visual stimulant, such as a painting, for inspiration).

Lyrically, it was the first significant sign that Waters was developing Floyd beyond its perception as space rockers, a label Waters never really embraced publicly, anyway. "Echoes" is a work of empathy, a clear forerunner to *The Dark Side of the Moon*. The *Meddle* sessions were also, purportedly, the first time the phrase "the dark side of the moon" bubbled over into the Floyd's collective consciousness. Said Waters, the multi-part twenty-four-minute composition was the "father and mother" of *The Dark Side of the Moon*. Alchemy.

Lines such as: *"by chance two passing glances meet"* could be interpreted as hippie dippy, yes, but Waters's role, if you like, the one he'd carved out for himself as a distant observer and satirist in songs such as "Set the Controls" and "Corporal Clegg," slowly receded with the appearance of "Echoes."

"Echoes" perhaps achieved both musical experimentation *and* the creation of a sonic-psychic journey for the listener, which could provide a kind of entertainment, especially if listening was/is accompanied by, say, some form of extracurricular activities. "Echoes" straddles two musical worlds, reverberating with commercial melodies and psychedelic sonic bursts. Most importantly, Waters's views of the human condition and universal consciousness are crystalized here and further explored on *The Dark Side of the Moon*.

Occupying the original LP's first side were "Fearless," "San Tropez," and "A Pillow of Winds," "Seamus" (appears as "Mademoiselle Nobs" in *Live at Pompeii*), and opener "One of These Days."

On "One of These Days," Floyd outdid themselves using the Binson Echorec delay effects unit, applying it to two basses—one each played by Gilmour and Waters. The pulse quickens as quarter notes repeat and are transformed into a funky triplet pattern feel via the Binson.

Winds whip up and there's a pre-echo of Wright's mysterioso/"horrorshow" or flying flare keyboard sounds, faintly heard at approximately 0:39, prior to Gilmour's initial bass riffs. Waters joins the fray on second bass at approximately 0:49.

The birdcalls or whale calls are made through a Cry Baby wah-wah pedal, the kind Hendrix used. Gilmour's throaty, crankin', steel guitar tone lends the piece its metallic rawness. The disturbing vibrato bass middle section was initially meant to be part of another song, but its menacing was so appropriate it was incorporated into "One of These Days."

Frightening sounds abound. In the studio, supposedly, Mason's vocals were recorded at double speed then replayed at a slower pace. Mason even changed his voice register—to something resembling Kermit the Frog at approximately 3:37—to match the alien feel of the lyrics. His voice may have also been sent through a ring modulator for the phrase "One of these days, I'm going to cut you up into little pieces."

"San Tropez," a nostalgic song that recalls the Beatles' "When I'm 64," was brought into the sessions by Waters nearly complete. Gilmour's Hawaiian-style guitar befits the sun-and-sand tipsiness of the tune.

When Floyd traipsed through France in early 1970, they and their extended caravan plopped down in a villa in San Tropez. Claustrophobia and family members created a powder keg of personal embarrassments. A lot was discussed at the villa, in front of family members, including what musicians do when on the road.

"I worked on the original version of 'San Tropez,'" Mike Butcher, former engineer at Morgan Studios told me in February 2008,

> which, in fact, is not the version on the album. They had actually finished the original version, and Roger Waters played guitar and David played bass. They spent all day on it, and then, I think it was the very next day, they re-recorded it with David Gilmour playing guitar and Roger Waters playing bass. They listened to it the next morning and thought they could do it better. I think that was the version they used on the album.

During the *Meddle* sessions at Morgan, Butcher had a front-row seat to what made Floyd tick, and witnessed the band dynamic in action. "The control room was above the studio," Butcher told me.

> Roger Quested [Morgan Studios manager at the time] was getting vocal sound, and he let Roger Waters carry on singing. Waters was thinking that Quested was taking a long time to get the sound. Whereas actually [Quested] was just letting Waters rehearse. Waters started to whistle, and [Quested] just let the tape roll. When the tape got to the end, I stopped it, rolled it back and [Waters] said: "So, Roger, have you got the sound now?" Very sarcastically, as if, you know, he was taking a long time. [Quested] said: 'Yeah, I have the sound. But are you going to sing or whistle?' Waters

said, "Well, you look like you've been in this business for a long time, what do you think I'm going to do?" Quested said, "Well, I don't think it really matters." And the band were like, 'Yeah, yeah, yeah. You tell 'em.'"

It seems Waters was already attempting to assume the command role in Floyd. "Underneath it all, I'd say there was something happening," Butcher told me.

Despite the intermittent session work, *Meddle* and "Echoes" would be not only fully realized, but also revered upon its release on Halloween, 1971. Not everyone was pleased, of course. At the time, *Melody Maker* called *Meddle* "so much sound and fury, signifying nothing," a confused affair with mixed results. In retrospect, *Meddle* is an important evolutionary step in Floyd's creative development, bridging the band's psychedelic sensibilities with their pop tendencies to create a kind of accessible progressive rock formula.

"It had a massive influence on us," says Martyn Ware, cofounder of The Human League and Heaven 17.

> I mean, we did a track for the third album, about the fear of nuclear war [Heaven 17's "Five Minutes to Midnight"]. When we were making it, we were thinking about it being a contemporary version of Pink Floyd. [Floyd] just wrote albums that people wanted to listen to over and over again. That's what we always aspired to: a kind of timeless quality. That's a template for great art.

POMPEII

In December, the band was filming footage for director Adrian Maben's film *Pink Floyd*, later known as *Pink Floyd at Pompeii*, also sometimes referred to as *Live at Pompeii*. For Maben the concept was simple: film Floyd in an atmosphere that was antithetical to the growing trend toward large music-festival events (i.e. anti-Woodstock). For all the talk about the mud-plied hippies getting back to nature and being "one with everything," there was something far more primordial, civilized, and cerebral, if less tribal, about *Pompeii* than *Woodstock*.

Maben had the band and its crew set up inside an empty ancient amphitheater in Italy, scene of their recent horrible experience with another film director. As *Pink Floyd and Philosophy: Careful with That Axiom, Eugene!* edited by George A. Reisch, astutely points out, the irony of Floyd performing for no one aside from the film crew, enclosed by a wall circulating the venue's parameter, is the knowledge that *The Dark Side of the Moon* is on the horizon. The subsequent years, and given Waters's growing sense of alienation, performing in an ancient, desolate arena may have been preferable to facing geezers falling about drunk and howling requests at the band from the front rows of packed North American sports stadiums.

It was a genius move. Among the rubble and ruins, Floyd blasted against the harsh Mediterranean elements—the blistering autumnal sun, choking microscopic wind-blown dust particles, bubbling lava pools, smoking hot springs—with all the sonic force they could muster.

Under the blinding stadium lights, Floyd took on the world. Were they prepared for what would follow?

CHAPTER 3

ASSORTED LUNATICS

Once you are out of your mind you can come to your senses.
—TIMOTHY LEARY

On January 20, 1972, at the Brighton Dome, Floyd had reached a turning point. It's the moment Floyd unveiled what would later become known as *The Dark Side of the Moon*. History should record this as a celebratory, monumental moment in time. Yet, despite the grueling effort they'd invested into tweaking this new material at both the Rainbow and the Stones's practice space in Bermondsey, the show was far from auspicious.

In the middle of their set, the PA conked out, taking the band with it. Audio and lighting running on the same circuit will do that. Floyd may have been forced to do so, but the fact remained: it was impossible to supply the two systems separately.

Gilmour flew to the sound engineer's location to investigate the enigmatic audio breakdown. By this time, the rest of the band had vamoosed. They were nowhere to be found when it became apparent that the band could not continue to play. Their grand work was grounded, and Waters made a brief statement explaining that the band would carry on with some familiar material. Pissed at circumstances that may have been beyond their control, the band proceeded with rocky, but ultimately superior and aggressive, versions of "Atom Heart Mother," "Eugene" and "Set the Controls."

It was a setback, even slightly humiliating, but the crew undertook a bit of troubleshooting the technical nuts-and-bolts problems. Of course, some of the band's new work *did* come off, at least according to a report from the ground by Tony Stewart of *NME*, even if during one song "not everything . . . flowed."

Although Brighton didn't happen exactly as planned, the Rainbow Theatre dates, February 17–20, is traditionally considered the unofficial unveiling of *The Dark Side of the Moon: A Piece for Assorted Lunatics*, complete with German Stuka dive bomber and all.

Graphic artist and friend of Nick Mason, Pearce Marchbank, remembers a certain prominent British guitarist in attendance at the Rainbow that night, "turning up, incredibly drunk," Marchbank says. "I and another guy helped him to the stage door where he drove off in a Lamborghini. Or something like that. I saw the Floyd quite a lot. They were proficient performers so they tended to do things much the same. I think it was a good concert, though."

As it so happens, another future Floyd collaborator, artist Gerald Scarfe, was in the audience for one of the shows and was impressed by the Nazi warplane and the band's various theatrical props. Scarfe would get to know a few of the band members, but it was Mason he warmed to nearly immediately. The two went on holiday together with their families in 1974 in France.

Floyd appeared on the cusp of a major artistic breakthrough. Meanwhile, in Cambridge, the band's former frilly-haired leader, Syd Barrett, appeared desirous of writing a new chapter of his career. For one thing, he granted interviews, planting the idea that new studio tracks could be forthcoming.

Barrett told *Melody Maker* reporter Mike Watts that he had been painting quite a lot and chasing a new muse. Although nothing could transcend the experiences at the UFO club, he said, Barrett was enthusiastic about his new role as artist. This interview is often cited as one of the various public testimonies of Syd's deteriorating mental health, but, honestly, it's difficult to tell if Barrett is scatterbrain, demented, or, frankly, playing with the interviewer, contradicting himself to see if Watts will notice and call him out.

Barrett admits to needing a job, presumably to get back to some kind of "normal" life. Yet in nearly the same breath, he says he's been living in Cambridge and would "suppose I could've done a job," he told *Melody Maker* in March 1971. "I haven't done any work."

"I was back in Cambridge for the birth of my daughter, but I later went back to college and did a degree in literature," says Jenny Spires, who'd married bassist Jack Monck. "When I was back in Cambridge in 1971, Syd was too, and he rang my mum to find out where I was. He told me he wanted to play. He said this to me in '69, and after *Madcap* and *Barrett*, he still wanted to. He was visiting our cottage outside Cambridge and jamming with Jack, smiling a lot, and not at all stressed."

In January 1972 he'd taken the stage at King's College Cellar at Cambridge, where former Delivery bassist Monck and former Pink Fairies drummer John "Twink" Alder, whom Syd remembered from the psychedelic rock band and UFO club regular Tomorrow, backed Motor City blues man Eddie "Guitar" Burns.

Barrett joined Monck and Twink again the next evening at the Corn Exchange, warming up the crowd for Hawkwind and the Pink Fairies, as the Last Minute Put Together Boogie Band, with ex-Apple Pie Motherhood Band vocalist Bruce Paine. Syd can be heard on *Six Hour Technicolour Dream*, a recording of the Put Together's January 27 show, featuring guest guitarist Fred Frith and released through the Easy Action label in 2014.

After the Put Together gig, Twink and Monck thought they had something special. Twink, for one, had returned recently from Morocco and was searching for anything heavy. Could they convince the Floyd refugee to, at least, rehearse some more with them?

Even asking the question, in retrospect, seems naïve, but Barrett accepted their invitation to jam almost immediately.

They rehearsed as a unit in Syd's basement in Cambridge, and even began attempting to play some of Barrett's classic material such as "Lucifer Sam." After investing more time together rehearsing as a unit, eventually they dubbed themselves Stars. All of this would seem to point to a very sane, very stable Barrett, capable of making decisions about his musical future.

Twink, who seemed to embody the ideals of free thought, personal expression, and exploration of the underground (and someone who had pioneered not only psychedelic rock, but later punk, and coined the phrase "acid punk"), was less ringleader than pied piper, convincing Barrett to make his first public performances outside the Floyd since his exit.

Stars played Dandelion coffee bar in late January and again on February 5. They also performed an outdoor concert in Cambridge, near Market Square in mid-February. Later in the month, Stars shared the bill at the Corn Exchange with the MC5 and Skin Alley on February 24. Skin Alley was soul or R&B to its core, with flashes of Traffic, King Crimson, and in some instances the softer folky/jazz moments of Jethro Tull. They were jazzy, at times sophisticated, but definitely vamp or jam heavy.

The Corn Exchange show was a testing of the waters as much as it was an attempt by Barrett to face a live audience again. The show didn't go, perhaps, as planned. Barrett seemed irritated at some points, lost and struggling at others. Technical equipment malfunctions also hampered the proceedings and helped clear the room.

Reports from those in attendance were mixed—some observers were confused by Barrett's erratic behavior and seeming lack of mental focus; others believed this kind of chaos was exactly what Barrett intended and what Syd fans relished. *Melody Maker*, which reviewed the show, presented the unvarnished truth as Roy Hollingsworth saw it, but was not totally unsupportive.

"Things had been going very nicely for Stars until we played a high-profile gig at Cambridge Corn Exchange when everything went wrong that could possibly go wrong," Twink once told me.

> The performance was reviewed in the music press in a negative light. When the review was published, which was after a second show we did at the Corn Exchange two days later, which went very well, Syd was called to his London music publisher's office [Bryan Morrison], who drew his attention to the negative review and told him to leave Stars. . . . Knowing Syd's vulnerability, they used it as a torpedo to sink the band.

Twink was convinced that circumstances and deliberate actions conspired against Stars—and Syd. It's also been suggested that Morrison was being used as a scapegoat to shield Barrett and camouflage Syd's flagging enthusiasm for the pop life.

Twink: "My theory is that it was good for Pink Floyd to have their 'Crazy Diamond,' and when 'Syd' did eventually surface with Stars, well, it had to be stopped. They couldn't possibly put up with Syd being seen to be sane, playing in another group with other respected musicians."

"None of the gigs was as disastrous as they were made out to be," says Spires.

> What were these people comparing them to? Syd wasn't too happy about playing at the Corn Exchange, but he went along with it. He had loved doing the smaller gigs, but I think, as I expected, he might be thrown. I know he had a flashback when we walked into the dressing room at one point, his collar went up and he went very quiet, but I can't remember which gig it was. . . . For him, just being onstage in a large, draughty venue again was enough, and then to be scrutinised by critics. . . . He felt betrayed.

Recordings supposedly exist of Stars' gigs and rehearsals, but no tracks have been released to my knowledge. If they had been, it would end the debate about coherency and musical quality, at the least.

Always with Barrett, we're confronted with a kind of multiverse of options and possible career paths; an endless string of "what ifs?" Had the timing been correct, the reviews been stellar, would Stars have developed into a proper band and thrust Barrett back to stardom? More importantly, if Syd was losing his spark, more rehearsal time would have done little to regain his confidence.

When dealing with an unpredictable leader like Barrett, the future of this musical project was uncertain at best. In any case, seismic changes were afoot for Barrett, and whether Stars had a good—or a bad—performance at the Corn Exchange might not have mattered in the grand scheme of things.

"By the end of February, Syd's mum sold the family home in Hill's Road," says Spires. "It had huge implications for Syd, because it meant he didn't have a base anymore, a place to work, and keep all his work, his paintings, writing, guitars. Much of his work evolved from this place. It was everything he identified with. It made him edgy. It was to be 'make or break.'"

"If I thought I could have done more, I would have, because it was at this time that he needed more support," Spires continues.

> But when I met up with him a few months later, it was a hot sunny day in late September, and we didn't even discuss [the move]. We spent half the day just sitting behind the Fitzwilliam Museum, playing with my daughter, and then we walked across Laundress Green, because he was heading back to London.

The next few years, Barrett's motivations would become increasingly inscrutable, his personal appearance more bizarre, and his presence ever more ghostly.

=

While Barrett's career may or may not have been intentionally derailed, Floyd continued to steamroll through what might be their most consistently collaborative and productive period in band history.

March and April were busy months for Floyd. After a tour of Japan and Australia, the guys entered Strawberry Studios at Chateau d'Hierouville in France to complete *Obscured by Clouds* for the 1972 Barbet Schroeder film *La Vallee*, a spiritual journey of self-discovery—a search for a hidden valley.

As they had done with *More*, Floyd watched a rough cut of the film and let a stopwatch run, to ensure that their work was synchronized—in terms of timekeeping, sequencing, and mood—with the visuals. The use of cross-fading was especially helpful here to transition smoothly from one musical idea to another.

Paris's Chateau D'Herouville was ground zero for Elton John's *Honky Chateau* and Jethro Tull's failed sessions prior to the recording of the concept record *A Passion Play*. Tull's Ian Anderson even famously referred to the studio as "Chateau d'Isaster" for the alleged technical issues during the band's stay there.

France plays a pivotal role in Floyd's career longevity. Knowing Floyd would and could go elsewhere for their American distribution of their upcoming record, *The Dark Side of the Moon*, Bhaskar Menon, chairman of Capitol, traveled to Marseilles as the band performed with ballet choreographer Roland Petit, to convince them to stay with the label. Bubbling up just under the surface was a frothing frustration with the band's Stateside distribution and commercial progress in America—a failing Floyd laid squarely at the feet of Capitol, EMI/Harvest's distribution in the US.

Not very many people were aware, outside the Floyd inner circle, that the band had been looking for other business partners in America to disseminate their studio recordings. In an era when cracking America meant virtually everything, Floyd, in this respect anyway, had very little to show. Still, the band knew it had an ace up their collective sleeve—*The Dark Side of the Moon*. But a great album could turn to shit—if distribution and marketing weren't handled properly.

Dark Side made it imperative for the band, if they were serious about leaving, to be expeditious about finding their American escape route. Step 1 was finding a label worth the potential financial pain and separation anxiety associated with jumping ship. One outlet, Columbia/CBS, practically the gold standard of the industry, offered a ray of hope for a better future. But just a few years earlier it did appear as though Columbia's magic touch had faded. By the mid-1960s, popular crooner Johnny Mathis had left Columbia for Mercury Records, and the company's cash cows, such as Broadway musical recordings, Mitch Miller, and classical works, were slowly losing earning power in the marketplace. In fact, the old standards were dropping like rocks into a bottomless well. In a complete miscalculation of forecasting trends, few CBS executives saw the need to court young rock bands. Although the label would soon see some success with Dylan, Simon and Garfunkel, and the Byrds, it was clear that Columbia Records was behind the times and in desperate need of an A&R overhaul.

By his own admission in his book *Clive: Inside the Record Business*, published in the 1970s, former CBS Records president Clive Davis seemed to get a vicarious thrill from reading the box office numbers in *Variety* and watching songs climb the charts in *Billboard*. "It's as if [the charts] represented a flow of energy," the Brooklyn native wrote.

In essence, there *was* a major energy flow: what Clive was feeling coursing through his veins (and perhaps other parts of his body) was the representation of pure power and wealth one can amass in the entertainment world.

After graduating from Harvard with a law degree, Davis was hired at a large New York City law firm, Rosenman, Colin, Kaye, Petschek, and Freund, where he handled the account for Columbia Artists Management, ironically unaffiliated with Columbia Records. When future CBS International president and head of Sony Records Harvey Schein left Rosenman's firm, he became general attorney for Columbia Records and hired Davis for the label's corporate law division in 1960.

Bronx native Schein increased company sales twofold during his time at Sony, but often ruffled the corporate feathers of his Japanese bosses. Schein also fought a losing battle in Sony's push for Betamax, introduced in 1976, in the home video entertainment market. The CBS Group was also responsible for distributing Fender guitars and Leslie speaker cabinets—both brand names Floyd used.

Davis did complain about the stuffy culture and its lack of empathy with the emerging rock movement, as well as the inability of higher-ups to scout for new, young talent and understand how to retain it by paying their workers what they were worth—or at least, give them a few extra bucks for their pockets.

The CBS culture also placed perhaps too much emphasis on its prestigious television division, which, like all of the companies composing the corporate conglomerate, was being carried for a time by the profits rolling into Columbia Records. Very little thanks were extended to the record company—or Clive Davis, personally—throughout the late 1960s and early 1970s.

Somewhere in the early 1970s, things began to fall apart for the record division, however. Sly Stone dropped out due to personal issues; Blood, Sweat, and Tears had lost David Clayton-Thomas; Santana was pursuing a more spiritual path than pop music could allow; Simon and Garfunkel had broken up; and Johnny Cash's and Andy Williams's variety shows were booted off TV. Although there was still good, if surprising, news from the Mahavishnu Orchestra, Loggins and Messina, and Dr. Hook and the Medicine Show, Columbia was going to have difficulty in attempting to recoup whatever losses they'd suffer from all of these seismic changes.

Instead of accepting a fated decline, Davis and his lieutenants signed established and up-and-coming talent, including Herbie Hancock; Earth, Wind and Fire; Neil Diamond; Mott the Hoople; and Liza Minnelli, not to mention Bruce Springsteen, Aerosmith, Billy Joel, Ten Years After, and Weather Report.

Floyd were watching these changes, sensing opportunity. Steve O'Rourke had met with EMI's L. G. Wood in 1971 wanting to be relieved from their obligations to Capitol, but Rupert Perry, who'd later become chairman of EMI's British division, struck a deal for *Obscured by Clouds*, bumping up the band's royalties. It wasn't significant, but it was enough to keep the band around for a little while.

"Over the years, and in retrospect, Capitol often failed to understand and exploit EMI UK's priority repertoire fully," says former marketing man at EMI/Harvest Stuart Watson. "The failure to release the Beatles's early singles provides a classic example of this. Some of the UK acts (i.e., Queen on Elektra) refused to sign to Capitol from the get-go and others that did—Floyd—made early arrangements to escape at the end of existing contract terms."

The scuttlebutt was that Capitol signed Floyd and had been pinning their hopes on the chance that the band might have a hit. A CYA signing, in other words, which relegated Floyd to Capitol's subsidiary, Tower Records—the equivalent of recording world Siberia. It would take *Obscured by Clouds* for Floyd to truly make any headway in the States, but by then Floyd had grown unimpressed with their US distributors and what the band perceived as lack of marketing expertise to tap into one of the biggest markets in the world. Strong ticket sales but moderate record revenue royalties plagued Floyd. They were largely known, if most music fans were aware of them at all, for their concert experience.

Bottom line? Floyd needed to be architects of their own future, and refused to be put in a position in which they were blaming the label for their lack of success.

Kip Cohen, an A&R guy at Columbia, was familiar with Floyd and knew Steve O'Rourke, and must have certainly been aware that the British band, in their early days, had appeared on the Columbia UK label. Cohen, former managing director of the Fillmore East and half the creative brain trust of the Joshua Light Show, had developed a relationship with the Floyd since the late 1960s and had kept tabs on the band.

Cohen hipped Davis to Floyd's growing commercial fortunes and their willingness to leave Capitol and set up a meet with Clive Davis, himself, and O'Rourke. Davis invited O'Rourke to one of the label's "singles meetings," in which marketing strategies were discussed and heads of various departments would voice their concerns as they listened to the music they were about to unload on the public.

Some label advisors failed to see the wisdom in wooing Floyd. Floyd was selling out some venues, yes, but they didn't have a breakthrough hit. Davis perceived Floyd, perhaps shrewdly so, as Columbia's Jethro Tull—a progressive act with a demonstrative ability to achieve chart hits, while generating sell-out crowds and sales figures in the millions.

Despite Warner Communications being competitive and A&M looming on the horizon, O'Rourke was impressed with the efficiency and professionalism at Columbia and reported back to the band. Floyd was reportedly offered a $250,000 advance for signing with Columbia in North America. Some reports have placed the sum as high as one million US dollars.

Although the contract with Columbia wouldn't take effect until the beginning of 1974, Davis and Columbia looked like geniuses when the industry experienced shock and awe from *Dark Side*'s retail performance. In time, and as a direct result of this signing, Columbia would claim ownership of some of the best-selling records in recording history, including Floyd's own 1979 double album *The Wall*, after further negotiations regarding contractual royalties.

Behind the scenes, trouble brewed for Davis, however. The "Drug-ola" and "Payola" scandals rocked the industry, exposing the ancient practice of quid pro quo, and indirectly ousted Clive Davis from CBS, an executive making upwards of $350,000 a year, according to a *Boston Globe* report from February 1975.

Radio/broadcast employees must disclose whether they receive and accept money or services to air songs. The person making the offer must report this information as well, of course. Failure to comply could lead to a fine and/or jail. Payola was a fact of life for every plugger in the biz. Eerily, of Floyd's first official single, "Arnold Layne," former comanager Andrew King reported to author Mark Blake, "We spent a couple of hundred quid trying to buy it into the charts."

"No questions," Peter Jenner, the other half of Floyd's early management, tells me. "This is what you needed to do."

"Frontline radioplay, where payola was rampant, was not something that Pink Floyd received until 'Money' and 'Another Brick in the Wall,'" Stuart Watson says.

> I remember taking a white-label test pressing of *The Dark Side of the Moon* to the Summer Ball at Exeter University prior to release and being stunned when, between acts, the students sat in silence and listened to every note. I guarantee at least 50 percent went out and bought the record on its release date. To answer your question: I largely ignored the scandals and got on with below the line promotion as usual.

The brewing Watergate scandal had opened the floodgates of public awareness to corruption. Critical, paranoid, conspiratorial, and cynical of many of our once-trusted institutions, we attempted to wipe the slate clean. Even the record business, *especially the record business*, wasn't immune to our extreme vigilance.

Syndicated columnist and investigative journalist Jack Anderson had reported in the early 1970s on evidence he'd found of payola in the music industry. Anderson spoke with Bill Ray, the head of the Division of Complaints and Compliance for the FCC, and uncovered that promotional men made payoffs in all kinds of ways, from sex, to expensive vacations, to automobiles, to bankrolling artists' drug habits—delivering bags of cold, hard cash as bribes to radio men to play new music. In the wake of these explosive revelations, the FCC wanted to downplay the entire affair in the media, even as it met with the FBI and the Department of Justice.

In the late 1960s, indictments had been handed down for payola at New York City radio stations, and by 1972, closed-door hearings had already been conducted by the Federal Communications Commission (FCC) into payola or, as *Billboard* dubbed it, "plugola." By June 1975, nineteen individuals were indicted and six companies brought up on tax evasion charges and suspicion of illegal payments to radio stations in a pay-to-play scheme.

Incredibly, the ink was barely dry on the Floyd deal when Davis was forced out of his position as Columbia Records president, due to alleged misappropriation of funds to the tune of nearly $100,000, including, allegedly, paying for his son's bar mitzvah and remodeling his apartment.

Over time, Davis found it difficult to combat the PR war waged against him. In the minds of many casual observers, Davis's legal issues, dealings with Columbia, and the payola scandal had been conflated. *Rolling Stone* magazine reported that at the time Davis was ousted, in 1973, he had a signed contract with CBS through mid-April 1975. It perhaps goes without saying that this document was barely worth the paper it was printed on when Davis was given his pink slip.

Davis was indicted for tax evasion, a charge, in reality, which had little if any connection to the government's payola scandal investigation. Davis, the feds alleged, failed to file taxes on the nearly $100,000 in question from his time as president of CBS. By announcing these charges at a press conference in June, a US district attorney overseeing the recording industry investigation may have given many in the industry and general public the false impression that Davis had been caught in a payola dragnet—and that the government probe was far more wide-ranging and successful than it was.

"Everything in the press is overblown, but the culture does appear to have been deep rooted," says Harvest's Stuart Watson.

> A lack of trust began to develop between artist and record company. I had been in the fortunate position of getting close the artists I worked with, and following much time together on the road, understood the way they tried to position themselves imagewise, and was able to influence the willingness to promote product in mediums in which artists were comfortable.

"In my experience, it was about *him* [Davis] and not the artist," says Peter Jenner, who managed Ian Dury, who appeared on Arista, and toured with one of the label's stars, Lou Reed. "That was what was so nice about working with EMI. It was about the artist, not about them. The execs were a bit civil servant-ish, but they were nice and did their job to sell records by the artist."

It wasn't completely positive for Floyd. New York attorneys Eric Kronfeld and Martin Machat sued Pink Floyd Music to the tune of $116, 675, charging that manager O'Rourke retained Kronfeld and Machat to represent Floyd in its negotiations with CBS.

The attorneys designed the deal as a tax shelter and expected to be slotted 50,000 pounds sterling for negotiating the deal—a sum they expected to be paid to them by September 1974, reported *Variety* in February 1976. I was unable to discover the details of the ultimate resolution in this case, but it was serious enough to warrant news coverage in the trades.

Back in Marseilles, in February 1972, it all seemed so innocent. After a long, boozy night, the drowsy and sauced parties—O'Rourke, the band and Menon—finally came to an agreement, a preliminary deal that was etched out onto proverbial bar napkins. Some of the details included the band claiming a higher royalty rate for the US distribution of the album and a sizable increase in their advance for the record.

With Floyd dead set against Capitol and O'Rourke willing to tell them such, Menon must have been quite the salesman. Floyd and O'Rourke agreed to stay with Capitol for *The Dark Side of the Moon*'s States-side distribution. "Whilst no one assumed Pink Floyd would leave, it was not a surprise to some when they did," says Stuart Watson.

It might have been cruel for the band and O'Rourke to indulge in a bit of subterfuge and not tell Menon that they'd signed on the dotted line with CBS. Menon, however, has gone on record as saying he knew very well that *Dark Side* would be the last record Floyd would distribute in the States through Capitol, but wanted the record anyway because of its potential. Besides, allowing the band's breakthrough record in America to slip away to a competitor was unthinkable. And O'Rourke knew that Capitol would clean house and jettison some of its signees. Meaning, for the first time, Floyd would get the full force of the label's promotional muscle, something the band felt it lacked for past efforts but long deserved.

In the wake of Floyd's departure, Capitol's dirty little secret was its desire to chase the one that got away. Michael Ponczek, one of the two keyboardists in the American progressive rock band Ethos (Ardour), sometimes simply referred to as Ethos, told me in an interview I conducted in 2009 that Capitol signed his band in the hopes of nurturing an American version of Pink Floyd. Ironically, Ethos (Ardour) were fashioned more in the Yes/Genesis progressive-rock mold and less the space rock/prog rock template Floyd perfected.

By the mid-1970s, the label was still distributing German prog and quasi-prog bands Triumvirat, Kraftwerk, Neu!, Jane (which appeared on the famous Brain label in their native country), and American/Latin American jazz-rock fusion outfit Caldera. Ethos (Ardour), while immensely talented, never had a breakthrough record. In addition, Canadian art-pop band Klaatu, it was revealed, was not the Fab Four in disguise, as was wildly speculated in the press, an auspicious sign that spelled trouble for the band and their label. Further, baroque prog-ers Gentle Giant had alleged that Capitol had not paid Alucard, the band's limited partnership, $40,000 it was owed for their *Free Hand* album.

The label's woes were temporary, however. By mid-1976, Capitol-EMI was going from strength to strength. Chairman, president, and chief executive Bhaskar Menon told the media in a presser on August 11, 1976, at the Hollywood Palladium, that the label's profits were up $5 million over the previous year.

=

The famous Floyd treadmill ride continued, as the band sandwiched work on *Obscured by*

Clouds between gigs in the United Kingdom, Continental Europe, and North America. *Financial Times* caught the band at the Rainbow Theatre and Antony Thorncroft noted that "the Floyd can create sounds and experiences completely outside the competence of any other group of musicians . . . in the country." Thorncroft did say, quite oddly, that the band was in a "creative rut," but have the "furthest frontiers of pop music to themselves."

They were proving it at every turn. As Graeme Edge of the Moody Blues and Carl Palmer of ELP would also do in the early 1970s, Mason laid his hands on a prototype electronic drum setup, offering him an expansive percussive palette.

Alternately, save for *Atom Heart Mother*, *Obscured by Clouds* might contain some of Floyd's most dreamy, pleasant sounds to date. The sedate folk-rock "Wot's . . . Uh the Deal" which opens in G, was written by Waters and Gilmour, and is infused with the spirit of American country rock, touching upon the alchemical theme at the heart of the film—the ability to "turn my lead into gold."

"Burning Bridges," which feels as though it's in 6/4 (some sources say 3/4), possesses a similar feel to Floyd's later masterpiece "Shine On," and features Gilmour's squawking slide guitar work, somewhat reminiscent of the seagulls or whale cries we hear in "Echoes." That's Gilmour, generally in the left channel, and Wright in the right channel, sharing lead vocal duties. The melody is reprised in "Mudmen."

The instrumental title track pulsates with VCS3 synth. There's a split-second pause following the track and leading into the instrumental mid-tempo rocker "When You're In," featuring at least two guitar tracks—generally one in each channel. Wright's staccato Hammond organ attack and the slight echo applied to Mason's snare drum and hissing cymbals carpet the track. This could be the hardest rocking number on the entire record.

"Childhood's End" is led by Wright's chordal playing and perhaps the VSC3—a compositional technique that would resurface on *WYWH* with "Shine On." We hear an acoustic guitar strumming and at least three other electric guitars—two main tracks panned left and right, layered on top of the musical proceedings. Waters's bass thumps away, providing the sonic-bed foundation along with Wright's keys. Mason's slashing and slushy partially opened hi-hat rhythmic patterns cut a path through the track and maintain its driving momentum.

During Gilmour's solo, beginning at approximately 2:48, portions of his playing are repeated (as early as 2:59) and (likely) used as echoed background audio. It harkens back to the raunchier moments of George Harrison circa 1968.

The jaunty quality of "Free Four" belies the reflective nature of its lyrics. The song addresses many of the issues we normally associate with the mid- and late 1970s Roger Waters—ambition, war, life as a merry-go-round, and so forth.

Waters sings of death being "a long cold rest" and touring the world and America to "make it to the top." The combat imagery runs amok: one can bury oneself in "fox holes," constantly being "on the run," leading to confusion over whether "the hunt has begun"—all themes later explored in more detail on *Dark Side* and *WYWH*.

Perhaps just as importantly, Waters also indicates, "I am the dead man's son," which could be interpreted as an extension of the "Corporal Clegg" or a preview of "Wish You Were Here" and the entirety of *The Wall*.

Obscured by Clouds appeared on June 2, 1972, and "Free Four," b/w "The Gold, It's In the," was released as a single in the US and in areas of Continental Europe. "Free Four" bears a passing resemblance to Norman Greenbaum's 1969 song, "Spirit in the Sky," a Top 5 hit in the US and No. 1 in Britain.

The cover Hipgnosis created was a blurry frame grabbed from the film, snatched by Storm. Over the years Hipgnosis has caught shit for this opaque cover image, but its vague overtures toward the cosmic befits the movie's plot. Upon its release, *Obscured by Clouds* just missed the Top 40, reaching No. 46 in August. In their September 30, 1972, issue, *Billboard* announced Floyd's success with the record on the French charts.

GOIN' FULL DARK SIDE

Just prior to the release of *Obscured by Clouds*, Floyd entered into EMI studio in early June to begin work on *The Dark Side of the Moon*. But how had Floyd gotten here? A look at the band's music and recording methods reveals clues to unlock the nature of Floyd's conceptual work and recording methods.

The Dark Side of the Moon began its life in a rehearsal studio—the Rolling Stones's spot in the Bermondsey district of London. Waters had brought in some musical and lyrical concepts, but the band hammered out basic musical ideas and improvised on them.

A band meeting was held in Mason's kitchen, in Camden, to discuss and solidify the direction of the new record. Mason told Tony Stewart of *NME* that "the piece is related to the pressures that form on us and other people generally," Mason said. "That is the very rough theme."

Mason and Waters jotted down life "pressures," and Waters took it upon himself to finally write the words to the emerging songs. On many levels Waters was hoping to move away from cosmic concepts inherent to the counterculture—those the band had been saddled with, perhaps unfairly, up to that point in their career. "I remember Roger saying that he wanted to write it absolutely straight, clear, and direct," Gilmour said.

Essentially, a distinct, if loosely connected, conceptual framework emerged and would explore all of the things that drive men mad: war, religious dogma, pressure to meet deadlines, need of attaining money, constant travelling, fear of flying, fixation on death and what lies beyond, even madness itself. This was not just armchair philosophizing. Waters admitted to *Melody Maker* prior to the release of *The Dark Side of the Moon* that the pressure and doldrums of everyday life, of touring and then recording—and repeating this vicious cycle—was driving him slightly insane.

Waters was working on a summation of the entire piece and envisioned "Eclipse," a moniker, which operated as the title of the entire work for a time. Floyd was forced, in a way, to use the title of "Eclipse," because the band Medicine Head had claimed the phrase *Dark Side of the Moon* for the title of their own 1972 work.

Whatever the record was going to be titled, Wright, for one, was unconvinced that the concept of madness could and should be sustained over the course of an LP's song cycle. Mental illness was a subject "I didn't feel strongly about," Wright was quoted posthumously by the *Sunday Times* in 2009.

Truth be told, *Dark Side*, or what would become *Dark Side*, felt different than other projects Floyd had undertaken. Instead of being led by their nose, there was a blueprint, a solid foundation and conceptual framework on which the band could build. The Beatles had led the way with their quasi-thematic *Sgt. Pepper's Lonely Hearts Club Band* from 1967, paving the pathway for conceptual rock records throughout the 1960s and 1970s.

Concept albums were essential to the growth of progressive rock, and Floyd became a leading light of this phenomenon. Much like theatrical (and musical) dramas for the last one hundred years or more, twentieth century (and beyond) concept records and rock operas present a discernable, chronological plot—a grand theme or a narrative thread infused with lead and minor characters, whether they be fictional or historical—that unfolds throughout a sequential track order.

Many other rock records sought to ape the Beatles's quasi-conceptual *Sgt. Pepper's Lonely Hearts Club Band*, either intentionally or unwittingly, which set the stage for far more involved, plot-based rock albums. The Who's *Tommy*, perhaps out of necessity, crystallized the working template for the concept record, or the "rock opera," and foretold the coming of *The Wall*.

"I did a show called *My Fair Lady* with Roger Daltrey," singer/actor/voiceover artist Jody Ashworth told me in 2011.

> He pulled out a guitar one day and we just started playing Who tunes. He had . . . an audience of one hundred people just standing there watching. We started talking about rock opera, and he said, "Jody, we didn't realize what we were doing at the time. The Who had put out three or four albums before *Tommy* and we were broke. We were $800,000 in debt." He said, "I'll never forget our manager came in and said, 'By the way, guys, I made a mistake; it is not $700,000 but $800,000 in debt.' He said, 'I'm glad he said it was another $100,000. Because if he had said $8,000, that might have been something we could have figured out how to pay off."

According to Ashworth, formerly of Trans-Siberian Orchestra, the Who were flouting convention by even associating the term "rock opera" with their musical project. Floyd's most comparable work, *The Wall*, wouldn't arrive until 1979, but *Dark Side* was clearly a game changer for the conceptual music world.

The Who were trendsetters in many ways, however. Richie Unterberger explains in his book *Won't Get Fooled Again: The Who From* Lifehouse *to* Quadrophenia, that working with an avant-garde composer at Cambridge University, Who guitarist/songwriter/vocalist Pete Townshend amassed biographical information on individuals who made themselves available for a battery of tests. The team then translated and charted the raw data they'd collected into music. What emerged were "pulse-modulated frequencies," Townshend said, that formed the basis, or basic rhythmic beats, for The Who's "Won't Get Fooled Again" and "Baba O'Riley" from 1971's *Who's Next*, an album that was largely constructed from the musical pieces of an abandoned conceptual project, the *Lifehouse* record.

Counterpoint rhythms were generated for these tracks via a 1960s organ driving an EMS VCS3 synth, with a filter and sample and hold capabilities. It's very much like the heartbeat motif running through audiovisual aspects of *Dark Side* and the hustle and bustle of "On the Run." Reportedly, Wright's Farfisa was sent through the VCS-3 for "On the Run," and this is partly what we hear on *The Dark Side of the Moon*.

Rhythm frames the entire record. Mason's kick-drum beater puffs softly to the timing of the human heartbeat—a pattern that both opens and concludes the album. It's a looped pattern, and actually, the pacing was slowed, perhaps more befitting of a monk or guru in deep meditation. Mason indicated that a sustained piano chord runs in reverse through-out the opening, creating further continuity via a drone bed.

The heartbeat pulse courses through Floyd's music—from "Heart Beat, Pig Meat" to "Shine On You Crazy Diamond." "The heartbeat alludes to the human condition and sets the mood for the music which describes the emotions experienced during a lifetime," Gilmour told Welch for an interview that appears in the book *Today's Sounds*. "Amidst the chaos there is beauty and hope for mankind."

Although this occurred late in the process, audio snippets of interviews Roger Water conducted during the recording sessions for *The Dark Side of the Moon* were recorded and used for the mix. Waters jotted down large-as-life questions on index cards and recorded spoken-word responses, to some surprising results. Floyd organized a coalition of the will-ing around Abbey Road studios and recorded them as they ruminated on questions such as, "Are you afraid of dying?" "When was the last time you thumped someone?" "Were you in the right?"

Participants included but were not limited to Paul and Linda McCartney, who were working on Wings's *Red Rose Speedway* at Abbey Road at the time; Wings guitarist Henry McCullough; Floyd road manager Chris Adamson; Peter Watts and his wife Puddie, mother of actress Naomi Watts; roadie Roger "The Hat" Manifold, and Abbey Road door-man Gerry O'Driscoll, who provided some of the best soundbites of the lot. Responses from Linda and Paul were rejected, it's been said, owing to the belief that their answers were too canned and guarded.

"Speak to Me," the first track on *Dark Side*, is a maelstrom of sights and sounds—an audio collage—of all the various "themes" we'll encounter during the sonic journey. It's a sampler of sonic components linked through a classic cross-fading technique and assem-bled by Mason at home and then later in Abbey Road studios. The cinematic qualities of the piece are self-evident—perhaps the very essence of "theater of the mind" or head-phones music—and provides the perfect overture and point of entry for the entire work.

We hear the ripping of paper and cash registers ring from "Money," vocalist Clare Torry's anguished orgiastic wailing ("The Great Gig in the Sky"), as well as portions of the audio from interviews Roger Waters conducted. Nothing sets the mood perhaps better than maniacal laughter and spoken-word gems of wisdom, such as "I've always been mad; I know I've been mad, like most of us have," and "I've been mad for fucking years."

What appears to be backwards organ and the hissing of a cymbal (reverse audio of a cymbal crash?) swells to a maddening, buzzing level as "Speak to Me" fizzles into "Breathe," which is largely shaped by Gilmour's droopy, mournful guitar and classic upstroked E-minor chord (or variation on it). Before long, the slide guitar work and ethereal drones have a sedative effect, inducing the sensation of sliding in and out of consciousness—the perfect entry point for this hallucinatory audiovisual journey.

The blue-dream quality of the song is further painted by Wright's jazzy chord sequence. When the instrumental section hits the G, the keyboards transitions through an E-flat chord. Wright tapped his memory for the chord, and applied a variation on a D-sharp seventh chord, something he'd heard on a Miles Davis record, *Kind of Blue*, quite possibly the track "So What?" (It should be noted that D-minor chords appear in more than one entry, as far as I can hear it anyway.)

Gilmour's double-tracked vocals and harmonizing serve to bolster Waters' lyrics, such as "all you touch and all you see," later echoed in the closing track "Eclipse." The stoic voice is somewhat creepy against the audio landscape and is effective despite lyrics urging listeners not to "be afraid to care." "Breathe" asks why we work so tirelessly and fruitlessly. It's only the opening salvo in a larger question posed by the record: do we make ourselves mad through life's constant chase, or are we predestined for insanity?

A drone links "Breathe" with the electronica of "On the Run," virtually composed on the sequencer on the EMS SynthiA KS. The SynthiA was the next step in the evolution of suitcase synthesizers, a gadget the boys *had* to check out. Gilmour fiddled around with it first and played a series of notes. Then he had the machine repeat the eight-note sequence and accelerate the rate at which it played them, shortening the space between the notes. Oscillators and filters were layered on top of this sequence, helping to develop the pattern as a quavering and quivering, almost living, breathing organism.

When Waters heard these dizzying, cyclical patterns Gilmour created with the SynthiA, he was intrigued. Waters tweaked what Gilmour had started and knew they were onto something. The piece known as "The Travel Sequence," once a guitar workout the band had been playing live onstage and one the author John Harris dubbed a piece of "jazz-rock fusion," finally had focus and had been transformed through a new synthetic complexion.

Through pitch manipulation and panning techniques these synths sounds sweep across the stereo spectrum, recalling the Doppler effect. The hi-hat type snaps, a kind of clipped rhythm, act as virtual timekeeping mechanisms threaded across the entire structure of the piece. An audio recording of Pink Floyd's show at the San Diego Sports Arena from April 1975, and another from Los Angeles, California, and Landover, Maryland, performing "On the Run" from *Dark Side*, reveals that Mason generated these sounds on hi-hats.

Played at a slower pace, but later sped up in the studio, these rhythmic circles were augmented by reverse audio bits, Abbey Road's considerable sound library, a found recording of assistant engineer Peter James' footsteps, synth-produced "chopper blades," the heartbeat pattern, and the whining noises of Gilmour dragging the leg of a microphone stand across the strings of his electrified guitar. This microphone stand whining, sent through an echo unit, was used in reverse for the final recording. We also hear maniacal laughter courtesy of roadie Roger "the Hat" Manifold, a nickname he earned through his frequent use of head-gear apparel while on tour. Audio snippets of Waters's interviews and airport announcements run throughout the track. There is no singing.

The SynthiA was far from being used as a space filler: the sounds it generated underscore the monotony, perils, reliance on machinery, and ironically, the human fears indicative of traveling in the modern world. The song literally comes to a screeching halt—signifying a plane crash—just after we hear Roger "The Hat"'s cackling in response to a question about death.

After the crashing sounds of "On the Run" dissipate, a series of ringing clock alarms jar and remove us from our slight hypnosis, brought on by the repetitive, minimalistic qualities of "On the Run." Recording engineer Alan Parsons was tasked with demonstrating the impact of quadrophonic sound and set out to record a series of clock alarm bells ringing. He found an antique clock store near EMI studios, brandished his portable tape recorder, and captured the ticks and alarms of each clock individually.

After Floyd had become aware of this fantastic sonic resource, they had to use it for the record. Parsons then had the meticulous and unenviable—maybe thankless—task of assembling these captured sounds into a coherent whole.

Musically, the track is quite a bit more involved than it would seem at first blush. Fairly sophisticated cross rhythms occur in the track's opening: the looped heartbeat pulse returns, a metronomic knocking pitter-patters away (courtesy of either a portable SynthiA synthesizer, VCS3, or bass pickup, whichever report you believe), and pitched Rototoms pop in time and tune with the sparse sonic elements.

Rototoms, essentially a single-head metallic drum shell frame that can be tuned by spinning the upper ring and twisting the drum itself, are treated with deep echo—the stuff of Dub musicians' dreams. The effect is cinematic: it's cosmic boogie, reverberating through the chasm of space.

After Mason's tom/snare pounding, Gilmour's venomous voice speaks to youth's relativism toward the concept of time, as Wright's dry, almost emotionless vocals offer a countervailing placidity indicative of a plaintive, even humbled, aging individual.

In an interview with Wright that ran in the *Boston Globe* in January 1997, the keyboardist said he was often uncomfortable with his voice, in large parts because he simply doesn't like the tone of it. Ironically, his somewhat ghostly, even shaky, voice works perfectly for the song. By song's end, it's evident that the speaker in "Time" believed he had more to communicate but can't seem to find the words to compose a coherent message.

Amid Gilmour's barking guitar lines, "Breathe Reprise," which is really just the second half of the song, the young "rabbit" of the opening appears no longer physically capable of sustaining long days in the fields. With the tolling of a church bell we are led to prayer, as "Breathe Reprise" spirals into "The Great Gig in the Sky." Wright begins the song in B-minor on piano and ends in what appears to be a G-minor seventh chord—and it's a wild ride getting there. The poise Wright exhibits and the inherent anticipation and pregnant pauses in the music all point to a seasoned artist who knows how to use color shading in chordal structures as well as stress the importance of space.

Gilmour uses pedal steel in the opening, just as he did for "Breathe." Ordinarily the steel would allude to a country rock or straight-up country and western style. What Gilmour and some of his progressive rock cousins did so well was use an instrument usually identified with American roots music and transcend this genre with something ethereal.

Audio snippets set the mood again. The song, once dubbed "The Mortality Sequence," is a cinematic sonic episode capturing the soul's journey into the afterlife. We hear O'Driscoll speak: "Why should I be frightened of dying? There's no reason for it; you've got to go sometime." And: "I am not frightened of dying. Anytime will do; I don't mind."

Prior to the interview voices being added to the track, Floyd and the production crew mused over the song. It was good, but they didn't know where to go with it: it had the feel they wanted, but still, something was missing. Having been familiar with vocalist Clare Torry's work at Abbey Road, Alan Parsons rang up Torry in January 1973 and asked her to come down for a session. Clare initially blew it off, saying she was too busy to accommodate his request. Further, she was not really a fan of Pink Floyd.

Torry did eventually show, and when she arrived at Abbey Road, Floyd attempted to explain what the album was about. Floyd had a general idea of what they wanted for the song, but couldn't explain in exact terms. Torry instructed them to play the track and began singing off the cuff. It was in a bluesy, R&B style. And totally inappropriate. Gilmour stopped her. Or corrected her.

The song needed something exotic, orgasmic, but not so bluesy per se. It needed to be something from the very depth of her soul; something "halfway between orgasm and terror," Barry Miles wrote in his book *Pink Floyd: The Early Years*.

Got it. Clare let 'er rip—a few times—and the band watched as she loosed with a string of anguished gospelesque screams, spanning a four-minute duration. Torry's voice never falters; the vibrato in her voice and the slight echo applied to it gives it an added presence.

If Floyd were satisfied with Torry's work, they showed no outward signs of such. Torry finished her takes, walked into the control room, and was met with silence. Nothing was spoken, not even "Thanks. That was great." No "Let's do it again." She thought she'd blown it and that her work would not be used.

"I was a big Pink Floyd fan but . . . Clare Torry was white? At one point I didn't even know that," says vocalist/actress Durga McBroom, lead choreographer for the *P.U.L.S.E.* tour who's performed the "Great Gig" sequence on stage with the Floyd. "When I met her, she said, 'I'm Clare.' I said, 'No, really?'"

It is a monumental performance and one that would send shock waves through rock music for decades to come. Countless rock bands and progressive rock bands have, it can be stated, followed Floyd's lead and incorporated similar soul elements into their musical opuses.

In retrospect, it seems silly that Torry would be surprised that she'd be featured on the record, and prominently, but that's the book on this track. Her contribution would later be a point of contention between herself and he band. After decades, Torry was awarded a financial payout and credit as a cowriter, along with Wright, the coauthor of "Breathe," "Time," "Us and Them," and "Any Colour You Like."

Interestingly, it is this writer's understanding that Torry's various takes were combined to make one composite "performance." This process was not unusual for the time, and is another example of Floyd manipulating tape to achieve groundbreaking results in the studio.

The song ends on a plaintive G-minor seventh chord and at approximately 4:33 we hear a warble, as if the Earth has been spun off its axis. For a few seconds the tonality of the entire musical structure skews higher, perhaps due to manual manipulation of the medium and representing an aura representation of the human spirit rising.

Early versions of "The Great Gig in the Sky," prior to the record being released, featured prerecorded spoken-word recitations from Pauline passages as well as the Lord's Prayer from the New Testament, the second part of the biggest best-selling book of all time, and British satirist-turned-moralist Malcolm Muggeridge. This type of appropriation was something Floyd had been accustomed to and would later continue for "Psalm 23" from the *King James Bible*, which appears in perverse but conceptual form in the song "Sheep" from *Animals*.

DARK SIDE, SIDE 2

In the early days, one would have turned the LP over and gotten onto side 2. In the digital and CD ages, there's a small pause and up comes cha-chings from a cash register, just one component of a looped collage composed of several different elements, including coinage sliding around Waters's wife's gardening/mixing bowl for clay, pennies being dropped, ripped paper and so forth. It was initially recorded by Waters on a two-track Revox A77 and Mason, in their respective private studios, but needed to be revisited by the band and recorded properly in the studio environment of Abbey Road. The loop of the sound effects recorded by Mason and Waters was put onto a four-track analog tape and later listened to in their headphones while recording. Essentially, they tracked to a loop as a timekeeping mechanism.

These sounds constitute, of course, the opening of one of Floyd's best-known tracks, and one that would garner much airplay: "Money."

As he had done for "Time," Waters recorded a demo for "Money," chopping out a 7/4 bass riff initially on acoustic guitar. In the official "finished" version, Gilmour shadows the bass line and eventually a couple more guitar tracks. Wright's funky organ was overlaid onto this matrix. Gilmour uses a Lewis guitar for his first, which was double tracked and ADT-enhanced as the movement progresses.

Although often mistaken as being sincere, the lyrics are actually an assault on the pursuit of material things—from cars and caviar dinners to paper money. "I just think that money's the biggest single pressure on people," Gilmour told music journalist Chris Welch in an interview appearing the mid-1970s book *Today's Sounds*, published by *Melody Maker*. "Remember the Pink Floyd were broke for a pretty long time. We were in debt when I joined, and nine months afterwards I remember when we gave ourselves thirty pounds a week, and for the first time we were earning more than the roadies."

For the middle section of the song, Floyd wanted a raucous rock number and thought sax would work wonders. Dick Parry knew Gilmour from their mid-1960s band Jokers Wild, and Gilmour admits that he was the only real sax player he knew.

In the early and mid-1970s, Parry had saxed for, among others, goofballs Bonzo Dog Band, John Entwistle's Ox, and the psychedelic/bluesy rock band Quiver, composed of guitarist Tim Renwick, drummer Willie Wilson, guitarist Cal Batchelor, and bassist Bruce Thomas, later of Elvis Costello. Gilmour would eventually produce Quiver when they merged with Sutherland Brothers. The tight-knit community appears to have helped contribute to the intimacy of these tracks and the comfort level the band and the session player seemed to enjoy.

After Dick Parry blows in "7," the time signature twists to 4/4 time for Gilmour's rock-style guitar solo. The guitarist was thrilled to not have to worry about soloing over an odd time signature—and just let loose. As Gilmour vocally scats we hear the voices of those interviewed by Waters at Abbey Road. Phrases such as, "I don't know. I was really drunk at the time," and "that geezer was cruisin' for a bruisin'" cycle as the song fades into "Us and Them."

The track "The Violent Sequence," originally written for Antonioni's *Zabriskie Point*, was resurrected for "Us and Them." *The Early Years 1967—1972: Crelation* lists the song idea as "The Riot Scene."

With "Us and Them," Floyd can reclaim the space rock title with pride. "Space," as it applies here, relates not to the cosmos per se, but the poise of the performances or *space* between notes. If any single song on *Dark Side* exemplifies this aesthetic, it's "Us and Them."

Little gestures go a long way. A change from D to Bm/D to Dm7 is pure magic, subtly shifting the melancholy mood like a soft, cool breeze. The icy musical complements the chilling lyrical imagery: young soldiers being mowed down as generals sit behind battle lines planning strategies, marking up maps, never counting the human cost of advance and retreat. It's not difficult to make the mental leap from these visions to the circumstances surrounding the death of Eric Fletcher Waters.

Later in the same song, the portrait of an armed man telling a youngster, "There's room for you inside" is quite sickening. It could evoke images of a military transport or the process of packing human beings onto trains and interring them in some far-flung POW work camp.

On the battlefield of another kind, an old man is starved to death, presumably due to societal neglect and poverty. No one seems to notice him, save for the narrator of the song. We rush through the streets—and our lives—and never give the old codger a second thought, so he dies. Stuart Shea, in his book *Pink Floyd FAQ*, pointed out that one of the main themes of the song is "emotional absence." It may also be commenting on how we fight for resources and time, with none to spare for the less fortunate.

The notion of "us and them" is based on common bonds and may merely be a construct of the mind. R. D. Laing, for his 1967 book *The Politics of Experience*, in a chapter titled, funnily enough, "Us and Them," discussed the psychological aspects of group and family dynamics. "If there is no external danger, then danger and terror have to be invented and maintained," wrote Laing. "Shall we realize that We and They are shadows of each other?"

Parry picks his spots to lay down his breathy performance: in between the verses sung by Gilmour. These saxophone blows, combined with all of these various other musical elements, seem to induce a near-comatose state in the listener. There's something interdimensional about the track. We're simultaneously floating and numb.

As sparse as the musical elements may appear to be, a simple gesture such as a manual repeat echo on the vocals is a brilliant touch by engineer Parsons. Words spiral off into infinity and Parry's sultry sax gently breezes through.

"I loved Parry's playing, and appreciate it now even more than I did at the time," says Tim Sanders of Kick Horns, a brass ensemble that would appear on David Gilmour's 1984 solo record *About Face*. "It's unbelievably hard to play so fluently through tempos as slow as 'Us and Them,' and so melodically. Both on *Dark Side* and *Wish You Were Here*, he was a kind of foil to the Gilmour raunch, and a very human voice within the electronics."

Rick and David sing lead vocals and Gospel voices, supplied by accomplished backing vocalists Lesley Duncan, Barry St. John (Elizabeth Thompson), Liza Strike, and Doris Troy, and inch toward something that could be described as audio overload.

Floyd makes use, again, of a D-minor seventh chord, which plays out the song and presages "Any Colour You Like," credited to Gilmour, Mason, and Wright. It's really (largely) an instrumental psychedelic rock jam awash with aquatic Leslie speaker reverb effects, not unlike "Echoes" and Eric Clapton's classic tone for the Cream offering "Badge."

Some of the scat vocals originally recorded were mostly scrubbed, but some remain. Tellingly, the original version was actually titled "Scat." Wright's repeating Minimoog synth lines ripple in what seems like concentric circles, surrounding the listener in bright sonic waves. They envelope you, and when the jam speeds to a halt, "Brain Damage" commences with Gilmour's lilting, partial chordal guitar work. Some, including Pink Floyd biographer Nicholas Schaffner, drew a link between the arpeggiated guitar lines of "Brain Damage" with the Beatles's "Dear Prudence." A guitar figure that was itself inspired by a technique Donovan taught the Fab Four while in India visiting the Maharishi Mahesh Yogi. Mason's heartbeat kick pulse pattern thumps away and Waters steps up to the mike, the first appearance of his vocals on the record.

The D chord during the verses of "Brain Damage" acts as a kind of grounding for the entire song. However, when the music moves to a G seventh chord—and back again—it fosters a subsuming darkness (an eclipse?) that shades the entire track in uncertainty, reflecting a kind of paranoia. Well-timed sonic droplets act as flaring meteor showers, but also conjure images of a battered and desolate lunar landscape.

Syd Barrett lives here, too, if not in the track, then in our heads. When being interviewed by Nick Horne for the Capital Radio's history of Floyd series, Waters did admit that the line "when the band you're in starts playing different tunes" is, in his words, "a direct reference" to Syd.

Then, again, the connection to Barrett hardly needs to be underscored: someone shouting and no one hearing it; voices inside the head. Waters equated the "desire" to walk on a nicely manicured patch of grass with being slightly mad. Equally inane is the idea that one would landscape such a beautiful plot of land and not allow anyone to walk on it—thus keeping the loonies on the (walk) path. Specifically Waters envisioned the grass between King's College Chapel in Cambridge and the River Cam. Could this have been a reference to Barrett, during summer, playing his music on the green lawns of Cambridge?

Other images are curious: Newspapers piling up, delivery never stopping. Our minds are crowded, stuffed, which may lead to insanity and even institutionalization. When Waters talks about raising a razor we think, for a minute, that maybe he isn't just discussing a cosmetic change, but a psychological one. Exactly how is the speaker (lunatic?) in the song being rearranged, and who is doing the rearranging?

A turn to an A seventh chord in the middle of the bridge or "chorus" section of the song, plus Peter Watts's crazed laughter, courtesy of those Abbey Road interviews, are heavy-handed decorations, but hilarious, effective, chilling.

As "Brain Damage" slides into "Eclipse," a sunnier day *seems* to be on the horizon. It's a psych-out. This mood is deceiving, however, as the chord sequence is sullied by the inclusion of a suspenseful B-flat major seventh figure. The rising swell of gospel-esque vocals whip up the howling specter of death, à la "The Great Gig in the Sky," just as Waters's lyrics speak of futility, numbness, and a letting go.

The word "all" appears as the lead word for a series of lines and often begins in one bar while the rest of the line continues into the next, without breaking the dynamic flow of the 3/4 rhythmic feel. Mason largely accents the triple feel here, but acquits himself very nicely, initially by crashing away on cymbals, then spraying beats around the kit, plying rhythmic patterns only in the space between Waters's sung words. Mason's playing isn't a drag on the pull of the emotional current created by a river of voices, images, and thoughts colliding and conspiring to conclude the song cycle. He goes with the flow.

The fixation on the sun and the moon in "Eclipse," seems an obvious nod to the notion that we're all mad. Deep questions remain, however: Does the driving ambition to collect material objects lead us to madness? Is the urge to gather wealth a natural human instinct? If so, then are we as a race inclined to insanity? Is humankind's natural or inert state madness, and is our notion of reality a reflection or manifestation of a form of mass hysteria?

As the song fades, Mason's looped kick-drum heartbeat reappears and we hear the virtual title of the album spoken by O'Driscoll: "There is no dark side in the moon, really. Matter of fact, it's all dark."

Some have speculated that the heartbeat at the end of the record signifies the end of a life, or perhaps even the cycle of life, death and rebirth—perhaps an audio representation of Nietzsche's concept of eternal return. Famously, the Floyd crew and even members of the band were left wondering what this ending, or lack of one, actually meant.

Gilmour told Chris Welch in 1973, "The songs are about being in rock 'n' roll, and apply to being what we are on the road. Roger wrote 'Money' from the heart."

But the songs are also about neuroses, Gilmour explained. "That doesn't mean that we are neurotic. We are able to see it and discuss it. 'The Dark Side of the Moon' is an allusion to the moon and lunacy. The dark side is generally related to what goes on inside people's heads—the subconscious and the unknown."

Despite what the band perceived as logical and clear messaging, some people, especially those engineering the record and part of the road crew, grappled with the overarching concept. The band was stunned by this, Gilmour said: that those closest to the Floyd "didn't see [Dark Side] was about the pressures that can drive a young chap mad."

The irony in presenting a record that focuses on the pressures of life is that the Dark Side period may have been one of the least stressful personal times for the individual members of the band. Mason was living with Lindy and would regularly see Waters and Judy outside the studio, even when not working on any material in particular. In Islington, Waters had built his own personal studio for the convenience of working on his own material without having to organize appointments with Abbey Road or even the other members of the band. Wright and Juliette and family were in Leinster Gardens, and Gilmour, the only unmarried member of the band, had moved to Essex, out in the country, where he renovated an old Victorian farmhouse, complete with a pool for his fish, which he dug himself.

YET ANOTHER MOVIE

Let's backtrack and pick up the story from 1972. Prior to the release of Dark Side, Floyd seemed consumed with film soundtracks. Between More, Zabriskie Point, Pompeii, and La Vallee, cinematic concerns were sandwiched between their recording escapades and stage work.

Filmmaker Peter Clifton shot the band at the Brighton shows on June 28 and 29—concerts that sprung up in the wake of Floyd's technical breakdowns in January at the same venue. "I was pretty good friends with Steve O'Rourke for a long time," Clifton told me.

> He came out to Australia for the first time with the Small Faces and the Who. . . . That's where I met him, and I stayed pretty good friends with him up to his death, which was a bit premature. Steve O'Rourke had these thick bifocals and they looked

like the bottom of Coca-Cola bottles. [He was] a lovely man and very honest. Not at all a hustler like so many other managers were.

"We used to play Cricket together," Clifton continues. "Roger Waters and David Gilmour were hopeless, but Po [Aubrey Powell] and Storm [Thorgerson] were really good. They were lovely intellectually artistic people. I got on really well with Roger, even though he's a hopeless batsman. I found him a wonderfully interesting person, and quizzical."

Clifton received permission from O'Rourke to film two songs on 16 mm negatives at the Brighton Dome: "Set the Controls for the Heart of the Sun" and "Careful with That Axe, Eugene." "I wanted to concentrate on what the boys were feeling as they were playing their music, and I got into a little bit of trouble with Steve O'Rourke," Clifton tells me.

He was happy with the light show, but you weren't seeing much of their light show [on film]. So, it didn't put me in the good books. They allowed us to film the sound check, or rehearsal, or whatever you want to call it. You can see they are at sound check, because Roger has a cigarette sticking out the axe of his guitar. He wouldn't do that in a live show. Afterwards when they performed the concert, our cameras went back into the audience and we filmed the wide shots and the long shots.

Clifton still has the negatives, tucked away in storage, and says the footage was eventually earmarked for *Rock City*, a film he cut decades ago. "I hired the Rolling Stones's 24-track mobile," Clifton tells me. "Roger came in and helped me to mix it down. I did a deal with EMKA, the company run by Steve O'Rourke, and I paid them 1,000 pounds for the rights to include them in my film, which at that stage was called *A Film Concert* and was eventually released by Columbia."

More Floyd film follies followed. Originally titled *Pink Floyd*, or *Echoes* according to *Variety*, the movie most know as *Live at Pompeii* had the scant running time of sixty-two minutes and was previewed at MIFED, Milan, Italy, on October 26, 1972. It was originally just over an hour, before Adrian Maben added footage. Scotland and France are thought to have screened the movie in October as well.

After the film's initial release in the fall of 1972, Maben coaxed the band to sit for interviews. He even convinced them to muck about the studio in what some observers have noted was little more than a mock recording of pieces on their upcoming record, *The Dark Side of the Moon*. The added footage bulks up the film, however, making it a Pink Floyd, rather than just a concert, experience.

Mason told *Sounds* in 1974 that he thought the band should have taken the interviews a bit more seriously and communicated "something about what's happening and what we do as a group." In some cases it seems as though the band is humoring or putting on the filmmaker.

Mason gets a lot of face, or skin, time onscreen. It's been long believed that Mason's front-and-center presence was the result of poor planning on the director's part. Some of the footage shot had been misplaced, so the director made do with what he had for the song "One of These Days."

In other iconic spots Gilmour mistreats his electric guitar, as if he had just discovered the thing, Waters smashes the hell out of his gong in "A Saucerful of Secrets," and Mason rocks his kit with an unprecedented aggressiveness.

The gong, in particular, an image of the gold circle, was emblematic of the sun and our search for it—a connection the film itself seems to make. Hanging onto the gong's circular support structure, smashing away at the gigantic metal disc, Waters allows the gigantic cymbal to violently sway back and forth as it endures blow after blow.

Gene Siskel reviewed the film upon its re-release in 1974 and gave it three stars, explaining that the movie was being screened in three separate theaters at the Marina Cinema in Chicago. Many critics disliked the film, however. Writing for *Newsday*, Dave Marsh claims it suffers from the "insurmountable problem" that nothing happens on screen. The *Boston Globe* complained that it was about as "engrossing as an Army training film" and as repetitive as a "television test pattern." The reviewer moaned that Floyd "deserved a better fate for their film debut." And in April 1974, the *Cincinnati Enquirer* took note of the "virtuoso camera work" and "effective" lighting, but claimed these factors weren't enough to carry a two-hour movie. The film's limited run at the Albee, the paper concluded, would cater only to Floyd fans and do little to convince neutral parties.

Waters, himself, gave an ambiguous endorsement of the film, saying it would gain a seal of approval of "Floyd freaks," but he doubted "anyone else would" find much interest in it. Waters even referred to the scenes in which the band walks Vesuvius as *Top of the Pops* glamour shots, or so Barry Miles reported.

This may have been a far sight better, however, than Maben's original cinematic concept of having images of Magritte, de Chirico, and surrealist paintings accompanied by Floyd's music. Upon hearing of this idea, Floyd turned Maben down. Intriguingly, Maben would later produce a documentary about Magritte.

Still, this was Floyd as few fans outside the UK had seen them. The film, assigned a G rating, proved popular with fans—as Waters predicted—and was still being screened years after its release. Waters may have been proven incorrect in the larger sense, however: today, the film is considered a classic of the rock film genre.

Floyd was off the road for most of the summer, and returned to North America late in the season. Curiously, and this speaks to the madness of Floyd's tour scheduling at the time, the band played in Vancouver on September 27 and again on September 30, 1972, with single dates in Portland and Seattle sandwiched in between.

With the help of a researcher at the Vancouver Public Library, I may have ascertained why there were two shows scheduled for the same arena, seventy-two hours apart. It appears there was an equestrian show booked at the Pacific National Exhibition fairgrounds, next to the Gardens. "Perhaps they booked the Gardens for an event?" the librarian asks. It was further theorized that Floyd split the dates for budgetary reasons: maybe it was more cost efficient to fly out of Vancouver than Seattle?

Floyd spent most of September in North America, in the American Pacific Northwest, Southwest, Texas, and California, including the Hollywood Bowl where the venue's follow spots created pyramid effects in the sky, foreshadowing the coming of *Dark Side*, but flew back to London to complete more sessions for *The Dark Side of the Moon* in October.

The October 17, 1972, charity event, the War on Want, was held at Wembley Park, as recording dates around this concert were cancelled. Subsequent sessions were planned for later in the month. By November, Floyd were in France performing for a Roland Petit ballet.

Petit, best known to Western audiences for his 1949 production of *Carmen*, choreographed a ballet in the 1960s, *In Praise of Madness*, boasting a libretto by Jean Cau based on Erasmus of Rotterdam's *Stultitiae Laus*, translated from Latin as "The Praise of Folly." Sounds like a title Waters, himself, may have envisioned.

Floyd was introduced to Petit during a French tour in 1970, a meeting set up by manager Steve O'Rourke, who'd been approached by the dance director about collaborating at some point in the future.

The band first played several shows for Petit in Marseilles in November 1972 and later in Paris, France, in January and February 1973. The ballet Floyd performed was supposed to be based on the seven-volume *Remembrance of Things Past* (or *In Search of Lost Time*) by Marcel Proust. Thought by some literary critics to be the finest fiction writing of the twentieth century, Waters, Gilmour, and Mason attempted to read it, but stalled long before the finish line.

Facts are a bit unclear, but it appears Waters gave up the Proust novel after either trying to absorb the first volume, *Swann's Way*, or only a part of it—or after reading the second volume of the book as a whole. Mason, in his autobiographical account of Floyd's history, *Inside Out: A Personal History of Pink Floyd*, credits himself with having gotten the farthest. Whoever holds the title of fastest speed-reader became irrelevant: Floyd chucked the thing and decided to go into the project with minimal background knowledge. Ultimately, and perhaps mercifully, Petit designed a three-part dance program to Floyd's music, which included performances of "Careful with That Axe, Eugene" and "Echoes."

THAT'S RANK

In one of the famous fuck-ups of the rock industry of the early 1970s, in November, the Rainbow Theatre was set to host a screening of *Pink Floyd*, the movie, but the invitation was rescinded by the club's owners, the Rank Organization. The reasoning? The film, even on a limited basis, would put it in direct competition with the live music the Rainbow presented. Pink Floyd's official website claims that "the theatre's owners discovered that the film had not yet been granted a certificate by the British Board of Film Censors."

Three thousand ticketholder couldn't have cared less, especially after it was too late for organizers to refund their money or find an acceptable alternate venue. The whole episode seems avoidable and unnecessarily harsh toward the film, the promoter Peter Bowyer, and the paying public. Questioned about the debacle, Waters simply pointed to theatre management's name, considering it apt.

The rest of the year the band spent on tour in France, from late November through early to mid-December, playing what would be titled *The Dark Side of the Moon*. "I believe the first time I saw Floyd was at Île de la Jatte, in Paris," says Clearlight's Cyrille Verdeaux, who saw Floyd over a two-day stretch in December 1972.

> Two days in the raw. I was with a group of moneyless fans and we had a trick to get in without tickets. But I can't reveal how it was a "trick." It started and the sound grew louder. People began clapping in time with the heartbeat [opening of *Dark Side*], and then smoke arrived. Then the show went on two hours of pure delight, especially because everybody was smoking or/and tripping in this music hall—including me, of course.

By January 9, Floyd was rehearsing its new material for the recording of *The Dark Side of the Moon*, only to return to France for another Roland Petit ballet. We, again, turn to Verdeaux:

"The choreography was well synchronized with the music," remembers Verdeaux, then a member of the French band Babylone, who saw the show in Paris in 1973. "It was starting with a deep-blue color smoke and then the first notes of the bass. I enjoyed every minute of it, and everybody else around, as far as I can tell, had obviously the same positive feeling. I remember the standing ovation that lasted several minutes."

By January 18, as well as 19–21, Floyd was in Studio Two at Abbey Road. Studio Three got a workout from January 24–27 and again from January 29 through Feb 1. By the end of January, however, it's believed that Floyd had finished what was left to do for their upcoming record, including the EMS Synthi A spectacular "On the Run."

Then, it was back, again, to France, for Roland Petit's ballet. Performing for the ballet was not as exciting or enjoyable as the band had first conceived. In fact it turned into a slog and a bit of a nightmare.

Gilmour said that being exacting was taxing: he couldn't or didn't want to count musical measures in his head while he was performing. Similar to the function musical spotters perform when musicians work in the Indian classical idiom, an acquaintance with only tenuous ties to Floyd held up sheets of paper noting the current musical bar. Nothing seemed to work like clockwork, least of all the timing by which the paper was lifted. The band muddled through, however, with some assistance from Floyd lighting director Arthur Max, who wielded a welding wand to help create the kinds of flying sparks indicative of a mad scientist's lab, adding visual effects.

The timelines have been variously reported, but some sources claim that after, others before, the Petit shows were completed, Waters, Mason, and manager O'Rourke were invited to the house of Russian ballet dancer Rudolf Nureyev where Petit, filmmaker Roman Polanski, and some film production crew were on hand to discuss a new project.

On the table: how to tie music and dance into a cinematic plot to be storyboarded, presumably by Polanski. Too much drink and too little talk of Proust caused the whole affair to descend into madness, however. Waters called the meeting a "complete joke."

One version of the story holds that the gang had suggested collaborating on a "blue movie" version of Mary Shelley's nineteenth-century cautionary sci-fi tale, *Frankenstein*. Upon hearing this outlandish concept, Nureyev became visibly nauseous—no doubt fearing he would be called upon to choreograph a (possibly pornographic?) science-fiction *horror show* involving an oversized, fleet-footed green goon composed of stitched-together reanimated body parts. You can practically hear critics sharpening their pencils, ready to launch a barrage of off-color puns.

Interestingly enough, Andy Warhol and writer/director Paul Morrissey erected a racy version of the Gothic classic, titled *Flesh for Frankenstein*, in the spring of 1974. Of further interest, Polanski appears in the Morrissey *suckfest*, *Blood for Dracula*, from 1974, starring Udo Kier as the HVIC.

ALAN PARSONS'S PART

Conflicting stories have circulated about mixing *Dark Side*, leading some, by logical extension to speculate about Alan Parsons's role in the recording. The band typically played down the technical assistance they received in the studio.

"It was almost unusual for engineers to get credits back then," says Parsons. "First time I remember seeing a credit on a rock record was on [the Beatles's] *Abbey Road*—and I didn't get a credit on that, it was just the main engineers, Geoff Emerick and Phil McDonald."

Parsons had worked with the Fab Four, as well as some of the individual members' solo projects. Certainly Parsons was well versed in how to achieve a fantastic sound from instruments in a recording setting. Although we should steer clear of revisionist history, one suspects that he deserves a bit more credit for his contributions than has previously been believed. By more than one account, it was Parsons who suggested Clare Torry for "The Great Gig in the Sky." It was also Parsons who recorded the clocks for "Time."

But making decisions about the final sound product was driving the band up a wall. In attempting to produce their own record, and knowing Parsons was right alongside them in the trenches through it all, Floyd clearly needed an outside presence to assess the overall production and what it might be lacking—or just to be a somewhat impartial referee. Usually in the past, doing multiple mixes would satisfy everyone's curiosity and an obvious choice would emerge. Not with *Dark Side*.

Division was rife among the creative ranks: Who wanted more echo . . . who thought the audio interviews should be handled more delicately. . . who wanted to emphasize the electronic or tape experimentation . . .

The decision was made to bring in Chris Thomas to "supervise" the final mix. Thomas was more than qualified to scale any obstacles the project would pose. After all, he'd worked with some of Britain's finest and most sophisticated rock and pop bands: the

Beatles, Procol Harum, and soon after *Dark Side*, Roxy Music. Thomas made a series of crucial, if not altogether earth-shattering, decisions about the record—adding or subtracting certain tracks and so on.

Perhaps more than anything, the fact that Floyd felt the need to bring in an outsider for the final mix might actually be the greatest, if only a tacit, endorsement of Parsons. This wasn't a slight to Parsons. Maybe the exact opposite. Parson was in the trenches or bunker with the band, an essential part of the creative team, and perhaps Floyd believed he did not have the proper objectivity.

It's doubtful anyone would disagree that *Dark Side* was a collaborative effort, and this teamwork has helped the record become a revered and an essential listen. Furthermore, *Dark Side* retains coherency through a combination of various studio techniques and conceptual layers.

The art of dissolving the audio of one song into the next, or cross-fading, was especially effective in this regard, and was used by a number of popular bands of the late 1960s and early 1970s to help pull together ideas and create cohesion, including the early Moody Blues recorded efforts. In fact, cross-fading would be pushed to the extreme during the mixing portion of the album, as tape loops, some measuring eight feet in length, were needed to seamlessly dissolve one song into another.

Methodical as the band and engineering crew were, fans have a strong emotional attachment to the record. The cyclical nature of *Dark Side*, its universal themes, its non-denominational mysticism, wrapped up in such minor-key music, has made the package irresistible to those inclined to repeat listens.

Future backing singer Durga McBroom remembers the record making an impact on her when she was in grade school.

> I would say eighth grade, junior high," says McBroom. "I was going to this very unique private school called Moboc, which stood for Mobile Open Classrooms. Our teacher was this fantastic man who was a former Beat poet from the Haight. Our classroom was a bus. The whole school would go around in these buses and vans, and instead . . . . of reading about how a newspaper is produced, we would go to the *LA Times*. While driving around, we had a great selection of music to listen to, and *The Dark Side of the Moon* was one of the albums we listened to.

"It's such a complete piece," McBroom continues.

> That is the pinnacle and the best balance of all of their talents, which is why it's such an iconic album, and why it sold so many copies. Just the soundscapes and the way one song flowed into another, and the use of sequencing in a way that had never been done before . . . it was so new to me. There was . . . one boy who I had a crush on. My friends and I were hiking up in the mountains and got him to take off his shirt. "Breathe" was on the radio. So, anytime "Breathe" would come on, my palms would sweat.

Floyd's records were masterpieces of sound engineering and design. *The Dark Side of the Moon* was one of the standards of audio fidelity throughout the 1970s, and certainly one of the best-sounding Floyd albums ever made. With Floyd remasters and various reissues, aspects of records such as *Wish You Were Here* have become equally crisp, pronounced, and defined. One could draw a direct correlation between the expanding fortunes of the audio industry, the retail electronics-store boom, the explosion of interest in stereo equipment in the 1970s, and the growing popularity of records, in general, such as *The Dark Side of the Moon*.

Obtaining a home stereo was a steadily becoming a suburban status symbol as upwardly mobile families had the cash on hand to spend on the latest technology. Mission One was experiencing a band like Pink Floyd at their finest, played on a delicate and sophisticated piece of equipment.

When absorbing *Dark Side* and 1975's *WYWH*, fans could fasten their chunky headphones, find a comfortable seat, perhaps chemically expand their mind (if they were so inclined), and become ensconced in the pastime known as "theatre of the mind."

Beyond the physical act of hearing the music, audiences enter into a social contract when they listen to Pink Floyd records. "I often felt with Pink Floyd that they were not prescribing the meaning of everything," says Martyn Ware. "The meanings of individual songs, or even the theme of a concept album, were deliberately left open. Floyd believed in the ability of their audience. It is something I always admired about Pink Floyd and it is something we always tried to emulate and incorporate into what we do."

=

Weeks before the release of the record, EMI hosted a press event at the London Planetarium. Gilmour had hoped to host a quadrophonic-mix listening party for the album's launch, but he either could not get it together in time or the Planetarium had not installed the proper equipment.

The details of the story have never truly been made clear, but the band refused to appear at EMI's planetarium press junket. In the band's certain absence, EMI's marketing division acted fast to produce life-sized cardboard cutouts of each of the guys, which were positioned around the building. Some say Wright attended the event but later appeared to backpedal about his presence there. Against the band's protests, EMI played a *stereo* version of *Dark Side*, with the sound no doubt bouncing off the cardboard Floyd fixtures.

"On 27th February 1973, I helped site cardboard cut-outs of the members on chairs situated in a darkened area of the Planetarium for the launch of *Dark Side of the Moon*," says former EMI/Harvest promotion exec Stuart Watson. "Contrary to many reports, following the argument with EMI management due to them [the label] failing to agree to the use of Quad sound, Rick Wright *did* attend and act as spokesperson."

Antony Thorncroft, reporting for the *Financial Times*, panned the publicity stunt and had a few choice words for the record. Calling the first half of *Dark Side* "formless,"

Thorncroft had to admit the second side "works," with a "climax which drives home why the Floyd are the most highly regarded group in pop."

Floyd certainly nurtured its mysterious public image. The packaging for *Dark Side* was case in point. No surprise, Hipgnosis got the call for album design. The brief, given to Hipgnosis by Wright, was that the band wanted to see a central image that was "simple, clinical and precise" or "clean, elegant and graphic," as it has been variously reported.

Other ideas had been floated and rejected, such as a cover featuring Marvel Comics' Silver Surfer. Only when the group saw the prism was the search completed. "We came up with the idea for the triangle and the prism after we saw a photograph in a book, a French physics books," Po says. "It was a prism by a window. It was actually a paperweight, a glass paperweight, and the sun was shining through the window, and the refracted light, creating a rainbow, was spread out across the paper."

Both Storm and Po rushed over to Abbey Road to show the band their idea. "We went up to Abbey Road and did a sketch," says Po. "They didn't want more of those surrealistic photographs. They wanted something like a chocolate box."

It took Hipgnosis several days to work up the appropriate initial illustration for the cover. Hipgnosis staffer George Hardie drew the sketch, which was later airbrushed by Bob Lawrie. Po says that when Hipgnosis met with the band again in Abbey Road, "they looked at the design and said, 'That's it, That's Pink Floyd. That's *The Dark Side of the Moon*.'"

On the cover, a beam of white light is refracted through a prism and bands of color continue into the album's inner gatefold, resembling the waveform on a display screen of a heartbeat monitor employed by hospitals.

"[The illustration] is what you call a mechanical," Richard Evans, former Hipgnosis staffer, once told me. "Basically it's instructions from a printer done on various layers of tracing paper, saying 'Drop black into this area and drop yellow into this area, and drop red into this area . . .' It was a mark-up for the printer. There is no illustration as such."

"Black with a singular image on it," Po adds. "It does sum up Pink Floyd. It's not my favorite Hipgnosis cover, but it's the probably the most successful one we ever did."

The striking visual, much like the later image gracing the cover of *Delicate Sound of Thunder*, was in homage to sound and light—elements or pillars of Floyd's live production. Beyond this, the triangle has multilayered meanings, too. The three-sided geometric shape is a universal archetype, tapping into our collective unconscious.

Diagrams in Sir Isaac Newton's centuries-old book *Opticks*, a tome on the qualities of reflected and refracted light and the University of Cambridge scholar's experiments involving (what appears to be) a *camera obscura*, bears a resemblance to the *Dark Side* cover.

Waters later described the conceptual core of *Dark Side* as notions of the pressures of modern life forcing us toward greed, insanity, death—everything we've already discussed. *Dark Side*, Waters theorized, implied a "Newtonian view of that physics."

There's no doubt that the final image is stark, sharp, and iconic, even if a tad bit clinical. Critics of Floyd seem to agree on this even if they don't quite grasp what it actually means. "Hipgnosis was always very beautiful and professional, but their covers never meant anything, in my opinion," says Pearce Marchbank. "I regard myself as a communications designer. [The cover of *Dark Side*] wasn't communicating anything. It was creating interest. It was [like] the Victorian use of painting, called 'Conversation Pieces.' I can't see any connection with the music at all. I mean, you have a record called *The Dark Side of the Moon* and then you have a prism with a rainbow. Can you help me, here? [laughs]"

"Well, it *does* have a connection," counters Po. "Only in that the band, who were very enigmatic, hid themselves from the audience. It really came down to what Roger Waters described as 'electronic theatre'—and nobody really knowing what Pink Floyd looked like."

One fun exercise involves juxtaposing multiple front and back covers and the gatefold of the original LP to create a continuous light wave or, as Storm indicated, a giant mandala. This diorama constitutes a pictorial representation of Floyd's stage show. Prior to the famous large circular projection surface Floyd used on tour, the band employed something called "Mr. Screen," a smaller version of the iconic forty-foot surface Floyd used later in their live shows.

A poster featuring photos of the bandmembers and shots of the pyramids on the Giza Plateau in Egypt, taken by Thorgerson, were included in the packaging. "I was sick and [Thorgerson] went out on his own," says Po. "Funnily I was looking at these photographs recently, some that had never been seen before, for a new SACD box. I have one picture, it was this beautiful picture I shot in the daytime. Because high-rise buildings now surround the pyramids, you could never get the imagery that we got in 1972. It was a privilege to shoot that."

The pyramids represent impermanence in the face of what could be viewed as a disposable popular culture. "As a symbolic image, the pyramid has been associated with extraterrestrial moments or Gods or sacrifices," says Po. "It's a potent symbol, the triangle, which is why there were posters [included with the original LP] featuring images that we shot in Egypt. It also has to do with something as basic and mystical as the mathematical figure pi. It added a bit more mystery into the ingredients."

ON THE ROAD

The *Dark Side* tour saw the appearance of two crucial additions to the Floyd live personnel lineup. Venetta Fields, along with Carlena Williams, was one half of the singing duo the Blackberries, who'd performed live with Floyd in 1973.

Fields was an Ikette and worked previously with Steve Marriott, formerly of the Small Faces. "We did an American and European tour," says Fields. "I had never heard of [Floyd] before. I had been in the business a long time and thought I knew everybody. We happened to already be in England and [they were doing dates] in Europe and didn't want to get their American girls to do it. So they asked Steve Marriott if they could borrow us. That was how it all started."

Fields seemed destined to have a career as a singer. Raised by a religious single mother and missionary (in conjunction with her aunt and uncle), young Venetta was instilled with a strong sense of faith and centeredness. Among her other gigs, in 1975 Fields became a cast member of the Academy Award-winning 1976 remake of *A Star Is Born*, featuring Barbra Streisand as up-and-coming singer-songwriter Esther Hoffman and Kris Kristoffferson as a drug addled and suicidal rock star. In the film, Fields is a member of the vocal duo the Oreos, backing Streisand's budding-superstar character.

Carlena Williams, the other half of the Blackberries, also had a stellar career. She was an Ikette, possessed an incredible vocal range, and racked up credits including Etta James, Humble Pie, Donna Summer, Van Morrison, and the Carpenters. Both Fields and Williams had the temperament and vocal skills to accompany the band while authentically reproducing its material.

Gilmour sent a tape of *The Dark Side of the Moon* to the Blackberries and later set up a meeting to get their feedback about the record. "I thought it was the craziest thing," Fields says. "It's in a minor key ... It was so weird and I was kind of bored when I started [listening], but I said to myself, 'Venetta, you are here for a reason. You must enjoy it.' I had never heard anything like it before. I grew a lot from that experience."

The Blackberries saw several opportunities to press their artistic thumbprints on the Floyd's live show. "The girls that they had before us [Black Grass] would sing a song or two and then they would go off [stage] and come back later and sing another couple of songs," says Fields, who now lives in Australia. "I said, 'When we get up there *we're not coming off*.' We made up backing vocals for 'Money' and 'Echoes' and Roger liked it at the time. He said, 'Keep doing it.'

"I remember our first gig in Europe. The hotel manager left the dining room open . . . and we were having dinner and drinking wine and under the table singing 'Summertime.' That broke the ice . . . It was very nice and a very unusual gig and friendship."

There seemed to be a bit of something for everyone in the *Dark Side* shows. Some who were active in the London underground scene in the 1960s had lost contact with or interest in the Floyd though the '70s but managed to catch the band's *The Dark Side of the Moon* performances, either in '72 or '73. Floyd played Earls Court, not far from the site of Syd Barrett's former apartment, and legend has it that the madcap actually showed up on a live performance of Dark Side.

"I saw the band a few times in the '70s," early Floyd producer Joe Boyd says. "I remained friends with them and also with Tony Howard and Steve O'Rourke, so I could go any time I wanted. I liked them, but Syd, for me, was the genius. Impressive rather than exactly my taste."

Across the pond, in Chicago, the *Tribune* made no bones about the acoustics being less than desirable at the International Amphitheater, but Floyd overcame adversity with its 360-degree sound system. The band complemented their sound with visual spectacle and "an array of gadgetry that looks like it could enable the crew to literally take off for outer space."

Mirrored reflective surface, dry ice rolling fog, and pyrotechnic flashes seemingly singeing the ceiling . . . It is "head music, trip music—easier to experience than to describe."

Cash Box posted a similar paranormal observation when Floyd visited America in 1972, pointing out that fans waded through "Eclipse," later known as *The Dark Side of the Moon*, equating the special effects and communal atmosphere with magic, even referring to the band's shows as a séance: "You come for the unexpected and you get it."

Undeniable success will make believers out of the staunchest critics. The *New York Times* filed a report on the Floyd show at Radio City Music Hall in March 1973, contributing to the uptick in positive vibes on the band. *Record World* estimated that as early as March 1973, *Dark Side* had moved over a million units in the States. (Sales were likely south of that number in the first quarter of 1973.) For the time being, a near-three-hour show that began *after* 1 a.m. EST garnered praise from the *NYT*, which called Floyd "one of the tightest acts in the business" and "precisely organized."

Back in England, Floyd was prepping in April for their Earls Court shows in May—the band's first concert in London after the release of *Dark Side*. A celebration it was, complete with fireworks, spotlights, and crashing planes. Spots tracked an aircraft until it took a nosedive and exploded into the stage, accompanied by a huge fireball.

Graphic designer Pearce Marchbank, largely due to his friendship with Nick Mason, was asked to produce the band's program for the Earls Court show, all the proceeds pertaining to which were earmarked for Shelter—National Campaign for Homeless People.

"I've known [Mason] since 1968," says Marchbank. "I published a magazine when I was at art school and he did some illustrations in it. Their first bits and pieces album, called *Relics,* which had a black and white line drawing—that was done by Nick Mason. It looks like some weird machine. He did something like that for me. Nick's stuff is quite architectural."

Marchbank recalls his relationship with Mason: "I used to meet [Mason] for dinner, once a month, and he was a very close friend of mine. He said, 'I have this charity concert at Earls Court. Will you do the program?' Nick is the historian of the band and he kept all the press cuttings and everything. I said, 'What information have you got?' He put all of this in a cab and sent them over to my place. I took all of the sexy stuff out [and used it in the printed program]."

The program or scrapbook was a "direct publishing" project, says Marchbank, who completed the job over a weekend. This process, a decade or so later, would be commonly referred to as *desktop publishing*. "We had a process camera in the studio rather than send it out to the printers to do all of the copying," says Marchbank. "It was pasted up and made up in-house and printed in one go."

The program was a hit, and so was the show. The *Financial Times*, fairly critical of Floyd over the years, called the band's performance at Earls Court "superbly controlled" and "trouble free."

HAVE YOU SEEN THE CHART?

By the end of May, Floyd was rehearsing for their second American tour in support of *Dark Side*. The band played Roosevelt Stadium in New Jersey, as well as Saratoga Springs,

New York; Pittsburgh, Pennsylvania; Columbia, Maryland; Michigan; Ohio; Kentucky; Florida; and other markets.

Fighting their artistic instincts, Floyd surrendered to the record company and decided, with the success of *Dark Side*, to release a single from the album—"Money"—in May 1973. Smart move: it soared to within the Top 30 on the *Billboard* Hot 100 chart, reaching No. 26 in the week ending June 30. *Record World* reported that key US radio stations added the song to their rotation, from WLS in Chicago and WQXI in Atlanta, to WIXY in Cleveland and KTAC in Tacoma.

And *Dark Side* was booming. The June 30, 1973, edition of *Billboard* shows *Dark Side* at No. 5, reflecting the week prior to the issue date. By the end of December 1974, *Dark Side* slipped and fell off the chart, only to return in April 1975 and score a combined total of nearly sixty weeks on the chart.

Dark Side was No. 1 for only a week, but it was subsequently in the Top 10 for months. Sales ran into the hundreds of thousands, a figure which would grow exponentially over the next decade and surpass 15 million copies sold in the United States alone, according to data collected by the RIAA. In 1984 the *New York Times* estimated that *Dark Side* was still moving a sizable amount of units, and in more modern times, the early twenty-first century, *Dark Side* sold short of ten thousand units a week. The thematic album would simply dominate *Billboard*'s Top 200 Albums chart in the rock era, having racked up a combined total of 741 weeks on the chart between 1973 and 1988. With *Billboard*'s expanded charts, that number ballooned to over 1,500 weeks. After the success of "Money," Floyd released a single for "Time," b/w "Us and Them," in February '74.

POSTCARDS FROM THE EDGE

In June 1973, an inebriated Robert Wyatt, former drummer for Soft Machine, tumbled out a third-story window, in a fall that paralyzed him for life. Wyatt began having suicidal thoughts and issues with excessive drinking *prior* to the accident, likely rooted in his lack of confidence and sense of direction in his career and as a songwriter. Hollywood film editor Alfie, who became his wife, described him as having a form of PTSD in Wyatt's authorized biography, *Different Every Time*, prior to his paralysis.

Wyatt's *The End of an Ear*, released in 1970, was the opening moments in a concerto of creative differences between the drummer/vocalist and his bandmates in Soft Machine. Like their underground music brethren Floyd, Soft Machine erupted in schism, having lost a towering innovative and inventive presence, while ushering in a decisive shift in musical direction.

The whistling shakiness of his voice made Wyatt immediately sympathetic, a musical trait his former mates failed to recognize and exploit to their advantage. Ironic, since it was on full display for "The Moon in June" from Soft Machine's 1970 double-album extravaganza, *Third*, featuring one extended track per side of LP, a concept that became a vast frontier to be conquered, the Manifest Destiny for prog rockers in the 1970s.

Soft Machine transitioned through various permutations, from a pataphysical psyche-delic art-pop band to an electric seven-piece with a four-man horn section to an experimental musical quartet. By the early 1970s, they'd slashed and burned nearly all ties to the more cerebral and playful moments of their late 1960s material and clearly cut a path toward experimental and muscular jazz-rock fusion.

Wyatt didn't stick around long enough for the full transition. Whether Wyatt was fired or shunned from Soft Machine is still cause for speculation, but doubtless the rift racked his self-image. Wyatt had been searching for an elusive combination of all of his musical tastes and interests: from "World Music" and jazz, to pop ballads and eclectic rock. Soft Machine, and few he'd collaborated with at the time, seemed to understand where he was coming from or understood how to fill this void in his musical life.

After recording hypnotic, vocal-laden, tape-based experimentations for *The End of an Ear*, Wyatt exited the Softs and formed Matching Mole (a Franco pronunciation for the English language phrase Soft Machine), a jazz-rock fusion band with minimalistic and avant-garde tendencies.

Not long after his stint with Mole, in a strange twist, the former Softs drummer had contacted Mason via postcard, inquiring about the possibility of having the Floyd drummer produce his next studio record. Eerily, Mason learned of Wyatt's accident the very day the message arrived. Mason agreed, and helped to stage a benefit concert for Wyatt, featuring Floyd and Soft Machine, on November 4, 1973, at the Rainbow in London.

The cause was enough to bring the press out, but Floyd stole the show. Martin Hayman, writing for *Sounds* in November 1973, explained that, despite Floyd navigating all their electronic gear, they were "master showmen."

It was enough to generate some serious cash for a good cause. In a letter to *Melody Maker*, printed January 1974, Wyatt's mother proclaimed that the benefit concert raised £10,000, a portion of which, of course, would be put toward government taxes.

Meanwhile, the former Softs drummer had begun working on some of the songs for his upcoming solo album, to be titled *Rock Bottom*. Although he had started work prior to the fall, the bulk of the compositions were constructed or reconstructed from memory when Wyatt was recovering in Stoke Mandeville hospital.

Wyatt massaged some of the music he had begun formulating in Venice, Italy, with soon-to-be wife Alfie, when she was working on the film *Don't Look Now*, starring friend Julie Christie and Donald Sutherland. It was Wyatt and little more than his voice and his Riviera organ, which produced sounds the songwriter said were inspired by Rick Wright's atmospheric "aurora borealis," according to O'Dair's biography of Wyatt.

For a brief time Mason's and Wyatt's musical eccentricities were synchronized and overlapped. The fact that Mason, a rising star in the business, decided to spend time rummaging through Wyatt's avant-garde musical playground said much about the nature of Mason's tastes and the drummer's willingness to present fresh, if noncommercial, music.

Upon the record's release in July 1974, *Rock Bottom*, at least in the press, was tethered to Wyatt's recent life-changing event. "The accident didn't in fact haunt me or in fact have half the effect on me that people might suppose," Wyatt told Charles Shaar Murray for a story that ran in *NME* in October 1974.

Even if Mason wasn't directly responsible for the material, he was supervising when elements *of that material* became Wyatt's sonic trademarks. We hear: vocal manipulation invoking the muted *whomps* of a cupped horn; multitracked organ; clipped backward audio; waves of Afro Latin brass blasts and squeals by horn player Mongezi Feza; percussive bass-string punches courtesy of Richard Sinclair (Wyatt's former bandmate in the Wilde Flowers); poet/comedian Ivor Cutler using an Eastern European or maybe Central African accent, and Mike Oldfield soaring with a multitracked, multilayered vibrato guitar solo in the second half of "Little Red Riding Hood Hits the Road."

This is speculation, but Mason may have seen redemption in *Rock Bottom*; a second chance and heroic comeback that escaped Barrett.

"[Floyd] wanted to be successful and they wanted to be rock stars, but they didn't want everything that went with it," says Marchbank. "When I heard from Nick via postcard, a kind of 'wish you were here,' *The Dark Side of the Moon* had taken off, and they were number five in the album charts. He was staying in a much better hotel than they normally would . . . That kind of success wasn't something they were chasing. It was something that happened to them, I think. Nick sent me a postcard saying, 'Hey, I'm a rock star, now.'"

The band had a No. 1 record, would soon be rich beyond even their wildest teenage dreams, suddenly found themselves the predators at the top of the food chain, and were able to tour the world behind the strength of *Dark Side*. But success can be a dangerous thing. What does one do when he/she outclasses nearly everyone? If you've reached the upper echelons of rock stardom, what inspires you? Do you continue to tour to stay relevant? If you do, are you serving your fans? Yourselves?

By early 1974 Floyd appeared to have no sense of purpose. They achieved what they wanted to: mission accomplished. "I think we were at a watershed then," Waters said in a *Wish You Were Here* documentary, "and we could easily have split up then."

For all practical purposes, Floyd was disengaged but also no longer an underground act. Their artistic tendencies were still in line with their previous cult-band status, but this schizophrenia had yet to register. The band may have had thought of breaking up but were afraid to leave the safety of the group—and the brand name they'd all built over several years.

The mid-1970s would be crucial in determining if the core band had the stamina to transcend life support or was waving the white flag in surrender, broadcasting to the world: "Do not resuscitate." It would take an act of self-reflection to both resurrect and exorcise ghosts of the past for the foursome to survive as individual artists and as a collective.

CHAPTER 4

SHAKING OFF THIS CREEPING MALAISE

4'33", which premiered in 1952 and is often cited as one of John Cage's most important works, directs would-be performers to disengage their instruments and allow the sounds of the music hall—the environment—to shape the work for the specified duration of four minutes and thirty-three seconds.

Cage's definition of music as "sounds heard," as well as the influence of chance methods and the application of the *I Ching*, is insightful in understanding this work. The noise encountered in the *absence*, or the perception of absence, of intentionally or unintentionally created sound, challenges notions of what we commonly think of as musical composition.

Cage was responsible for more than just *4'33"*, of course. In the mid-'70s, Cage completed an eight-minute piece, *Child of Tree*, for which the solo performer prunes and pricks a plant (or fondles a cactus) and manipulates other discretionary natural objects and vegetation in his/her hand to create shuffling, crackling, scraping, and rustling sounds.

Cage gives scant instructions about how to proceed but indicates that sections are to be approached and divided in accordance with chance methods—the *I Ching*. "[I]nstruments are allocated to the different parts by the same technique," writes David Revill in *The Roaring Silence: John Cage: A Life*.

The title was taken from *Finnegans Wake* by James Joyce. Interestingly, the word puzzle employed by Joyce (i.e. the opening and closing lines of the work completing one another), a kind of literary loop, is similar to the cyclically lyrical approach Waters uses for *The Wall*.

Cage also foresaw a future music via electronics or electric instruments, preoccupations directly relevant to Floyd's creative activities in the mid-'70s. As if taking a cue from Cage, astoundingly, Floyd's first instinct following *Dark Side* wasn't to err on the side of another conceptual blockbuster, but to generate avant-garde music using experimental gear or found objects.

"[*Dark Side*] was probably the easiest album to sell in that it was the easiest to listen to, but its success has obviously put some kind of pressure on us, and that's what to do next," Wright said.

According to some sources, including Steve Peacock of *Sounds* in August 1974 and John Harris's book on the making of *The Dark Side of the Moon*, the band had spent a few days recording experimental tracks at Air Studios during the making of *Meddle*, and, later, Abbey Road was transformed into a sonic laboratory.

Floyd imagined stretched rubber bands as strings. Clamps were fastened to a table to hold the strings, a cigarette lighter acted as a bridge, and matchsticks, presumably used as frets, became the body of an electrified found instrument. Different lengths of cellophane were ripped to produce tonal pitch and later combined to create a scale of notes.

"We used a yellow bristle broom," legendary producer/engineer Alan Parsons tells me. "That was the hi-hat, and it was that broom against the wooden floor. The snare drum was an aerosol can and that was cut to a very tight piece of tape, probably no more than about half an inch of linear tape length to get that short snare drum sound. The kick drum sound was Nick's foot on the carpet in the studio, with the mike very close. I furthermore made the suggestion that we make the album using one microphone. Everything was layered and everything was recorded separately. It was possible to record everything with one microphone. I kept it locked up so that I knew that it was that same mike we used every time."

One of the experiments, with wine glasses, produced an eerie effect. "I'm sure you've tried this yourself," Parsons tells me. "You can get a pretty good note from a wine glass, running your finger around the edge. Different pitches could be obtained by pouring more water into the glass. It might have been wine, I don't remember. [laughs] You can literally draw up a scale of notes, and that's how the band was able to reproduce chords off wine glasses. We . . . carefully tuned each note to be in tune using a device, which was quite new then. There was a device called a Strobo tuner."

Recording dates for these sessions seem to vary, but Pink Floyd's official site reads that the twenty days of intermittent tracking began at Abbey Road on October 1, 1973. Floyd toured Europe in October and continued with recordings from October 22 through 26, and again from October 29 to the end of the month. Work continued from November 12 through 14, as well as November 19 through 21, and November 26 through 28.

In an interview with Waters conducted by Nick Segdewick during the fall of 1975, the music journalist recalled that he'd visited the band in January 1974 and that Floyd was still working on *Household Objects*.

Why is running through these reported recording dates significant? It demonstrates the effort Floyd exerted to cross the finish line for this experimental project. It may not have been the throwaway recording some believe it to be.

"I recall that when we did *Wish You Were Here*, we weren't allowed to cash in on *Dark Side*," former Harvest label co-manager Mark Rye told to author Brian Southall. Rye, who passed as this manuscript was being written, called *Dark Side* the "elephant in the room."

"'Cashing in' was not even on the table," adds Stuart Watson. "Floyd's members were, as always, very reluctant to get personally involved in promotion, as they had never needed to before. Suddenly they had sold so many records that every journalist and DJ in the world wanted access. But it wasn't necessary."

Most sources indicate that the abandoned recording was largely incomplete. It's been reported that *Household Objects* included material titled "Carrot Crunching," "Papa Was a Rolling Floyd," "Nozee," and "The Hard Way." Miles, in his book *Pink Floyd: A Visual Documentary*, said that the band had tweaked three tracks. Whichever possible version is true, strangely enough, the band painted itself into this corner. They were not being pushed into recording a follow-up to *Dark Side*, and yet a self-imposed pressure was applied to get them back into the studio and do *something*. Because *Dark Side* had been so monumentally successful, Floyd allowed a countervailing avant-garde instinct to run wild in an attempt to maintain their creative edge and shatter listeners' expectations.

Perhaps the real reason for recording sound and not constructing songs was the simple fact that it delayed any serious decision about what would follow up *Dark Side*. If they had to put off the inevitable to give themselves a little creative space, so be it. Had the band seen the project through to fruition it would be, arguably, one of the most daring releases Floyd could have ever released in their career. The fact that it could have followed *Dark Side* only demonstrates the severity of their desire to be taken seriously and break the commercial mold they'd fashioned around themselves.

"It was the concept," says Watson. "Just as the sounds of 'Grantchester Meadows' created a mood on *Ummagumma,* the lawn mower, drill, or broken glass potentially could have created similar moods/feelings of peace, anger, and/or frustration on *Household Objects.* The group were perfectionists so had to get things one hundred percent right."

Surely EMI were nervous about *how* the band would follow up *Dark Side*. "There was a trust that developed whereby Harvest/EMI didn't need to get directly involved in the follow-up," says Watson. "We left them to it."

Floyd, EMI, and Columbia may have skirted certain commercial disaster when *Household Objects* was set aside. It was believed at the time that the record couldn't be fully appreciated by listeners lacking the proper stereo equipment needed to hear nuance in the recordings. Besides, how well would this go over with Floyd's new American label, Columbia?

Ultimately, the band realized it would simply be easier to use a standard-issue guitar than to build a facsimile of one from scratch. "I think they just said that it's just all too much, spending days working on one individual sound, which was, effectively, what it was," says Parsons. "I think they just said, 'We have better things to do.' I think that was the attitude."

Questions still remain, however. Was abandoning the recordings prudent or a sign that Floyd hadn't the stomach to do something controversial and avant-garde? "I was disappointed it got abandoned," says Parsons. "With a bit of determination, perhaps not a whole album, but one really good track could have come out of it."

Floyd would return to *Household Objects* and put their experimental tendencies in perspective for what could be their greatest single composition. Still, says a onetime close musical associate, *Household Objects* wasn't the only project swirling around inside Waters's brain.

"I have a vague memory that he was talking about *The Wall* already," says Alan Parsons, "in the brief post-*Dark Side of the Moon* period I was with them. I knew nothing about what it was. He just mentioned this project called *The Wall* and I knew nothing about it. He had it in his head."

THRIVING ON MADNESS

Hard economic times had befallen the United Kingdom and even worse days were ahead. OPEC raised the price of crude oil and constrained supply, contributing to the energy crisis of the 1970s.

Similar hardships had hit the United States around the same time, as OPEC's oil embargo and United States' own economic policies, as well as ballooning inflation, led to a mid-1970s recession and long lines at gas stations to fuel our automobiles.

Economic woes might seem a luxury in relation to other societal ailments. In November 1974, Roy Jenkins, the Home Secretary, visited Birmingham the day after tragic bombings by the Provisional IRA killed twenty-one people, largely young tourists. Jenkins recalled that the atmosphere in the middle of the "unusually deserted" city was marked by "unforgettable and oppressive ingredients." In the wake of the tragedies, and in light of police zealousness in finding the perpetrators, six apparently innocent Irishmen were beaten by the police, eventually sent to prison, and not released until the early 1990s.

The British stock market tanked in December 1974, but by early 1975, miners used the threat of strike for pay increases. Railway workers used the same tactic to negotiate higher wages. Later, in 1975, the pound weakened, unemployment levels soared, nationalized businesses received the go-ahead to lay off workers, British Steel's operations were cut by nearly half, car sales dropped precipitously, and, increasingly, Middle Eastern oil money fled for the States. Economists were perplexed by Britain's monetary and financial ailments, and it appeared the United Kingdom was stuck in an economical downward spiral.

The madness spread to the general populace and even to idyllic settings such as Cambridge, the Floyd's spiritual home. Much like Son of Sam in New York City a few years later, Peter Samuel Cook terrorized Cambridge from autumn 1974 through spring 1975.

Ex-con Cook perpetrated a series of sexual assaults in Cambridge, a university town with very few incidents of physical violence in recent memory. Cook broke into flats, bedsits, and buildings on the University of Cambridge campus, where he often rendered his victims unconscious through the noxious agent chloroform.

The bike-riding perpetrator eluded authorities for months by wearing female wigs and escaping via the back alleys and byways of Cambridge. Police eventually cooked the crook's goose, and it was revealed that he had not only committed these dreadful assaults but was a serial burglar and had a history of snatching ladies' knickers, much like "Arnold Layne" in Syd's song.

The Cambridge neighborhood home to the Barrett and Waters was plagued by a spate of incidents involving undergarments disappearing from washing lines. As Cambridge was a college town, both Winifred Barrett and Mary Waters took in young-adult female lodgers. It's been suggested that the fictional portrayal of kinky panty raider "Arnold Layne" was actually based on someone who snatched knickers and other unmentionables from Cambridge clotheslines.

Waters surmised that the suspect had ceased seizing undergarments for a while—a pattern of behavior coinciding with the spotty nature of Cook's lengthy criminal career prior to 1974–75 (i.e. the serial offender was repeatedly arrested and jailed before reentering society).

Cook could have easily been scouting for skivvies while cycling around Cambridge. It seems Cook, who died in 2004, fits the profile and did have the means, opportunity, and motive.

It's been said that "Arnold Layne" was one of the original inspirations for Arnold Korns—a transvestite character Bowie envisioned and claimed to have entertained as a lead character in an upcoming concept record, before Ziggy Stardust touched down on Planet Earth. Future Sex Pistols manager Malcolm McLaren and fashion designer Vivienne Westwood marketed a T-shirt with the image of a masked man identified as the Cambridge Rapist. Could a man who terrorized a city have inspired the soundtrack of the British counterculture, circa 1967, as well as one of rock's leading lights and the architects of the British punk movement?

Clearly chaos reigned by the mid-1970s, and Floyd seemed to thrive on it. Whether fans needed escape or believed on some unconscious level that Floyd was tapping into dark, collective motivations, an explosion of interest in Floyd—past, present, and future—led to a EMI/Harvest and Capitol repackaging and rereleasing the boys' first two records in the form of *A Nice Pair*. If nothing else, reissuing the band's early albums, at a special price (no less), would introduce fans of *The Dark Side of the Moon* to Floyd's more obscure material and help Syd Barrett attain some financial boost.

As was typical for critics reviewing post-*Dark Side* Floyd, the *Boston Globe* presented a mixed review of *A Nice Pair*, describing the experimental sounds of the band's first two records as something between a "symphony orchestra tuning instruments to Dr. Spock [*sic*] and company 'beaming up.'" The article does point out that the band is "effective" in "making bizarre the focal point" of the music and that these avant-garde noises aim to "separate the mind from the body."

One of the benefactors of Floyd's newfound fame was Barrett. It's been said that he was rolling in cash due to David Bowie's cover of "See Emily Play," a track on Bowie's 1973 album *Pin-Ups*. The 1971 compilation *Relics* also helped pique interest in Syd on both sides of the Atlantic, and Barrett's "Terrapin" had appeared on the 1970 Harvest label compilation *Picnic: A Breath of Fresh Air*, along with Floyd's "Embryo."

New interest brought growth opportunities. Barrett returned to London, first staying at Park Lane Hilton and then, in a move facilitated by Bryan Morrison, at an apartment in Chelsea Cloisters where he squirreled away most of his musical equipment in the building's requisite storage space. With his purported newfound riches, Barrett barricaded his apartment with modern appliances, some of which he barely used.

Lots of wild stories about Barrett emerged both from his time in London and just before, in Cambridge, solidifying the notion that Syd was losing touch. "In 1974, I was walking down Cherry Hinton Road in Cambridge and [Syd] came along on his bicycle and he stopped, got off the bike, walked up to me and said, 'One day you won't need that beard,'" says Nigel Lesmoir-Gordon. "Got on his bike and cycled off. I mean, it's a classic thing. It's a real Syd thing."

When asked what message Syd may have been trying to deliver, Lesmoir-Gordon says, "I did actually have a beard. I don't have a beard very much in my life. It was just two or three years that I did. I think he remembered me without a beard. . . . [Floyd biographer] Mark Blake talked about Syd possibly looking up to me. Thing is, I was slightly older and I was holding poetry readings and poetry and jazz sessions. I think he for a while looked up to me."

Syd was spotted around town and outside London. The volume of many reported sightings increased just as Barrett, it was said, had gained weight and shaved his head, looking less like the curly-haired, pale-skinned Pharaoh of psychedelic rock than a nine-to-five insurance actuary who survives on fried chicken and mashed potatoes and gravy.

It's difficult to know with any certainty what Barrett was doing during these days. Some reports indicate that Syd had little to occupy his time other than TV and food. Relative inertia and lack of employment meant he was burning few calories and evolving into someone physically unrecognizable from his former self. Some who saw him about town said he resembled Aleister Crowley.

Despite his added girth, Barrett was still known to gingerly step on the pavement around London or (supposedly) become quite triggered and cross with associates. He would show up at Bryan Morrison's office, which was handling his publishing royalties, with allegations of financial malfeasance. Syd thought he was being cheated out of payments.

One of Morrison's employees tried to explain to Syd that he'd collected a check just the day before. Believing this was a lie, the madcap caused such a commotion in the office that Morrison came from his back office and tried to shame Syd and shout him down, pointing a finger in Barrett's face.

Threatened by the offending appendage, Barrett supposedly gnawed the tip of Morrison's finger—literally biting the hand that fed him, an observation that has not escaped many. Morrison was not someone who scared easily, but as the story goes, Barrett never made an in-person appearance in the office again—and Morrison was no doubt relieved.

Then there were the odd tendencies of giving away his cash and worldly possessions. If Barrett personally picked up a royalty check or had been sent one in the post, he'd disburse cash as fast as he received it. Strange, considering that he seemed to fall hook, line, and sinker for the materialistic aspects of the disposable mid-1970s culture. He'd go on to buy furniture and a large TV but would also freely pass off his musical equipment and appliances to complete strangers—whoever might come calling to his apartment.

"Dave told me that Syd didn't want money," says Pat Martin of the country-rock band Unicorn, once produced by Gilmour. "Apparently, one time, he went up to Abbey Road studios and there was a guy at the door with a uniform; he connected a guy in a uniform with someone in charge. Got hold of this guy by the lapel and said, 'Stop sending me the fucking money.'"

Most of the Western world view material objects purchased through a form of monetary currency as having value. We have been told, generation after generation, to work hard and own a house and, if you're so inclined, live the American Dream. Do Syd's actions reflect an individual who grew bored of material goods and believed he could exist without the stuff cluttering his home? If someone places no importance beyond the fleeting emotional enjoyment worldly and consumer-based items can give, should we consider this person crazy?

A Floyd press release in 1968 intones that Syd was "quietly removed from the world of us normal ones." Harvest may have failed to recognize what was staring them in the face. Incredibly, the Harvest label thought it was a great time to reissue Barrett's two solo albums in one package for the European and US market, which would be officially released in America for the first time, in the hopes of capitalizing on the popularity of *Dark Side* and Syd's growing mystique.

A fresh face was commissioned for the *The Madcap Laughs/Barrett* double album. Perhaps in the hopes of securing an actual photoshoot with the reclusive former Floyd frontman, Hipgnosis got the nod to design the cover of the double-LP compilation. Some accounts say it was both Storm and Po who traveled to Syd's flat for the shoot; others say it was just Storm. Whoever was present, when Hypnosis representation arrived at Barrett's apartment, Syd refused to open the door, flatly issuing an admonition: "Go away."

Offended and slightly humiliated, if amused, the Hipgnosis team needed another plan of action. Storm turned to the photoshoot by Mick Rock. It was the famous set shot at Syd's Earls Court Square apartment, with its alternately orange- and blue-painted floorboards and Syd's girlfriend, an Inuit named Iggy, dancing *au naturel* for Barrett's debut, *The Madcap Laughs*.

Legend has it that Syd painted himself into a corner, but it's also been reported that he brushed one color at a time, across alternating slats, right over the dust and dirt on the floor, making it easier for him to maneuver around the room.

Using one of these images, Hipgnosis opted for a conceptual design, displaying objects Syd was fixated on during his first or an early acid trip with friend David Gale—namely a box of matches, a plumb, and an orange.

Newfound marketplace viability notwithstanding, some failed to see the wisdom in unearthing old material. The *Chicago Tribune* called the music "dated" and suggested it be viewed as nothing more than a relic of the past.

Cruel press, perhaps, and certainly out of step with generally accepted rock-fan thought, even at the time. In the interim years, the Barrett mystique had transmogrified into legend. Syd was such an influential figure that his reach exceeded his music or lyrics. For example, T. Rex's Marc Bolan idolized Barrett and picked up on his fashion sense in regards to eyeliner and dark clothing.

Because the *Madcap* compilation did modestly well, it convinced EMI that they should act on a clause in their contract with the artist, which stipulated that Syd still owed the label recordings.

EMI/Harvest's marketing scheme, it appears, was to have both Floyd and one of their founding members—someone who many considered to be a mad genius—creating new work for the label. It's a variation on an old record industry trick: sever a lead singer or the most recognizable face of a band from the rest of the group, groom this talent to be a solo artist and then allow the surviving members of the act to carry on using the name. What you'd have, in theory, are two lucrative, legal, and independent acts performing similar, if not the exact same, popular material. You'd think this would saturate the market, but it actually feeds interest.

It's believed that in August 1974 Syd entered Abbey Road studios to record new material for what could and should have been a third solo record, or what some have referred to as the "Chooka Chooka Chug Chug" sessions.

Some sources place this incident earlier in the 1970s, circa late 1972 or early 1973, and at least one book on Barrett tells us these sessions occurred in November 1974. Perhaps there were earlier attempts to bring Barrett into Abbey Road, in addition to the above-mentioned one from 1974, but it is too difficult to say authoritatively.

"I did two lots of sessions with [Syd]," Jenner offers. "One with Malcolm [Jones] earlier on, when he left the band. Then . . . two or three years later, Bryan [Morrison] asked if I'd have another go with Syd, because he said something about Syd having a good vibe on me."

For their part, Barrett's former bandmates and Jenner thought Syd making music again would be remedy for the soul and psyche. It was a kind of therapy that would help him to break free of whatever had taken hold of him since before his exit from Floyd. From the available evidence, the sessions went nowhere, and famous tales, true or not, have passed into myth about them. For instance, when lyrics for Syd's songs were typed up, for some reason the copyist used the red ink strip of the typewriter ribbon. When Syd was handed a sheet of white paper with red lettering, he assumed it was a bill and, according to reports, may have become violent and accusatory toward members of the staff.

"It was a very upsetting experience," says Jenner. "It was a disappointing experience."

Jenner told author Nicholas Shaffner that "[f]rom the doodling of a sick mind, bits of clarity would emerge." As it seems, those moments of clarity were not enough to hold the project together. The story goes that Barrett kept overdubbing guitar parts, endlessly, either due to his perfectionism, self-doubt, and lack of confidence, or some mental block or defect that prevented him from completing the song.

If the last of those possible scenarios proved to be the reason why the record, or the song, wasn't completed, it was "Have You Got It, Yet?" on steroids. Syd's possibly diseased mind was setting himself up for a fall. Author Palacios called it a "soundtrack of mental illness."

Funny: as his former bandmates in Floyd were frittering away tediously and ultimately nearly fruitlessly for *Household Objects*, Barrett and his benefactors were forced to abandon their well-intentioned sessions. Rumors have circulated that Syd recorded informally with Steve Peregrin Took, but these failed 1974 sessions are believed to be Barrett's final and official attempt, as it were, at professional recording.

It's a wonder, given the rumors circulating about Barrett, that EMI would risk such an undertaking as late as the mid-1970s in the first place. Was there belief at the label that Syd's career could be revived?

"Of course there was," Stuart Watson says, "but [Barrett] was almost impossible to rely upon to support such a revival. We tried to set up promotion but it proved to be in vain. So sad, but there was nothing anyone could do about it."

What often escapes scrutiny is the notion that Syd was, at the least, partially lucid of his surroundings and was fully aware of the rising commercial fortunes of his former bandmates. Could this success have had a crippling impact on his creative process, much as it impacted the post-*Dark Side* Floyd? Did Barrett feel the old pressures of having to come up with a single—again?

In the absence of public information, gaps will be filled by sheer speculation and conspiracy theory. It's inevitable. Some artists are able to fight through self-doubt, bouts of depression, and constant second-guessing to live a productive and long life. Others lash out at the world or go mad from its dizzying and seemingly infinite complexities, injustices, and cruelties. Which was the case here?

This may seem like an obvious point to make, but the Pink Floyd studio recordings circa 1967 were psychedelic-pop that bore only *some* resemblance to the improvisational group that dabbled in wild exploration onstage. With each passing year, Floyd moved further and further away from these beginnings. In some ways, so had Syd.

Ironically, and reportedly, Boyd's name didn't come up when it came time to pick producers for Syd's solo material. When asked if he was ever asked to produce any of Barrett's solo material, Boyd flatly denied: "No."

Thematic releases, successful in spite of their weighty concepts, were miles away from psychedelic pop, or Top 40. It's impossible to know if Syd would have adapted to the AOR version of Floyd, or been absorbed by it, although ambitious tracks such as Syd's "Opel" offer tantalizing possibilities. Point being, the post-Barrett Floyd flipped the script—never living or dying by the hit single. Floyd sidestepped "the system" designed for the lowest common denominator, joining the ranks of the progressive rock bands with whom they are so often associated.

The contradictory nature of the industry was not a puzzle Barrett logically ever solved, if he was inclined to do so. In some sense, by not bowing to *every* commercial concession, Floyd skirted the Jungle, even if they hadn't fully tamed the industry monster or approved of its predatory practices. Barrett was lost despite his songwriting ability and helping Floyd achieve early success. Quite paradoxically, *Dark Side* taught us that chasing dollar signs drives us insane.

"[Barrett] didn't like the music business or what it was, but it is a tragic or great loss, I still feel to this day," Jenner says. "My feeling is if he was happy, I don't mind what happened. But if he wasn't happy I do feel bad about it."

A comparison between Barrett and Yes's early guitarist, Peter Banks, reveals an eerily similar self-destructive energy and unpredictability during live performances. Actions taken to remove Banks and Barrett no doubt helped to contribute to their shrinking from the public eye. Except for a short period of time when Banks spearheaded the promising Flash, Yes's fortunes grew exponentially while Banks's dwindled. In fact, as Yes became more and more famous, the guitarist grew ever more incapable of sustaining a viable creative outlet.

Peter Jenner relates Barrett's reported behavior in the mid-1970s to his interactions with him years earlier. "In some sense if what you want to do is optimize your career choice, is that insane?" Jenner asks. "Is bad business the same as insanity?"

THE FOUR NOTES

Once Floyd abandoned the *Household Objects* project, they started anew—this time in The Unit, a rough-and-tumble rehearsal studio in Kings Cross, perhaps better suited for up-and-coming bands than a million-selling supergroup.

Practice followed a kind of format with room for improvisation factored in. Floyd might warm up with some Hendrix covers and Derek and the Dominos "Layla." They'd even stretch their scope and encompass songs from the Top 20 UK, such as "How Long" by Ace, a band led by singer/keyboardist Paul Carrack, who'd later perform live with solo artist Waters. Interestingly, the Ace single is believed to have been written about bassist Terry Comer, who Carrack claimed was sneaking around, performing with other bands, including the Sutherland Brothers and Quiver, which David Gilmour would produce. Quiver guitarist Tim Renwick toured with Floyd, and drummer Willie Wilson appeared on Gilmour's debut solo album and with Floyd for live dates supporting *The Wall*. Eric Clapton, of course, collaborated with Roger Waters in the 1980s. A big circle.

Then, it happened: the defining moment in the band's mid-1970s period and perhaps their entire career. Gilmour was fiddling around on guitar and struck upon four notes of a G minor thirteenth chord.

It stunned Waters: "What's that?" he asked. Gilmour, in an off-handed remark, simply said he'd just found this riff. The guitarist just liked how it sounded: bold but mournful, clear and unapologetic, but reminiscent of a distant past. Waters, always the conceptualist, heard something rich with self-referential meaning.

"Somehow those notes evoked a song about Syd and his disappearance, absence if you like, in Roger," David Gilmour said in the documentary *Pink Floyd: The Story of Wish You Were Here.*

Waters wanted to pay homage to Syd, to recognize his creativity as well as express sadness over his mental absence. Mason agreed that Syd should not be forgotten, and that they should "not write him out of history," as the Floyd drummer said in the documentary. The four-note phrase—the Syd Sequence—would become a seminal part of one of Floyd's most memorable songs, known as "Shine On You Crazy Diamond."

Like a bolt out of the blue, after hearing Gilmour's guitar phrase, lyrics began to surface in Waters's mind. Something triggered Waters and the floodgates opened: the sadness, the regret, and the guilt. "I think the world is a very sad fucking place," Waters told Nick Sedgewick. "I'm very sad about Syd; I wasn't for years. For years, I suppose he was a threat because of all that bollocks written about him and us."

"[Syd was] just a symbol for all the extremes of absence some people have to indulge in because it's the only way they can cope with how fucking sad it is—modern life, to withdraw completely," Waters told Sedgewick.

Waters does contradict himself a bit here, however. In the past he said that Syd, the subject of "Shine On You Crazy Diamond," was merely a representation of one kind of absence we encounter in life. He is. And was. But in the *WYWH* documentary, Waters makes clear that "there are no generalities, really, in that song . . . It is about Syd."

"Shine On You Crazy Diamond" seems to implore Barrett to maintain his visionary status and illuminating ideas and reject the shadows and tendencies to hibernate and recede from the public.

Wright told *Melody Maker*: "Did you realize that 'Shine On You Crazy Diamond' is about Syd?" Wright said. "We don't see much of him now since he left and we're definitely a different band since his day. Thank God we're not the same. I know it's very fashionable to like Syd these days, but I think we have improved immensely since he left, especially live. He was a brilliant songwriter and he was fantastic on Piper, but he was in the wrong state to play any music."

Waters tweaked and retweaked the lyrics, poring over his words until they conveyed exactly what he wanted them to. Not very many people knew the "Real Syd," said Waters, and daring or attempting to understand him from the outside was very nearly impossible.

Judging by the struggle Waters had in pinpointing what it was that made Syd tick was difficult enough. Waters was also responding to what he perceived or described as Barrett's general withdrawal from the world. For the band, despite the fact that Barrett was still alive, somewhere, he was no longer with them in mind or body.

So much has been written about Roger Waters's character from *The Wall*, Pink, whose transformation into a kind of catatonic Syd Barrett—*Barrettonic* or *Syombie*—

zombie rock star drew from personal experience with the troubled visionary. It's likely the nuts and bolts of Pink's origins stretches back at least to 1975, with *Wish You Were Here.*

The song "Nobody Home" seems particularly self-defeating and self-referential. The character of Pink speaks about "powers of observation" and "second sight," which could easily refer to Waters or Barrett—perhaps both at this point (1979). Tantalizing clues could lead to Barrett and his stunning appearance at Abbey Road in June 1975, such as the line "a bag with a toothbrush and a comb . . . ," but might simply refer to Waters's travel pack and the meager possessions he keeps with him on the road when moving from city to city, hotel to hotel.

Pink, reflecting Waters's autobiographical recounting of his professional life, wallows in self-pity. He also raises the specter of a grand piano "prop up my mortal remains," recalling Waters's dissociative episode and the strength of black-and-white keys to pull him through. More about this later.

And while we're at it, the track "What Shall We Do Now?"—which appears in the film *The Wall* and on the *Is There Anybody Out There?* live collection—rattles off a series of questions pertaining to the band's options in the immediate future.

The rock star mask slips in what might be one of Floyd's most uncomfortably honest tracks. Of course, Pink is a fictional character, but one has to wonder if conversations between Waters and others took place, and whether questions, such as the following, really were asked: Should they break up homes and contract venereal diseases? Argue among one another and/or see a psychiatrist? Buy expensive sports cars and horde cash?

We get the sense that these speculative "to do" items don't necessarily need to be accomplished at all, in their entirety, or in that order. Just as "Cymbaline" was a window into, or a day in the life of, a musical group, "What Shall We Do Now?" offers insight into the guilt-ridden mind of a bored rock star.

In 1974, Waters was still formulating these ideas, and "Shine On You Crazy Diamond" was the result of the band locking themselves inside a rehearsal room in Unit Studios in Kings Cross and beginning a process of looking at themselves in the mirror.

Floyd had developed two other new songs, "Raving and Drooling" and "You Gotta Be Crazy," both of which were initially earmarked for their upcoming studio album, and both unusually driving and aggressive by Floyd standards.

They had three potential songs—actual songs, not *household* experiments—for a new album. The band appeared to be making progress. Yet, despite some breakthroughs at Kings Cross, the band turned down the heat on producing a new record and rushing material out into the universe too quickly. Fact was, Floyd was fatigued, having spent weeks on an abandoned recording project, which did little to instill confidence in their ability to complete a traditional album full of songs.

Stardom did have its advantages, however. Floyd could be more choosey about the shows they did, for one thing, and how long they'd need to be on road. They liked the idea of cutting down on the number of dates they were playing, and in what type of venues they appeared. This weeding out process, presumably, was to help them to focus as a songwriting unit.

Gilmour, as if channeling Barrett, said that he didn't want the band to get in a rut of playing show after show, performing the same material, night after night. This meant changing set lists, even, if they must, and lopping off *Dark Side* altogether. For the time being, of course, the entirety of *Dark Side* was the centerpiece of their post-intermission second set, albeit with slight variations and allowance for guitar solo improv in "Money," for instance.

The band would eventually put a moratorium on playing the whole of the concept album, but individual tracks from the song cycle surfaced on various tours from 1977 and beyond.

Ironically, performing a commercially viable record onstage, night after night, hit the band's wallet pretty hard. A new projector and sound engineering console, and the sheer size of the ballooning tech and operations crew, were not cheap to maintain on tour. The thinking? A respectable ROI would be substantial enough to warrant the cash outlay.

So, in the summer of 1974, Floyd embarked on its infamous French jaunt, partially sponsored by soft drink brand Gini. As per a business agreement, Gini expected Floyd to write music for company advertising spots. Not realizing what it had gotten itself into, Floyd had come to despise the deal and rued the day they became corporate shills hawking a product.

Fittingly, Waters wrote the song "Bitter Love" in connection with the marketing campaign. Although, *The Rough Guide to Pink Floyd* author Toby Manning and *Pink Floyd: In the Flesh* authors Povey and Russell point out that the band were seen with Guinness beer T-shirts on tour around this time and didn't seem to be particularly bothered by corporate endorsement. In addition, and reportedly, Floyd entered into an endorsement deal with Avis circa 1973. The marketing campaign slogan was: "Make Tracks Like Pink Floyd—Rent an Avis Truck." I attempted to contact Avis to get the scoop on this marketing campaign on the off-chance that an executive involved would still be employed by the company. Calls went unanswered.

Waters would also write "How Do You Feel?" in Morocco in 1974, perhaps in response to Floyd's interfacing with the advertising world. Interestingly enough, the title was a line from "Summer '68."

Reports that Floyd shunned corporate partnership are greatly exaggerated. Years after the Gini debacle, Gilmour's Floyd entered into a deal with Volkswagen for a special Floyd model of the car, and Mason helped design the vehicle's interior.

I'M A BELIEVER

By the mid-1970s Floyd had spread its tentacles across several creative fields and rock spectrums. Not only were they a major draw and an ongoing concern, but as individuals, they were lending their talents to lesser-known artists. Mason, for instance, may have been the most active outside of Floyd, and in the fall of 1974, he found himself supporting pal Robert Wyatt.

Let's backtrack a bit: The story goes that guitarist Andy Summers, later of the Police, joined Soft Machine as a replacement for future Gong leader Daevid Allen. Summers was fairly close with Wyatt, having jammed, explored genres from jazz to minimalism, toured America, and even partaken of a few extracurricular activities so common to the era.

Summers exited the tight-knit quartet, however, on the say-so of then bassist/vocalist Kevin Ayers, who envisioned the group as a trio. Summers would later tour with Ayers, but prior to this he resurfaced with the paralytic Wyatt on *Top of the Pops* in September 1974 for a cover of the Neil Diamond-penned "I'm a Believer," perhaps best remembered as a No. 1 UK hit for the Monkees in 1967. Wyatt's own version, produced by Nick Mason, cracked the Top 30 in the United Kingdom in 1974.

On the TV program, Summers appeared to be playing acoustic guitar, and Henry Cow's Fred Frith mimicked electric guitar riffs accompanied by bassist Richard Sinclair, piano player Dave MacRae (of Matching Mole), and Mason on drums. Wyatt was out front "singing" into a handheld microphone, rocking back and forth in place with his eyes closed.

Some of the musicians were miming and some appeared to be playing *something*, but the audio heard for the broadcast was the recorded version of the song. Frith, for one, recorded the violin solo on the original but does not appear to be playing one on *Top of the Pops*. No one does.

Prior to the show, in one of the most spectacular public turnarounds of the classic rock era, *Top of the Pops* had reservations about allowing Wyatt to appear in a wheelchair. As it turns out, the BBC's fears and concerns for offending viewers appeared to be unfounded, not the least of which because the studio audience seemed to sway along with the spritely music and pantomime display.

Fred Frith once told me that it was Virgin Records label head Richard Branson who stepped up and made the call to *Top of the Pops* to rectify what could have been a PR disaster for the BBC.

In 2007 I interacted with the long serving, and now late, Soft Machine bassist Hugh Hopper, who recalled his experiences with Mason and Floyd:

> I only saw them play once, on the same bill as [Soft Machine] in late '67. [It was] OK, if you were stoned. I liked the two singles with Syd, "See Emily Play" and "Arnold Layne." . . . The Floyd and [Soft Machine] did a lot of gigs together in the early days, and the two bands were good friends, but I wasn't in the band at that time. I got to know Nick Mason in the 1970s, and even did the Robert Wyatt gig at Drury Lane in [September] '74 with him, and recorded at his studio a few times. A witty guy and a pleasant fellow by then.

The Drury Lane show was the first solo performance Wyatt gave in the wake of his accident and after the release of *Rock Bottom*. Wyatt was said to be mortified prior to the concert, but a recording of the show, staged on September 8, 1974, once licensed and released through Joe Boyd's Hannibal Records, seems to tell the opposite tale.

Wyatt's vocals on "Sea Song" and "Calyx" in particular are delicate, but the horn-inspired, idiosyncratic vocal manipulation is unmistakable. He even playfully interacts with trumpet player Mongezi Feza for "Little Red Riding Hood Hit the Road." Mason appears on several tracks on the recording, including the second half of "Little Red Riding Hood Hit the Road," featuring Ivor Cutler.

Mason, as musician for hire and producer, continued to work with a wide range of artists. In 1974, producer Mason rekindled his professional relationship with Principal Edwards Magic Theatre for *Round One*, tracked in late 1973 and early 1974. The band first worked with Mason on their 1971 studio album, *The Asmoto Running Band*, a follow-up to their 1969 *Soundtrack* album on John Peel's Dandelion label.

Principal Edwards appeared on the bill with Floyd a few times, as well as with Dandelion labelmates Medicine Head, right around the time Medicine Head's album titled *Dark Side of the Moon* was released—a year before Floyd's. Principal Edwards also appeared with Floyd at the College of Commerce in Manchester on May 2, 1969, one of the concerts recorded for Floyd's *Ummagumma*.

"Dandelion were reluctant to let us record a second album, but eventually said we could go ahead if we found a producer who inspired confidence on their part," says former Principal Edwards guitarist Root Cartwright. "We had met [Mason] on the road and become quite friendly, and so it seemed like a good idea to ask if he was interested. He was, and we were delighted."

Mason was likely attracted to Principal Edwards for some of the same reasons Floyd signed on with Roland Petit: it tapped the art-snob instinct they had to rise above the accepted artistic limitations the industry often imposed on mainstream rock bands in those days. "I don't think there was any great similarity between the two bands' music—a common desire to do our own thing aside, but [Mason] was obviously sufficiently interested in what we were doing to commit some time to the project," says Cartwright.

Principal Edwards's stage show was a combination of theatrics and knotty, dense sonics. A narrative flow was wrapped up in esoteric mystique—factors that helped bolster their progressive rock cred. "If the founding impulse of the progressive thing was to move beyond three chords and three minutes, then the next stage for many people seemed to involve stringing together a sequence of songs with shared lyrical/musical themes," says Cartwright. "Thus, the 'concept' album, too often stretched to ridiculous length. . . . The first side of *The Asmoto Running Band* is generally regarded as 'conceptual' in this sense: the five tracks sketch a conflict between evil real estate developers/countryside despoilers and the [Asmoto Running Band], an innocent tribe gliding secretively through the forest. There's a slight topographical infelicity in that the forest is atop the hill from which we view the nefarious goings-on—and where we, who of course are the Asmoto Running Band, actually lived."

Cartwright stresses that there is "no explicit verbal narrative conclusion." He says, "This, together with two of the tracks being completely instrumental, indicates that the narrative or concept had been designed in three dimensions with the dance and imagery, which are obviously absent from the record."

Given the theatrics of the band's music, Mason would be sure to capture the live aspect of their show in the studio. In a way, one could be forgiven for making a connection between their more dramatic slant and Floyd's stage production, both in the 1960s and 1970s.

"I think Nick Mason summed this up a few years back when asked about producing us, and said that as with Pink Floyd you had to forget about the stage show when you went into the studio and just concentrate on making the best possible record," says Cartwright.

"[Mason] was endlessly patient and encouraging, though also good at reining us in when necessary—and full of helpful suggestions," continues Cartwright. "Essentially, his role was to help us get the best possible performance onto tape."

There are quite a few interesting audioscapes on 1971's *The Asmoto Running Band* album. In fact, the entire record has a kind of fairgrounds or carnival atmosphere.

Floyd's and specifically Mason's love of sound effects and *musique concrète* is evident, and in "McAlpine's Dream" we hear an auctioneer's voice, which Carwright says was a "reedy, tannoy effect achieved by speaking into a vacuum cleaner hose." Backward audio can be heard in "The Kettering Song," and there's an impressive, almost twenty-first-century digital-audio dissolve in "Asmoto Celebration."

"I think it's fair to say that the ideas were generally ours, but we had no idea how to do cross-fades and the like, so Nick Mason's expertise was indispensible in making them happen, pointing out possibilities and certainly producing a more sophisticated result than we could have managed alone," says Cartwright. "One thing that Nick Mason introduced us to was ADT—automatic double tracking. We used that a fair bit on *Asmoto Running Band* on vocals and fiddles. Obviously not just a mathematical multiplier, this produces a subtle thickening, smoothing effect, which, if you wish to deploy such terms, might be described as ethereal, otherworldly, unnatural, etc."

By the time the band hooked up with Mason again, for the production of 1974's *Round One* at De Lane Lea Studios, it had shortened its official name to Principal Edwards. As such, *Round One* was perhaps more rock-oriented and accessible than *Asmoto*—the overall sound a bit sharper, crisper.

"You're really looking at two different bands," says Cartwright. "New people, new sounds, new approaches to their instruments. There's a wider instrumentation—we hadn't used synths before, although interestingly mandolin also made it on to record for the first time. The studio was better. Also with the new line up, the theatrical side had been scaled back: there were just the six of us, with some of us at times performing in character, so possibly more of the drama was condensed into the actual music rather than depending on being augmented by additional staging."

Round One was more of a production than *Asmoto*, says Cartwright, which may explain why, despite the mega-track "The Rise of the Glass-White Gangster," tracks such as "Triplets," "Milk and Honeyland," "Juggernaut," and "The Whizzmore Kid" were more accessible than some of the material on *Asmoto*.

"It's worth pointing out that we always went into the studio with a set of material written and ready to be recorded and developed," says Cartwright.

Principal Edwards and Floyd occupied opposite ends of the music biz spectrum. Yet each, in their own ways, was obliged to deal with the burden of the business circa mid-1970s.

"The business side of things was in the hands of Clive Selwood who, for whatever reasons, took a dislike to us right from the start, interpreting our reasonable requests for a modicum of essential support as the expression of unbridled greed," Cartwright says. "We were trying to support a large crew on gig income that would barely have kept a trio alive, and operating in an environment where rock bands were the tulipmania or dot.com boom of the day, with labels vying for headlines by announcing bigger and bigger advances. We had no such expectations, and were simply trying to keep the show on the road. There did seem to be a conflict at the heart of the operation, at least as it affected us, between the artistic vision and the money. But when isn't there?"

NO WAY OUT OF HERE

Spotting a unicorn is a metaphor for experiencing the impossible in this world. Yet in the early 1970s, David Gilmour was on the lookout for just that. The guys in the British country-rock band Unicorn were hired to perform at the wedding reception in Kent for Cambridger Rick Hopper, an executive with Transatlantic Records. In lieu of payment, the band was told that bigwigs of the recording industry would be attending. Starved for attention and in need of a record deal, Unicorn agreed. As it happened, there was at least *one* special guest . . .

"[Gilmour] came up to us and said he liked our original songs," says Unicorn bassist Pat Martin. "He also said he really liked Neil Young."

The legend has it that Unicorn jammed with Gilmour on Neil Young, but something far more permanent was cemented between the budding producer/emergent rock star and Britain's up-and-coming, perhaps premier, country-rock band.

"[Gilmour] took my number and called a few days after this wedding. He had this studio [in Essex], and [he said,] 'Would you like to demo some of our original numbers?' There would be no charge, but he would be 'experimenting.'"

Unicorn assembled in Gilmour's home studio and had the run of Gilmour's guitars. "[Gilmour] said he didn't have a separate control room and he would mix using headphones," says Martin. "He had a drum kit set up, which we used. We did about four or five numbers. Then he called me up again and asked if I wanted to do some more. His girlfriend at the time [Virginia Hasenbein, a.k.a. Ginger] cooked us a nice meal and . . . I remember getting really stoned and watching *Monty Python's Flying Circus*. We were just rolling about the floor, almost in agony, in laughter."

Unicorn, not to be confused with the Cambridge band White Unicorn, had galloped onto the scene initially as a 1960s-era Byrds-esque folk-rock band dubbed the Late, a name their former label, Transatlantic, rejected. "They said, 'You have to come up with a name, or we'll call you the Armadillos,'" says Martin. "We said 'Armadillos' sounds heavy, doesn't it? One day Ken [Baker, guitarist/songwriter] said, 'How about Unicorn?' David [Gilmour] said to me, 'When you think about it, Pink Floyd isn't a good name. After a while the words just become a sound.'"

The band's country-rock bent gave the erroneous impression to naysayers that Unicorn was composed of bumpkins and simpletons, motivating some to throw around derogatory terms in a failed effort to describe their style of music.

"Dave was down to earth," says Martin. "He took us to get a meal once, and they put us in the basement part of the restaurant, because we had long hair and there was this awful music being played. Dave called the waiter down the stairs to this basement area and he said, 'Can you turn that music off, please?' He said, 'Afraid I can't. It is on throughout the restaurant.' Dave got up front the table and ripped the [leads] out from the back of the speakers."

While it's perfectly valid to compare Unicorn to the West Coast folk- or country-rock sound, the funkiness in the band's songs also faintly recalls Little Feat, a favorite among many musicians in the mid-1970s.

America had been bombarded by country- and folk-rock acts ever since the mid-1960s. By the 1970s, however, there were a few standouts, including Firefall, Eagles, Poco, Michael Martin Murphy, and Pure Prairie League, with its evergreen and Top 30 hit from 1975, "Amie." Folk-pop and country-rock icons—from James Taylor to Lobo—ruled the AM radio airwaves. Linda Ronstadt, in particular, experienced a breakthrough in 1975 with "You're No Good," a No. 1 song. Meanwhile, Emmylou Harris kicked off a string of Grammy noms and wins with a cover of "If I Could Only Win Your Love" from her WB debut, *Pieces of the Sky*.

"We were heavily influenced by the American West Coast thing, but [our] lyrics were incredibly English," says Martin. "I personally think one of the strong points is Ken Baker's lyrics. That was one of the aspects of the music that drew Dave Gilmour to us in the first place."

Gilmour fell in love with Unicorn's sound, so much so, that he appears on 1974's *Blue Pine Trees* and its follow-up, 1976's *Too Many Crooks*, issued as *Unicorn 2* in the States with different artwork.

"[Gilmour] said that on his last American tour he bought a pedal steel guitar and he had been playing about with it, and would we mind if he dubbed some pedal steel licks on some of the songs we recorded," says Martin. "We said no, we didn't mind at all. He put some pedal steel riffs on there and he said, 'I'm not very good at it. I only use three pedals.'

"There is a track on *Blue Pine Trees* called 'Autumn Wine,' and [Gilmour] plays on the outro of that. There's a pedal steel on that and he used backward echo where you record the echo with the tape turned around the wrong way. It sounds like something from science fiction. It was his idea—and it sounded great."

Gilmour bankrolled Unicorn's initial recordings and Steve O'Rourke's EMKA management company secured a deal for the band with EMI globally, Capitol in the States, and Charisma in England. "Around this time Dave bought his first nice house, first nice car and studio, he saw us and liked our music," says Martin. "Steve O'Rourke went to see Transatlantic . . . to get out of the deal. The only way they would let us go is if they were given half of the publishing rights. That was 1973. Once we got the deal from the record company they put us on a weekly wage. It was about 30 pounds a week or something."

Gilmour had specific plans for how the band should sound and where they should be recorded. "We recorded Olympic Studios, A and B, and then David Gilmour wanted to mix in Air," says Martin.

> I remember I was standing at a microphone and using this wind chime as an effect in one of the numbers. Someone was standing behind me, I think, and in this really posh voice says, "Eww. That sounds rather lovely." It was George Martin. I nearly dropped the bloody thing. I couldn't believe I was standing in the same room as him. Geoff Emerick engineered on a couple of [songs]. [Comedian] Spike Milligan's son was one of the engineers there, and he was just as mad as his dad. Spike was on *The Goon Show*. I remember on one occasion our guitarist was overdubbing a solo and he kept cocking it up, and all of a sudden he did a blistering solo, and we were all jumping around . . . I said, "You did record that, didn't you?" He said, "No, but I think I can remember it." Peter Sellers, another member of the Goons, his son was a tape operator there, too.

Things were looking up for Unicorn. When the band toured the United States in the fall of 1974, supporting acts as varied as Billy Joel, Linda Ronstadt, and Bob Welch-era Fleetwood Mac, *Blue Pine Trees* went to No. 3 on *Billboard*'s FM Action chart in late October.

"I remember doing a few interviews on different FM stations and . . . getting in this big American car and listening to the radio and hearing our music on our way to [a] gig," says Martin.

Aside from Gilmour, some very influential people took notice of Unicorn. "Pete Perrier [sometimes credited as Perryer] used to do this thing on drums and he went passed where the beat was and normally where people would stop. It may be over-the-bar playing or something. David used to really love that and liked Pete's drumming. There's a track on Fleetwood Mac's album *Rumours* in which the drummer does something similar. The song was 'Don't Stop.'"

After their US tour, Unicorn returned home to England and shared the bill with Sutherland Brothers and Quiver in London, at the Marquee Club, with Gilmour taking the stage to jam. Interestingly, "Ain't Too Proud" by Sutherland Brothers and Quiver—a song that was released as a single—would feature pedal steel guitar by Gilmour.

Sutherland Brothers and Quiver jammed with one another back in 1973 and decided to merge. Their combined talents scored a Top 5 UK hit in 1976 with "Arms of Mary."

By the mid-1970s Unicorn was tracking 1976's *Too Many Crooks*, containing some of the band's greatest material. "No Way Out of Here," written by guitarist/vocalist Ken Baker, has become a popular song in some music circles largely due to Gilmour having recorded it as "There's No Way Out of Here" for his self-titled solo debut from 1978. It's since also been covered by Iron & Wine and Ben Bridwell.

Portions of Gilmour's version seem almost jazzy: Gilmour tracked a "fuzztone-distorted" guitar part with a harmonica and had the assistance of saxophonist Raphael Ravenscroft when performing the song live.

Both versions are exceptional, but Unicorn's original take is subtler, *twangier*. Carlena Williams, Debi Doss, and Shirlie Roden offered vocal support and a distinctive Floydian sensibility.

"When we recorded 'No Way Out of Here,' David phoned up and said he couldn't make it, but the studio was booked," says Martin. "Ken had written two songs the night before . . . including 'No Way Out of Here,' and I think it was only about the third take, and we got it. We put it together, more or less, there. It was magical. David went into the studio the next day and phoned me up and said, 'That is the best thing you've ever done. I'm going to record this on my first solo album."

"No Way Out of Here" *may be* discussing some of the same topics Waters tackles on *Wish You Were Here*, but even the band members are unsure of the details of the song's seemingly profound message. Is Baker discussing life and death? The music business?

"I've asked Ken about it many times," says Martin. "He gets out of things by saying it's all a stream of consciousness. The song 'Too Many Crooks' has amazing words. I asked him about certain references in that, too, like 'Roll up, roll up window cleaner. What a big man you must have been . . .' Ken was writing in his bedroom at home and all of a sudden a head appeared in the window. The guy was on a ladder."

Too Many Crooks was released in March 1976, predating some pivotal commercial country-rock records, such as the Eagles' omnipresent *Hotel California*. Unicorn drew from a reservoir of great material, but without a hit single it became increasingly difficult to justify the expense of representing the band and distributing its music. "When punk came in, [EMKA] said, 'We can't do anything for you anymore. We're going to have to let you go,'" explains Martin. "They said, 'You owe us some money, but we'll let you off.' The New Wave thing, I mean, we were so unfashionable. There was some talk that we would live in the States, but not everybody could get that together. So, that was it, really."

1978's *One More Tomorrow*, co-produced by Gilmour and Muff Winwood, was tracked at Island and Floyd's then-new Britannia Row recording studio. Harvest needed a single and Muff suggested "Slow Dancing," which did garner airplay but not enough to convince the label to keep pouring money into their future.

"It hit Ken [Baker, guitarist/songwriter] really bad," says Martin. "He found religion and I think it knocked the rock and roll out of him.

"In fact, David asked him to put the lyrics for three other songs he had written. Ken said he couldn't put lyrics to someone else's songs. If I had been a songwriter I would have locked myself in a room . . . Roy Harper did the lyrics for one of them, 'Short and Sweet.'"

In recent years, Cherry Red rereleased some of the Unicorn material, but Unicorn are victims of both self-destruction and circumstances conspiring to undermine its initial success. Some of Baker's behavior is eerily similar to a certain prominent former Floyd member. Martin says:

> The thing is he won't talk to anybody. He comes to see me sometimes, but he only stays for a half hour, and he can't handle sort of being around people. A couple of years ago a guy phoned up and asked us to do a festival. I asked [Baker] about it. He didn't want to at first. Then he wanted to. He finds it very difficult to communicate with people. He said he would do it, only if he could stay in his hotel, go out and do the set, and go back to the hotel. That's what we did. Dave Gilmour lent him a really nice guitar and amplifier and we did this gig. We would never do another one, because Pete, the drummer, had passed away in 2005.

The fallout from Unicorn's disbandment hasn't impacted the relationship Martin keeps to this day with Gilmour. "David always had a great sense of humor," says Martin. "Sometimes he asks me to move a car for him. He might be going to fly down to the West Country in England in his plane, but he wants his car down there to drive around in. He phoned me up recently and I said I am going to Greece on holiday, and I can't move the car . . . He said, 'It's alright for some, isn't it?' This is a multi-millionaire saying, 'It's alright for some,' who can afford to go on holiday. We had a great time working together."

Unicorn may not have been a huge commercial success, but they were a tight, intelligent band with obvious talent. Another statistic of the unforgiving music business.

For loads of failures there is a success story, however. Gilmour's radar was beeping, again, in 1973, when he was introduced to a teenaged songwriter named Kate Bush and recorded her at his home.

Bush's angelic "Wuthering Heights," written on the top floor of an apartment building on Wickham Road, reached No. 1 in the United Kingdom in 1978—the first time in the history of the British charts that a female had written and performed a top song.

As a child Bush was given wide latitude to be herself—whatever that might be—and it was this freedom that's so often evident in her rich compositions. Coupled with her coquettish and almost witchy sexual allure, her musical attributes have fused to create a public persona that has elevated her beyond the status of pop icon and delivered her to the rarified confines of art-rock cosmic whisperer.

Her doctor father played piano at home, introducing young Kate, or Cathy as her family had known her, to the likes of Beethoven, Chopin, and Schubert. Kate listened to

Bowie, Roxy music, some King Crimson, and other progressive rockers. Elton John was a favorite as was Irish folk music. Kate soaked up just about anything she had heard with a magpie's curiosity and skills.

In the mid-1970s, only a few in the recording industry, very early on, had fallen prey to the potency of her spell. Bush was rejected on a regular basis, but her champion, Richie Hopper, the aforementioned "plugger" for Transatlantic Records, was determined to make her music stick. A handful of listeners, including Hopper, had not easily forgotten the scent of her simple but enchanting barebones compositions, scores of which had been captured with her father's AKAI tape recorder.

"Richie Hopper, the plugger I was talking about from Transatlantic, went to Cambridge University with Kate's brother [Jay]," says Unicorn's Martin. "He was always going on about his friend's sister, who was a songwriter, and likened her to Joni Mitchell."

The stripped-down music recorded to cassette tape found its way to Gilmour. Intrigued and looking for new talent to mold, Gilmour heard the demo in 1973, as reported by Graeme Thomson, author of *Under the Ivy: The Life & Music of Kate Bush*, and was won over. Something nagged at him, however. The audio fidelity and other factors dampened its commercial value.

"The demo was not saleable," Gilmour told the *New Statesman* magazine in February 2005. "The songs were too idiosyncratic: just Kate, this little schoolgirl who was maybe fifteen, singing away over a piano. . . . But I was convinced from the beginning that this girl had remarkable talent."

The story goes that Gilmour met with Bush at her home to witness the artist at work. He *may* have recorded her himself at this point; documentation is unclear. Further impressed, the Floyd guitarist invited Bush to his private recording studio at his home in Essex in the summer of 1973. "[Hopper] sent a tape to Gilmour, who then phoned me and Pete, and said, 'We have this girl Richie has been going on about for ages, will you come and play?'" says Martin.

Martin was hesitant at first to sign on to this improvisational jam, not knowing what he, and drummer Pete Perrier, would encounter once they interacted with the prolific but shy songwriter. "She had never played in any settings other than on the piano on her own," says Martin.

Any fears were allayed when Bush sat down in front of a Wurlitzer, an instrument she had never played, crossed her legs, and tapped about the keys. "We just said, 'You should just play the song and we would just join in,' which we did," says Martin.

After some joking and taking each other's temperature, the ice was broken and the room began reverberating as tape rolled. "I think we did about four or five songs," says Martin.

They sat and talked about musical instruments and experimenting with such. A friendship grew between Gilmour and Bush, and periodically they'd see one another. Reports are that Bush popped in to see Gilmour during the recording sessions of *WYWH* at Abbey Road.

Not much progress was made getting Bush signed to a recording contract, however. Then, Gilmour decided it was best to bring her into a professional recording environment and track her music at George Martin's AIR Studios in the summer of 1975. The problem was that Gilmour was going back out on the road to tour America with Floyd at the same time, and he could not personally supervise.

Wanting the process to move forward, Gilmour reached out to his longtime friend from Cambridge, arranger Andrew Powell, to help produce a few songs for Bush, including the soft and enigmatic yet tension-filled piano and string ballad "The Man with the Child in His Eyes."

Gilmour listened to these polished demos and liked what he heard. Claims that Gilmour is the "Man" referred to in the song are based as much on educated guesses as sheer speculation.

The story goes that Gilmour was listening to them at some later date, in the early morning hours at Abbey Road, when a rep from EMI slipped into the studio and was amazed by what he was hearing. He was treated to the song "The Man with a Child in His Eyes."

Convinced Bush was something special, the label tracked down the teenager's father. There is evidence to suggest that Bush, her family, and the record label were cautious regarding the artist's schooling and age. Eventually, however, EMI sealed the deal and released Bush's debut, *The Kick Inside*, in early 1978, and the rest, as they say, is history. Gilmour and Bush would remain friendly and even collaborate professionally onstage and in the studio into the twenty-first century.

"In 1980 she used this song called 'Passing Through Air' on a single, and she sent us a check," says Martin.

NOVEMBER TO REMEMBER

This should have caught no one by surprise—but it had. The band was having a falling out with Peter Watts, head roadie and father of future actress Naomi Watts. Watts's substance abuse, unbeknownst to the band and management, made touring an untenable situation. Watts had been with the group since the 1960s, and the band felt not only a sense of sympathy but loyalty to him. They gently pushed him to clean up.

Arthur Max, who worked at the Fillmore West and whose temper could flare up at a moment's notice, was given the nod to head up the crew. Given Max's tendency to erupt, some in the Floyd believed this was a bad choice, but there were few other options available. To top it all, their sound engineer had very little experience in the field and had to learn a new Andy Bereza mixing desk practically on the spot.

Unsurprisingly, problems ensued. Nothing seemed to mesh very well: not the crew with Max, not the crew with certain pieces of equipment, and not members of the crew with one another. Film projectionist Peter Revell reportedly threatened to—and did— walk out on the job more than once in protest. Ironically, Max seemed to work well within an ensemble cast, so to speak, on the set of movies, as he turned into a fine production designer for Ridley Scott films such as *Gladiator, Kingdom of Heaven*, and more recently *The Martian* and *Battle of Britain*.

Floyd could negotiate periodic personnel spats, but lack of confidence in live audio tech was cause for grave concern. Getting it right was essential. Not being mixed properly—not pumping out the best audio to an audience—would be deadly to Floyd's rep. When the live sound reinforcement engineer had spent his final minute as a deer in the headlights, it was obvious what course of action was needed.

Enter Brian Humphries, tape op/assistant engineer at Pye studios, where he recorded a number of singers, including Sammy Davis, Jr. and Nancy Sinatra. Humphries worked with Floyd on *More* at Pye, and when Pye relocated to Basing Street, he picked up with them again for the live tracks on *Ummagumma* and performed engineering duties for the *Music for the Body* album.

In an e-mail to the author, Brian Humphries reported:

> I worked for Island Records at Basing Studios, where I'd recorded Traffic, amongst others. They also had a Mobile Recording truck, which I got to record some great bands. Early in 1974 I was asked to record Stevie Wonder at the Rainbow Theatre [London]. The first gig was OK, but Stevie wasn't happy with the sound system, so he asked me whether I knew of a better one. Having worked with the Floyd on the *More* album, then *Ummagumma*, plus going to Rome to work on *Zabriskie Point*, I was able to phone David [Gilmour] and ask the availability of their PA system, which they rented out when not on tour. Stevie Wonder hired it and was happy with the gig.

It's been suggested that Humphries had to pass an audition of sorts, as Chris Thomas was on hand observing how this potential sound engineer operated. Humphries must have received an exceptional grade, because he became the band's live mixing engineer for the following tour dates and would eventually follow the band into Abbey Road studios for the *WYWH* recording sessions.

"Originally I was asked to record the Floyd gigs, but was asked to take over the live sound mixing the next night [at Empire Pool]," Humphries told me.

The band ran through "Shine On You Crazy Diamond," "You Gotta Be Crazy," and "Raving and Drooling," and would play these songs in July and August when they toured France. The plan was to record these numbers after the British tour in 1974.

Wright said, "[T]here's enough material in those three songs for an album, but I don't know yet. We may do something else as well which we haven't actually played yet." Wright even intimated that there was material he was working on, in his home studio (reportedly in Royston, outside Cambridge), that he'd like to see get the nod for the album.

Tweaking songs on the road was not unusual. Floyd had aired out *The Dark Side of the Moon*, after all, long before it was recorded and released. "A [song] changes so much when we do it live over a long period," Wright said. "'Shine On' had changed a lot since we started already."

In an interview with Nick Sedgewick, Waters said that some of his lyrics could be about the record-buying public, not just the industry, but those lyrics had yet to be recorded. Wording for "You Gotta Be Crazy" and "Raving and Drooling" would change once they appeared (with new names) on the *Animals* record. For instance, the phrase "raving and drooling" doesn't actually appear in the later incarnation of the song, retitled "Sheep." "Bleating and babbling" does, however, to describe the gruesome auditory sensations of a mass sheep attack.

Waters's emotional release and observations on mass thought and mass production, addressed on both *WYWH* and *Animals*, lead to the Floydian's own psychological regression, back to some of the sources of his pain and childhood fears. While this is *not* the same type of "scream" Lennon induced in his primal therapy with Dr. Janov, there are therapeutic qualities to both the former Beatle's sessions and Waters's angst.

Melody Maker reported that the album was expected in March—a guestimate given Wright's optimism and the progress the band appeared to be making. Floyd was contractually obliged to hand the record company seven records over a five-year stretch, which could include film scores. To see this through, the plan was to spend more time in the studio, from the holidays through to early spring, and then hit the road.

A Harvest record ad appearing in the Knebworth official festival program from July 1975, and a *Boston Globe* article from June, hyping the new record titled *Wish You Were Here*, also reported the August release date. This, too, was premature.

Strangely enough, Floyd was once again beaten to the punch by a British music artist, this time Badfinger, when it released *Wish You Were Here* in the fall of 1974, produced by Chris Thomas, of all people. Unlike the circumstances surrounding the titling of *The Dark Side of the Moon*, evidently there was not much cause for concern regarding overlapping and redundant album names, and tragically, Badfinger vocalist and guitarist Peter Ham committed suicide in April 1975.

Floyd kept rolling along. By the end of September and early October the band was filming footage for the tour as rehearsals continued at Elstree. The production studio, increasingly, had available rental space for Big Name rock acts as film business was drying up. And it's believed that Queen, for instance, partially shot their promo for 1975's "Bohemian Rhapsody" at Elstree.

For Floyd, dealing with technical difficulties, working out audio equipment bugs, and putting in time merely learning the songs was grueling, bordering on the ridiculous. Rick Wright said, "Dave had to have the words of the songs stuck on the top of his guitar."

In November the band played Scotland on their first extensive British tour since 1972. Floyd played dates in the United Kingdom, including at Sophia Gardens, Cardiff, where rock shows were prohibited due to disturbances and vandalism at a Who concert. The demand for tickets was through the roof. A week later, Floyd were back for three days in Liverpool before launching a quick tour in December.

Floyd were always masters of visual accompaniment for their live shows. During 1974, in addition to their lauded stage show, this meant making available a comic-strip program.

Illustrator Joe Petagno, supervised by Hipgnosis, had the honor of drawing Rick Wright (a.k.a. Rich Right) in one of the 1974 tour program's fantasy sequences. Despite Wright's shy and reserved manner, the keyboardist gained a reputation for throwing wild parties. Nothing on the magnitude of the comic-book strip dedicated to him, however.

"Storm was responsible for the portrayal of Richard as a Hefner-type party animal," says Petagno, an American who arrived in London in the early 1970s in search of work in the booming book- and LP-cover illustration businesses. "He and the Floyd were close friends. He is also suggested to use a Little Annie Fanny-type style. I think we both talked about the comic book concept for the tour book."

Time was tight, and Petagno recalls the creative process taking two days to complete. "The *Ummagumma* back page was done in about four hours with pencil and gouache paint," Petagno says.

Dating back to their fascination with Gerald Scarfe's early 1970s cartoon, Floyd infused their tour program with hints of iconic images of pop and American mainstream culture. We recognize famous individuals, from John Wayne, Malcolm McDowell (as Alex in *A Clockwork Orange*), Hugh Hefner, Charlton Heston, and so on. "Storm had a witty story to illustrate with lots of puns and innuendoes for me to include in the art-work," says Petagno. "Since we were in the celebrity world of the rich and famous, as it were, we might as well milk it for what it was worth."

Understandable, but what's up with the Phenis—phallus phone—in Rick's hand? "Just a little joke of mine," explains Petagno, who also designed Led Zeppelin's Swan Song LP label logo. "I've used lingam and yoni symbols quite extensively through the years to poke fun and provoke the status quo. Why not make a penis phone?"

Wright's bandmates received a similar caricature treatment. Action/adventure strips were drawn for daredevil motorcyclist "Dave Derring," star footballer "Rog of the Rovers," and "Captain Mason" of the Royal Navy, matching wits with a WWII German U-boat commander. Vital information about the band was also included, such as listing off-the-cuff remarks dubbed "Life Lines."

Further work needed to be done for the program as rehearsals for the 1974 tour took place at Unit studios in Kings Cross. Illustrator Gerald Scarfe was on hand to discuss ideas as the band was munching on Wimpy burgers. While the band played, Scarfe sketched Roger, Rick, Nick, and David in a style similar to the Beatles illustration he'd completed several years earlier for a *Time* magazine cover. Ultimately, Scarfe transferred his initial doodles into grand grotesqueries in October 1974.

Mason concluded that the tour program design was one of the most successful ideas the band ever had—even if it didn't do very well commercially. Of course, the secondary market has made the original quite collectible, carrying a hefty price tag.

The 1974 shows in England and Continental Europe featured major pieces from what would emerge as some of the band's strongest releases of the 1970s—*Meddle* ("Echoes"), *DSOTM* (in its entirety), *WYWH* ("Shine On You Crazy Diamond"), and *Animals* ("Raving and Drooling," "You Gotta Be Crazy").

By November, given a public starved for new Floyd material, a bootleg recording of the band's 1974 tour had emerged. Is it any wonder that fans would pay top dollar to gobble up material that the band never intended for anyone, much less the buying public, to hear?

Floyd learned the hard way the perils of not properly protecting their intellectual property. By performing material for their upcoming album, or *albums* as the case may be, the band inadvertently helped to fuel a booming, and quite illegal, business. Nefarious though it was, some fans were faced with a conundrum: despite their ignoble provenance, these bootlegs offered a view of the future Floyd.

Although handheld tape recorders and even video cameras existed at the time, they were not always affordable or practical for everyday use by the masses—and even less desirable for bootleggers. If you were lucky enough to pass through security without being detected, chances are you tucked a device into a jacket or a pocket, possibly obstructing the microphone's ability to capture clear audio. For that matter, handheld devices were not state-of-the-art equipment, even by 1974 standards.

For fans, tape traders, and the "underground-market" consumer, however, quality wasn't always the determining factor on whether they should purchase an unofficial release. The mere appearance of a tape that froze an important moment in time was intoxicating and irresistible and imbued the audio object with occult power. Floyd knew this and perhaps, at least publicly, were totally against the idea of bootleg recordings.

Bootleggers took their jobs seriously, however. Some even went to extremes to capture audio of top rock bands of the day. Mike Millard, who some consider one of the best bootleggers of the classic rock era, captured Floyd on their 1975 tour of the States. Wily enough to slip passed security with his equipment, Millard feigned paralysis by appearing at the LA Sports Arena in a wheelchair with recording gear tucked inside his bag. Millard did not record bands for profit, it's been said, but the bootlegger was a deeply troubled man. Depressed, Millard left an incomplete legacy when he committed suicide in 1990, after having rummaged through his tapes and destroyed much of his work.

Bootleggers have commented that there are marketing and even financial benefits in having these types of recordings released, regardless of their audio quality. The audio pirates would, of course, make such obviously self-serving claims, but there is a grain of truth in what they were saying. The financial detriment these releases have on the overall bottom line of a record company or the band in question is difficult to quantify, and bootleggers themselves could fall prey to enterprising pirates who'd independently produced versions of well-known unauthorized recordings. Whatever else we say about bootlegs, these underground items promote interest in the bands. Some artists understood this. Others didn't.

The Paris convention in 1971—which had nothing to do with America's withdrawal from Vietnam—gathered record industry and government types to draw up a plan of action focused on what can legally be done about stemming the tide of counterfeit records. In the early 1970s, the authorities went on the attack. The pirating industry needed to be wiped out for good, said the FBI, and they teamed with local law enforcement to conduct raids targeting small-time operators and visible retailers, such as Richard Branson.

Despite the fuzz's crackdown on illicit material, bootlegging experienced a resurgence of popularity thanks to underground releases and fan fervor over the fomenting punk cultural revolution in the United Kingdom. While some mainstream names were threatening and even following through with legal action, other more populist artists seemed to look the other way, boosting the illicit cottage industry.

For a time, bootlegs were even seen as being superior to official releases. In fact, some believed, and still do, that *Spunk* rivals the Sex Pistols' official Virgin debut, *Never Mind the Bullocks*. Since 1977 material from these sessions has popped up on other legally sanctioned titles, including on CD by Castle Music.

Although Floyd could afford to take some financial hits—*Dark Side* was moving millions, after all—they were incensed by the *British Winter Tour '74* bootleg, recorded on November 19, 1974, at Trentham Gardens. Featuring tracks "Raving and Drooling," "You Gotta Be Crazy," and a twenty-plus minute version of "Shine On You Crazy Diamond," the item reportedly sold in the neighborhood of one hundred thousand copies. This number does seem inflated, and some have questioned its validity. More likely it sold in the tens of thousands—astounding for an illegal audio product, at any rate.

Floyd had been stung previously by at least one unofficial release—a bootleg of the band's third night at the Rainbow, February 1972. Numbers vary as to how many were sold, but stopping bootleggers may have been a luxury regarding Floyd's 1974 dates.

The worst was yet to come.

Nick Kent and Pete Erskine reported for *New Musical Express* on the Thursday (Nov 14) and Friday (Nov 15) Floyd shows—the first two appearances of the band's four-night stand at Empire Pool, Wembley, London, on *The Dark Side of the Moon* tour. There had been talk, so the story goes, of promoters wanting Floyd to play a mid-afternoon show on Sunday, but allegedly, the band flatly rejected the offer.

Erskine and Kent wrote that "Raving and Drooling" did little to warm the cockles, and the band fell back on old habits, with Waters "doing his whole 'Careful with That Axe, Eugene' tormented, horse-faced routine." As for "You Gotta Be Crazy," the band allowed the song "to sprawl out to last twice as long as it should." In addition, the rock quartet lacked a certain human element, if not enthusiasm. They seemed remote.

The article was especially brutal to Gilmour in that it purports to know his motivations as a professional musician. The authors perceive Gilmour's versatility, or "malleabililty," as not a virtue but a sin, and that he fell into his position in Floyd by sheer luck. Gilmour appeared to be a "lucky geezer," with the "it's only a gig philosophy," they wrote.

After skulking over the review, Gilmour vented his disgust at one of the article's authors. "I've just read the piece," Gilmour said, "and I'm very angry about it."

Erskine backtracked a bit, and Gilmour confessed that audio difficulties on Thursday night, anyway, hampered the performance. Decades later Kent admitted he likely "overreacted" but defended his right to keep Floyd honest by saying "they partly deserved it [the bad review]." Kent maintains that the Wembley show was "a bad gig."

The damage was done, however. "I'm afraid we were a little rude about them," Pete Erskine conceded in the January 11, 1975, issue of *New Musical Express*.

Whether or not the review displayed poor taste or bad judgment, others seemed to pick up on a similar energy surrounding the band. The *Financial Times* chimed in as well, being the latest outlet hopping on the Hate Floyd Train. Antony Thorncroft floats the idea that the Floyd are the greatest band in the world, but confesses that the group's appearance on the opening night of their at Empire Pool run had left him wondering if he should reassess his proclamation.

The first half of the show was populated with new songs that demonstrated "little coherence and too many passages of random noises." Returning to *The Dark Side* after the intermission was predictable but comforting. The visual aspects of the show, from the large circular screen and lighting, produced a "most impressive exercise in mixed media." However, the band's almost automaton-like demeanor and lack of dialogue with the audience chills their performance.

The thirty thousand-plus people in attendance for the shows may not have cared what was written about the band. However, something profound was afoot: the great divide between critic and fan, artist and audience, and rock star and media widened. Just as Floyd was withdrawing from, even denouncing, rock stardom, their fanbase was growing to astronomical levels, idolizing the band. Floyd became superstars in an era when the Rock Star Machine was burning at full blast—and the press demonized them for it.

Yet, the press may have actually put its fingers on a certain truth about Floyd. Waters explained in psychological, even Jungian, terms that he was "scared of his own shadow." Performing onstage did little for his self-worth and only added to the considerable pressure he already felt as the band's self-appointed leader and main creative source. Pleasing the audiences who invested their time, money, and energy in seeing Floyd was almost a separate issue. Waters began to feel "very disconnected."

"I think there is something wrong with that . . . people needing hero figures like that, thinking that rock musicians have all the answers," Gilmour mused during an *NME* interview from 1975.

Both the *NME* writers and Gilmour seem to be working at different angles for the same result: lifting the veneer on rock stars and getting down to something real. Erskine quotes a *Sunday Times* reporter who, in "florid prose," praised the band's debut performance at Wembley. Gilmour seemed uncomfortable with being praised, nearly as much as absorbing the critical barbs he received from his detractors.

The press—willing accomplices in the band's rise to power, such as it was—also pulled the rug out from under them and watched as the band lost its balance and slipped. At the time, media outlets in large cities seemed foremost concerned with giving rock stars, like Floyd, not a pat on the back but their comeuppance.

In the time period of 1975–1978, prog rockers' shtick—composing self-indulgent, expansive, and complex material—once considered a radical act, grew tiresome for some reviewers, and carried less the weight of revolution than the well-tread tracts of common-place artistic formulas.

Of course, we'd be remiss if we did not reference that the blowback traveled in two directions. Waters went on a tirade when speaking with *Q* magazine in the early 1990s, lambasting their contributors and records reviewers, or lack thereof. Waters didn't hold his tongue and disdain for the music press, and some of this may have been frustration at how commercially viable Floyd was in the wake of the mid-1980s split—and at the lack of good or any press he was receiving for his solo efforts.

In retrospect, the Kent-Erskine grievances, memorialized in print, is a microcosm of the growing storm about to blow through the music industry. Punk wasn't a fully formed musical force yet, but it was the inevitable and cultural byproduct of government distrust and economic decline. In the months prior to the explosion of punk, this activity can, in retrospect, be interpreted as a pre-echo of the storming-of-the-palace revolution that punk represented to the established recording industry. Never mind that some in the recording industry were funding and actively fomenting this revolution in search of the "next great thing."

The recording industry, or sectors of the record business establishment, pushed a populist revolt in consumer buying habits. Some of the biggest and hippest names signed so-called New Wave acts, from Virgin Records (and A&M before them) to Sire and Clive Davis's new label Arista, which inked a deal with punk poetess Patti Smith and generated a media blitz around her 1975 John Cale-produced *Horses*, heralded by the *New York Times* and *Village Voice* as one of the best of the year.

Punk changed the trajectory of pop music, but we shouldn't underestimate the power of Britain's tight-knit musical community—the complicated web of interpersonal and professional relationships—in redirecting the course of artists' careers. Johnny Lydon wrote in *No Irish, No Blacks, No Dogs* that Nick Kent "used to jam with [Sex Pistols] from time to time," adding, "That's what Steve [Jones, guitarist] told me."

Gilmour provides another prescient point: "[Kent's] still really involved with Syd Barrett and the whole 1967 thing," Gilmour told Pete Erskine. "I don't even know if he saw the Floyd with Syd."

All of this presents startling possible insight into the psyche of the mainstream press as a whole. Maybe all the brutal blows Floyd received were motivated by something else other than a bad performance? And the clot thickens: it's unclear exactly what happened, but some kind of verbal altercation led Sex Pistols bassist Sid Vicious to whip Kent with a motorbike chain, swung around like a Roman flagellum.

Granted. Rotten, who was given his nickname by Steve Jones, made it clear that he did not want Kent around and was confident of his position in the band only when the Pistols severed ties with the journalist. "They never made him a band member, although he considered himself as such," said Lydon. "He's never written a good word about me ever since."

Still, some journos appeared predisposed to accept and promote the street noise of punk. Class warfare was indicative of societal, political, and economic strife, and Kent even raises the specter of Orwell by referring to Floyd's "morose laziness" and "pallid excuse for creative music" that would be "touted as fine art" in a *1984*-style totalitarian society. Machines are plugged in, programmed, and are allowed to run, as the band plays snooker or watches a football match backstage.

That's probably a "polite" way of calling Floyd the archenemy of freethinking people everywhere. The zonked-out masses who followed Floyd had no idea of the putrid nature of the music they were hearing, or not hearing. The lines were being drawn: not only had the reviewers attacked the texture of Gilmour's hair but also audience members who projected the same personal appearance. In addition, Kent said he couldn't think "of another rock group who live a more desperately bourgeois existence in the privacy of their own homes."

Gilmour, like Waters, wrestled with the socialist instincts instilled in them of a better, brighter future through collectivism. Mason and Wright seemed less affected by their newfound wealth and even reveled in it. "Sure, I'm cynical of our position," Gilmour told *NME*'s Erskine in 1975. "I don't think we deserve it. But I'm no more cynical of our position than I am of anyone else's on our level."

With the first shots of the punk revolution already fired, music critics, with increasing regularity, deemed Floyd unworthy. At least they could agree on *something* . . .

Clearly, there was deference to the Syd Barrett-era Pink Floyd vis-à-vis the British music press. Just by being successful, Floyd were targets, but the band's audiences were also targets for ridicule. In his book *Pink Floyd: Bricks in the Wall*, Karl Dallas speculated that it was the "working- class nature of [Floyd's] following that alienates the media."

It seems incredible, but the press engaged in class warfare—something that was under the exclusive purview of reviews of progressive rock shows of the time. "Some people dislike the basic premise of what we are all about," Gilmour told Chris Welch in 1973. "Then their criticism is a waste of time. For someone to criticize you who understands you, and can say where you have fallen down—that's valid."

=

Factions within Floyd remained dissatisfied for years on the issue of the band's live performances in the mid-1970s.

Floyd lamented never having released a solid live rendition of *Dark Side* back in the 1970s. Apparently it ate away at the band enough that the infamous show at Empire Pool, Wembley, from November 1974, was released as a two-CD package of a *Dark Side of the Moon* reissue. The feeling of loss or inadequacy may have been compounded by the fact that Floyd did not have the best of luck post-*Ummagumma* with live recordings. For instance, Floyd began organizing *Live at Montreux* in the early 1970s, only to abandon it.

P.U.L.S.E., recorded at Earls Court twenty years later in the 1990s, contains *Dark*

Side in its entirety. Anyone with access to the Internet or with the cash to buy the 2011 two-CD Experience edition of *The Dark Side of the Moon* has rock-solid evidence, for or against, the claims made by the press at the time. Although other recordings I've heard were made on Saturday, November 16, and I have found them agreeable, but readers can decide for themselves about the quality of at least one Floyd performance at Empire Pool.

WHEN YOUR LIFE'S YOUR OWN

Straight from the Wembley show, Gilmour headed over to Air Studios to meet his old friend Andrew Powell and new acquaintance, songwriter David Courtney, perhaps best known for his association with Leo Sayer.

Courtney's old band, the Urchins, backed singer Adam Faith when the baton was tossed to them by the Roulettes, featuring drummer Bob Henrit, later of Argent and the Kinks. Faith, a pre-Beatles hit-parading pop star, known for his all-night sessions at Abbey Road, converted musical know-how into record industry acumen.

While recording at Virgin Records' Manor studio in Oxfordshire, the Sayer crowd worked with engineer Tom Newman, of *Tubular Bells* fame, who introduced Faith and Courtney to the Who's Roger Daltrey. Henrit explained, in his book *Banging On!*, that it was Faith's wife, Jackie, who rechristened Gerry Sayer as Leo Sayer because of his curly mane.

"[Newman] said . . . Roger Daltrey lives down your way, and he's just built his eight-track studio in the barn of his house, and I'm sure you would get on great with Roger," says Courtney. "Adam and I went along and played Roger what we had already recorded, and he couldn't believe what he was hearing. He said, 'Not only would I like you to record the rest of the album here, but I want you guys to write my solo album.'"

Daltrey was so hot to release his own music that his self-titled debut actually predates the Sayer effort *Silverbird*, sessions for which piqued the interest of Hendrix drummer Mitch Mitchell and Pete Townshend, who supposedly popped in to say hello during the sessions.

Due to his success with Sayer and Daltrey, Courtney signed with United Artists in the United States and EMI in the United Kingdom. Sessions for *First Day* took place at George Martin's Air Studios and Abbey Road with legendary Beatles engineer Geoff Emerick.

For his personal project, Courtney revisited "Silverbird," a song he had always envisioned as "something more grandiose," he says. With the help of co-producer and arranger Powell, Courtney realized the orchestral coloring he'd heard in his head years earlier.

"When Your Life Is Your Own" features Gilmour on guitar and addresses topics ranging from mental illness, isolationism, the global economy, and doomed business relationships.

This was also the era of riots. University of Warwick student Kevin Gately was killed in June 1974 during the Red Lion Square disorders, demonstrations, and counterdemonstrations involving the right-wing group National Front and the communist International Marxist Group (IMG).

"'When Your Life is Your Own' expressed what I felt was political at the time," says Courtney. "It captures the feel of what was going on at the time in this country, with strikes and that sort of thing. It seemed to rub off on me, but I never consciously sat down with a big burning desire to be heard on a political level. I just didn't feel comfortable with how things were out there, and at that time I had this burning desire to live in America. England, at that point, had been controlled by the unions, and I felt that this was not what I want to be part of."

"When Your Life is Your Own" already had a Pink Floyd vibe even prior to Gilmour's involvement. "Having been a big Floyd fan, there was only ever one man to ever play guitar on that—and that was David Gilmour," says Courtney. "I played Andrew 'When Your Life Is Your Own' and said, 'You can hear that it is very Floyd influenced. What are the chances that we could get someone like David Gilmour to play on it?' As it happens, Andrew was friendly with David and he said, 'I'll phone him up.'"

Gilmour showed up at Air Studios, guitar in tow, ready to play, record, and, as always, chat. "I remember clearly that David was at Wembley that night, with Floyd doing the *Dark Side of the Moon* concert," Courtney says. "He came straight from Wembley with his roadie, amplifier, and guitars and he probably arrived about eleven o'clock at night or something and set it up and we went through the song and we were there for a good part of the night."

Gilmour cut his guitar track relatively quickly but spent most of the night in the studio with friends. "When you say you were there most of the night, it was not that we were going over and over the song," Courtney says. "It would have been because we were chatting and doing other things. You are just tripping because you're all there together. Tripping in more ways than one, I think—if I remember rightly. It would have been maybe one or two or three takes, at the most. . . . I think the song spoke to him in the same way that he didn't have to really give this a lot of thought. It could have been a Floyd song; the chord structure and everything about it was right in that pocket."

Once Gilmour's tracks were recorded, the symphonic element was added, expanding the scope and sonic dimension of the track. "That's when the song really came to life," says Courtney. "It's the best song on the album, and the one I'm most proud of. Not just because of David Gilmour, but everything about it. It's the one that speaks to me the most."

Another song, "Everybody Needs a Little Loving," was inspired by Courtney's friend, someone who had gone insane and was committed to a mental institution. A familiar story in the Floyd universe. "I used to go and visit him," says Courtney. "He used to think he was in the music business, but he really wasn't."

First Day may not have been a huge hit, but it deserves a second look, if for no other reason than its diversity of moods and sounds. "It has that slightly *Sgt. Pepper*-ish thing about it, in that it's like a variety show," says Courtney. "It has the big opening, and it takes you on this journey. That's what albums used to be like. I appreciate that now you can only download the songs you want, and that's fine on a practical level. Albums were experiences and we lost some of that."

PURGATORY

More extracurricular activity occurred in the fall of 1974 as Floyd continued to flirt with the international film industry. Originally released in Sweden in November 1974, *Skärseld*, a.k.a. *Skaerseldan*, or *Purgatory*, starring Jan Blomberg, was distributed in the United States in early 1975.

Skärseld follows the exploits of a professional writer named Dante, portrayed by Blomberg, whose life is coming apart. Director Michael Meschke intersplices elements of Dante's *Divine Comedy* with the psychological, spiritual, emotional—and even physical—journey the writer undertakes during the creative process. The journey *could be* metaphorical or actually track the progress of the writer's soul through the afterlife.

I obtained a copy of the film directly from Meschke and heard snippets of the music appearing on the then-recently certified Gold record, *Ummagumma*, including live versions of "A Saucerful of Secrets," "Astronomy Domine," "Careful with That Axe, Eugene," portions of Wright's original "Sysyphus," emphasis on Parts One and Four, and the noisier textural passages of Gilmour's "The Narrow Way." A contemporary chart documenting the songs used in the film also confirmed this.

The Swedish Film Institute was kind enough to send paperwork relating to the film from their archives, including a handwritten report noting the running times and sequences in which the partial songs appear. "A Saucerful of Secrets" gets the most screen time, at 516 seconds or thereabouts.

"The music corresponded to the mood in certain scenes," Meschke tells me. "I . . . remember, particularly, [it worked well] in the beginning when Dante, halfway in his life, gets lost in a wild forest where he meets Virgil, his mentor."

A typed letter dating from April 1974, addressed to producer Bengt Forslund at the Swedish Film Institute in Stockholm and sent from EMI's copyright department, clears the producers for usage of Floyd's music for the film. Forslund, a screenwriter, received an Oscar nomination for 1971's *The Emigrants*, which chronicles the saga of Swedes crossing the Atlantic and settling in eighteenth-century Minnesota, America's Upper Midwest, and stars Max Von Sydow and Liv Ullmann.

EMKA Productions had asked for £1,000 just for Floyd's name to be attached to the film, with an additional £500 to be paid to EMI for the actual appearance of the songs. Nordisk Copyright Bureau would do the honors and clear the actual music.

A sum of £1,000 may not have been exorbitant, considering the kinds of money a band could make for signing, say, a record deal, but everything is relative. In 1974, making over £1,000 for virtually greenlighting the use of your music in a film is not bad work if you can get it. To put this in perspective, Floyd were paid eighty pounds by Peter Whitehead for allowing their music to be used for *Tonite Let's All Make Love in London*. If nothing else, this proves that Floyd's cinematic ambitions *could be* financially lucrative if they pursued this path more aggressively.

At one point, Floyd's music was practically synonymous with film soundtracks, and music listeners would continue to hear the band's work in film into the mid-1970s. Along with Arthur Brown, Floyd's music appears in *The Committee*, a British satire released in 1968, which includes a version of "Careful with That Axe, Eugene." Some of the material, which has been labeled as "The Committee, Part 1," was actually used in reverse for the film. "Echoes" was used for *Crystal Voyager*, an Australian surfer documentary, which opened in Melbourne in December 1973, and a portion of "Shine On You Crazy Diamond" appears in Walerian Borowczyk's erotic flick *La Marge* (a.k.a. *The Streetwalker*), released nearly a year after *WYWH* surfaced, starring Andy Warhol/Velvet Underground chum Joe Dallesandro and Sylvia Kristel (of *Emmanuel* blue movie series fame).

Floyd was also tapped to do the music for *Rollo*, a TV series that was never completed and apparently never aired, as far as I can tell. The planned animated film project told the story of a boy named Rollo who seems to live in, or creates, a fantasy world. Eventually the adventure takes Rollo—and the viewer—into outer space, where it appears the Moon is smoking a cigar.

Perhaps the problem with Floyd recording scores for films, or licensing their music, is that Hollywood—or any movie industry—is fickle. There's an ebb and flow to taste, and if Floyd was "in" one year, they may be "out" the next, possibly relegating their future to the fickle fortunes of a film's failure or success.

Furthermore, if a film tanked, their music may not have been viewed as being effective—or even useful to prospective directors. Why Floyd didn't pursue soundtracks with more vigor could be down to Floyd, and in particular Waters, not wanting their music to be controlled or interpreted by someone else—used, if you will, toward an end other than the audiovisual soundscapes the band, itself, had created for the listener.

Ironically, Floyd had turned down Stanley Kubrick when he came calling to request usage of "Atom Heart Mother." "The only thing I knew about Kubrick was that, after 1970, he was interested in using at least part of 'Atom Heart Mother' for a film [likely *A Clockwork Orange*], but was refused by Steve O'Rourke, probably because the Pink Floyd machine would know that, once 'Atom Heart Mother' was associated/identified with a film, it would have a more limited life," says Ron Geesin.

Kubrick may have wanted full discretion in how the song, or any parts of it, would be used. This was unacceptable. Ironically, Roger used audio from the HAL 9000 death sequence, from *2001: A Space Odyssey*, for his "Perfect Sense, Part I," which appears on his 1992 solo record, *Amused to Death*.

Floyd could have pursued any number of avenues, but bad reviews, a half-baked movie career, and an unfinished studio record positioned them in a twilight world of uncertainty. "Purgatory" may be an apt phrase to describe the band's existential predicament as artists—and perhaps that of the larger world circa late 1974 and early 1975.

If the middle years of the 1970s were a watershed moment to take stock of where we were and where we were going, Floyd was certainly going with the flow. Set adrift by Watergate, terrorist bombings in Britain, and news trickling through of the Khmer Rouge's Killing Fields, claiming the lives of well over a million Cambodians, the cruelty and uncertainty of life came at us so fast and furious that we became disoriented by, and occasionally numb to, the darker aspects of the world.

The constant drumbeat of negativity had a cumulative psychological impact. The mid-1970s signature was one of reckoning, rage, paranoia, madness, surrealism, sickness, and need for accountability.

Nick Kent correctly points out in that infamous *NME* review from 1974 that the Floyd are "definitely the quintessential English band" summing up "the rampant sense of doomed mediocrity in this country's outlook right now." Very few bands could act as a mirror to the events of a historical era, but Floyd, the centerpiece of Maben's Anti-Wood-stock cinematic creation earlier in the decade, is one of them.

Teetering on the edge of progressive rock and pop worlds, Floyd's music was no longer considered psychedelic, but it retained certain hallmark qualities of the style they'd helped to pioneer. Some of their 1960s devotees had abandoned them years ago. Mainstream audiences adored them, however, rushing to record outlets and screaming at arena concerts till their throats were raw—a constant irritant to a certain lead vocalist bassist.

Indeed. The true mantel of the psychedelic experience of the 1960s was passed not only to Floyd's arena shows but also perhaps to the dance clubs and the discotheques largely in urban areas of North America and the United Kingdom, where sex, personal freedom, and illicit chemicals flowed freely.

During the band's show at Empire Pool, Wembley, on November 16, about forty minutes into the performance, Waters engaged in a revealing interaction with the crowd. When a fan, romanticizing Floyd's past, shouts out "1967!" Waters corrects him—"1967? No, you're wrong. This is 1974."—to great applause and whistles. Waters continues: "And this is another new tune, especially for *you*, and it's called 'You Gotta Be Crazy.'"

Both the fan and Floyd made valid points: We *were* going slightly mad both as a people and as a culture, with little reason to invest in the future. Floyd was quickly learning a very hard and valuable lesson—no one can outrun his or her past. The faster and harder we sprint, the farther away our goals appear to be. In the case of Floyd, one historic figure still loomed large, even years after his exit from the band. The defects of the era, and the ghost of one of Britain's greatest underground music idols, continued to stalk them.

CHAPTER 5

VANISHING POINT

Homer said it best. No, not the Greek bard of grand ancient tales, such as the *Iliad* and the *Odyssey*, whose work has survived centuries and continues to regale us with sagas of heroism, war, tragedy, and triumph on an epic scale. Not *that* Homer.

Homer *Simpson*, who may someday be viewed with equal reverence for his profound and popular philosophizing, proved his worth when, ruminating on the mid-1970s music scene, he blurted out, "Everyone knows rock attained perfection in 1974."

Time may prove Homer correct. The turn from 1974 to 1975 may not have been a particularly drastic one, but it signaled the moment our Western society had crossed the point of no return.

Marinated in a malaise of confusion, distrust, distress, and escapism, the music of the era was a diverse blend of seemingly contradictory attributes, a stew of uncertainty spiced with a diversionary dash of hope and possibility.

Picking up on the mood of the times, *Melody Maker*'s June 28, 1975, cover line asked, "Is Rock Finished?" There was a shift in the collective consciousness, possibly owed to a general sense that something was slightly amiss.

For starters, the Beatles dissolved their partnership in 1975. The Fab Four had ceased operation as a band years earlier, and the glow emanating from the Summer of Love had long ago faded. It wasn't returning. And neither were the Beatles. For many, this simple fact alone meant pop culture was rudderless, set adrift in the choppy depths of an uncertain world. No words of wisdom, no new "Let It Be" for our weary world consciousness.

Secondly, rock music was steadily becoming a commodity. The recording world had always been a business, of course, even from the dawn of the industry and the appearance of so-called "race records." But the industry—the Machine—was growing at incalculable rates in the 1970s, seeding offshoot, parallel, and cottage industries, from music publishing, music journalism, and live audio reinforcement to ticket distributors, sound recording and production companies, graphic design, advertising, musical instrument manufacturing, and trucking.

There may be nothing at all inherently nefarious about the above industries, but with increasing regularity, the focus was on the bottom line, which gradually drained the individuality of mainstream, if idiosyncratic, artists.

Being mavericks of style, substance and vision was no longer good enough to get a record deal or financial backing. In short, being different held little currency.

"I often get reminded, when I think about that time period, that there was not this thing of selling out before 1974 or 1975," says Trey Gunn (ex-King Crimson, Security Project). "I don't think we even listen to records this way, anymore. Just by listening to a record, right away, you could tell whether the band sold out. I can't even conjure that for myself, anymore. It wasn't the hype, the image, presentation or advertising—you could hear it in the music. Something was missing. It was empty where it was once full. It wasn't personal. Everybody could feel it. Man, that is a striking difference to the world we live in now."

On some level we were operating on intuition more than we are now; we could *feel* if a track lacked musical dimension and emotional depth. "There was something about a song being written that became popular, but its purpose was not to just be popular," says Gunn. "Somehow Pink Floyd avoided all of that. They're classic rock forever. I can't ever imagine they'd be off the radio until there is no radio anymore. Zeppelin is the same way."

This isn't to say that 1975 was a terrible year for music. Just a schizophrenic one. We witnessed the rise of punk rock; Paul McCartney and Wings' arena-ready *Venus and Mars*; the Bay City Rollers' bubble-gum rock; Elton John's homage to "Lucy in the Sky with Diamonds," which went Gold in '75 and soared up the charts in advance of *Captain Fantastic and the Brown Dirt Cowboy*; Earth Wind & Fire's sophisticated spiritual funk; the Eagles' peaceful feelin' country-rock; and Alice Cooper's Bob Ezrin-produced *Welcome to My Nightmare*. (Interestingly, in 1976, *Alice Cooper Goes to Hell* was a continuation of the theme from the previous record, featuring a song titled "Wish You Were Here.")

Led Zeppelin unleashed the sprawling double LP *Physical Graffiti*, encompassing elements of blues, British folk, funk, R&B, classical, jazz, and Indian music.

The Sweet crossed so many genres it was difficult to categorize them. Presupposing the explosion of disco and punk, they strung together a series of hits throughout the 1970s with some help from production and songwriting team Mike Chapman and Nicky Chinn. We were treated to "Fox on the Run," "Ballroom Blitz," "Teenage Rampage," "Little Willy," "The Six Teens," "Blockbuster," "Wig Wam Bam," and "Love Is Like Oxygen."

Queen's extended operatic six-minute single "Bohemian Rhapsody," scaling the depths and heights of a tortured and anguished soul, reached No. 1 in Britain. Queen began recording it at Rockfield Studios in Wales just prior to the appearance of *WYWH*. Track upon track were later overdubbed for the pop masterpiece, hundreds of them by some reports, to complete what many fans consider their masterwork.

While some historically significant music and cultural bright spots did pop up, by the mid-1970s we, as a society, appeared to not only be fatigued but haunted by some of our greatest and most celebrated musical works of the day. If we indeed sensed some ghastly presence in our popular music, it may only have been a reflection of our own lingering, unresolved issues.

It's no accident that the ten-year period, beginning roughly in 1963 with the assassination of JFK and continuing through to 1973, when William Colby had assumed the role of director of central intelligence in the United States, might have been the most topsy-turvy era in modern world history.

The unfortunate events in Dallas provided the initial sparks that ignited the explosion of the counterculture, one could argue, just as conflict was the new global norm. At least three presidential administrations, including the Kennedy, Johnson, and Nixon administrations, spanned the life of the Vietnam conflict. This despite peace talks, a Commander-in-Chief being assassinated, one retiring from politics, and a third forced to resign.

When portions of the so-called Pentagon Papers were published in major US daily newspapers, Americans, at least those who cared enough to pay attention to what their government was doing in the shadows, were shocked by the duplicitous nature of politics surrounding the Vietnam War. It was revealed that American presidents, dating back to Truman, Eisenhower, and JFK, had not been fully forthcoming regarding the United States' involvement in Southeast Asia and what role the French had played at the outset of the conflict.

Although not appearing in the Pentagon Papers, the Nixon administration unsuccessfully dealt with the fallout from the potentially explosive and politically poisonous revelations revealed by the document dump through political operatives, called "the plumbers."

Ken Kesey, author of *One Flew Over the Cuckoo's Nest*, was traveling cross-country when news of the JFK assassination—and the ensuing chaos surrounding the capture and arrest of Lee Harvey Oswald and his own very public murder at the hands of Jack Ruby—filtered out to him and his buddies via car radio. In an article called "The Loss of Innocence," published in *Newsweek* in 1983, Kesey dubbed Kennedy "the last person we could believe in" and claimed that "this was a real loss of [a high] opinion of ourselves as an innocent, wonderful, above-board nation."

Perhaps this crystalized the view of many in the country, and all over the world, until a certain kind of cynicism invaded the public consciousness in the early 1970s—and the veil had been lifted. We no longer believed what we were being fed by our government or the media. We began to demand the truth from our leaders.

Kesey, who said he volunteered for government drug testing in the 1950s, would tour the country again the year following Kennedy's assassination. This time it was in a bus with his band of Merry Pranksters, immortalized in Tom Wolfe's book *The Electric Kool-Aid Acid Test*, witnessing the nascent stirrings of a hippie movement as a nation was in the process of healing.

Kesey, an author and pop culture icon who had hosted multimedia light shows and acid tests years ahead of the pop culture curve, decamped to Oregon to become a farmer in 1967 at the height of the hippie movement. Kesey retreated. As did America.

America's presence—and notable absence—around the world was no laughing matter, as it contributed to the ultimate and unceremonious collapse of the entire military misadventure in the Southeast Asian theatre.

By the mid-1970s, prolonging the agony of war was not something US President Gerald Ford was willing to do—and he certainly wasn't going to become a hapless victim to never-ending overseas conflicts, as at least two previous occupants of the Oval Office had been. More likely, Congress simply did not think it wise to continue to pour money, treasure, and lives into Vietnam.

Yet, America's rolling withdrawals left South Vietnam vulnerable, including capital and crown jewel city Saigon, eyed by the North for years, which was a sticking point in peace negotiations. In 1975, communism advanced, perhaps as many in the military and federal government had foreseen.

Saigon, no longer in the grip of South Vietnamese control, was lost in late April 1975 to the communist North, even as eight Americans and many others were reportedly still being held captive in the city as of June 1975. With all military and political options exhausted, the United States seemed powerless. Even upon leaving, US planes were being fired upon. American and sympathetic South Vietnamese evacuees climbed a metal ladder to freedom and were choppered from the roof of the US embassy in Saigon to the relative safety of Navy ships.

It was dizzying. In the wake of the Watergate scandal, there was a general lack of faith in the righteousness of Western military power, government, and even the entertainment industry, as supposed secrets were revealed in Kenneth Anger's *Hollywood Babylon*.

Corruption and exhaustion reigned. This sickness infected popular music, and the record business soon found itself under scrutiny. As we've discussed, payola and drugola were a way of life, and the radio and record business, such as it was and is, thrived on such activity. It would be very difficult in 1975 (and prior) to break a single through sheer word of mouth or press coverage. It *could* happen, but radio airplay was the most powerful and perhaps the most effective way to get music in front of the masses.

Numerous popular bands were affected by this mid-1970s "sickness," or curse, as it were. American road warriors and tragic heroes, the Allman Brothers Band, were fatigued and thrown into disarray by a brewing storm of inner turmoil. Gregg Allman even found himself on the wrong side of the law due to his "rather long bout with drugs." Their soap opera saga was textbook "unmaking a rock 'n' roll band."

The band's fifth studio album, *Win, Lose or Draw*, did little else but highlight the strained partnerships negotiated by the various bandmembers. Allman's title track and Dickie Betts's fusion-esque instrumental "High Falls" are standout numbers, but on the whole, the record teases with the prospect of something greater emerging from the song cycle. It never does. The album seemed constructed more by treaty than chemistry. Something was missing from this project, a certain spark *absent*.

Even the LP cover imagery, a view of an empty Muhlenbrink's Saloon in Atlanta, questioned the band's commitment to their music, their new record, and each other. Other big-name artists were falling into mid-1970s rock music misfortune. The October

1975 issue of *Creem* magazine reported that Led Zeppelin lead vocalist Robert Plant and his family were involved in a vehicular accident on Rhodos, off the coast of Greece, on August 4, 1975. Plant broke bones in his foot and fractured his elbow, forcing Zeppelin to cancel its upcoming tour. Ironically, Rhodes or Rhodos was the same island Floyd and their family members chose for holiday in the mid-1970s.

The Who was consumed with their own case of mid-1970s burnout. Guitarist/songwriter/sometimes singer Pete Townshend had strong feelings about growing up and growing old in the public eye. He intimated that he could sense a sea change in attitude toward rock stars. "[N]owadays it's considered very passé to admit that you've got a burning ambition to stand on stage and be screamed at by fifteen-year-old girls," he told *NME* in May 1975.

Townshend confessed that as early as 1974 he felt that he—and maybe the entire band—were at times going through the motions and almost parodying a Who performance when they took the stage. "Slip Kid," from 1975's *The Who by Numbers*, illuminates the agitated discourse between the young rebel and the elder. The teen protests, the adult looks for clues. No matter how old, each attempts to break free of the Matrix and liberate his mind and spirit of an oppressive world.

While rock stars were thrown into confusion and disarray, with increasing regularity the general population just stopped . . . being there. Floyd talks about being physically present but mentally absent. By 1975, salt-of-the-earth individuals and high-profile personalities were quite literally *disappearing*.

Consider a wave of mysterious absences: All the reported MIAs in Vietnam, for one. Secondly, in Italy through the early fall of 1975, the Mafia and a shadowy organization calling itself Kidnappings Incorporated snatched dozens of children of wealthy families for ransom, murdering some. Women and men were abducted, bringing the total to eighty for 1975. Italian police were puzzled by the public's seemingly apathetic attitude toward the wave of crimes.

Newspaper heiress Patty Hearst fell off the radar and resurfaced in 1975. Hearst—christened Tania by her kidnappers, the Symbionese Liberation Army, an urban guerilla terrorist group that may have forced her to participate in the most heinous of crimes—could have been a victim of some form of Stockholm syndrome. Her disappearance triggered a nationwide FBI manhunt, while wild speculation ran rampant.

Lesley Whittle, referred to as an "heiress" in the press, vanished in January 1975 and was found dead two months later, a victim of Donald Neilson, or the "Black Panther." We were also informed of the kidnapping, later proved to be a staged hoax, of Samuel Bronfman II, son of Seagram's beverage magnate Edgar Bronfman.

Jimmy Hoffa, the former president of the International Brotherhood of Teamsters, disappeared. Hoffa's last known whereabouts was a Detroit-area restaurant parking lot. A 2014 documentary, titled *Killing Jimmy Hoffa*, speculates that the former Teamsters honcho was going to spill his guts before the Senate about everything he knew, all of it, including the Mob and its possible involvement in the JFK assassination and the long-believed connection between the CIA and Mafia in snuffing out "The Beard," Cuban dictator Fidel Castro.

One of the United Kingdom's most famous missing persons, Lord Lucan, vamoosed after the nanny of his three children suffered a fatal blow to the head. Lucan was found guilty of murder *in absentia* on June 19, 1975. After decades of conspiracy theories and possible sightings, Lucan was officially declared dead in 2016.

We were besieged with still more high-profile disappearances. With his financial house in complete disarray, John Stonehouse—Labor party pol and junior minister under Harold Wilson—apparently faked his own death by drowning in Miami, Florida. Observers were suspicious of these reports even before American lifeguards debunked aspects of the story.

Stonehouse's audacity knew few bounds. Speaking before the House of Commons in October 1975, he attempted to objectify his behavior by referring to himself in the third person. An Australian psychiatrist tasked with diagnosing Stonehouse described his actions in terms of "psychiatric suicide." Stonehouse may have been suffering from some form of mental illness, but it was later revealed that he had lived a double life: he was likely having an affair with his secretary and was a communist spy in the House of Parliament, passing state secrets to the Czechs.

Stonehouse eventually surfaced in Australia, apprehended by authorities already on the lookout for Lord Lucan since December 1974. As Francis Wheen wrote in his book *Strange Days Indeed: The 1970s: The Golden Age of Paranoia*, "[W]hen the Australian police found [Stonehouse] hiding in Melbourne a month later, they assumed he was another missing person, the fugitive Lord Lucan." Was the decade so mired in uncertainty, so weighed down in its "miasma of confusion," that we couldn't even keep track of our missing persons?

=

As the hangover from the 1960s receded, a shroud of paranoia and distrust loomed. In 1975, art in the realm of literature and film imitated life as much as music did.

Clandestine societies, covert activities, and secret messages abounded. We became more conspiratorial and saw the world as full of mystery, intrigue, and danger. The historical events surrounding the Cambridge Five would later be dramatized and immortalized in the mid-1970s espionage page-turner *Tinker Tailor Soldier Spy* by British novelist John le Carré.

The cult conspiratorial fantasy series *Illuminatus!* kicked off with *The Eye in the Pyramid*; Philip K. Dick was awarded a Hugo for his dystopian, post-Second Civil War sci-fi tome *Flow My Tears, the Policeman Said*; Saul Bellow grabbed a Pulitzer for his exploration of art and commercialization in *Humboldt's Gift*, and Charles Berlitz sold a boatload of nonfiction books purportedly investigating sunken ships and lost aircraft in the deadly area known as the Bermuda Triangle.

Cinematic releases such as *One Flew Over the Cuckoo's Nest*, *Barry Lyndon*, *Monty Python and the Holy Grail*, *Jaws*, Ken Russell's *Tommy*, *Three Days of the Condor*, *The Day of the Locust*, Gene Hackman in search of a runaway girl in *Night Moves*, and being on the trail of international drug runners in *French Connection II* speak to various themes Floyd addressed or alluded to with *WYWH*. Addressed were issues involving everything from absence, surrealism, and isolation to corruption, madness, fear, and the perils of pop culture deification.

In *Rollerball*, James Caan portrays Jonathan E., star player for the Houston roller derby team. Emotional retreat into a virtual world frames the plot of the film and Jonathan appears almost willfully zoned out at times. He wishes to be numb, even envies his comatose, fallen teammate Moonpie, portrayed by John Beck, a jockish cut-up who refused to take the bloodsport too seriously—and paid the consequences. Despite being a professional sport, there are no victors in the "game" of Rollerball.

In the final scene, after virtually all the participants on both teams have died or been wiped out, Jonathan E. zooms around a smoking circular track and posts the match's lone goal. A once-hushed crowd slowly builds toward the rousing chant, *"Jonathan, Jonathan . . . ."* Feeding off their intensity, Jonathan takes a victory lap. The game is all he has—maybe all *he ever had*—and is compelled to continue, regardless of what he, or his bureaucratic overlords, had planned.

Bach's "Toccata and Fugue in D minor" provides the film's unofficial soundtrack, but "Welcome to the Machine" could have easily fit the bill. Indeed, the hellishly clinical future of *Rollerball* is a different kind of science fiction than we were used to, or we'd see two years later in *Star Wars*. But it represented a reality some feared we'd experience in the not-too-distant future.

For all of Waters's denials that Floyd is "space rock," the notion of being absorbed by a soulless organism, or being the victim of machines of our own creation, to the point we become mindless drones subservient to our devices, resonates through "Welcome to the Machine" and popular culture of the 1970s—as much as it does today.

In a sense, "Welcome to the Machine" is the perfect sci-fi song for the automated 1970s. Threats from outer space or from a nuclear attack had become passé in the late Cold War years of the 1970s. Following Apollo 11, even venturing to the Moon *seemed* commonplace. But in the wake of HAL 9000, the threats of computer malfunction or malignant machines going haywire were hardwired into our collective conscious.

As we moved through the 1970s and our once-trusted institutions had failed us, paranoia inevitably festered. What would be the next phase of our social evolution? Would we face certain economic collapse and could we successfully check rogue scientific experimentation? Would we have the wisdom and strength to avoid forming a global surveillance state, eradicating individual liberties, and spewing falsehoods through mass media propaganda?

The messages were clear: If we were not careful we would no longer be in control of our own lives. To concerned observers, someone, some governing body . . . had already overridden the system.

One Flew Over the Cuckoo's Nest, directed by Milos Forman and starring Jack Nicholson, was released in November 1975, and offers yet another example of how Floyd's muse was reflected in the popular art of the day. Bizarrely, Jack Nitzsche composed music for the film's soundtrack with, among other instruments and objects, wine glasses for an award-winning movie that focused on mental health.

It's not difficult to see Syd in Nicholson's rebellious and charismatic McMurphy. Syd wasn't a criminal like McMurphy, of course, but both represented a threat to the status quo. Both waged battles against soulless societal "machines" before slipping into mental stupor.

Opposed to the stranglehold communism had on Eastern Europe, director Forman was once rumored to have signed on for a Syd Barrett biopic. That's a tantalizing thought, given the director's humanistic treatment of doomed antiheroes. A "sense of the power of institutions to crush radicals and truth-tellers permeated [Forman's film projects]," read the Czech director's obit in *Variety* in April 2018.

Although based on the 1962 Ken Kesey novel of the same title, *Cuckoo's Nest* is not merely a stinging indictment of the mental health profession and a sobering view of the insanity of American life, but a haunting portrait of the destruction of the outlaw spirit. The message was clear: "The Machine" crushes outcasts and nonconformists.

"I guess we are, to a certain degree, obsessed by both the way the music industry and society eat up people," Gilmour told the *Chicago Tribune* in 1978. "As for how to change society for the better . . . well, those kinds of changes have to come from the inside."

Somehow Floyd managed to reflect on their current condition and their own past, as well as the capture the zeitgeist of the times. Motivated by absence, madness, and malaise, Floyd was one of the few rock bands of the era to look into the abyss, see it in themselves, and create enduring musical elements greater than the sum of its parts. *WYWH* is, arguably, more intimate than *The Dark Side of the Moon* and the most humanistic in the Floyd catalog.

≡

A crash was inevitable while fighting a Hippie Hangover. A rebuilding process was slow in evolving as we escaped into willful numbness, warbling through life in search of fantasy. Floyd reflected some of this dark-light dynamic in their mood and in their moody expansive music.

"You had mentioned the malaise of the 1970s and some of the images of my mind of Cleveland and New York City in the 1970s," says Eric Sosinski of the Cleveland-based band Wish You Were Here. "I've been on a Sex Pistols kick lately and you see the partying going on with Studio 54 and on the backside of that, here's all the garbage heaps and the underbelly of New York in the 1970s—at least that was the view of it at the time."

We were living a paradox and existed in a kind of No Man's Land: we could no longer look to the past for guidance, but weren't sure what the future held, either. It's no wonder that the music fans in the United Kingdom and even in the United States took to the thrashing and wailing of punk, or New Wave, and the sweaty, hedonistic four-on-the-floor beats of disco in the latter half of the 1970s.

We needed our escape; we needed some reassurance as a culture, as a society. We needed to start feeling good again, even if this meant indulging our senses in wanton excess and deluding ourselves.

Disco, or what would be later identified as the disco *sound*, began seeing success in the charts as early as 1972. By the mid-1970s, artists such as Donna Summer, Gloria Gaynor, KC and the Sunshine Band, and European record producers not only paved the path for the crossover sensation *Saturday Night Fever* but were the foundations of a cultural movement.

New discos were opening on a weekly basis in New York City and around the United States, and a growing dance/DJ culture in the United Kingdom developed. The records spun in discos were what the kids wanted to dance to and likely buy, circumventing any record company's standard radio promotion strategy.

The improvisational nature of underground music and the feedback loop it created among the band and the crowds were similar to the relationship nightclub DJs and nightclub goers had. The master of ceremonies—the record spinner—"read the room" to keep nonstop energy in a club.

Disco or nightclub-based dance music hypnotized us with flashing lights, choreographed dance steps, chemical stimulants, and the possibility of physical interaction with a dancing partner—on and off the dance floor. Both the rock audiences and their clubbing cousins possessed the urge to transcend so-called musical, cultural, and social boundaries.

"A transition was made from [the] psychedelic era into the 1970s and loft parties and dance music," says former NY/LA DJ and current radio news reporter Jeff Baugh. "Number one, mobile DJs started in London. That's how I got hip to it. Late '60s and early '70s, the lighting was all the gel and lava lamps, and that's what you had in clubs. That faded away as the sound and lighting systems in clubs got better. I remember people dancing for hours, on end, without stopping, you know? [laughs] . . . People would go into these clubs and lose themselves for a good three or four hours. You would open at eleven and play till dawn. It was an almost trance experience."

"Drugs were all over the place," Baugh continues. "It sounds hokey, but there were also those who were high on the scene and the music and the atmosphere."

If disco seduced us by appealing to our pagan instincts, then punk, or the New Wave, as it was initially dubbed, was a slap in the face, desperately attempting to wake us from our complacency.

Amid mining disasters, strikes, and terrorist bombings, we witnessed populism in the British mainstream culture—an underclass raging against The Machine, refusing to accept economic disenfranchisement.

It was in 1975 that Sex Pistols' future singer John Lydon, a.k.a. Johnny Rotten, wore his now-famous tattered Pink Floyd T-shirt held together with safety pins. He'd scribbled the words "I Hate" across the words "Pink Floyd" in an act of schoolboy defiance.

Sex Pistols band manager Malcolm McLaren was immediately impressed by the youth, despite Lydon's future band members being skeptical of the aspiring singer's stamina.

The Pistols trolled an industry, a TV commentator, a Queen, and a nation. They seemed to exist for the sole purpose of surging against so-called dinosaur acts, who appeared to have a corner market on rock music. At first, anyway, punks were equated with disrupting the industry, holding anti-establishment perspectives, and purging rock of moldy stock. The DIY ethic, which shunned formal training and technical ability, slowly democratized the business. Owning expensive equipment was perceived as elitist. Anyone could play in a garage rock band if he had access to a guitar.

This sentiment was going viral on both sides of the Atlantic. Debate rages as to punk's true origins, but few would argue against the notion that vibrant scenes developed in London, New York, Southern California, and even Cleveland, Ohio, supporting Sex Pistols, New York Dolls, the Clash, X, Generation X, X-Ray Spex, Black Flag, the Damned, Ramones, Television, Suicide, Blondie, and Rocket from the Tombs.

British music paper *New Musical Express* caught one of Patti Smith's shows at CBGB in Lower Manhattan in April 1975 and marveled at how the punk poetess's slight and effortless movements onstage were more powerful than the intensity level most rock bands on the scene could muster. Smith's *Horses* appeared in the fall of 1975 on Clive Davis's new Arista label. In 1974, Smith released as a single the sexually charged version of "Hey Joe," dedicated to Patty Hearst.

Onetime Pink Floyd producer Joe Boyd drew a passing comparison between the punks of the 1970s and the so-called hippies of the 1960s underground British music scene in his book *White Bicycles*, calling the former the "spiritual (and perhaps literal) progeny" of the social and political protestors, who took to the streets a decade earlier.

"Punk hated hippies and psychedelia," Boyd tells me now, "and I had little use for most of punk, aside from Johnny Rotten. But both were certainly anti-establishment."

Floyd, too, was at one time. Contrary to conventional wisdom, most if not all of Floyd didn't register the new sounds of the underground as being a threat. "I did like the Sex Pistols, I confess," Gilmour told the *Chicago Tribune* in 1978. "I think Johnny Rotten has definitely got something." Said Wright, "You can't be underground when you sell out every concert hall and your album goes to Number One."

Other industry big wheels believed this as well. Virgin Records once supported acts that were progressive, innovative, idiosyncratic, and experimental, such as Clearlight, Mike Oldfield, Henry Cow, Robert Wyatt, and Hatfield and the North.

"They signed *Tubular Bells* [Mike Oldfield], and do you think they knew it would successful when they signed it?" says Martyn Ware, producer, founder of Illustrious, as well as co-founder of Heaven 17 and Human League.

> They signed it, because they liked it. At the same time they had bands like Henry Cow, Hatfield and the North, and obscure artists like Ivor Cutler. They signed them because they thought the public would like them, but they didn't expect them to

be massively successful. *Tubular Bells* comes along and they have all this money flooding in and they have to spend that money, otherwise they have to pay taxes on it, and they wind up signing a band like us [Human League] and Culture Club and the Skids etc. etc. That was it, in a nutshell, how that post-punk New Wave boom happened in Britain.

But as the punk movement gained momentum, Richard Branson's mail order-turned-record label welcomed the New Wave and soon began making business decisions that would impact countless careers.

From a purely business standpoint, punk could be produced at cheaper rate than experimental rock and take a fraction of the time relative to progressive rock albums. These are generalizations, of course, but the idea of a golden return on investment and a wave of political and social change forced shifts in popular tastes, which helped to shift the business direction of the companies who were claiming and distributing this music.

Clearlight's Cyrille Verdeaux says:

For the reggae, I could understand, but to be honest, the punks at Virgin? I was not happy about it. After Gong, Tangerine Dream, Klaus Schulze, Robert Wyatt, etc., how could it end with punk's music? I should say that I only stayed two years at Virgin, '74 and '75, doing two albums, but after that, my pregnant wife delivered my son and she didn't want to live in UK. Branson ended my contract, because he wanted me to stay in London and you don't say "No" to Richard without consequences. But my group and myself had a real good time at the Virgin's Manor for two weeks . . . I wish it could have lasted a lot longer with Virgin, but the birth of my son stopped my promising English music career. I must add that my son died of an accident five years later. After this absolute drama, I went to India and California, started yoga, meditation, and forgot about progressive rock to try new age music.

Even Floyd's label, EMI, was swayed by the punk revolution. EMI and, more specifically, Harvest had a reputation for promoting cutting-edge or progressive artists. It gradually caught wind of what was happening in the British music underground.

"We had a lot of friends in the media at shows like *OGWT* [*The Old Grey Whistle Test*] and magazines such as *Sounds*," says Watson.

John Ingam at *Sounds* was, I believe, the first person to give us a "heads up" on punk . . . and [having] hung out at the 100 Club, witnessed and believed in the trend.

As you know the *Sex Pistols* were signed to EMI at a very early stage, but proved to be too controversial for the company so, I guess, the directors saw the act as a threat following the Grundy incident, not to music but to the company image. Harvest was not a label to follow trends. We tried to set them. When the Damned approached us on *Phantasmagoria*, we saw huge potential and the record was, I believe, the group's bestseller. Looking back this act, next to the Pistols and the Clash, were very close to a breakthrough at the time so to the company did recognize a definite source of potential new revenue.

Imagine attempting to create in this chaos. As if batting down the hatches and preparing for a storm, Floyd returned to their home base, EMI Studios, Abbey Road, in early 1975, where they were piecing together ideas for new songs.

The huge success of *The Dark Side of the Moon* brought fame, fortune, FM airplay, throngs of fans, and global tours. This whirlwind experience was like no other in the band's history. Yet, this exhilarating period did little to energize the quartet and, in retrospect, may have been the beginning of their undoing.

Recording engineer Brian Humphries said that the band's dry spell was really due, in part, to Floyd riding the wave of success from the popularity of *The Dark Side of the Moon*. They were apprehensive about the reception of their follow-up studio album, so they were taking their time to get things precise.

Truth be told, the band was running on fumes prior to *The Dark Side of the Moon*, despite the record's commercial success. Returning to EMI was less of a moment of triumph and catharsis than a gesture in sheer habit. Floyd were conquering heroes to the outside world but were slowly losing the plot privately inside the confines of Abbey Road.

The members of Floyd were going in four different directions. Complicating matters, Mason and Waters were having difficulties in their marriage, further putting a strain on their lives and alienating them from other members of the band.

Wright admitted that he and Gilmour wanted Floyd to play more live gigs, but Mason and Waters were complacent to keep live shows at a premium. Keeping dates to limited runs "saved [Floyd] from going mad," Wright admitted.

The plan was for the band to take two three-week tours in the United States with a long break—two months—from the road in between. Wright seemed genuinely concerned that the band was not playing onstage enough and that this could be remedied by the band members spending half the year with Floyd and the other portion undertaking whatever endeavor they so chose—even playing with other bands. "I think we might be reaching that stage now," Wright said. "Every one of us wants to do other things but at the moment we don't have the time."

Well, that was the official cover story. It's closer to the truth to say that Floyd had plenty of time, but not the motivation, to do anything that was not sanctioned by Floyd Inc. Hunkering down together was a way of insulating themselves from the outside world.

Floyd had been faced with insurmountable odds—the critics gunned for them, rock-stardom fatigue was setting in, and creative entropy was nothing short of paralyzing. Furthermore, in what seemed like a potential disaster, Alan Parsons had not signed on for the new Floyd record.

Parsons performed the sound engineering duties for the band's *DSOTM* tour, and it was believed Floyd would be working with him again, but the rising-star producer had other plans. Although he was asked to help design the audio setup for Pink Floyd's Britannia Row studio, Parsons was busy producing John Cage, Al Stewart, Ambrosia, and Dutch prog rockers Kayak, among others, and churning out albums and hits by Pilot, Cockney Rebel, and Steve Harley.

More significantly, Parsons had established a clandestine organization, the Alan Parsons Project, with songwriter and then manager Eric Woolfson, who held honest discussions with Parsons to assess his career direction.

"The irony for him was that I was a pretty unknown session man or producer and I was probably doing better than him in terms of making a living," Woolfson told me prior to his untimely death in 2009. "He was on the staff of Abbey Road. People used him, but they didn't pay anything for his services. He found it very hard to get a reasonable deal, so he asked me to become his manager."

Woolfson counseled Parsons to resist the temptation to work for big-name artists. "The first week I was working with him, I had turned down both Paul McCartney and Pink Floyd," Woolfson said. "I said, 'Alan, you're better off with someone off the street. You've already done *The Dark Side of the Moon*. How much more can they do for you?'" With Woolfson's relative anonymity as a songwriter and producer and Parsons's behind-the-glass talents, the APP studio beast could potentially metamorphose into whatever musical setting the two protagonists wanted. APP's plan was to tap a pool of band and session talent to realize their collective visions.

For a time, at least, APP was kept largely undercover. Not even Floyd was entirely sure of what Parsons was up to. The Project was, in fact, gearing up for their debut record, 1976's *Edgar Allan Poe: Tales of Mystery and Imagination*, full of pop hooks and majestic art-rock orchestral washes and released by 20th Century Records in Europe and North America and Charisma in the United Kingdom.

Recording took place at Abbey Road beginning in July 1975 and continued periodically through the early part of 1976. Woolfson once told the author that he left the track names vague or misidentified on the tape boxes, camouflaging APP's true intent and helping to ensure that other musicians wouldn't get wind of the grand concept of the record.

"I remember being petrified that Pink Floyd would get hold of the idea," Woolfson told me. "We called everything by fake song titles."

Nearly a year later "(The System of) Doctor Tarr and Professor Fether" entered the charts and became a Top 40 hit, spending two weeks there, and Parsons didn't look back. The Project eventually signed with Clive Davis of Arista and were intimate with the US charts for a solid decade, with songs such as "I Wouldn't Want to Be Like You," "Time," "Games People Play," "Eye in the Sky," and "Don't Answer Me."

"I remember Clive Davis said to us, 'I've got a friend Neil Diamond, and every day he wakes up he wants to be Beethoven. But then he realizes he's Neil Diamond,'" Woolfson told me about signing with Davis's Arista Records for 1977's *I Robot*. "'But you guys could be anything you want to be. You're anonymous.'"

Ironically, Floyd had been accused of being the very same thing: faceless. In the past, they may have relished this aspect of the public persona they had constructed, but now, in mid-1975, being anonymous was synonymous with the reality of being truly absent, of lacking face time with other members of the band, which was impacting the direction of their careers. Cracks in the façade were apparent.

"Punctuality became an issue," Mason was quoted as saying in *Guitar World* in 2012. "If two of us were on time and the others were late, we were quite capable of working ourselves up into a righteous fury. The following day the roles could easily be reversed. None of us were free from blame."

Squash games were a favorite diversion, as was planning social commitments and competing in air-rifle darts matches. Putting it mildly: music was not a priority. There were entire days in the studio, Brian Humphries recalled, when the band did little more than horse around, flop, and drink.

Wright told *Melody Maker* that the band "sat around" and discussed why they were still a band. "We got into a bad period when we didn't do anything at all creatively," he said.

$$\equiv$$

The studio album that would become *Wish You Were Here* was essentially recorded in two spurts—from the middle of January 1975 through the middle of March, and then from May through most of the summer—to complete recording, overdubs, and mixing. Getting there was not unlike an Olympic adventure.

Floyd began recording on January 6, 1975, and worked through January 9. They continued recording in February at Abbey Road and again on March 3. Sessions would begin at 2:30 p.m. and would end mostly when the band knocked off for the day, whenever that was.

Acoustic guitar, synthesizers, bass (which was a direct injection input, not altogether different from how Waters had done it in the past), and, of course, Mason's drum tracks.

At Abbey Road Studio Three, a twenty-four-track Studer A80 had just been installed, the same one, presumably, that recorded *Household Objects*. EMI custom modified the Neve desk in the studio, but few in the place were familiar with the ins and outs of the machine. This would come back to haunt the band and the engineer, as few were properly equipped to debug the unit.

From January through the end of March, Floyd worked some four days a week to make progress on the new album. But for the "first six weeks" the band was in the studio, Waters said it was as though Floyd were wading through quicksand.

Some of the biggest obstacles to our heroes' success were lethargy, timidity, and low-level enthusiasm, which did little more than snowball into a psychological barrier that most certainly *wouldn't* have been there had *The Dark Side of the Moon* been as successful as, say, *Obscured by Clouds*. Claiming the success of *Dark Side* was the rock music equivalent of the real-life lottery nightmare. The minute you think you've got it made, it all falls apart.

Waters, for one, was not the type to watch his band's project drift away. It was time for action, for getting the band to snap out of it. It was high time the band gazed upon its own reflection in the mirror.

A meeting was called wherein members of Floyd talked about their lives, what was happening to their group recording, their concerns, and what transpired in the last year or so. Waters was studious, writing down all he'd heard in the conversations and monologues, and he formed ideas about what he could write about.

One dilemma was the organization of the material. Floyd actually had quality songs, and a fair amount of them. In 1974, Floyd had jammed on a few ideas that would form the basis of "Shine On You Crazy Diamond," "Raving and Drooling," and "You Gotta Be Crazy."

Gilmour liked "You Gotta Be Crazy" and "Raving and Drooling" and wanted them to appear as soon as possible on a band record. Waters had been listening to the band's conversations, its collective frustrations, its candor, and even its internal arguments, acutely aware of his own personal issues. Waters even speculated that the kibitzing and backbiting would make for great releases some day. It was in these thoughts that he began to formulate an overarching concept for the record.

Then an epiphany: the only way Waters could say anything meaningful was to structure the new material around the band's current predicament (i.e. how they were operating and feeling at the moment).

Waters envisioned the new record as an opportunity to make broad, sweeping statements about the toll of the business, touring, and the creative process. Floyd were exhausted, drained, and creatively depleted. In short, the band was just . . . not . . . there. The treadmill effect of having to continually kick out new material, bigger and better than their last, is of course the curse of success.

This also meant anything not associated with the theme was to be chucked, and "Shine On You Crazy Diamond" was getting an overhaul. It was to be split into two major segments: Parts I through V were assigned to the album's opening track while movements VI through IX closed the record, bookending the work and making it seem more coherent and thematic.

Gilmour objected, however, wanting to make "Shine On . . ." one monolithic track occupying what was the entirety of Side 1 of the original vinyl LP, similar to how the band handled "Echoes" on *Meddle*. Mason and Wright agreed with Waters that the two songs that did not fit should be ditched in favor of an overarching concept.

Since the general musical direction of the band's albums was largely shaped, at least in the mid-1970s, by democratic vote, Gilmour was outnumbered. Besides, symbolically, breaking "Shine On..." in half, in retrospect, represented Syd's life up to 1967 and his post-Floyd life.

"Shine On . . ." was recorded in the first six weeks of sessions and tracked in three separate chunks. Although the band had the concept squared away, from the early goings, there were mishaps.

Firstly, the initial two divisional pieces were not edited together smoothly. When Humphries attempted to fuse two parts of "Shine On . . ." together, the tempos didn't match. The first part had to be rerecorded. It seemed monitor echo was applied to guitar, keyboards, and tom tracks, making them unusable. Wright hated the echo on his keyboards and wanted it gone. Recording engineer Humphries couldn't accommodate because the echo did not originate with the desk but with the recording machine.

"[W]hen we played it back we found that someone had switched the echo returns from the monitors to tracks one and two," Gilmour was quoted in Miles's *Pink Floyd: A Visual Documentary*. Mason, in *Inside Out*, makes similar statements about echo being applied to backing tracks for the song.

There was no way to get rid of it, short of rerecording it. Once Humphries said he was at a loss, that he could not remove the echo, he thought his goose had been cooked. Working through the finer points of the new twenty-four-track console surely meant that Humphries would get the heave-ho.

Humphries slinked out of the studio for the weekend, fully expecting to get a phone call saying, "Don't bother coming in on Monday." Surprisingly, that call never came. As luck would have it, the band wanted to redo the first of the "Shine On . . ." sections anyway, feeling they could improve upon it—and Humphries, if his job was ever in jeopardy, lived to EQ another day.

"Shine On . . ." went through further permutations. Even after laying down backing tracks for the song over several days, some reports said weeks, Floyd didn't like the result. The band was exhausted from working on the track day and night. Then, as if by magic, the band decided to cut the bullshit and do their level best—in one day—to cut the song. In all, the song was supposedly recorded three separate times.

This story is not totally out of character for the band. Floyd were notorious for recording a track, playing it back, feeling OK about it, going home, returning to the next day, changing their minds, and rerecording it. "They'll keep on recording a track, scrapping it and doing it again," tour manager Mick Kluczynski told Floyd biographer Rick Sanders. "They flog themselves. They will spend four days, eight hours a day, on a new song."

All well and good, but Waters was not entirely happy with the length of the song. After all, *Dark Side* is the epitome of directness and economy. *WYWH* harkened back to a time of excess.

The "drawn out nature of the overture bits," Waters said in a Capital Radio interview from 1977, deeply disconcerted him. His instinct was to edit the instrumental sections of "Shine On. . . ," for instance, and get to the meat of the vocals more quickly. He also acknowledged that working in reverse—writing lyrics first and then the music—may have been a mistake.

While Floyd was busy making these important decisions, the wolves were at the door. Eager to report anything about Floyd, who had gone dark for two years, *Record World*, in its March 1, 1975, issue, claimed the band's new studio record would be released in April, with the working title *You Gotta Be Crazy*. Wishful thinking, of course, and they weren't alone. The *Montreal Gazette*, in late 1974, speculated that the new Floyd record would surface in March. The truth was that the band was still slogging through material in Abbey Road, and it wouldn't be until nearly the first official day of fall before the record would see its release.

≡

Waters thought he was going mad; he began to feel his mind slipping. Having sat down with his bandmates to eat in EMI's canteen during a break from the intense *WYWH* sessions, he suddenly felt out of sorts and not himself. The world around him had changed—or perhaps he had. Without excusing himself, he got up from the dinner table, clutched the walls of the building, making what was nearly an impossible climb up the stairs, and gravitated toward Studio Three.

Waters walked into the recording studio where a piano awaited him. He slinked down in front of it and hunted and pecked a few bars. Gradually, as the tones pierced his ears, the disorienting fog lifted. "This is what having a nervous breakdown must look like," Waters told Gerald Scarfe.

To this day, Waters is uncertain what caused this episode, aside from the notion that maybe he was going slightly crazy. Some reports put this incident earlier in the 1970s, during one of the various recording sessions for *Dark Side*, but Waters recounted the story to Scarfe for his book on the making of *The Wall*.

Waters's mid-1970s waking terror may have been the first steps in a process mental health professionals know as a psychotic break. Perhaps in clinical psychological terms, what Waters momentarily experienced might be called a mild dissociative episode, which may have manifested itself due to the appearance of some kind of stressor in Waters's life.

Add to this the fact that Waters was an avid reader of the *Guardian* and became convinced that the world itself had gone mad. For Waters, the protest generation was once all-powerful but absent a message—all while the crazy, crazy world spun in its elliptical orbit around the sun.

The Mayo Clinic identified symptoms of the abovementioned disorder—two being "[a] sense of being detached from yourself and your emotions" and "[a] perception of the people and things around you as distorted and unreal"—which could explain this category of "depersonalization" and "de-realization."

According to the Mayo Clinic, one of the complications of this at-risk behavior includes "major difficulties in personal relationships and at work," which was likely the case for a stressed-out Waters, who was then in the final death rolls of his unsalvageable marriage to soon-to-be ex-wife Judy.

Extreme cases of this condition include identity disorder—the classic multiple or "split" personality. Although some would associate this type of condition with combat fatigue or PTSD, we might be surprised to learn how many civilians have dealt with such a break, even if only on a momentary or hourly basis. It's all in how we receive and react to life's events that make the difference between a sense of connectedness and a fugue state.

Ron Geesin composed the piece "To Roger Waters, Wherever You Are," which appears on Geesin's 1973 album, *As He Stands*, and I posited that the title was a way of implying that Roger's personality could be a bit schizophrenic. "I think you're pushing the issue with your suggestion," Geesin says. "The title is because we were close friends in 1970, but had moved apart by 1973, in some ways regrettably in my view then."

If the story is to be believed then Roger, on some level, quite incredibly sought a quick remedy through music and was able to pull himself away from the edge before tumbling over a potentially psychologically damaging cliff.

It's no wonder Waters made the connection between his current decrepit mental state and Syd Barrett's alleged psychical deterioration, a circumstance that served to partly inspire the mega-successful *The Dark Side of the Moon* and the album they were now working on, *WYWH*.

Brain fog or not, for a band that appeared to be running out the clock, eating the meter with no real purpose, suddenly they were working efficiently: the basic tracks for major chunks of "Shine On . . ." were cut and virtually done—from the guitar solo through to Dick Parry's sax solo and beyond. A mega-track stitched together.

The band had been working on another track, penned by Waters, called "Have a Cigar," the most lovable snarky hate letter to an industry likely ever recorded. They'd also played it on the road in April 1975 during their North American tour.

Roy Harper was on the road in the United Kingdom from late May through mid-June, backed by his band Trigger. It's unclear if the band had invited Harper to sing prior to Floyd's North American tour or after.

Floyd returned to North America for the month of June and played Knebworth in England in early July. It's likely, but not certain, that the band had recorded its vocal version within the March or April time frame, went on tour, returned to Abbey Road in May, made changes, added overdubs, and had Harper sing for them.

Unlike most British and American bands of the era, Floyd decided to tour the States and Canada *prior* to the release of their record. In retrospect, seeing the band's itinerary, perhaps they themselves believed the news reported by *Record World* regarding the album's release date. This could be one reason why the tour was scheduled so far in advance of the eventual release date for the record: Floyd assumed they'd be done with it by then. It could also mean that Waters's brainchild—constructing *WYWH* as a concept record—was hatched as late as March.

Floyd were finally hitting their stride, but this fragmented creation, typical of the Floyd recording process, may not have been the healthiest choice for recording the follow-up to *Dark Side*. Wright, in particular, became disillusioned, and even recording engineer Humphries was unsure where it was all going next.

MYSTERIES AND MANDALAS

There was little that could be done about it, though. Tour plans had been made. The band was expected overseas in April, beginning in Vancouver, for a swing through the Pacific

Northwest (Seattle and San Francisco area), then onto the mountain regions of Colorado and desert of Arizona. Floyd would swoop down to Southern California and then fly out to the Southeast, Mid-Atlantic, Northeast, Midwest, and lastly Hamilton, Ontario, Canada.

By mid-April, *Dark Side* had reentered the charts at No. 179. Over the course of two weeks, the album picked up some serious steam and jumped *up* the charts—to the tune of nearly a hundred or so positions, to rank among the Top 100 albums, edging out Kansas's *Song for America*.

CBS/Columbia, a record label to which Floyd had recently signed for its American distribution, ran radio spots hyping the shows in major metropolitan areas in the States. While print ads were the norm and the tried-and-true marketing path, Columbia went a different route altogether and engaged the audience via the airwaves and promised to simulcast their performances live. Unorthodox, yes, but no one could quibble with the results: tickets flew out the door—and the band's record for the label had yet to be released.

This Floyd tour aligned all the trappings of the previous *Dark Side* jaunts—and then some. For their live spectacle, Floyd relied on special effects man Derek Meddings, who'd just finished work on the James Bond film *The Man with the Golden Gun*, starring Roger Moore and Christopher Lee. Meddings, another creative wonder fostered by the art school culture that flourished in Britain post-WWII, was a graduate of the Hammer Films' school of matte-design atmospherics and brought brilliant, reliable pyrotechnic effects to the Floyd shows on a nightly basis.

Snippets of *Crystal Voyager* and Ian Emes's animation for "Speak to Me," "On the Run," and "Time" had already been incorporated into their live shows to accompany *The Dark Side of the Moon* song cycle. Emes experimented with synching animation captured on Super 8mm film with Floyd's music years before he was asked to collaborate with the band. His work was broadcast on *The Old Grey Whistle Test*, seen by Wright, who clued in O'Rourke and told Emes that the band requested a screening of his work.

Emes rented a movie theatre, invited the band for a private screening, and Floyd watched *French Windows*, a short movie synchronized to an edited version of "One of These Days" from *Meddle*. Although Gilmour noted the shortened length of the song, O'Rourke informed the young artist, then all of twenty-three years old, that the band was fond of the flying clocks in his film. When Floyd began using the now-iconic forty-foot circular film screen for their 1974 and 1975 tour dates, supported by heavy-duty steel trussing, Emes's imagery was projected onto the screen by Peter Revell during live performances of "Time."

Emes wasn't the only visual designer for the band's mid-1970s tours. Floyd used a variety of images, including people walking the streets of London during rush hour, South African miners, politicians singing along to "Brain Damage," an actual eclipse, flowing lava, ER doctors brandishing butcher knives, the image of Earth from outer space, Castro, Nixon, and a jet airliner in flight ("On the Run").

Director and friend Peter Medak shot new footage for "Money" and "On the Run," working with Floyd at Elstree in the autumn of 1974. Medak had directed *The Ruling Class* and the TV movie *The Third Girl from the Left* with the alluring Kim Novak, and he would go on to direct the cult horror classic *The Changeling* with George C. Scott as well as episodes of a slew of popular TV shows from the 1980s through the 2000s, including *Breaking Bad* in 2009. He may have been connected with an abandoned Syd Barrett/Pink Floyd biopic, stories about which have floated around the film industry for years.

Prior to collaborating with Floyd, Medak directed Peter Sellers and Spike Mulligan in the seventeenth-century pirate farce *Ghost in the Noonday Sun*. Rumor had it that Sellers was hot to make *Ghost*, but when shooting began, his enthusiasm waned and he became difficult on set. Medak shot a behind-the-scenes documentary about the making of this cinematic debacle, titled *The Ghost of Peter Sellers*.

The cinematic aspects of the show were handled under the supervision of Medak, yes, but respected industry vet Ray Lovejoy, who'd worked with Stanley Kubrick, most notably on *2001: A Space Odyssey*, was Medak's trusty editor. Tim Hampton produced.

The band was also impressed by Gerald Scarfe's animation for *The Long Drawn-Out Trip: Sketches from Los Angeles*, a seventeen-minute animated short that was broadcast on the BBC two years after it was completed.

It was Mason, a bit of an amateur illustrator himself, who was impressed with Scarfe's work. Mason told Waters about Scarfe, and with a little investigation, Roger concluded that the man was "obviously fucking mad." The Floyd *had* to enlist him and set up a meet at Mason's home in Camden Town.

Scarfe's fluid images can be classed somewhere between cubism, biomorphism, and abstract art. It's impossible to guess into what a figure will next be transformed, once the sequence of evolutionary steps is undertaken.

The band thought this style perfect to accompany their music. Scarfe began creating animation for "Welcome to the Machine," but as far as I am aware, the song was played live for the first time in 1977 on the North American tour to support *Animals*. Scarfe no doubt related to the message in "Welcome to the Machine," even if on some abstract basis. Scarfe liked to take the piss out of authority, which was right in line with Roger's sense of humor.

Mason slowly receded to the background as Waters became the point man for Scarfe and his fantastical visions. Scarfe and Waters would forge a lasting friendship and creative partnership grounded by a mutual cutting wit. It was a trait that no doubt helped to diffuse any potential arguments. Much like Waters, and so many others in the Floyd universe, Scarfe was fatherless in his youth—at least for a time. His dad went off to WWII, as Roger's did. Scarfe was brought up in wartime Britain and remembers the air raids, an intense fear of which is portrayed in "Goodbye Blue Sky" from *The Wall*, later animated brilliantly by the illustrator for the 1982 Alan Parker film.

For Floyd's 1975 tour, Scarfe oversaw the creation of animation depicting a man defying gravity, somersaulting into the air, which, again, was used later for the movie *The Wall*. Mike Stuart did design honors. Interestingly enough, the tumbling Leaf-Man cracking the sky, as if glass, seems like a motif that is straight out of the surrealistic mind of Magritte, a Hipgnosis favorite. Another creation, the Sandman, or the disappearing man, may have been a visual reference to Syd, but also echoes Hipgnosis's eventual album packaging.

A red blood cell, or a blood clot-looking thing, mysteriously finds its way onto the business end of a large fishing hook in the animation sequence for "Shine On You Crazy Diamond." (It, too, was used for the film *The Wall*.) Dogs then materialize out of clouds; one of them rips up a blood clot or what appears to be a slab of meat. Then a larger dog eats a smaller one.

Other snippets include a faceless man ejecting a clear box encasing a naked prisoner, who appears to be spooked by a giant spider. The arachnid evolves into something resembling an octopus and finally what appears to be a red blood cell.

All of the images commissioned for the 1975 tour were projected onto Floyd's forty-foot circular upstage screen. The images and the sheer size of the screen transported us to a different world. One could say that the projection surface is as much film screen as giant mandala.

Like a window into another dimension, video content and a simple play of light and shadow on the surface of the screen often resulted in interweaving geometric designs. Given that the halls Floyd played were often intentionally kept dark during their performances, the screen was the main visual component for most of the shows; it was difficult to look away and not to be transfixed by it.

There have been hints of Indian spirituality throughout Floyd's lifespan, whether it is the guru Syd sought to follow or the back cover of *The Piper at the Gates of Dawn*, designed by Barrett, depicting a series overlapping silhouettes that could pass for a crude representation of a Hindu deity.

More specifically, the projector screen "mandala" used by the band in the 1980s and 1990s was augmented with programmed lighting fixtures running along its parameter. In addition, Floyd created a similar effect via the so-called "mirror flower"—a series of circular overlapping flaps with half a disco ball stuck in its center. When clear light was thrown onto the mirror flower, it radiated blinding beams inside a music hall, resembling a gleaming "machine." This was topped off by smoke rolling across the stage in blanketing blue lighting. In some cases the fog rolled off the stage like rapids rushing toward a waterfall.

Floyd's stage presentation was perceived as mystical, by some fans. Critical reports of the shows, from Los Angeles to San Francisco and from Detroit to New York, however, never fail to criticize the band's use of props at the music's expense. In some cases, ironically, the large-as-life production provided a diversion for the reviewers, who were none too thrilled with the music anyway.

The April 15, 1975, review of the band's show at the Cow Palace, for instance, which ran in the *San Francisco Chronicle*, dubbed the band's visuals little more than "theatrical diversions in a show that never escaped its own tedium." The show lacked "intellectual continuity" and "conceptual integrity." Even Floyd's lighting designer wasn't immune from criticism, as it was believed that as the music ramped up in intensity, "the lighting flashed through its spectrum of colors, calling more attention to itself than its intended subject."

Floyd both procured and ambled into its faceless public image. Legend has it that, in a ruse to beat gridlocked traffic, the band walked unmolested back to its hotel room after performing at Three Rivers Stadium in Pittsburgh, Pennsylvania, in 1975. "And not a single person recognized any of us," Waters told the *Washington Post* in 1993.

"Pink Floyd was never an image band," says Eric "Eroc" Sosinski, bassist and co-founder of the long-running Floyd tribute band Wish You Were Here, which introduced a flying pig and large circular projection screen into its act years ago. "It was more about the multimedia presentation."

"I didn't get a sense of the band at all," says former King Crimson Warr guitarist and Chapman Stick player Trey Gunn. "I didn't know who they were or jump on board until *The Dark Side of the Moon*. I was twelve years old. For me, they were almost personality-less. I didn't know who played what. It was just the atmosphere."

"Floyd were wise enough not to use themselves as the model," says Joshua White, principal of the Joshua Light Show, which took up residence at the Fillmore East in New York City during the late 1960s. "They avoided all the posturing that was such an unpleasant part of that era."

Combine mind-altering drugs and expansive music, multi-colored stage lighting, humongous theatrical props, and the expectation of emotional release, and a rock concert is nothing less than a religious experience. This could partially explain why, in regions where populations prided themselves on their Catholic faith, such as Montreal, and Quebec in general, music fans were evangelical about progressive rock, testifying to the sacred qualities of this music.

George Dennis O'Brien—author and former president emeritus at the University of Rochester and former president of Bucknell University (as well as former dean at Princeton)—once mused that rock music is "anti-educational" insomuch as audiences seek instant gratification, an idea O'Brien admits is based on those of Rudolf Otto. According to O'Brien:

> Since the African-Americans were famously put down and discriminated against, at least in a church service they could be in heaven by the kind of ecstatic scene that was typical of black gospel music. A lot of that pours into rock and eventually gets into advanced rock. Rudolf Otto, German scholar of religion, referred to the "Holy" as something, which is . . . mysterious, tremendous, and fascinating. Well, any big rock concert, particularly when it is a big production such as the Pinks would do, is something that is mysterious, tremendous, and fascinating. You are caught up in it. The rhythm catches you and so . . . it has the characteristics of a quasi-mystical experience on the one hand or sexual orgasm on the other. That is kind of a quick line of what I thought about rock music all along.

NORTH AMERICAN TOUR

Floyd's North American tour in 1975 could have been a spiritually uplifting experience, but, like so many other aspects of life during the era, it was often a steady stream of chaos, ultimately delivering moments of both escapism and sobering reality.

Electricians and stagehands, members of Canadian Union of Public Employees, picketed outside the Pacific National Exhibition coliseum and nearly derailed Floyd's first show of the tour, staged in Vancouver, Canada. Local 686 was on strike against radio station CKLG, which aired advertising promos of the upcoming event.

Promoter Jerry Lonn, president of the Seattle-based Northwest Releasing, rebuked this, saying the spots were unpaid public service announcements. "We aren't choosing sides in a Canadian dispute," Lonn told the *Vancouver Sun*. "We just want to put on a show."

A potential physical showdown and political disaster was averted at the last moment, but only after a court injunction was issued, outlawing picketing of the venue. The union lifted a ban on its members working the exhibition center. Apparently, striking was not in the public interest and could not undermine the wants and desires of nearly seventeen thousand paying ticketholders.

If critics had any say in this matter, they'd continue to stoke the fires of division, decree labor negotiations a stalemate, and postpone Floyd's show indefinitely. Don Stanley, in his review for the *Vancouver Sun* published on April 9, 1975, described the Floyd concert the night before as "fitfully pleasing, consistently dull." The effects seem to get their props, so to speak, although the plane normally released during *Dark Side* performances evidently was never launched.

Waters and Gilmour possess "undistinguished voices," Stanley wrote, relative to the support vocalists in the Blackberries. Dick Parry performed the hottest soloes of the evening but he could just as easily have been "a robot and a tape."

A bootleg from Floyd's Vancouver show on April 8, 1975, tells a slightly different story. "Raving and Drooling" builds tension via rumbling of guitar, drums and bass, and droning keyboards. "Shine On You Crazy Diamond" and "Have a Cigar" were somewhat faithfully delivered to the standards the band set in the studio. Also fascinating is how the band seems to change the complexion or even meaning of a song through simple vocal inflection. Upon listening, several times, to "You Gotta Be Crazy," you realize the title might be less like an indictment than a pep talk: what you need to succeed in a cracked world is to be crazy . . .

Despite a lack of audio clarity, the Vancouver recording I'd heard is an important document, if for no other reason than it presents a robust and energized Floyd, belying what had been written about them in the press. In addition, the music doesn't drag as much as the critic would have us believe. There's a certain amount of "noodling," yes, but that often works in the music's favor. These interludes only serve to accentuate moments of band synchronicity, such as harmonized lines played by Gilmour and Wright.

Of the recorded performances from 1975 I've heard, the band does seem to be tighter on the *Dark Side* material. This should not have come as a shock or surprise. Floyd had been working at the *Dark Side* tunes, literally, for years by the time 1975 rolled around. For their 1974–75 live dates, the band had a considerably shorter length of time to perfect prototypes of tracks that would appear on *WYWH* and *Animals*.

Seattle, on April 10, was up next. Once again, *Dark Side* material was delivered with power and even emotion, including Gilmour's extended solo in "Money" and the Blackberries' anguished and soulful cries in "The Great Gig in the Sky."

The shows may have been magic, but Seattle holds a particular sting for Waters, dating back to the late 1960s. With no money and no prospects, Floyd had been marooned in the Emerald City during their second US tour in late summer 1968. Seven years later, on yet another sweep through the States, Waters was again on an island.

Feeling homesick (perhaps even suspicious?), he places a call to the United Kingdom from the coffee capital of the country, just as trouble was brewing in his marriage to Judy Trim. As the story goes, Waters phoned home to explain the details of the tour, how things are going. He'd expected to hear his wife's voice. Instead a man answered.

The awful truth was staring Waters in the face. He and Judy had, more or less, been leading separate lives, but this may have been a deathblow to the relationship. The couple agreed to move ahead with divorce proceedings. It's not difficult to see the parallels between this story of staggering humility and the transatlantic phone call placed by Pink at the conclusion of "Young Lust" from *The Wall*.

Still, Waters wasn't alone in this sense: He, like so many other married adults in the United States and the United Kingdom, were getting divorced at a staggering rate. According to figures kept by the US Department of Health, Education, and Welfare, over one million couples untied the knot in 1975—the highest number recorded to date, up six percent from 1974. Although divorce rates in the United Kingdom fluctuated, slightly, the statistics tracked by the *Guardian* through 2012 reveal that divorces in 1975 were up from 1974 by a four-figure differential. Numbers wouldn't settle down to 1975 levels until 2008.

"By this point, the band members were older and they were trying to figure out their marriages," says Venetta Fields, member of the Blackberries, who were traveling with Floyd on the 1975 tour. "But it was all breaking off for some reason. They had their work cut out for them. . . . You reach the peak of your career and you get so selfish that you ignore your family. Sometimes the wives can endure and sometimes they can't. In that case some of them were going through that. David was not married yet. He was dating Ginger [Virginia Hasenbein]. It really is lonely at the top."

As a collective, however, Floyd was just as sharp as they'd been on the *Dark Side* tours of 1972–1974. Perhaps sharper. Waters's vocals in San Francisco on April 13 (the last of a two-night stand) were fairly strong despite Waters performing some tricky vocal acrobatics in "Raving and Drooling."

It's all the more impressive considering the stage volume and loony, cinematic Wright keyboards. Billowing sound clouds envelope the bassist and lead singer, and Waters had to overcome this. It should also be noted that in some instances during the San Francisco show, the integrity of the audio of one of the unofficial recordings is challenged. The sound, in spots, actually warbles, creating a spaced-out, psychedelic effect.

At the Cow Palace, there were some crowd disturbances just before the start of *Dark Side*. These could be a few in a long list of similar incidents that fueled Waters's disenchantment with large venues and the fans who attended Floyd shows. For the life of him, Waters could not comprehend the behavior of the intoxicated or stoned, insulting one another, calling each other names, wantonly tossing beer bottles on the ground or lobbing them at the performers onstage, and constantly yelling for people to "sit down." None of this has anything to do with the performance onstage, and the tense atmosphere often escalated toward violence.

Waters conceded that it was difficult to perform under such circumstances but said, "I felt at the same time that it was a situation that we have created ourselves, out of our own greed."

These rows recall the band's earlier days: In early 1967, at the California Ballroom in Dunstable, audience members had the bright idea of attempting to electrocute the band by throwing beer onto them. In another episode, perhaps a more famous one, at the Feathers Club in Ealing later that year, someone threw a coin at Waters's head, drawing blood. Later in the evening, the audience pummeled a patron simply for expressing his love for Floyd. Waters said, "[The mob] spent the evening beating the shit out of him, and left us alone."

These vulgar displays of disapproval were not exclusive to the crowds in the United Kingdom or Continental Europe. In 1973, at the outdoor venue Merriweather Post Pavilion in Columbia, Maryland, some of the patrons who were relegated to lawn tickets were so furious that they could not upgrade to the reserved seating area. When they were denied access, they began tossing chunks of turf at security, at least according to an eyewitness for the *Baltimore Sun*. No one was hurt.

In an article titled "Pink Floyd Rises Above Audience," the *St. Petersburg Times* covered the band's show in late June 1973 at Tampa Stadium, in Florida. The music played by Floyd was perfect, the paper gushed, but *anti-socialites* in the stands shot off fireworks and watched them sail into a cluster of concertgoers close to the stage.

It seemed as much violence was happening outside the arenas as inside them. While the band was on tour in April, a series of bizarre suicides were occurring in England, the most high profile of these, perhaps, being Lady Lucy Russell, who died in an act of self-immolation.

Even in crossing the Atlantic, Floyd couldn't escape what appeared to be a world in decline. Just after notorious English serial killer Frederick West had committed his last known crime for three years, Floyd's rock and roll caravan cut a path through the frontiers of the American wilderness, plains, and mountainous regions, likely oblivious to the violence virtually under their noses.

Floyd played Denver on April 17, two days after a (likely) victim of serial killer Ted

Bundy went missing in Nederland, Colorado, fifty-some-odd miles or so outside the Mile High City.

Floyd truckers likely took Route 80 across the Western states and headed in a northeastern direction from San Francisco, through the outskirts of Boulder, and into Denver, traveling within miles of Bundy's hunting ground. With a three-day advance, Floyd's roadies would have been tasked with striking the show that evening after the concert was finished and loading eleven tons of hardware, props, and equipment in trucks in the early morning hours of April 14.

Roadies either got some much needed rest, or headed out, at a moderate speed, for Colorado—nearly 1,300 miles and a day's drive away (with no stops), even at a fairly moderate clip. Either way, the tour bus likely pulled up no later than April 15 for setup, to prepare for the show the following evening. The point of all this? It's not out of the question to imagine Floyd's touring caravan passing through Boulder as Bundy was literally committing his horrific act.

Floyd couldn't possibly have known the hotbed of villainy they had driven into. The murder rate in America rose to unmanageable rates in the 1970s, and, perhaps for the first time in modern history, we witnessed a glorification of violent crime.

Super-psychopaths were a twisted variation on the archetypal rock star—a strange manifestation in the era of malaise. Bundy, Gacy, Son of Sam, and Manson, who faced justice at the dawn of the 1970s, transcended the bounds of criminal to become folk or cult heroes to some. They were nearly deified through mass media coverage, which fed some deep-seated psychological need for pornographic violence and sexual sadism in the public's collective consciousness.

Jack the Ripper may have fathered the modern-day serial killer phenomenon, but Charles Manson held a deeper personal connection with his devotees, especially in the years following his conviction. From prison Manson was communicating with his misguided children, such as Family member Lynette "Squeaky" Fromme, who stood in the Los Angeles Hall of Justice and read a letter that Manson penned to the DA, whch compalined about the biased coverage in the media of his trial. Charlie played the victim, but he had more destructive, divisive long-range plans.

Although he escaped the clutches of the death penalty, he was securely behind bars (and eventually died there) and had counted on Fromme and other followers to act on his orders to stage an anarchic event in the near future. At the time, either the authorities were not aware of his grand designs or did not take him seriously.

As far as I can tell, the show in Denver went off without a hitch. I could not find any coverage of the concert event in the major Colorado newspapers of the time, and have received no negative feedback about the show from future professional musicians in attendance.

One would have to say that, regardless of what was going on around them, Floyd seemed to deliver night after night. It was business as usual. "They were not rude," says Fields. "They were just serious. They weren't friendly like Humble Pie. I knew they were . . . older than the other bands I had been with, as well. They were cordial to one another. After I read the book by the drummer [Nick Mason's *Inside Out*], that's when I realized there was friction. It didn't affect me at all, though."

≡

Arizona, including Tucson and Arizona State University (ASU) in Tempe, and San Diego, California, were the band's next stops. According to Glenn Povey and Ian Russell, authors of *Pink Floyd: In the Flesh*, the Floyd show in Tempe was slated for April 15 at ASU's Activity Center but had been cancelled and rescheduled for the 20th.

There's a difference of opinion on why this show was rescheduled: One theory holds that safety and power-supply issues were the culprits—meaning the show would not be set to a volume necessary for the size of the venue. The other possible reason, at least according to the activity center manager Warren Sumners, was simply that there was not enough cable for all of Floyd's equipment.

Sumners maintains that the university fulfilled their contract with the promoter, Dan Bowley, but said that had they "known about the cable, [they] would have rented it" prior to the band loading in for the gig on Tuesday, April 15.

Moving the concert date was relatively painless, although one wonders why the band was booked in two different spots within the same state, barely a two-hour drive from one another. Ultimately this may have cut into Floyd's overall haul. Roughly a hundred ticketholders arrived at ASU's Activity Center expecting to see Floyd on the 15th. Of those hundred fans, four made the fifteen-hour drive from San Francisco to Tempe; a little more than a handful demanded their money be refunded.

A campus activities board, Associated Students of ASU, as well as an organization called Arizona Family and an unnamed financial sponsor, produced the event. You begin to see why the university needed a benevolent benefactor: Floyd was not cheap. They raked in $40,000, no questions asked, just for appearing. Ticket prices ranged from $7.50 to $8.50.

The *Arizona Daily Star* reported that the band was pulling into Tucson on April 19 with a large production show, for which the 4,800-square-foot stage alone cost $15,000. The *Daily Citizen* of Tucson noted that the ten thousand in attendance paid an average of $8.50 each for admittance into the Community Center on Saturday, April 19.

The production was so visually rich that even in the darkness of the intermission, the flower mirror or "giant circular saw," began to "twinkle and sparkle." "Green fog" swamped the stage and confetti fell from the rafters during the encore "Echoes."

There may have been some misunderstanding surrounding ticket sales for the show on the 20th, but this is unclear. Otherwise, Arizona appears to have been a highlight of the tour. The same cannot be said for Los Angeles, however.

Just as the UK authorities had cracked down on the UFO club years earlier, US law enforcement had gotten wind of the purple haze wafting out of metropolitan arenas when Floyd toured major cities. Fifty thousand tickets were purchased within hours of their availability. This was going to be a major rock music event for the area and era. The police smelled the opportunity for action.

The police deemed Floyd fans a target, and because of the event's high profile nature, seventy-five police officers were out in force for each of the five nights the band performed at Memorial Sports Arena, from Wednesday, April 23, through Sunday, April 27. More than twenty of those officers were off-duty cops employed to police the events.

Predictably, on Friday night alone, police rounded up 125 people. Prior to Saturday's show, there were almost 350 arrests in total. On Saturday night, 104 more people were charged with possession of drugs and ticket scalping. Overall, nearly 90 percent of the people were charged for possession of dope, and most of those were people under eighteen years old. One, an underage runaway from Covina, was escorted into police custody.

In total, over five hundred people were arrested at the arena during Floyd's five-night stand, with charges as far ranging as drug possession, battery—including a physical altercation with a police officer—concealing and carrying a loaded gun, and "sexual perversion."

Lieutenant John Salvino explained that the arrests made by police were not meant to harass concertgoers. Former USC quarterback and arena manager Jim Hardy did not approve of the full court press the police were executing for the spate of Pink Floyd shows at the arena and made his displeasure known to authorities. The public spat made headlines in LA, and police chief Ed Davis shouted at Hardy, "He's sort of a crybaby."

On the surface, anyway, the dispute seemed to spring from Davis and his belief that Hardy had not obtained the proper permit for a rock show, but for "café entertainment." Mr. Davis also seemed to signal that he was defending the city, on one level, from the swarming of rock 'n' roll potheads. The whole affair had the whiff of internal political gamesmanship and squabbles.

Hardy maintained that the Coliseum Commission had complied with all the city regulations necessary to produce the event. Peter Hagan, a police spokesperson, said that concertgoers were "warned that law violators would be arrested." Ticketholders for shows at the Hollywood Bowl, the Greek Theater, and the Shrine Auditorium, he reasoned, are barely aware of police presence.

Letters to the *LA Times* penned by concerned citizens, some of whom had actually attended the show and others who'd allowed their children to go, show some support for the five hundred arrested. However, this was far from unanimous. Public reaction to LAPD tactics, at least as evidenced by these letters, seemed to be mixed.

Waters, himself, in a recording I'd heard from one of the LA shows, berates the security guards just before the band leaves the stage at the time of intermission. Waters tells the crowd that, when the band returns to the stage for another set, he'd "appreciate it" if "you people in yellow shirts stop fucking wandering about in front of the stage." The crowd roars.

Waters continues: "So, just sit down somewhere and enjoy the show, if you can. Leave everybody alone; everything will be all right."

It's difficult to discern, but Waters may have viewed security and police as a fascist presence at his show—something his socialistic tendencies had instinctually repelled.

Lost in the shuffle was the music quality. On Wednesday, April 23, 1975, the first night of the stint, *LA Times* reviewer Richard Cromelin came . . . saw . . . cried. Cromelin ripped into the band, calling the show pointless. Cromelin rationalized that if the Floyd kept bringing up Syd Barrett by promoting "Shine On You Crazy Diamond," then it was fair game to state that "a few bars of any Barrett-Floyd song you'd care to name would be worth more than the hours of zombie electronics purveyed by the current outfit."

"Raving and Drooling" and "You Gotta Be Crazy" were singled out as "typically faceless and morose excursions"; Mason's drumming was "spineless," Gilmour's guitar paying was "pedestrian," and the entire band was just plain "lifeless." The group, speculated Cromelin, seemed to have as much difficulty "staying awake as this reviewer."

If this performance was any indication of what's in store for fans eagerly awaiting the release of *WYWH*, the *LA Times* surmised, Floyd should erase its new recorded material; much in the same way, the reviewer surmised, Barrett used to operate when working in the studio.

Cromelin notes that on synth, presumably during "Shine On . . . ," Wright plays a portion of "The Scarecrow." Could be. However, the studio version of "Shine On . . ." from *WYWH* features a snippet of "See Emily Play," and a live version of the song I've heard certainly features the "Emily" snippet.

Legendary bootlegger Mike Millard, revered for his high-quality audiotapes, likely recorded the April 26, 1975, show, which I'd listened to. The audio on the Millard LA show is better than some official live releases from the 1970s.

Floyd seemed to take a few minutes to tune up before actually presenting the music. Then the show, as far I can tell, opened with "Raving and Drooling," and the familiar bass riff, à la the Binson amp of "One of These Days," gallops out.

In fairness it's difficult to divorce the aura and legend surrounding the well-known future studio versions of these songs from their cruder live cousins. In other words, I fight the urge to "hear" the finished product in my head when I listen back to the recordings. A live review, of course, is just that. It needn't take into account what songs *may sound* like once they are officially released, but how well they go over on the night in question.

Having said this, there seems to be plenty of whistles, shouts, and orgiastic screams emanating from the crowd, egging Floyd on and anxiously awaiting the band's next number—"You Gotta Be Crazy." The crowd seems, at least in part, enthusiastic about hearing the new material. Yes, Wright's whining keys do grate at times, the vocals could be tweaked, but Mason is rock solid and not spineless at all.

Of "You Gotta Be Crazy," Waters said, "It was a cruel song, but fair." He then said, "The next tune we're going to do is another new number . . . 'Shine On You Crazy Diamond.'" "[Diamond]," Waters said casually, "has something to do with Syd Barrett, who some of you might remember . . . and some of you probably won't."

Not exactly a ringing endorsement of the latest band material. But this was Floyd in the spring of 1975. All in all, it was an unceremonious end to a tour that may have completely slipped off the rails.

If not for the revelation of infidelity, technical glitches, police crackdowns, ticket scalping, and bad press, the road might have been a friendlier place.

And Floyd's touring woes were not behind them. Trouble was dead ahead as the second leg of their North American tour and a stop at Knebworth festival in England, scheduled for the spring and early summer of 1975, would prove far worse . . .

MONO LAKE

While on the West Coast swing of their North American tour, the band and Storm Thorgerson discussed the visual possibilities for the cover of the upcoming Floyd album. Upon reading the lyrics to "Shine On . . . ," Storm had brainstormed with Roger over the concepts of absence and presence.

Once off the road, Storm gave the matter more thought. Along with the concept of absence, Storm was convinced that the number four was crucial to understanding the album and Floyd. Four seemed to define everything having to do with the recording, from the four words in the eventual title and four band members to the four-note Syd Sequence Gilmour played at Unit in Kings Cross. There are four classical elements—air, earth, fire, and water—and Storm wanted to visually depict them while commenting on absence. Each element might also correspond to each of the Floyds:

Earth: Nick Mason, for keeping the music grounded and giving fans something to grab hold of.

Wind: Rick Wright, for his airy keyboard sections.

Fire: Roger Waters, for his demeanor and inextinguishable enthusiasm.

Water: David Gilmour, for fluid musicianship and life-giving melodicism nourishing Floyd's art, but also providing the perfect foil for Waters's burning and perhaps all-consuming passion. The evangelical musical and lyrical fire never burns out of control thanks, in part, to Gilmour's countervailing, accessible musical ideas.

Psychologists and music historians have said that each member of the Beatles symbolizes different quadrants or aspects of a single male personality. Perhaps. But if this is the case, we could further insinuate that the four-member Floyd, circa 1975, represents a perfectly balanced band, in the classical sense.

These ideas echo through the imagery for the packaging: a business man getting "burned" in a business deal (fire); an empty suit hawking the Floyd record, foot propped up on a bestickered suitcase in the middle of the desert (earth); a red veil floating in the wind (air); and a "splashless" diver in California's Mono Lake (water). Three-dimensional frame designs on the cover (front and back), as well as on the LP's inside sleeve, reinforce the theme.

For the cover, it was agreed upon that the act of a handshake was emblematic of an empty gesture. You can "shake on it" to seal a deal, but little can keep men from straying from the pretense of honorable contracts. But how to attack this? Should the band use photographic imagery, or something else?

It's been said that Hipgnosis picked exotic locales for photographic shoots, not only for the opportunity to photograph unusual geography and scenery but for the adventure faraway lands could deliver. Powell and his crew spent a considerable amount of time in Northern California, and other regions of the Western United States, scoping out locations.

"I was there for a month, shooting," says Po. "[Floyd] knew the ideas I was looking for and I had carte blanche to spend whatever [money] was necessary to do what I wanted. I rented a private plane and flew over Lake Powell, Pyramid Lake, Lake Mead, and different lakes in Northern California. While I was flying over Mono Lake [California] I saw the [tufas] sticking out of the lake. We flew low over the lake and thought it was the most extraordinary and surreal place I'd ever seen for this kind of picture."

After his airborne excursion, Powell touched down in Reno, Nevada, and traveled to Los Angeles, where he rented a car to drive out with his crew to Mono Lake. When they arrived, the area around Mono Lake was desolate. It is, in fact, an isolated, remote location in which only several hundred people live year-round. NASA purportedly tests its Mars rover in this area to simulate the rigors of traversing rocky alien terrain.

"The lake is terminal, so it has five different streams that feed into it and none that flow out of it," says Arya Degenhardt, communications director for the Mono Lake Committee. "It's been around for somewhere in the million-year range and over that time it's accumulated a lot of salt and carbonate, so it has a very unusual chemistry. There are volcanoes and springs [that] come up from cracks in the earth. That water is full of calcium, because it runs off the Sierra. When the calcium and the carbonates in the water come together, calcium carbonate precipitates out and you get limestone rock in this funny formation. That's what those iconic tufa towers are."

Mono Lake was at the center of legal battles for years regarding water rights, occupying the line of scrimmage in the great Water Wars of California. "Starting in 1941, the Los Angeles Department of Water and Power tapped the streams that feed Mono Lake, and there's a whole interesting and intriguing story about that, if you've ever seen the movie *Chinatown* [1974]," says Degenhardt.

Field reports dating to 1978 indicate that the water level of Mono Lake, at least in the area photographed by Hipgnosis, was barely five feet deep. That was a sufficiently shallow level for the paradoxical "splashless diver" image Po snapped for the LP.

"I had a special yoga chair built [for the diver]," says Po. "The diver said, 'What I need for this lake, because it is very muddy, is a chair built that we can put onto the lake that I can basically do a yoga stand in and put my shoulders onto.' We had this special chair built for him and . . .we dropped him into position from [an] aluminum boat."

Stories vary about the diver and whether he used any breathing apparatus while submerged. "He was a yoga guy who could hold his breath for a long time underwater," says Po. "I had to look through all the stunt agencies to find the right guy. He also had to have a good body and look good and he could do incredible yoga underwater. He put the chair down into the mud and then just reversed himself up and he held his breath for about one and a half minutes, two minutes."

On the evening the *WYWH* LP sleeve photo was snapped, Po remembers the conditions being nearly perfect. "The late afternoon I flew over the lake, it was absolutely still," says Po. "Funnily enough I was there for a couple of days and it was very windy. The lake was very choppy and the evening I did the photograph, for about two hours, it suddenly stopped, absolutely stopped dead. I was in a little aluminum boat, a rowing boat, with my assistant, who was up to his waist in salty water and mud."

The ability of the yoga guy aided in creating something of an optical illusion, making us believe a diver plunged into a bottomless mountain lake. "The ripples just cleared and there is no retouching on that image at all," says Po. "It's amazing. It was a magical moment."

Po's good fortune continued through the photoshoot for the invisible businessman— the empty suit—haunting the back cover of *WYWH*. "I photographed him in the Yuma Desert, south of LA, the Yuma Sands," says Po. "I wanted to get out onto the sand dunes, and just by chance these guys came by in dune buggies and took us out there. As all good things happen by chance, I did the shoot and then they came by and picked us up, and our equipment, again and brought us back to our cars."

"The facial features and arm and leg on the desert man were bleached away and blended back with photographic dye," Richard Manning, retouching expert formerly with Hipgnosis, told me. "The technique was learned at a chemical retouching studio, Meyer Arron, that I was employed at, 1969–70, in Oxford Street, London."

"He appeared to be the invisible man," says Po, "which was for an album all about absence and insincerity in the music industry."

The image of the veil and windswept poplars is perhaps the greatest symbolic photo of the entire packaging. Sunlight, which ordinarily mitigates the chilling effects of environs depicted in photographs, actually adds to the eerie setting captured by the camera. "It's quite spooky," suggests Po. "It's Norfolk, UK, and it looked like an area of France: straight tall poplar trees that you see all over northern France."

This area is steeped in the Cambridgian psyche. In describing a close encounter with an extraterrestrial race, Waters name-checks Mildenhall, located in the Fens, in "Let There Be More Light" from *A Saucerful of Secrets*. "Because I come from Cambridge in England, which is where Pink Floyd came from, we all knew the area very well, and we just thought of one of the areas around the Fenland, where you have giant poplar trees," says Po.

Jenny Spires eloquently explained to me that the geographic location—known alternately as the Fen, the Fens, or the Fenland—is "the north of Cambridge, [which] borders on ancient marsh and bog between Cambridge and the Isle of Ely, up into

Lincolnshire." Spires continued: "In days gone by, Windmills were used to control the water levels. The light is a delicate watery yellow, at times very eerie, and many supernatural tales in folklore have been passed down . . . But if, as you say, the Floyd used the 'border' imagery of the Fen, in the '70s, they may well have used it in relation to Syd's breakdown and loss, which at the time had such a huge impact on us that none of us really understood."

The "woods," as an idea, is deeply rooted in Barrett mythology. "One day Syd Barrett got lost in the woods and never came back," wrote Julian Palacios in *Lost in the Woods: Syd Barrett and the Pink Floyd*. "Roger Barrett came back instead, leaving his invented alter ego out there somewhere. The ghost of Syd Barrett remains there, and also in his magical, mysterious songs."

If nothing else, Po's image is a visual reminder, a photographic representation, of how haunted this entire production was. Po diffuses all this heavy talk with lighthearted banter: "The thing is, have you spotted the naked girl behind the red scarf?"

Some speculated that the scarf was overlaid upon a background image to create a composite, but Powell refutes this. "I threw a scarf up in the air and it was windy and [I] shot a thousand rolls of film," Po says. "It was an awful lot of footage on a Hasselblad and I eventually got the shot. There were plenty of shots without the scarf in it. It was as simple as that. As simple as throwing a scarf in to the air. And because it was a sunny day [and] it was at a high shutter speed . . . it captured it. No trickery."

In fact, Hipgnosis applied a similar technique for the cover of Unicorn's 1976 studio album *Too Many Crooks*. The colors are unnatural, but don't let this fool you. Look closely: over a blue cornfield, you'll see a hat flying through the air, against a yellow sky.

There was indeed no trickery used for the iconic cover—an image of two businessmen clutching hands, closing a deal. This, of course, also spoke to the recording industry tirade Waters launched with "Have a Cigar." Interestingly enough, the idea of a handshake sealing a deal can be found in the lyrics of what was titled "Dogs," originally "You Gotta Be Crazy": "Like the club tie, and the firm handshake . . . You have to be trusted by the people that you lie to."

Stuntman Ronnie Rondell was actually set aflame for the shoot in Warner Bros.'s vacant Hollywood film lot. A trained staff of about twenty people, Po estimated, were on hand and were vigilant should anything go horribly awry. When it was time to start shooting, an effects man took his pyro wand, touched Rondell, now flammable, and *presto!* He was on fire.

Wind cooperated at Mono Lake, but on a purportedly empty movie lot, Powell was less than fortunate. At one point a gust of wind picked up and nearly burned Rondell's face. Rondell dropped to the ground and extinguished himself with the help of his training, the discharge of the fire extinguishers, and blankets. When Rondell recovered, he called the shoot off. No more, he pleaded. As it happened, Po had what he needed.

Stills from that day show Rondell walking off as Po kept shooting. In one frame, Rondell's leg is the only thing visible: a good representation of absence in and of itself.

Another image of a diver in a white swimming cap, attempting to part waves of sand, was not used for the original LP packaging, although it does appear in later CD reissues. Intriguingly, Hipgnosis's freelance photographer, Howard Bartrop, reports this wasn't the only image to fall by the wayside.

"It could have been for *Wish You Were Here*," Bartrop says, "for which we had a couple embracing in a room . . .We had four wind machines and about a hundred sheets of paper that we had thrown into the air and [we] just fired a flash and [waited to] see what happened. Those images I really liked but they didn't get a place. It was obviously a real image and not a montage, because of the way the paper interacted with the couple, creating shadows on them, with very strong lighting but that never really found a home. Pity, really, because I would love to have that image now."

Further surrealistic touches were added. "I cut up a piece of cardboard in an L shape and photographed the sand as it flows through [the back cover]," says Bartrop. "We did that in the studio to give it a slight 3-D effect. As far as the burned edges [on the cover image], we just burned something in the studio."

Without exception, it's the imagery for *WYWH* that most closely aligns with Hipgnosis's *raison d'être* and its connection to surrealistic artwork of the twentieth century. The link we make between surrealism and Hipgnosis is largely due to the company's work on *WYWH*. The cover of *Ummagumma* is surreal, to an extent, but the record didn't have the commercial impact *WYWH* did.

Beautiful, impossibly clean, surrealistic, and/or white-bordered album-cover imagery became a style in and of itself, one that was echoed through legendary packaging for Led Zeppelin, Yes, Bad Company, Novalis, Brand X, Peter Gabriel, and Def Leppard. This voice, this style, was solidified with the appearance of *WYWH*, and undoubtedly, it influenced younger artists, such the Mars Volta, Audioslave, Phish, and Muse.

Hipgnosis was rock music's answer to Belgian surrealist René Magritte. Indeed. Magritte's *The Lost Jockey* and its main subject, the faceless bowler hat man, bears an uncanny resemblance to the record salesman on the back cover of *WYWH*. Furthermore, Giorgio de Chirico, an influence on Magritte, constructed paintings using the artistic technique known as vanishing point to create the illusion of infinite space. The best example of this on the *WYWH* packaging is the row of trees stretching to the horizon in Po's red-veil image, printed on the original LP's inside dust cover.

Although Gilmour's ire rises when these types of romantic comparisons are made, vanishing point is a metaphor for the life of Barrett, lost in the woods. "Hipgnosis were big fans of René Magritte and Salvador Dali," explains Bartrop. "Surrealism was very much what they were after."

=

By my estimation, finalizing vocals for "Have a Cigar," featuring progressive folk rocker Roy Harper, occurred no earlier than May, before Floyd would embark on the second leg of their North American tour and before Harper went gallivanting throughout the United Kingdom.

Floyd began, as far as I know, at Abbey Road on May 5 and continued through the 9th. Throughout the month of May, actually, Floyd worked five days a week, virtually until they were set to hit the streets of North America again in June.

One listen to unofficial live recordings from Los Angeles and Seattle captured in April 1975 demonstrates that although the song is nearly fully formed—months prior to the release of the record—the guitar solo bears only a passing resemblance to its studio-version cousin. Another recording, from the Nassau Coliseum in mid-June 1975, reveals a very similar performance but contains a solo (relatively) more in line with what we hear on the record.

May was a make-or-break month. It brought constant reminders of what had alternately unnerved and comforted Floyd for the last two years. On May 3, *Dark Side* climbed up the charts again, this time to No. 63, and for the week of May 17, it had jumped to No. 41. The following week, *Meddle* reentered the chart at No. 162, and *Dark Side* moved within the Top 40 at No. 37, climbing over that *other* major conceptual rock record, the Who's *Tommy*, which had charted for nearly a year at that point.

If that weren't enough, the band needed to gear up for more recording and be mentally prepared for another tour of the States in a few weeks. If anything put the band in the mindset to properly record "Have a Cigar," it was the comings and goings of the spring of 1975. The band could not escape the Machine firing up once more or their role in it.

We know Harper is ultimately credited with singing lead vocals on the song as it was originally released on the classic album, but this was not by design. In fact, both Gilmour and Waters made a pass at the song.

Gilmour tried but wasn't feeling it, and recording Waters's vocals was an excruciatingly painstaking process. Tracking him one line at a time was the best way, Humphries and his assistants believed, to capture the best performance from Waters.

Waters, quoted in *Guitar World* in 2012, said he had to sing it "over and over again just to get it sounding reasonable."

Waters was already afflicted with the curse of the ambitious musical artists: to make the best record—perhaps the perfect record—every time he walks into the studio. For Waters, vocals were an Olympic level exercise in self-doubt. Working line by line, he undoubtedly began seeing cracks that may have been wisely ignored had he been able to belt out the tune in one go. In this case, vocals are suddenly thrust under a microscope and too thorough an examination makes one second-guess choices, even one's own talent.

Waters admitted that he did not have a traditionally pleasing voice but could hear in his head what *needed to* be done; he knew what he wanted to do with his vocals but didn't have the technique to pull it off. So there was a kind of compromise wherein both Waters and Gilmour would share lead vocals. The result? Their combined voices create an overall strained and, dare we say, ill-suited soundtrack to a song about the industry's smarmy, smooth operators.

Granted. The vocals did have a slightly agitated, punk-y quality—appropriate given the subject matter—but still, the band was not satisfied. To rectify this situation, Waters suggested they bring in an outside voice. To his surprise and dismay, the rest of the band agreed, and he begrudgingly conceded that someone else could deliver the vocal performance needed for the song.

Harper, who had been hanging around Abbey Road checking out some of the Floyd session and had been working on his own *HQ* record, was present when the band was mulling over their next step regarding the vocals for "Have a Cigar." Sensing their dissatisfaction, Harper suggested he have a go.

"I'll do it," he said, but he wanted to be paid for his time.

A deal was struck: in lieu of cash payment for his contribution to the "Have a Cigar," Harper would receive lifelong tickets to cricket matches at St. John's Wood, Lords. Harper stepped behind the microphone, assumed the role of the smarmy record executive, and sang his ass off. It was the role he had spent his lifetime preparing for.

Because he'd heard the song so often, he had committed most of it to memory. Roy banged it out.

We've become accustomed to hearing Harper sing the vocals, and it becomes difficult to properly assess the "Floyd version" of the song. Having said this, the Gilmour/Waters delivery seems rushed, almost forced. At last count, Waters still feels he should have used his own version—and it's likely why, after all these years, he decided to release the band's rendition of the song. His interpretation, he has said, is more "vulnerable" and less "cynical."

Perhaps, but Harper's "method acting" approach—much more closely aligned with storytelling than the Floyd template—gives substance to the song. Gilmour has said that Harper's version is pretty much the definitive one, and it is difficult to argue to the contrary.

Apparently there has not been any public acknowledgement that the band's rather gentlemanly debt to Harper, if we can rightly deem it as such, was paid. In short, Harper was never compensated, or so he explained in October 1990 to Mark Saxby of *The Amazing Pudding*, a Floyd and Roger Waters fanzine. One wonders if Harper and one or more of the band members shook hands on the deal . . .

SYD RETURNS

Apathy was the prevailing attitude in Britain, it seemed, during the mid-1970s. If Genesis's "Supper's Ready" and Emerson, Lake & Palmer's version of "Jerusalem" were unofficial English prog anthems for the early 1970s, then Harper penned an antinationalistic requiem of sorts, summing up the malaise with a snapshot of British contemporary life in the mid-1970s with "One of Those Days in England," from 1977's *Bullinamingvase*.

Manchester United fans riot during the World Cup after a devastating and some might say controversial loss, just as other acts of arson, violence, and destruction of property happened to and from football matches throughout 1975. "The poor performance of English cricketers and other representative teams undoubtedly added to the sense of national malaise," wrote Mark Garnett in *From Anger to Apathy.*

Garnett repeats the now-legendary story of someone seeing the phrase "Apathy is the curse of Britain" on a bathroom wall. Another individual, at a later time, scribbled underneath it, "Who cares?"

The United Kingdom entered the European Communities or Community in January 1973 but voted to ratify their initial vote via a referendum in June 1975. Conservative leader Enoch Powell, who was branded everything from hero to racist due to his oratories, was leery of Britain in Europe. He was fighting a losing battle against members of his own party, including future Prime Minister Margaret Thatcher, and a well-funded, celebrity-studded, message-coordinating media machine, which did its best to convince voters of the benefits of the EEC.

The star power of everyone from athletes to violinist Yehudi Menuhin, president of the International Music Council, may have helped contribute to the electorate voting to remain. Decades later, Britain found itself in the midst of a Chapter 2 of this story. The steps of the process appear to be painful, even frustrating, but over forty years later, the United Kingdom is on its way to a so-called Brexit . . .

Harper, by this point a kind of barometer of the national consciousness, chimed in on the subject, having recorded "Referendum (Legend)" for his 1975 record, *HQ*, while being, it appears, either cautious of the impact of economic melting pots or parodying the condescension and soft bigotry of elitists. Harper and others were curious as to how Britain's voters cast their ballots and why. It was suggested in the media that voter apathy suppressed turnout or caused some to be ill-informed on the economic and political ramifications of the issue.

On the same day, June 5, 1975, Britons were deciding to remain part of a union, Floyd had inadvertently engineered a kind of reunion. It's one of the most mysterious chapters in the annals of rock history.

As the band was mixing "Shine On You Crazy Diamond," a eulogy for Barrett, a man waltzed into Abbey Road Studio Three. The bandmembers didn't recognize him at first. Either Gilmour or Mason pointed out the portly, nearly bald fellow with shaved eyebrows. Facial recognition kicked in and Waters winced, covered his mouth, and nearly broke into tears.

The man was Syd Barrett.

"Alright, Syd?" Gilmour asked as Floyd's former leader fumbled about the studio. Members of the band have argued amongst themselves as to who actually detected that the strange chap was Syd. The end result was the same, no matter whose recall was the best: total shock.

Once a handsome, curly-haired young man, Syd had changed so dramatically and his demeanor shifted so radically that he'd been reduced to a mumbling and portly so-and-so, waddling about, stunning and saddening everyone at Abbey Road who cared to notice him. He would sit down, stand up, brush his teeth, put his toothbrush away, take it out again. He wanted to know when he could lay down his guitar parts, despite not having an instrument with him.

This stout murmuring man, clutching a plastic bag and toiletries, explained how he's been gorging himself on pork chops, claiming he was ready to hear the playback on the track, "Shine On You Crazy Diamond."

When the track was played: "Sounds a bit old," Barrett said upon hearing the song.

Reports that Barrett attended the reception of Gilmour's marriage to American model Ginger may or may not be founded. Some have placed that momentous event as having taken place over a month later, in July.

When the band wanted to hear the mix again, Syd chirped: "Why bother?" This was an interesting choice of words: supposedly this same exact phrase was uttered before the fateful decision was made *not to* pick up Syd when Floyd was travelling to a gig in the late 1960s . . .

During the research process for this book, I spoke with Blackberries singer Venetta Fields, who claims to have remembered the incident. We talked about Syd materializing on the day the band was mixing, or prepping for overdubs in the studio.

The exchange went as follows:

What can you tell me about the famous story involving Syd Barrett coming to Abbey Road during the making of WYWH?

Fields: He happened to come to the session that day. It freaked everybody out the way he looked. They almost didn't recognize him. That put another vibe into the session . . .

Did you see Syd?

Fields: Yes, I saw him. He came to the session that day, and things were quite tense. They didn't know what to do. They had not seen him in a long time and they were surprised to see him and the way he looked . . . They all were in the studio for a while, not doing any new music, because Syd was not in the musical mood at that time. He was looking for his friendship with the guys. He was there for a while and then he left . . . Then we worked on . . . "Shine On You Crazy Diamond," and the song was about him. I didn't put two and two together.

You hadn't realized that they were writing the song, more or less, about Syd . . . ?

Fields: Yeah. I didn't know about him at all . . . When he came to the session, it was the first time I saw him . . . I didn't know how amazing it was at the time. But through the years it became an amazing encounter.

Were you actually in the control room? Were you recording or listening back to the track?

Fields: I don't think we [Blackberries] had started recording. We had just gotten there. I think they were playing the track for us. We didn't hear that music before. We were not in the room while they were making the music. We were there [in Abbey Road studios] listening to the track and that's when Syd came in. He wasn't there for the session.

A picture exists of Barrett, supposedly taken at Abbey Road at this time. So there's actual "tangible" proof that this story is true. Even Gilmour had to admit that Syd dropping by was not a rare occurrence. Ron Geesin has attested to this.

This leaves us with several questions and possibilities: If any of this is true, could Syd have known that the band was working on a song that was inspired by him and decided to drop in? What are the chances that he turned up on the exact day Floyd was mixing "Shine On . . ."? Was he tipped off to the progress and substance of the songs because he was still in contact with the band?

Usually the BS meter goes off when stories describing the same event mutate as they circulate. *Cash Box* magazine, back in October 1975, even seemed to think Barrett helped "to mix the 'Shine On . . .' track." Maybe this type of shifting narrative is to be expected when dealing with the human psyche. For instance, several people who are witnesses and innocent bystanders to a car accident often describe the same incident in different ways. The shock of the unexpected may facilitate false memories.

In his book *Inside Out*, Mason, ever the pragmatist, diplomatically splits the difference and preserves a key component of the Floyd legacy. He doesn't dismiss the entirety of the scenario out of hand; he's just not sure what song Floyd was working on when Syd reappeared. He *is* confident, however, that the band was sufficiently distressed and distracted by Barrett's presence, his roaming around the studio, listening to tracks the band were working on.

What we have here, then, is truth that exists along a sliding scale of probability. It's doubtful this could be chalked up to psychological phenomena or simple faulty memory. Syd was likely there, but why and the circumstances surrounding the visit are still a mystery.

TRAGIC, "APPALLING" TOUR

The second leg of Floyd's North American tour would last through the spring and into early summer, and the band would cap off their run with a single-show appearance at the Knebworth festival in England in early July.

Subsequently, Floyd was scheduled to head back to Abbey Road for approximately three weeks to finish off *WYWH*.

The band's first stop on the tour was Atlanta, on Saturday night, June 7, followed by sold-out shows on June 9 and 10, in front of nearly thirty thousand, at the recently opened Capital Centre in Landover, Maryland.

Once again the visuals were praised but the sound and compositions, being "ponderous" and "lacking in passion," were critiqued. The *Washington Post* even called out Floyd for its "laughable clumsiness" in their attempt to move from their familiar "space rock" sound to a more philosophical one attempting to illuminate the "inner mind" in their performance of "Raving and Drooling."

In Philadelphia, at the Spectrum on Thursday, June 12, it was a similar story. Echoing Nick Kent's sentiments in the UK press (perhaps attempting to play a game of one-upmanship), *Inquirer* reporter John David Kalodner was not impressed with the mid-1970s Floyd, to say the least. "The 1975 Pink Floyd show seems to be little more than going through the motions of creating music," Kalodner wrote on June 14, a day after the band's two-night stint.

Kalodner identifies "sloopy playing, off-key vocal," and "poor transitions" between songs. He even went so far as to call "Raving and Drooling" and "You Gotta Be Crazy" "gluttonous." The review also makes a veiled indictment of the nineteen thousand fans, claiming they aren't discerning, "mistaking tricks for talent and accepting Muzak instead of music."

Kalodner, who'd go on to sign pop-prog supergroup Asia to Geffen Records in the early 1980s, had no real context at the time for the songs "Raving and Drooling" and "You Gotta Be Crazy." Considering these songs as standalone tracks, without the benefit of hearing them within the context of *Animals* (which appeared in early 1977), it might have seemed as though Floyd had gone weird and completely inaccessible.

Kalodner's stinging review accused Floyd of being a "tediously mediocre supergroup" that survives through "media 'hype'" and "reputation," mapping "plodding, lumbering pieces," such as "Raving and Drooling" and "You Gotta Be Crazy."

It is interesting, however, that when Floyd swung through Philly in late June 1977, the *Evening Bulletin* reported on the big-production trappings and the fact that songs predominately from *WYWH* "proved most impressive."

Jack Lloyd, entertainment writer for the *Inquirer*, acknowledged that Floyd virtually introduced England to the concept of "integrated light and rock shows" but pointed out that some of the gags Floyd gets away with are sometimes "cornball." The band's brand of "progressive rock" (he brackets the term in quotation marks) trades heavily on "monstrous repetition on a glorious scale." Any variation in the "hum-drum" musical set, such as an acoustic interlude, represents only half-hearted attempts at "artistic flexibility." The acoustic variations Lloyd refers to are the two sections of "Pigs on the Wing." Waters wrote those tracks as a way of commencing and ending *Animals* on a more positive note.

The irony in picking up on a folk vibe can't have been lost on Waters. The instinct that possessed John Lydon (a.k.a. Johnny Rotten) to scrawl the words "I Hate . . ." on his Pink Floyd T-shirt was likely the very same one that motivated Waters to deface the visage of '70s folk icon John Denver on his own T-shirt. A close look at Waters's shirt reveals that Denver's eyes were "burnt out" as a "bit of a joke," Water said to Scarfe for the illustrator's book, *The Making of Pink Floyd: The Wall*. "John Denver, to me, sort of epitomized everything that was lame about middle of the road, you know, lovey-dovey stuff."

While critics believed Floyd had to justify their position at the top of the rock music heap, we shouldn't lose sight of the fact that the recording industry churned out rock stars through its rigorous internal filtration system, which weeded out acts (fairly or unfairly), limiting competition for those at the upper echelon of the food chain.

Whether we're talking about Floyd or Led Zeppelin or Elton John or any artist who became an international musical phenomena in the mid-1970s, amassing sold-out show after sold-out show was accomplished when it mattered the most—against what seemed almost insurmountable odds. They broke through, with a bit of cajoling, good luck, arm twisting, palm greasing, and very hard work.

In addition, the slog of touring is rarely discussed. At a certain point artist do give of themselves, regardless of the rewards, and are expected to perform. No matter what. Fans wait, family members sacrifice, livelihoods are on the line . . .

Case in point: It was a backstage at the Spectrum where Waters was administered a shot of tranquilizer. Waters suffered from stomach cramps prior to Floyd's performance, partially inspiring the song "Comfortably Numb," which once existed under the working title "The Doctor."

A June 29, 1977, review of the show, appearing in the *Philadelphia Inquirer*, points out Floyd's light-and-sound concert motif but doesn't mention anything specific about Waters's performance either as lead vocalist or as a bassist.

The *Evening Bulletin* reported on the same show but there was no mention of Waters and his performance outside general praise for the band and its "tight interplay." It'd difficult to tell what impact the tranquilizer had on Waters. (What does this say about Floyd?)

=

Rock concerts and the number of concertgoers flooding the town of Jersey City had so worried local business owners and area residents that there was serious consideration given to banning rock shows.

Back in 1973, the city council was willing to write legislation to this effect, due to rock shows' destructive environmental footprint. The trouble was the shows at Roosevelt Stadium grossed tens of thousands of dollars for the city.

Despite the $225,000 advance Floyd reportedly received for the sold-out, 30,000-seat-capacity Roosevelt Stadium show in June 1975—a $100,000 jump in the band's asking price relative to 1973 when the band played the same venue—this was easily the low point of Floyd's tour.

The first concert event of the summer season, and part of promoter John Scher's "Garden State Music Fair," saw issues with wind at the outdoor venue, which may have cut into the band's sound, virtually blanking out the highs. Gusts rendered the "UFO"-shaped stage covering, a pyramid formation designed and created by Jonathan Parks and Mark Fisher, inoperable for safety concerns. In addition, the spitfire stopped short of the film screen before video showed it exploding.

If this was all that had gone wrong with the Roosevelt Stadium show, one would chalk it up to *Spinal Tap*-level galactic misadventure gumming up the works of the rock 'n' roll machinery. This was not the case. One man, who attempted to scale the stadium walls to gain access, died in a freak accident.

The deceased was identified as twenty-eight-year-old William F. Morgan from Yonkers, New York. Morgan and others had constructed a "human ladder," propped up via a tipped-over concrete bench. When the authorities spotted the gatecrashers, they ran to the scene. Maybe from a sense of panic, or maybe from an inability to negotiate the space, the human ladder collapsed and Morgan sustained fatal injuries to the head.

Strangely, the Jersey incident has nearly slipped away into the mists of time. Seemingly, it's an abomination most would rather forget. At the time, Jersey City mayor's aide Arthur C. Delo told the press: "I feel troubled that a human being is dead, but I also feel the city was in no way negligent."

More bad news in Jersey. Reportedly fires were set at the Roosevelt Marina, causing a danger to everyone in the area. Two of the attendees, who'd OD'd on narcotics, were hospitalized, although according to reports that number may have been magnified by an order of six. At least fourteen people—allegedly all from out of town—were arrested on Saturday night (June 14) and Sunday morning (June 15). *The Dispatch* claimed the number of those arrested was as high as eighteen, all on drug-related charges.

A sad irony in all of this is that some bureaucrats, against the concert series to begin with, believed that Alice Cooper, set to appear later in the summer schedule, would be the *real threat* to public safety. The master of madness was approved only after he assured the council that he had watered down his highly theatrical (and some said violent) act. I have not heard of many issues with the Cooper show. In fact, Cooper had not been operating at 100 percent: he'd been nursing a head injury and six cracked ribs, the result of having fallen in a freak accident nearly two weeks prior, in Vancouver.

Perhaps one of the reasons this Jersey City tragedy has slipped from collective Floydian memory is due to simple misunderstanding: Some reports have the show as being canceled. Jersey newspapers I've read all refer to the concert as having occurred on Saturday, June 14. A ticket stub I've seen also confirms this and lists a possible rain date at June 15. This could be the source of the confusion . . .

Further clouding the issue, in May 1975, a Jersey paper had previewed Floyd's show as upcoming on June 19. It may have been rescheduled, but more likely this date was a misprint. As far as I am aware, Floyd did not play on June 19—in Jersey or anywhere else. In addition, both *Variety* and the *Jersey Journal* refer to the sold-out show as occurring on Saturday June 14, 1975, at Roosevelt Stadium, Jersey City.

Whether the band was aware of the death at Roosevelt Stadium is unclear. Had they been, it undoubtedly was another nail hammered into the coffin of Waters's morbid view of live performance at the time.

Maybe Waters was right. Something had to change. If Floyd couldn't alter the behavior of their audiences to suit itself, then maybe the band needed to shift its presentation to them.

Waters began toying with the idea of erecting a wall across the stage, one built of black polystyrene, to be a physical barrier representing the festering isolation he was feeling toward his audience. Waters would bring this idea to fruition a few years later with *The Wall* tour in 1980 and 1981.

Undoubtedly, it was incidents such as the one in New Jersey and others on the 1975 and 1977 tours—even the stampede at the Who concert at Riverfront Coliseum in Cincinnati, Ohio, in December 1979—that shaped Waters's increasingly negative view of the vile nature of arena rock shows. Waters, during a 1977 Capital Radio broadcast, complained that "the last tour [1975 tour] was absolutely appalling," an off-the-cuff remark.

It was as if misfortunate, infidelity, police surveillance, and even death were shadowing Floyd in the summer of 1975. The song remained the same as the band trekked through the New York metropolitan tri-state area and launched a two-night stand on Long Island. Sixty people were arrested on drug charges in Uniondale at the Nassau Coliseum. A handful of concert attendees had overdosed on either THC (cannabis) or an opiate, and fourteen were hauled off on felony charges involving the sale of drugs, including LSD. The majority of the arrests occurred on the second night—Tuesday, June 17. At press time, a Freedom of Information Law (FOIL) request I filed with Nassau County, regarding these arrests, went unfulfilled.

In 1975, the Nassau County DA made his displeasure known, stating publicly that the police's decision to deploy thirty-five officers to the Coliseum for the two-night stand was excessive. "There has been no change in the police department's drug enforcement policy," a police spokesperson said.

The author can attest to a strong police presence at Floyd's New York area shows, dating back decades. I attended the 1988 Waters-less Floyd concert run at the Nassau Coliseum, the same string of performances in which the band recorded *Delicate Sound of Thunder*.

With the newspaper reports of arrests in the 1970s and images of frenzied fans cracking the Coliseum's large glass windows in 1980 (for *The Wall* tour) still fresh in their minds, Nassau County police were on high alert by the time Floyd rolled around again in the late 1980s.

Everywhere we looked, mounted police patrolled the perimeter of the Coliseum. At one point we were standing outside the arena before the show and cops engaged us, demanding to know what we were doing. Like something out of a bad trip, the horse's face grimaced and morphed into something quite menacing. These kinds of forceful tactics will make even the innocent feel guilty—*of something*.

You'd think that with a police crackdown critics would cut Floyd a break. The *Newsday* review of the band's show at the Nassau Coliseum on June 17, 1975, was perhaps the most brutal of all. According to the article, titled "Lost in Space," Mason and Gilmour were out of sync, actually "playing different songs"—an attempt at mocking the band with its own lyrics to "Brain Damage." Again, the crowd was chastised for confusing "skill with endurance," and the article claimed, "Just because a band plays loud and long doesn't mean they play well."

There's also a whiff of elitism in the review, which challenges Floyd's legitimacy as recording artists, because they'd succeeded in generating a "grassroots phenomenon," inspiring fans to (in part) get stoned. The reviewer was mystified that most of the crowd gave the light show a standing "O." He seemed baffled at how the crowd "were capable of standing."

Record World, in attendance for the Roosevelt Stadium and Nassau Coliseum shows, did not share the same opinion. The review identified "Shine On . . ." as concluding with the lights hitting the mirror flower, "filling the auditorium with thousands of shafts of bright light."

Ironically, of the live versions of "Shine On . . ." from the era I've heard, the Uniondale show stands out; the band seems poised and more precise than on previous evenings. Granted, Floyd's vocals could always use some tweaking during live performance, but the band got tighter as the tour wore on, and the Uniondale show is a great example of Floyd's energy. Raw, at spots, but not nearly as dreary or dull as some would have us believe.

≡

Floyd hugged the East Coast. On June 16, a night before the band's appearance at Boston Garden (now TD Garden), Mason Condon, a chief engineer for the Metropolitan District Commission (MDC), now known as the Department of Conservation and Reservation, was convicted of extortion, conspiracy, and filing fraudulent income tax returns, in a trial lasting over two weeks.

When hauled before Judge Walter J. Skinner, Condon opened a briefcase, burnished a firearm, and shot himself in the head—in front of the jury that had deliberated over his fate. Condon died in the early hours of June 18 at Massachusetts General Hospital, the very day Floyd was set to perform at the Garden.

Due to sentencing standards in federal court at the time, the *Boston Globe* theorized that Condon may not have seen much, if any, jail time for his crimes. Eerily, and as far as this author can tell, Boston Garden was under the purview of the MDC. Death had, once again, preceded Floyd. Add to this the fact that the city had been divided by racial tensions involving busing and desegregation, and a Led Zeppelin show, months earlier, was cancelled due to pre-show violence. Pardon the pun, but this powder keg of hot-button issues had the makings of a new Boston Massacre written all over it.

However, a large percentage of the fifteen thousand ticketholders were likely unaware the public suicide had an even remote connection the venue. Fans were more likely to know that *Dark Side* was back in the Top 30 Albums chart in *Billboard*. After all, Floyd had wowed a sold-out crowd in Bean Town previously, at the Music Hall in 1973, and a year earlier presented a forerunner to *The Dark Side of the Moon*, then dubbed "Eclipse," for a performance the *Globe* called "smooth" and "superb."

By 1975, Medak's films were mentioned as being a strong point of the night. The band's lack of "raw musicianship," the *Globe* reasoned, was balanced by "imagination" and "taste." Floyd played a strong if typical set: "Raving and Drooling," "You've Gotta Be Crazy," a sublime "Shine On . . . ," both sections of which were divided by a noisy, even raunchy rendition of "Have a Cigar." As the band grew into the new material, it became groovier, more menacing, and hypnotic.

Atypically, Wright took some of these songs by the balls, his slinky lead keyboards carrying the tone of a snake charmer's pungi. Moments in which Dick Parry's wonderfully squeaky sax, Wright's whining keys, and Gilmour's twanging guitar meld are pure magic, if not completely unusual. And while vocals were always the band's weakest link live, especially in "Raving and Drooling" and "Have a Cigar," at least from a critical point of view, the show was a success.

≡

Floyd escaped Boston, but Pittsburgh law enforcement was hip to the band's concert on June 20. Pittsburgh authorities were no doubt aware of the attention and crowds Floyd concerts attracted. Large stadium events that held thousands of people coursed with free-flowing drugs and psychedelic rock music. The safety and well-being of the general public wasn't just a talking point: there was a real possibility that something very wrong could happen. The irony is that Waters admitted he was smoking hash heavily in the early 1970s but had given it up in 1975.

Three Rivers Stadium certainly had its share of misfortune in the recent past. A seventeen-year-old intoxicated fan had fallen more than eighty feet to his death at a Pittsburgh Pirates game just a few years prior. His blood-alcohol level was .02 over the legal limit, the city coroner Dr. Cyril Wecht told the *Post-Gazette*. Prior to this, in 1971, a twenty-two-year-old baseball fan, attending the Pirates game at Three Rivers, died in a similar manner . . .

In the early goings, it did appear as though there would be some serious issues with crowd control. Ticketholders formed a line outside the venue hours prior to the event. More die-hard fans, some traveling from outside Pennsylvania and as far away as West Virginia and Washington, DC, camped out in the parking lot. The volume of people in a confined area . . . hopped up on whatever . . . some full of testosterone—it was a recipe for disaster.

Pittsburgh Post-Gazette reported that the forty-five thousand on hand were fairly well mannered, but some fighting broke out; there were a few casualties, but no fatalities. Attendees who OD'd were first treated on site and then shuttled to a hospital for further observation. In a bizarre complaint, exemplifying the sociological aspects of mainstream teenage life in the mid-1970s, some drug users blamed the venue for not providing adequate medical centers for ODs.

Floyd was experiencing its own issues. The production didn't run as smoothly as it should have. Back before the band had hit the road, Waters had scribbled on paper the initial design sketch for an inflatable, helium-filled pyramid "roof"—the triangular prism being the central image associated with the album cover of *Dark Side*—which would fly away at a certain point in the show. Mark Fisher ultimately had a hand in designing the prop.

Atlanta is generally accepted as the first sighting of the flying pyramid, and conflicting reports reveal that the inflatable geometric piece was accidentally let loose over Pittsburgh, foreshadowing what was to come for the *Animals* cover shoot in late 1976.

As the air-filled pyramid was free of its restraints, it went up, up, and up, and was lost in the ether. Well, only momentarily. It touched down in the parking lot of Three Rivers Stadium, causing some automobile damage, at which point a free-for-all ensued: fans savaged the stage prop in the hopes of taking home a great piece of Floyd concert memorabilia.

MORE ARRESTS

According to *Performance* magazine, when Floyd performed in Milwaukee on June 22, 1975, the concert sold out more quickly than any other concert in the history of County Stadium. Concertgoers flooded the stadium's parking lot nearly a day before the event, eating, sleeping, playing, and sunbathing in the hot summer sun.

The sudden lack of availability of tickets took even die-hard fans by surprise. One poor distraught soul from Green Bay placed a wanted ad in a local newspaper, screaming, "Desperation!! Need 2 tickets to Pink Floyd concert." Similar classified ads cropped up in areas of Wisconsin weeks prior to the show.

The fan missed a dandy: the crowd was treated to a good old-fashioned Midwestern summer day, with temperatures climbing above ninety degrees. Young men and women discarded their garments and sunbathed in the parking lot hours before the show, soaking up the rays and making the most of the summer season, barely a day old.

The heat and humidity, pressure in the atmosphere, and a coming cold front coalesced to create a major summer storm, with winds exceeding forty miles an hour. Power outages were recorded throughout the state, lightning ignited at least one house fire in Milwaukee, a small twister ripped the roof off a school in Fennimore, and tornadoes were spotted in Green Bay and other areas of Wisconsin.

A storm was brewing in Beer City in more ways than one. A torrential downpour stopped action onstage at County Stadium around 9 p.m. and intermittent lightning and rain caused frequent delays throughout the night. Few left or were affected by the weather, however.

To fans, Floyd were icons they'd go to any lengths to see—including looking into the eye of a hurricane. To the cops and mayors, Floyd was a plague of locusts swarming through towns across America, causing irreparable damage. Police frisked and searched over fifty thousand Floyd fans for illicit substances. Concertgoers' personal possessions were confiscated and/or trashed.

Given that law enforcement in New York, New Jersey, California, Pennsylvania, Wisconsin, and other states were ready to take punitive action against Floyd crowds, one begins to wonder if these local police departments were in communication with one another.

As it stood, one of the attendees was arrested and dragged before a judge. When the concertgoer was given a pat-down by authorities, he was found with a vile full of amphetamine tablets. The charges were dismissed when it was ruled that the officer's arrest was illegal and a search warrant was needed. Only the existence of a crime or the threat of an imminent crime would make the search legal, said circuit judge Hugh R. O'Connell. However, this ruling did not apply to charges being brought against other defendants.

To add insult to injury, the outfield at County Stadium, home to the Major League Baseball's Milwaukee Brewers, was pockmarked with holes. The Detroit Tigers were stunned by the condition of the field when they played the Brewers the following night. Some American League teams protested and others wondered if the grounds crew would rectify the situation in time for the All-Star Game at County in July. (They did.)

Floyd fans can't take all the blame, however: the weather ruined some of the field, and the Stones played the same venue earlier in the month, leading to damage to both the infield and outfield.

Despite police arrests, lightning strikes, and runaway props, for the most part, America's Heartland was fairly good to Floyd in the 1970s. Floyd played quite a bit in Michigan throughout the first half of the 1970s, including the Eastown Theatre in Detroit in the early years of the decade.

Floyd fans certainly got bang for their bucks. At Cobo Arena in 1973, the band's flash-pots were stuffed with an overload of black powder. Minor injuries were recorded. Later a speaker malfunction rendered more than half of the band's surround sound or "circle of sound" from operating properly, or so said the *Detroit Free Press* in 1973.

"At concerts we have quad tapes and four-track tape machines so we can mix the sound and pan it around," Gilmour told Chris Welch in 1973.

The Detroit area band the Frost, formed in the late 1960s, shared the bill with Floyd at the Eastown Theater in April 1970 for two nights, and were the toast of Motown—and the headliner that evening.

The Frost packed in crowds at venues like the Eastown and the Grande Ballroom. Management and booking agents were sure to strategically pair touring British rock bands with popular regional American acts. It's a common industry practice, even if didn't always sit well with the local musicians.

"Some Detroit musicians would be angry, like, 'Damn English bands, taking all the work,'" says Donny Hartman, guitarist for the Frost, spearheaded by a Detroit rock institution, the late guitarist/vocalist Dick Wagner. "I said, 'Wait a minute: we're all in this together boys.'"

Hartman remembers Floyd's ingenuity and pre-show prep. "The crowd fell in love with them," says Hartman. "We did a lot of concerts at the Eastown. It was a great sounding room; it was an old theatre. The crowd went nuts, but I remember something but I don't know if I should tell you this. . . . [Floyd] did one song and all I know is a girl did a swan dive right off [the balcony]. I said, 'What?' She gets up like an angel and takes a dive. Everyone was yelling and about fifteen people right underneath her caught her."

Detroit crowds were certainly primed for Floyd by the mid-1970s, even if things were a little less exciting. For one thing, there were no swan dives in '75, but the crowd seemed to be head over heels for Floyd in the sweaty, air-conditioned-challenged environs of Olympia Stadium for the band's two-night stand at the venue. Packed in like sardines, the seventeen thousand concertgoers in attendance were forced to comply with the contract demands of Floyd's desire for festival-style seating.

Aside from the heat, the show was marred by issues with the projector. The Medak film shown during the band's onstage performance of *The Dark Side of the Moon* was damaged due to its exposure to the elements at the show in Wisconsin the preceding Sunday. Despite some of the technical malfunctions, Floyd "kept the crowd cool with their jazz-inspired rock," read the *Free Press*.

Next, Floyd visited Montreal, Canada, to play the outdoor arena the Autostade—an admittedly elusive show that has frustrated connoisseurs of unofficial recordings for years.

Built for Expo 67, the Autostade possessed an unusual, modular architectural design, reportedly with mobile seating sections, resembling petals of a humongous flower. Interestingly, the band's own saw blade-shaped flower mirror prop echoed, if only slightly, this structure.

In retrospect, the seating sections seemed so odd that it's difficult to wrap one's head around Floyd even playing there. It should be noted that the Who didn't seem to have a problem when they rode into town in 1968. But a lack of recordings circulating in audio circles tested one's sanity for decades and made some question whether the show ever happened. Apparently it did: promoters Donald K. Donald and Jean Bertrand boasted about having scored a major coup, photos of the event have emerged in recent years, and twenty-one thousand tickets sold in one day. (The final ticket tally was upwards of forty thousand.)

Even Floyd was surprised that they could pull off a show of this size and magnitude. "I had no idea we were this big in Quebec," Nick Mason told the *Montreal Gazette*.

Quebec, in general, and Montreal specifically, have been big supporters of experimental, jazz-inflected, and classically inspired rock from Europe—what music critics of the region referred to as "Cosmic Rock." Genesis, Gentle Giant, Moody Blues, Supertramp, Germany's synth-heavy electronic bands, and of course Floyd had rabid followings there in the 1970s.

Import records stores, such as Phantasmagoria and L'Alternatif, and radio station CHOM, promoted this music back in the day, although one suspects Quebecois music fans, likely in both the French- and English-speaking quarters, would have gravitated toward this style of music naturally. I have not heard any audio from this show, but there is no reason to believe that the band performed under par or any differently than the recorded concerts I've listened to from '75. Given the fervor of Quebec music fans, still imbued with L'espirit de Montreal, memories of the show might be skewed—a refreshing change from the critical barbs Floyd absorbed in 1975.

The *Gazette* noted technical problems early on but reported that Floyd recovered and "dazzled" the forty thousand or so in attendance with "Raving and Drooling" and "You Gotta Be Crazy," which, at that point, were thought to be previews of an untitled, upcoming studio album.

The concert felt like a celebration: ticketholders, seated on the grass, tossed frizbees; lighters were flicked and matches were struck during the band's performance of *Dark Side*, radiating a liturgical glow typical of a sacred ritual.

Bill Provick, of the *Ottawa Citizen*, attended the show and was surprised by its intimacy, beauty, and precision. Well-positioned speakers added spatial dimension to the music, and, as always, the visual effects received top marks: "After an hour the group set spinning its silver sunburst, with thousands of tiny, revolving mirrors throwing fireflies of light hurtling up from the crowd like a snowstorm in reverse."

The show was anticlimactic for some, however. The *Gazette* let it slip that after Floyd returned to England and performed at Knebworth in July, they were breaking up. It's difficult to check the veracity of this report, as the source was not ID'd, but if unrest ran rampant in the organization, even as the band neared completion of their next studio record, it wouldn't be a complete surprise.

While the timing and the nonchalant manner in which the report was presented are suspect, if this information accurately reflected the attitude of the band at press time and was provided to the newspaper by O'Rourke or even one of the band members, then perhaps there was even more going on behind the scenes than we imagined.

Then again, if a Floyd went to the media with the tidbit, "We are breaking up by summer's end," it may have only been the musings of one man out of sheer frustration in the dying days of a grueling tour. In other words, the guy didn't really mean it or it could easily have been a play for leverage of some kind. It's difficult to see a financial angle, as well: if Floyd had disbanded at this time, it's doubtful the business-savvy quartet would have obscured their actions. Their farewell tour likely would have been advertised as such. Either way, this discussion may be academic: Floyd stayed intact, at least for one more studio record, and released *The Wall* in 1979, although sans Wright.

After Montreal, Floyd traveled 'round Lake St. Clair and continued in a northeast direction through Canada for their show at Ivor Wynne Stadium on June 28, where area residents protested the rock group's very presence. The fifty thousand who attended may have taken issue with the town's stance, however.

On a Hamilton, Canada, Floyd bootleg I've heard, prior to "Shine On . . ." being introduced, someone close to the microphone actually calls for the song to be played. Although this was the last date of the second leg of their North American tour, the song hadn't been officially released yet. This was proof that Floyd's new material was penetrating and preoccupying the minds of fans. As the first icy and monumental atmospheric tones of "Shine On . . ." reverberate in the building, Waters tells the crowd: "This is a song about not being here."

Unlike in the States, there wasn't much of a police presence at the show. According to a May 30, 1975, edition of the magazine *Performance*, the town was lucky that "the parks and recreation committee of Hamilton does not have the same prejudiced and shortsighted opinion."

The fact is, there *was* trouble, but it couldn't be blamed the band. An explosive amount of pyro detonated well after the Hamilton show had ended, and the Ivor Wynne Stadium's scoreboard had exploded in smoke and flames. Reportedly, the blast had busted up glass in nearby residences. Two electricians were sent to the hospital and kept overnight for observation. In addition, groundskeepers developed a headache while picking up the heaps of discarded beer bottles strewn all over the ground in the wake of the show.

The North American tour may have ended in a bang, but it was a slog for most of the trek, what with the human and economic toll. Floyd were no doubt glad to leave North America and return home for their final show of the year: Knebworth, in England, on July 5, for the festival's second anniversary.

Steve Miller Band, Linda Lewis, Captain Beefheart, Roy Harper, and between-set entertainer Graham Chapman of *Monty Python's Flying Circus* populated the bill. BBC Radio's John Peel and Pete Drummond were also on hand. Harper performed "Have a Cigar" with Floyd.

"Knebworth stands out," says Venetta Fields. "There was something like eighty thousand people there. What fascinated me the most was that I had been with other bands before, like Humble Pie, and they could fill out fourteen thousand-seaters. But Pink Floyd would fill out football stadiums, with thirty-six thousand or forty thousand people. That was my biggest crowds at that time. Humble Pie would go out, and they would pump the audience up so much. Steve Marriott. But [Floyd] floated out. They seemed to be on a cloud—they just floated out like the music."

There seemed to be as much, if not more, action backstage. Prior to his own Knebworth appearance, Roy Harper had performed on July 3 at the Theatre, a show recorded by the BBC. The very next day he was taken by limo to the backstage area of the Knebworth stage. Not long after, it's been reported by *Melody Maker*, Harper threw a fit backstage, because his limo was raided. Audio and musical equipment gone. "One of My Turns" from *The Wall* is said to be based, in part, on Harper's public blow up.

At least one author has reported that Barrett appeared backstage at Knebworth but fled the scene. This is a curious fact that never seems to get much traction in the press. Scarcity of information about this alleged sighting could be explained through a few simple factors:

1. Barrett or someone else in the Floyd circle wished not to explain his appearance or disappearance.
2. It was a case of mistaken identity.
3. Barrett appeared at a similar event, not Knebworth.
4. The few who witnessed it can't offer details.
5. It never actually happened.

Had Barrett been seen backstage with Floyd, it would make, by some counts, three separate instances of Syd being sighted in the span of about a month—including, quite possibly, Gilmour's wedding.

This alone should have made Floyd's set at Knebworth a triumphant return to a home crowd. But a series of mishaps maligned what could have been an otherwise outstanding show.

Spitfires buzzing the crowd, a spectacle meant to open the show, occurred too early in the program, when the road crew was still assembling the stage. This meant Floyd was obliged to perform sooner than they'd planned. In addition, because of intermittent AC current, Wright's Hammond organ was continually thrown out of tune. Wright had to switch to the Farfisa and the band then had to tune to this instrument, causing long pauses between songs.

"I'll tell you what's happening," Waters said. "The Hammond depends for its tuning on the frequency of the AC cycle that's coming in, which is varying. So the Hammond is a quarter-note flatter than everything else. Now, myself, and David are tuned to the Hammond, which means that Rick can't use any of the other keyboards. So, we have to tune to the Farfisa and *fuck* the Hammond, and then we'll carry on. This will take two or three minutes. So, be patient and we'll be with you . . . [trails off]."

The press called their appearance a disaster. Not everyone agreed. The October 1975 issue of *Circus* magazine held the contrary opinion, having published a piece titled "Floyd Wows 'Em at Knebworth." The publication was critical of some of the opening numbers but dubbed the spitfire stunt "stunning" and praised "Have a Cigar." The second half of the show, in which the band presented *The Dark Side of the Moon*, was "magnificent."

Indeed. One listen to the boot from the show, and it was not as horrendous as it was once believed to be. The consensus among the media class? Floyd had a tough time at Knebworth, and that was the narrative. Critics didn't always have the best track record regarding Floyd. On one level, anyway, it was a richly symbolic end to their tour: Floyd was a slave to their machines and victim of their own devices.

≡

After the tour Floyd decamped to Abbey Road, and they mixed the record from July 7 to 11 and again from July 14 to 19. The last weeks of putting the record together was a mad dash to the finish line, leaving the band nearly breathless and listless.

Despite some disagreements, the band eventually saw eye to eye, and the entire mixing process was completed in a week or so. By comparison this was a whirlwind—and just the opposite of what you'd expect from such a long, drawn-out recording procedure.

Unlike with *Dark Side*, Floyd did not feel the need to bring in an outside ear. They handled it in-house—just one of the many signs that Floyd, despite all of the uneasiness at the beginning of the recording process, had gained clarity of vision and grown confident in their perspective about the quality of the album. It was also perhaps a sign that Floyd could handle debate among the ranks without lunging for one another's throat.

It wasn't full agreement all the time, of course, as Gilmour intimated that there were different mixes made and the group debated the merits of each one. This seems to confirm some of the evidence available: photos taken by a young Jill Furmanovsky clearly show Roger at the mixing console, but Gilmour indicated that he preferred mixing.

Once the final product is realized, a musician can sit back and appreciate all the work that went into the making of it. But while in the process of creating music, one can't see the forest for the trees.

The band's own site says they reconvened at Abbey Road on July 7, 1975, for three weeks of recording and mixing to finish the album, putting the completion of the project around the first week of August, or thereabouts. Then, the band spent the early fall—September 29–30 as well as October 1, 6, 9, 13, and 29–31—in the studio doing the quadrophonic mix of *WYWH*. Nine days in total.

Finally, mercifully, *WYWH* was finished.

CHAPTER 6

THE MUSIC: SYD SEQUENCE

Side 1 of the original LP of *Wish You Were Here* opens with the centerpiece of the album—
the first half of "Shine On You Crazy Diamond."

Credited to the songwriting trio Gilmour, Waters, and Wright, the track has it all: steel
guitar, synthesizer leads, Clavinet, Mason's economical drumming, some of Waters's most
paradoxical lyrics, Gilmour's gut-wrenching solo that effectively neutralizes the metastasized
sickness inside the band, and a conclusion dedicated to the man for which the song was
written—Syd Barrett.

From the first line, Waters's lyrics take us through the mists of time—recalling a different
era, when Barrett was young, a beacon of creative purity and innovativeness. Syd's experimentation with mind-altering drugs as a way of seeking truth had left him with eyes that remind
Waters of black holes—empty, lifeless, even dangerous.

Lyrical imagery, such as Barrett being "blown on the steel breeze," speaks to the invisible,
invincible, yet impermanent. Waters was very sly in using the poetic image of a diamond: the
precious stone is flawed but the hardest substance known to man—and a universal symbol
of wealth.

Syd is both a "prisoner," confined to his home, and "piper," leading countless followers.
"Piper" is, of course, *The Piper at the Gates of Dawn*, but is also a reference to Syd's carefree
spirit, love of nature, and the influence of British children's literature on his art and life.
Barrett, says Waters, was caught in between "childhood" and "stardom," forever frozen in
1967, at the moment he became a Romantic hero of the British psychedelic movement. The
"black holes" where his eyes once were are outward and physical manifestations of a human
attempting to reach "for the secret" or truth through hallucinogens. This chilling line slightly
changes the texture and tone of the song.

Waters is observing Barrett, but he's not doing it clinically or as a gawker would, peering at a
zoo animal through bars of a cage. Syd might actually be in a cage, of sorts, but Waters appears
to be giving Barrett a pep talk: telling him to shun the outside world and not change, stay
creative and full of curiosity . . . Maybe Waters is telling the world that Syd really *can't* change.

"Shine On You Crazy Diamond" begins in a G-minor chord, with Wright's keyboard notes trumpeting forth from our speakers. Wright piles on Parsons's wine-glass multichord, creating a drone via (what is most likely) a Hammond C3 organ, ARP string machine, Minimoog, Taurus pedals, and a spring or bird-cawing sound (0:14) on an EMS SynthiA.

Tinkling, or twinkling bells, likely some form of glass from *Household Objects* or a glockenspiel, can be heard in the mist, adding to the song's mystique. Minimoog takes the lead (0:46), soaring above the twenty-four-track glass chord, turning this entire section into something approaching symphonic, psychedelic blues-rock.

"The wine glasses would have been compiled as continuous loops of tape," Alan Parsons tells me. "That was fairly painstaking to get a good loop. You could only hit the note for ten seconds. We had to make a physical tape loop of each note and then transfer that to a twenty-four-track. What you had was a scale of notes on a twenty-four-track tape; a major scale, for the sake of argument. By pushing up faders with each channel containing a track of those wine glasses, you could make chords."

It was during these same sessions that seeds of a new instrument, similar to the tape-based demon called the Mellotron, were planted in Parsons's innovative musical brain. "I actually remember Roger saying, 'Wouldn't it be great if we had a keyboard that played the twenty-four-track?'" says Parsons. "That stuck in my memory, and I had an American electronics engineer design that very thing—something that could play loops from a multi-tracking machine on a keyboard. That's what affectionately became known as the Projectron. [It was] essentially an early digital Mellotron, although it was of vastly superior quality to a Mellotron, using multi-track tapes instead of individual tapes."

Amid the glass-chord backdrop, Gilmour's first solo, marked by clean tones and string bends, beginning approximately 2:11, feels both expansive and in your face—cosmic, Eastern, and mystical yet earthy and gut wrenching. The freeness of the playing, the global scope of the modes—a Blues/Indian crossover—and the overall musical atmosphere contribute to the listener's sense of weightlessness.

For certain, the Syd Sequence was recorded to a click track in the big room, Studio One, at EMI, and Gilmour's rig was miked at a distance. He was using his famous black Fender Stratocaster. Future guitar tech and backline crewmember Phil Taylor was in attendance at the Bath festival in 1970, where legend has it the Black Strat made its live debut. Taylor admitted to *Guitar Player* magazine, for their November 1984 issue, that Gilmour often tuned the low E string down to D.

Although it's difficult to quantify such an influence, it's known that Waters saw Ravi Shankar in the 1960s. Waters's interest, even if it was a passing interest, in Indian music may partly explain how and why the presence of drones became a signature sound for the band.

In the documentary *What Ever Happened to Pink Floyd?: The Strange Case of Gilmour & Waters*, author Chris Ingham points out that the active musical agent shaping the main melodic line of "Set the Controls" is essentially a minor-key drone. The use of drones was a compositional technique that reemerged to structurally support "Shine On You Crazy Diamond" and frame the band's biggest single, "Another Brick in the Wall (Part 2)."

When Floyd toured North America in the early 1970s and stopped in Chicago, they played "Heart Beat, Pig Meat" from *Zabriskie Point*. The *Tribune* reviewer observed that the music "oozed out in concentric circles, lulling and attacking the listener at once." At the Aragon Ballroom a year earlier, in April 1970, Floyd's drone was actually compared with a "raga."

"There's hints of those in there," adds Damian Darlington, co-founder of Brit Floyd, a UK-based Pink Floyd tribute band, who spent time as a youth in the United Arab Emirates and Africa. "Take a very early track like 'Set the Controls for the Heart of the Sun' and you can argue that there is an Indian influence in a piece like that. Even something like the opening to 'Shine On . . . ,' the way it's basically a drone on one chord for a long time, with decoration on top of it—that is a very Indian idea, isn't it?"

At the opening of "Shine On . . . ," Part III, Gilmour's solo fades, and we still hear the buzzing and whining of wine glasses. The amalgamated effect of the multi-track mix mimics a church organ. Once this complex sonic soup recedes, the famous four guitar notes that define the song—notes of the G minor thirteenth or G minor seventh add sixth chord—appear at approximately 3:55, virtually almost out of nothing.

The electric guitar signal, sent through a Leslie cabinet with rotating speaker heads, generates shockwaves that shatter the buzzing, layered atmosphere. Gilmour picks strings and grabs the vibrato arm to manipulate the notes to great shimmering effect.

The classic four-note riff, or Syd Sequence, is performed several times until drums, slapped with a forward echo, rumble to a dull roar at approximately 4:25. Gilmour was known for overdubbing, and a possible fourth guitar, a rhythm track, rife with jolting vibrato, joins the four-note "Syd" riff.

Gilmour takes a second, somewhat "clean" solo (at 5:11), and throughout, some of the rhythmic phrases Gilmour played earlier in the song are reprised. These repeated elements may have been put on a loop, or Gilmour played a distinct performance with each pass.

Rife with piercing clean notes, emotional bends, fretboard slides, sustained and ringing notes, and trembling vibrato, the "Shine On . . ." guitar solo could quite possibly be the best extended recorded-guitar performance Gilmour ever committed to tape. Although the nearly tear-inducing "Comfortably Numb" solo bristles with life and is brilliant, "Shine On . . ." has the feel of something much less conceptualized.

Gilmour's work on "Comfortably Numb" was the result of his taking several passes at the solo and then jotting down on a piece of paper the best bits and pieces he wanted to keep, so he could construct one from his notes. Although recording engineer Brian Humphries would not reveal to me if Gilmour did, indeed, operate in a similar fashion with "Shine On . . . ," there *seems* to be an improvisational aspect in the playing here, which lends the performance a sense of immediacy. In split seconds, Gilmour demonstrates superior command of dynamics—he transitions from a harsh sonic grind to a whisper.

"Regarding your question: David was always the one who decided when his guitar parts needed beefing up," Humphries told me. "Roger was always thinking of the effects that went with the lyrics he'd written or had in mind."

Mozart was said to have composed music in his head and have it hit the page perfectly. Gilmour might have this same instinct. We should point out that, in fact, the band had been playing "Shine On . . ." on the road for quite some time before the song was recorded, likely adding to the perception of Gilmour's composure as a guitarist.

While this *might not* be an example of superhuman skills in the art of spontaneous composition, Gilmour's poise is vital to the overall feel of "Shine On . . ."—he doesn't rush things but does ring nearly every possible emotion out of the tones he picks, clustering notes and leaving space between them to help the music breathe.

Other progressive rock guitarists of the day were busy foraging in thick thatches of knotty note-laden woodshedded workout wildernesses, while Gilmour freed our minds with Prog Rock fusion. The solo's combination of space, cross-genre sonics and coloring, and emotional rawness places it somewhere between Freddie King, Ali Khan, Eric Clapton, and John Cage.

"There's a handful of guitar players where their touch is so clear and I think Gilmour is one of those guys," says Warr guitarist Trey Gunn (Security Project, King Crimson). "[If] you are trying to emulate that touch, as well as all the technology . . . shit. Find something else to do with your life. It's too unique. Gilmour, Jeff Beck, they somehow expressed it through the guitar. It is down to fingers on the strings."

Like Eric Clapton, Gilmour rarely blows you away with the sheer speed of his riffs. More often than not, Gilmour's "moments" work toward building up the song or creating atmospherics through soaring notes or experimental noises. It's about stirring a *feeling* inside the listener, rather than impressing with technical chops.

"Fundamentally [Gilmour] is a blues guitarist, and he wasn't afraid to experiment with all the effects that were becoming available at the time and creating all these different textures and a different guitar tone," says Darlington. "I think, ultimately, it boils down to the fact that he was a wonderful blues guitarist and also had a wonderful sense of melody. These are the things you learn about him when you are trying to recreate these songs."

As smooth as the solo or soloes are, the song is kept slightly off-kilter by its 6/4 time signature, not an altogether unfamiliar tempo in the Floyd music world. It opens in free time and moves to 4/4, but the cyclical arc of the "6" is sufficiently hypnotic that it adds to the meditative effect of the song without crossing over into major boredom.

It's part of Floyd lore that Gilmour was not impressed with the drumming tracks for *WYWH*. Some sources have said Gilmour was not thrilled with the elaborate fills Mason was playing. For the Capital Radio interview series, the band indicated that Mason was being too "flowery" and not straightforward enough.

Ironically, Mason's drumming on the record tends to be economical, not excessive, and in retrospect, quintessential Floyd. When asked if he wished he had taken more drum lessons, Mason was quoted in *Classic Rock* magazine as saying, "Not *more*—any."

There is a certain drone—an "om," for lack of a better phrase—that Floyd threads like a needle through the fabric of their most epic tunes. When I questioned Humphries about it, he was mum about this "om," if it existed, or how it might have been created in the studio.

The transformational quality, a tendency toward inner searching, reflection, and time-lessness embedded in Floyd's compositional approach, is enhanced by innovative use of musical instrument and recording studio technology circa 1975. The music *is* meditation.

Floyd, perhaps as much as any of its progressive-band contemporaries, was greater than the sum of its parts. Unlike, say, Yes and Emerson, Lake & Palmer, Pink Floyd was not driven by virtuoso performances. Floyd's music was truly "space," or spaced, rock.

"It is not just the architecture of the notes," says Trey Gunn. "You can play the archi-tecture of the notes for Beatles songs, and the music is there. Nothing is missing, in a way. I don't know that you can do that with Floyd's music. It seems like there's a presence in the recording that is down to the recording, more than it is the notes."

As we move into Part IV, there's lots of musical interplay. Wright tracked a Steinway, a Hammond, and a synth in a slow keyboard passage (6:27) that features two rhythm guitar tracks, piano, and an organ drone, supporting the Gilmour solo starting at 7:34. Framed by an economy of phrasing, numerous string bends, and fretboard slides, this Leslie-effected solo is momentarily joined by a harmonized guitar, at 8:28, which is likely yet another Gilmour guitar track. Part IV also introduces the support singers, the Black-berries.

When in production for the 2011 Super Audio version of *WYWH*, mastering and mix-ing engineer James Guthrie discovered that a piano track underpinning Wright's nautical, ship horn-like Minimoog solo in the first half of "Shine On . . . ," present on the original stereo mix, went missing, or, in the language of the land, was totally *absent*.

Guthrie made a bold decision to rerecord Wright, which was done at British Grove, Mark Knopfler's recording studio, and the song was fully restored for the version appear-ing on the reissue project.

The band winds down at the opening Part V as the last held, descending notes of Gilmour's solo fade. We hear droning organ and Mason's hi-hats producing the classic jazzy "chick" sound, and then a dry thump on the toms, before Waters introduces the vocals—"Remember when you were young . . ."—for the first time on the record.

The chordal underpinnings of the verses in "Shine On . . ." make subtle overtures to jazz and gospel, harking back to *The Dark Side of the Moon* and earlier efforts, and fore-tell more rock-operaish material on *The Wall*, such as the grand emptiness of "Nobody Home."

There may be some double-tracked guitar at approximately 9:00 and approximately 9:45, which sounds like harmonization. Gilmour plays arpeggiated notes, a variation on the Syd Sequence, to root saxophonist Dick Parry's solo. Parry switches between tenor and baritone saxes as ARP strings join the musical fray. Onstage, and we can see this clearly on the *P.U.L.S.E.* video, Parry engages with one and keeps another slung around his neck.

At approximately 13:02, the first half of "Shine On . . ." is joined with the next track, "Welcome to the Machine," via the technique of crossfading. We hear machine noises, humming, whirring and throbbing, which builds in volume . . .

"WELCOME TO THE MACHINE"

Zonked, self-absorbed, insulated, and operating on autopilot, Floyd were little more than wind-up or mechanical drones when they arrived at Abbey Road in the winter of 1975.

Recording the follow-up to *The Dark Side of the Moon* was never going to be easy, but perhaps no one in the band could have foreseen the struggles that would beset them or the troubles they'd face by grappling with stardom and personal heartache at the edge of professional burnout.

Unclear on what the future would look like—or even if a collective one would emerge—Floyd operated on autopilot, as if programmed either by their label, the industry at large, or sheer self-hypnosis to check into Abbey Road . . . *to do something.*

Were they assembled again because they wanted to make music? Or did they simply want to keep the ongoing concern that was Floyd Inc. from going under? Did they even know why they were in Abbey Road other than occupying space there as a force of habit?

Their drive to be innovative may have been lost through sheer exhaustion. Gradually, after months of slow progress, the daily grind of work accelerated as the band careened toward a North American tour. The band spent parts of May and into June completing "Welcome to the Machine" and "Have a Cigar."

Credited solely to Waters, who had started writing the verses prior to entering Abbey Road to record the track, this studio creation once dubbed "Machine Song" spoke to the foibles of the recording industry and the fairy dust that execs often sprinkle on the wide-eyed artists who willingly sign on the dotted line. The image of the rock star lifestyle looks appealing, but it's a trap.

One response to the industry, what Waters deemed the "Machine," is completely Pavlovian. Musicians, from an early age, have been conditioned to strive for a dream of wealth and happiness—sex, drugs, and rock and roll, basically. If these things do exist, and they do, they can often come at the expense of the dreamer and destroy him/her.

"Some people are fortunate enough never to really make it in their lifetime," Anthony Stern told me. "Being a successful artist is really simple: you just learn to play the publicity machine. But to be a great artist you have to turn your back on all of that."

Floyd may have wanted it every which way: to achieve fame *and* be artistic. Most recording artists or painters or novelists or actors have to choose. Our sympathies extend so far. No one forces the young musician to sign on the dotted line, to feast at the "steak bar," or drive a precision luxury car.

The rock world "game" exists as a giant pyramid. The business builds this monument, brick by brick. It looks impenetrable, imposing, and constructed upon a sturdy foundation. Perhaps from the industry's standpoint this is true. The capstone—the artist—is then slid into place largely for cosmetic purposes, completing the edifice. In this "pyramid scheme," the artist is not fundamental to the structural integrity of the building and is incidental to its massive scale and purpose.

"Businessmen have realized the market," Mason told *Record Mirror* in 1971. "A lot of these record company businessmen know nothing about music . . ."

"The capitalist obsessive profit-making thing that goes on in the world would have to be changed," Gilmour told the *Chicago Tribune* in 1978. "People seem to strive obsessively for profits, but it can't do them much good, really, in the end."

"Machine Song" not only emphasizes the dehumanizing aspects of the industry but puts the focus on artists becoming increasingly subservient to MI electronics. Ironically, the "pyramid scheme" seduces you to experiment with music-making machines, rendering you a cyborg, or worse: a redundancy in your own creative process. Truth be told, if record companies had their way, they'd much prefer dealing with automated robots to flesh-and-blood creative beings.

Prior to the official start of "Welcome to the Machine," at 12:52 into "Shine On . . . ," the humming of mechanical devices builds in volume. At 0:03 we hear a door buzzing—a young artist gains access to the "Machine." The door shuts (at 0:06) and eight seconds later, an icy blast is followed by a second door clicking open and then closing. Chopper blades stutter, reminiscent of the SynthiA KS-produced whirring of "On the Run," accompanied by a low drone and an electronic throb.

The throbbing is composed of each pulse of the VCS-3, followed by an echo, creating a ping-ponging effect. The synth was sent direct to the board—direct injection (DI)—to give a saturated, unwavering, almost claustrophobic tightness in the musical atmosphere that you can feel in the pit of your neck. The icy blasts or wind effects are (likely) the VCS as well.

At 0:48 a twelve-string acoustic guitar is strummed, standing in contrast to the AI-stalked musical proceedings. At 1:05 vocals enter: Gilmour screams, "Welcome, my son . . . ," possibly the amalgam of, at least, two voices—one lower register and one upper. Double tracking was done and tape-speed manipulation was applied to at least one vocal line. Gilmour couldn't reach a sequence of notes, so the tape was dropped half a semitone to accommodate his voice. Despite his yelling, there's something utterly dispassionate about Gilmour's vocals that borders on inhuman.

As Floyd often does, they juxtapose a minor and a major chord throughout the verses, bolstering the song's sinister quality. Time signature switches, from 4/4 to 3/4, further hypnotize the listener by placing him/her in a "zone" and creating an otherworldly atmosphere.

Mason's kit drums and timpani rolls are cyborg in nature: they bring a human, aggressive quality to the track but burn with the freezing sting of metallic sheets slicing your brain. Gilmour complements this sensation with the metallic sound he extracts from his electric guitar as beeping and pulsating synths swirl.

Wright created some of the most frightening and psychically scarring sounds of his entire career for "Welcome to the Machine." He tapped Minimoog, Moog Taurus pedals, and most likely an ARP string machine. A VCS3 is used as well, perhaps by Wright, but more likely by Gilmour or Waters. The overwhelming, glassy synth leads, likely generated with the Minimoog, are downright nasty. Nothing in the Floyd universe comes close to its overt menacing quality.

Floyd has used synth prior to *WYWH*, but "Welcome to the Machine" solidified the band's reputation as pioneers of an electronic rock form. In fact, Floyd may have opened the floodgates to Kratwerk, Faust, Can, Neu!, and in particular Tangerine Dream. Not to mention Hamburg native Michael Hoenig, Ash Ra Tempel/Ashra's Manuel Göttsching, and Klaus Schulze. For that matter, it's difficult to imagine many of the great ambient, trance, and electronic artists of the 1990s on Peter Kuhlmann's German-based FAX label without the existence of Floyd's spaced "Us and Them" and layered "Shine On You Crazy Diamond."

Waters intimated that had Floyd flopped in its attempts to fuse *musique concrète*, electronic instruments, and recording equipment of all sorts, perhaps Tangerine Dream may never have come to the attention of Richard Branson's musical mavens at Virgin Records.

"They're into a sound we were into a long time ago," Gilmour told the *New York Times* in 1978. "They have all this sophisticated technology at their disposal; we did it all on crummy electric organs."

We would have to acknowledge that Germany has produced some of the most well-known electronic innovators in modern history, however. For instance, Stockhausen and his work continues to inspire generations of composers and musicians.

The Nazis euthanized Stockhausen's mentally ill mother, and Simon Stockhausen, Karlheinz's father, died in WWII, in Hungary, biographer Michael Kurtz theorized. It was an altogether too familiar song for a generation of European children in the wake of the Second World War.

Throughout the 1950s and 1960s, new music's notions of rhythmic time, chance, use of silence, and radical revision of standard musical notation were being reconfigured in electronic pieces, percussion compositions, and other works, such as the Stockhausen's circular *Zyklus*, *Prozession*, and *Kurzwellen*, and the global fusion of *Telemusik*. With *Hymnen*, Stockhausen employed short-wave radio signals and improvisation to electronically fuse national anthems in a kind of social commentary.

At the end of the 1950s, Stockhausen began publically expressing a desire to create a "spherical auditorium for music," infusing spatiality as an integral part of the musical equation. Just over a decade later, Stockhausen and members of his ensemble created a multimedia event inside a spherical auditorium at the West Germany Pavilion at the 1970 World's Fair in Osaka, Japan. Stockhausen controlled, from a mixing console, the direction and amplitude of the sound within a three-dimensional space more so than when he performed in, say, the caves of Lebanon.

The groundbreaking electronic work, *Gesang der Jünglinge*—melding voice, electronic pulses, and tape speed—explored what has been dubbed "spatial music," which Stockhausen envisioned for a surround-sound environment. This fusion of electronics and concepts of spatiality challenged contemporary views of how music was experienced, defined, interpreted, and created. This is, of course, faintly echoed through Floyd's propensity for quadrophonic audio and, later, its application of the Azimuth Coordinator in a live concert setting.

Nonetheless, Floyd's music completed a circle of influence. German rock bands of the 1960s and 1970s idolized Floyd for their ability to infuse their popular rock recordings with something that resembled a Continental European avant-garde sensibility.

A direct line can be drawn between the improvisational and atmospheric aspects of Floyd's earlier sound and the so-called Space Rock of Amon Düül II, as well as later German bands Eloy and Novalis.

"A lot of people did appreciate these new ways to get high on music," muses French musician and composer Cyrille Verdeaux of Clearlight, sometimes tagged with the Space Rock label. "Yes, it was strongly evoking Space and was suggesting extraterrestrial visions, but it was music . . . ."

When Waters was asked if he heard or listened to German progressive rock or Krautrock, he denied he did but paradoxically said, "[I]t bored me."

"Pink Floyd was probably the first group to use synthesizers, sequencers, and other machines able to generate cosmic and spacy atmospheres," says Verdeaux, whose work appears on a Virgin compilation, titled *V,* from 1975, which also features Robert Wyatt and Nick Mason on "Yesterday Man." "They also took the visual aspects of their presentation to a new limit, all part of their tremendous popularity and record sales. 'Inner space' and the 'outer space' music are for me the same, since my extraterrestrial source is also within my consciousness, and I suppose I'm not the only one to experiment with it. A lot of composers even from centuries ago said the same . . ." In the ensuing years, it seems, "Welcome to the Machine" has taken on many meanings. Audio bites and synthesizer sweeps have classed Floyd in musical strata all their own, as masters of the audiovisual.

Case in point: By song's end, we hear the protagonist step into his car and close the door. It's a bit artificial, and, funnily enough, it's been revealed that the sound we're hearing in this sequence may not have been attached to an automobile at all. In fact, if Mason remembers correctly, that sound was the door to his refrigerator opening and closing. Gilmour expressed belief that he believed the droning mechanical noises at the end of "Welcome to the Machine," prior to the roar of the party crowd, were actually those of a car lift.

"If you do it right," Gilmour told Gerald Scarfe, "that opening sounds as though the door's opening up and you're coming into a party, and all you're doing is pushing up faders."

Suspending disbelief, our doomed musician protagonist steps into a car, no doubt the Jaguar mentioned in the lyrics, and speeds at an ungodly pace along what we imagine is a deserted winding road in the pitch dark of night, toward some secluded mansion or beach house where a party is well underway. Individual voices are indistinguishable; it's just a mass of humanity (or is it inhumanity?)—faceless and perhaps soulless industry types and hangers-on looking for a ride in the fast lane. This clusterfuck fades as Side 1 comes to a close . . .

SIDE 2

In the spring of 1975, Floyd was hard at work on one of their latest creations—"Have a Cigar." The lyrical subtext of "Have a Cigar" is one of victimhood, continuing the theme stated so vividly and clearly throughout Side 1. Floyd *may* have been a victim of the system, but Syd certainly was, and the subtext is there—Syd is present in spirit.

The Prince of Psychedelia wasn't the only one floating around the Floyd universe with the crown of victimhood, a casualty to the perils of the music business. Progressive folk-rock cult hero Roy Harper fit that bill very nicely, perhaps just as well if not better than Syd.

It's Harper who sings lead vocals on "Have a Cigar," so it would be worth evaluating various aspects of the cult figure's career and what circumstances led him to, or placed him in, Abbey Road in 1975 for the recording of the Floyd's most cynically wicked, hysterically insightful song about the record business . . .

Although Harper's earlier music bore more obvious connections to Dylan and Donovan, the freaky folkie synthesized various influences fluidly, particularly in the 1970s. There's no doubt that Jethro Tull's Ian Anderson, Led Zeppelin's Jimmy Page and Robert Plant, Paul McCartney, the Who's Pete Townshend, and David Gilmour viewed him as a national treasure, a true English rock music eccentric.

Albums such as *Led Zeppelin III*, the untitled but so-called *Led Zeppelin IV*, featuring "Stairway to Heaven," *Houses of the Holy*, as well as Jethro Tull's *WarChild*, *Minstrel in the Gallery*, *Songs from the Wood*, and efforts dating back as far as 1969's *Stand Up* owe some debt to Harper's eclecticism.

The story goes that Harper met Jimmy Page at the 1970 Bath Festival of Blues and Progressive Music, which eventually led to a kind of tribute to Harper, "Hats Off to (Roy) Harper," from the largely acoustic album *Led Zeppelin III*.

"Roy was and continues to be a great talent and character," says former EMI/Harvest promotion exec Stuart Watson. "Many of today's new-wave folk successes, such as Fleet Foxes and Joanna Newson, cite him as a major influence. I worked with him on *Lifemask*, *Valentine*, and *HQ* and visited him at his Hereford farm on several occasions. He's used to people being baffled by him, but musicians love him. Zeppelin's 'Hat's Off to (Roy) Harper,' Paul McCartney's cameo on *Bullinamingvase*, and Kate Bush's relentless cheerleading, together with his vocal on 'Have a Cigar' speak for themselves."

In the late 1960s, Harper appeared to have everything going for him—all the connections, the talent, the admiration of famous friends . . . Superstardom was not in the cards, however.

Harper's early life was less than auspicious. For one thing, Harper's mother died in childbirth, and his stepmother, a Jehovah's Witness, quite possibly helped to foster young

Roy's aversion to organized religion—a frequent target of his lyrical attacks, as in "The Spirit Lives" from *HQ*, a song in which Indian, Celtic, and Delta Blues styles seem to intermingle. ("The Spirit Lives" also seems to yearn for the pre-Christian British days, an epoch in which men were not poisoned by dogma and did not flock like singular-minded "sheep.")

Music offered a reasonable level of personal comfort, and the young Harper counted Skiffle, Leadbelly, and Elvis as early influences. His childhood didn't last long, though. Reportedly, he joined the Royal Air Force to escape home, but soon found a different kind of hell in the service. Harper wanted out and even entertained thoughts of going AWOL. Feigning madness, Harper hoped he'd be granted an immediate discharge, but he was ordered to check into a RAF psychiatric hospital in Wendover.

Harper was in for a shock—a literal one—after being subjected to a session of corrective electroshock treatment. "I was just together enough to know that if I had any more it would destroy my brain," Harper told *Rolling Stone*, UK edition, in December 1972.

A physical altercation, perhaps by design, led to a trip to Lancaster Moor Medical, a now-closed mental health facility. Lancaster was said to be one of the more humane mental asylums, but Harper complained about being physically abused for simply not following orders. According to his own account, he slipped out a bathroom window, and he was gone.

When he trekked up Blackpool, a town Harper once called a "cemetery with bus stops," trouble followed him: he was arrested (mostly) for drug use and theft. Some accounts report that Harper was given three years probation and a year in jail in Liverpool, where he supposedly began writing poetry. Once released, or when enough time had passed allowing him to legally travel, he busked his way through Europe, having earned a considerable amount of money playing largely American blues and roots music on the street and in clubs.

Upon his return to England, Harper became a rising star on the British folk circuit, having caught the eye and ear of the English music cognoscenti and influential recording labels. Harper's growing technical skill on guitar and commanding presence meant he held his own among names as legendary as the Incredible String Band, Donovan, John Renbourn, and Bert Jansch.

By the same token, in 1965, anyone with an acoustic guitar, offering social commentary, was being hailed by record companies on both sides of the Atlantic as the "Next Bob Dylan." While Harper never quite fulfilled this role—and there's no evidence he desired to take up this mantle foisted upon him, anyway—his acerbic wit and weighty lyrics offered a form of psychotherapy, one thinks. Unresolved personal issues and disdain for authority and religious institutions likely helped to shape an eccentricity foreign to the denominative acoustic folk and baroque folk crowds. In short, Harper was an outsider even among the perceived freaks, loners, exiles, and hippies quickly populating the roots music circuit in Britain.

After the release of his debut album, *Sophisticated Beggar*, Harper's manager, Jo Lustig, had partnered with the Who/Kinks producer Shel Talmy for 1968's conceptual *Come Out Fighting Genghis Smith* and 1969's *Folkjokeopus*. Harper's vision for *Ghengis Smith*—a narrative shaped by a theme of succeeding against incredible odds—was the sort Talmy had been familiar with in his dealings with the Kinks. It's also the kind of conceptual effort that another Talmy-produced act, the Who, had pioneered.

The songs on *Folkjokeopus* seem to hang together through some loose conceptual threads. From "One for All," which is emblematic of Harper's signature triplet pull-offs, to "Mañana," a politically incorrect piece of irony, taking aim at violence, homophobia, and record industry cynicism.

"At the start, Roy provided me with a rough tape upon which he played the songs acoustically, in the order he wanted them," Shel Talmy tells me. "[The track order] was more or less in the sequence that the album took form. I don't think he did the same for *Folkjokeopus*. I didn't contribute to composition, but always did the arrangements working with the artist, which could mean getting him/her to rewrite lyrics, add or delete parts, and change the song sequence.

"The sessions for *Folkjokeopus* were not as focused, with a lot of rambling moments courtesy to the influence of his lady friend, Janey, who sings on the record."

Prior to the release of his fourth major studio record, Harper met former Floyd co-manager Peter Jenner, who negotiated a deal for him with EMI's new progressive music subsidiary, the Harvest label, which saw the release of *Flat Baroque and Berserk*. The future seemed full of possibilities.

Recorded in 1970 at Abbey Road studios and titled for a bird that sings through inclement weather, *Stormcock* is an epic folk entry served with a dash of autobiography, mixed with a ton of biting social criticism. Harper also gets a little help from his famous friends: Led Zeppelin's Jimmy Page appears on the record but under the conspicuous pseudonym S. Flavius Mercurius.

The overlap may not be immediately obvious—Harper's jaundiced eye and confessional lyrics make his music more personal than Floyd's—but *Stormcock* is much like *The Dark Side of the Moon*. It's part of a grand design that ties together all of its disparate musical ideas.

This was a golden age for the singer-songwriter, on both sides of the Atlantic, and Harper was hitting his sweet spot. The trouble was that the troubadour's instincts could be counterintuitive and even self-destructive. Live, for instance, he appeared to unravel, showing signs of physical deterioration, before an audience's amazed eyes. At other times he'd been full of energy and regale audiences with a mixture of coherent anecdotes and non sequiturs, often confusing listeners, motivating them to exit the building, shaping the legend of Harper's intersong rambling verbosity.

One incident has been etched into the memory of record company execs, and it seems Harper has never fully recovered from it. Harper was booked into the Troubadour in Los Angeles in what may be his most fateful gig overseas.

"Roy was on as a support," says Peter Jenner. "He came out and he saw this sort of glitterati at the front of the [stage], and he realized that there were people in their mink coats and diamonds, not there to see him. He decided that he would slag them off. He threatened or said he would piss all over the front row."

"I'm very stoned and very tired and if you don't like me you can come back tomorrow night," Harper reportedly said.

This behavior was unacceptable to Capitol Records, which had set up the gig, hoping to break Harper in the States. "They were outraged by him," says Jenner. "You've heard that 'Gigs at the Troubadour made your name in America'? Well, Roy's was the reverse. From that point on, Harvest was not able to spend a penny on him in America. He was never able to do that crossing-the-Atlantic thing successfully."

Fateful as Harper's American appearance seemed to be, Jenner's former client shouldn't and couldn't take full responsibility for the US market being virtually closed off to him. Jenner admits that he'd have knockdown, drag-out fights with Rupert Perry of Capitol over promotion, further vaporizing Harper's chances of making headway in North America.

Telling was Harper's dedication on *Lifemask* to Jenner's Blackhill Enterprises: "[Blackhill] sometimes works for us, sometimes against."

Harper made no secret of his disdain for the business and, in the liner notes to *Lifemask*, proclaimed the music scene, circa 1973, to be "brainless, thoughtless and just a hype, which is probably a reflection of a lot of what is going down in the world at this time."

"I think it was the frustration that Roy had, and I did to a lesser extent, that Roy wasn't as famous or as rich as he probably deserved," says Jenner. "Other words, you had [Ian Anderson], who was also brought up in Blackpool and was very influenced by Roy. Led Zeppelin, both Page and Plant were . . . I think Roy was deeply pissed off, and I sympathize. But on the other hand, he didn't play the game. Stubborn."

Harper would have several bites at the apple, however. In a career makeover, Harper attempted to relaunch himself as an actor when material on *Lifemask* was performed live or used in part for *Made*, a film in which our folkie hero portrays self-centered rock star Mike Preston.

Landing a co-leading role in a movie could catapult talent to the upper echelons of pop culture. Roy gives a great performance, yes, but appearing on the big screen did little to facilitate his crossover appeal. Even though younger generations have discovered Harper, access to the film or a DVD copy has been difficult.

There were other factors contributing to why Harper's profile was so obscured. For one, he fought a hereditary blood disease that doctors told him was a death sentence. He was expected to live no further than into the mid-1980s. Aside from the possible psychological shell shock Harper experienced from this diagnosis, Harper's medical condition slowed him down considerably.

"He went ill at one stage," says Jenner. "He was never the healthiest person. He had gone very ill and that was the whole problem with a tour he had to cancel."

But something else was eating away at Harper, too. "We were trying to sell something that was an album product, which I thought you could do because the Floyd had done so well and so did Led Zeppelin," says Jenner. "But Harper didn't do it. It didn't resonate with the public; he was too weird."

Medically ill, spiritually poisoned by a paradoxical society, Harper seemed resigned to his fate. However, and quite ironically, when the world seemed mired in malaise, Harper lived by the laws of contrary public opinion. A (slightly) new musical direction, a new band, and presumably a different mindset seemed to indicate that Harper was bringing the hope of new life.

Harper's 1975 album *HQ* can be viewed, in part, as an attempt to change his fortunes. The first course of business was to hire a stellar band. The whole point was to move Harper slightly away from his solo artist/folk figure public image and into the arena of rock bands. Thus, expanding Harper's reach beyond England to Continental Europe and, more precisely, North America.

Pairing Harper with a band was intended to gently curb the wordsmith's acerbic bite through the dissolving solution of band chemistry. The moniker Trigger was supposedly chosen democratically among the band members. Funnily enough, former Trigger guitarist Chris Spedding, in the book *Chris Spedding: Reluctant Guitar Hero*, does appear to take credit for the Roy Rogers-esque moniker as a phonetic send-up of Harper's cowboy-style get ups.

Legend has it that in March 1975, Spedding turned down what was touted as a temporary gig with the Rolling Stones to do Harper's 1975 tour, a business proposition to which he'd already committed. Spedding had recorded for Harvest under his own name and the Battered Ornaments banner, with Pete Brown, longtime friend of Harper, and he had hooked up with former Velvet Underground multi-instrumentalist John Cale for a UK tour supporting *Slow Dazzle* in May 1975. Spedding seemed to always be busy, but his band, the Sharks, was disintegrating; the time was right for Spedding to jump on this new musical opportunity.

On paper it was a phenomenal coup of sorts: Harper would be backed by one of the United Kingdom's greatest session guitarists as well as the stellar progressive rock drummer Bill Bruford, late of Yes, King Crimson, and Gong, and former Sharks bassist Dave Cochran, who'd spent time in the American South on the Chitlin Circuit playing with blues and roots musicians such as Albert King. When the Sharks said sayonara, Cochran lost his footing in music business, but Spedding recommended him to Harper.

"The band for *HQ* was astonishing and really good," says Watson.

EMI was onboard and even invested in ads via their Harvest label for placement in the music press. "We loved Roy at Harvest," says Watson. "He had many champions in the press, and we regularly obtained cover stories such as the one in *Melody Maker* where he is depicted sitting on Trigger backstage at Knebworth in '75."

Contemporary publicity shots of Trigger show the band brandishing toy (?) guns and Harper swinging an axe, slashing down at the camera. The belligerent band name aside, this was over-the-top, and Bruford, with eyes cast downward, seems as though he wishes to be anywhere but at this photoshoot. *Careful with that axe, Roy.*

Despite all the show biz-y marketing ploys, *HQ* might be one of Harper's strongest releases to date—musically and lyrically. The opening, multi-sectional song—Harper's own "Shine On . . ." you could say—is a whopping thirteen-plus-minute track titled "The Game (Parts 1–5)," which tackles complex issues of isolationism and society's perpetual slide toward corrosion and corruption. We think we see progress but life is a zero-sum game. As the song says, "The rules are set to paradox."

"The Game" features drummer Steve Broughton, Led Zeppelin bassist John Paul Jones, and David Gilmour, who'd played with Harper for a free Hyde Park concert in late August 1974.

"[Roy] had met the Floyd and they knew each other," adds former Floyd and Harper manager Peter Jenner. "It was a small world in London . . . He'd been on the Hyde Park concerts with the Floyd. We were all part of the same gang, partly going back to Blackhill."

Bruford plays marimba beginning approximately 7:27 into the track, and continues for well over a minute as Broughton plays kit drums for the main body of the song. Spedding's wacked out, slide-luscious guitar solo—what sounds like the whirring of an electric drill applied to a pickup—is "a wonderful piece of spontaneous Rock and Roll," Harper said in liner notes to the album.

Spedding, dressed in a white suit and red carnation, with a miniscule amp positioned in the middle of the room, cut his solo in one take in EMI's Abbey Road Studio One—the same location Gilmour used for "Shine On You Crazy Diamond," usually reserved for large-scale orchestras.

Foreshadowing the circumstance surrounding Harper's own performance for Floyd's "Have a Cigar," a Floyd band member had demurred when it was time for the little red light to go off in the studio. Gilmour had thought about the solo for months, and even had a go at it, legend has it, but he couldn't pull a track together.

"I knew nobody could have done any better than [what Spedding did], including [Spedding]," Harper says in *Reluctant Guitar Hero*. "From having David Gilmour struggle with it for three or four months to having Chris come in and do it in first take was sublime."

"I really dig Chris Spedding as a guitar player, and he has done great solo albums," says Steve "Boltz" Bolton, former guitarist for the band Headstone, which supported Harper on tour in 1975. "He's the consummate session guitar player."

"The Game (Parts 1–5)" could be interpreted as an indictment of the hippie movement and its failure to make real foundational societal changes beyond the 1960s. Harper admits, on his blog, that a particular strain of artistic protest, what he called "musical journalism," waned in the 1970s and, finding the movement's lack of progress dispiriting, that "the '60s had become increasingly embarrassing." Any gains in the cultural, political, social, environmental, spiritual, and sexual revolutions promulgated by the so-called

Flower Power Generation had fallen woefully short of the promises made by the peace-and-love crowd. "It was all over, bar the shouting, which was continued for a time by things like flying pigs, and increasingly larger flying rigs with decibels that kill," Roy wrote. "Decadence set in."

What Harper has done so well is point out the utter farcical existence and psychical disaster a conscientious individual must experience just to survive life's inherent contra-dictions. How does one accept the world, and live, without going crazy?

Five years later Harper followed up the song with the quite mysterious "You (The Game Part II)," from Harper's *The Unknown Soldier* album, featuring co-leading vocals by Kate Bush. If the first installment of the track was about survival, then, perhaps, the second is about faith in someone else.

Abbey Road's Studio One was also the site for the recording of the reflective and largely acoustic "When an Old Cricketer Leaves the Crease." Ripples of melancholy brass, so instrumental to the nostalgic aspects of David Bedford's arrangement, and beautifully performed by Grimethorpe Colliery Band, made "Cricketer" a fan favorite upon release.

Framed by an emotionally stirring sports analogy involving final acts and loss, "Crick-eter" penetrated perhaps like no other Harper song in a divided and drowning England. Dedicated as much to this life as the next, "Cricketer" operates as a national eulogy. BBC producer John Walters promised to play the song at legendary DJ John Peel's funeral and on air as a tribute, but Walters died before he could see this through. Peel, instead, played the song as a dedication to Walters after the latter died in 2001. Three years later it was, indeed, spun in memory of Peel and at Peel's own public funerary service in 2004.

Floyd speaks about absence with *WYWH*, but it's Harper, perhaps just as embittered as any Floyd lyricist, who presents a more positive view of death and absence than the songwriter's commercially successful friends. For Harper, the emotional hole resulting from death may just be a state of mind. No one truly dies—if we keep the spirit of the deceased alive. Of course, Harper himself, in his lyrics, is open to the possibility that the "sting in the ale" is so overwhelming that he's given to an overflow of nonsensical thoughts.

The material on *HQ* is simply brilliant and beautiful. The issue *HQ* faced was the same dilemma Harper had faced for years: How could he market himself outside England and the United Kingdom?

Despite helping to promote the release of *HQ* through a cricket match pitting Pink Floyd against Harper and members of Trigger, Jenner, in retrospect, believes very little could have been done to improve the nearly insurmountable odds Roy faced in his quest for stardom. Jenner now believes Roy likely didn't even get a fair shake inside his native country.

"[*HQ*] was buried in the UK," says Jenner. "EMI was a very old-fashioned company. . . . I think I had enough friends at EMI that they would have spent some money, but they said, 'We haven't got the money . . .' It killed the record."

For that matter, *Wish You Were Here* was still months away from release. Any promotional tie-in would be deferred, at best. "It sold well, but not well enough, as the sudden change in musical direction confused the *Stormcock* fan base of old," counters Watson. "This was indeed the issue. It was like a first LP from a new artist. We tried very hard to break that record and marketed it aggressively. It was difficult, however, to connect it with 'Have a Cigar.'"

Chrysalis, nurturing a smashing success with Tull in the States, distributed *HQ* in North America. One would think that, given the history of Tull in relation to Harper, *HQ* would have it made. The label, however, mysteriously saw fit to change the record title from a relatable *HQ* to the mouthful *When an Old Cricketer Leaves the Crease*. This was a strange misstep and an ironic one, since Chrysalis was viewed as a pathway to Americanization and more mainstream acceptance.

Success and failure, breakthrough and invisibility are relative terms, of course, and not every deterrent to Roy's celebrity was erected of Harper's own doing. There may be deeper issues here that are better left unexplored and unsaid. "Ten Years After, Jethro Tull, all those Chrysalis bands broke in America," says Jenner. "But [Harper] managed to fuck off his American label. He could make a good living; we were able to play thousand-seat venues but not beyond that."

"[Harper] was very difficult to work with because he was always very argumentative," adds Hipgnosis's Aubrey Powell.

Hipgnosis's cover for *HQ*, in England, reflected this. "He wanted to be like God, so we suggested that he walk on water and would be like Christ," says Powell. "I went up to Scotland. I was shooting a car commercial, or something, and I thought I'd kill two birds with one stone."

If management thought selling and recording Harper's music was a hoot, lensing the image for the UK version of the cover was a photographer's equivalent of a lost weekend. "I shot some water and then I shot [Harper] in the studio and I made a montage of the two things together," says Powell. "The only other thing I remember about this cover is that I got the car stuck on this tiny island in northern Scotland. It was stuck in sand . . . We left it there, which amused Roy to no end."

Harper's mid-1970s career was in the same predicament—immobile, stuck in the muck of an ungrateful recording industry. Perhaps in an act of self-medication and catharsis, Harper admitted that he wasn't shutting down any possibility of achieving fame and fortune—just that he didn't want to "make it" in an atmosphere that fostered so much hype (i.e. the lame state of the popular recording industry and its values).

This was likely a defense mechanism triggered for Harper's own protection. Was this all Harper licking his wounds and putting on a brave face? The Harper-as-madman angle has been projected by the media virtually since the singer-songwriter's early days as a professional musician. For instance, an ad for a pair of concerts staged in the Purcell Room at the Royal Festival Hall in September 1969 describes shows headlined by Harper, Ron Geesin, and Ralph McTell as "two days of . . . Anarchy, revolution and madness."

"I mean, the old game of genius and madness are very closely related," says Jenner.

"Was he a genius or was he crazy? Both are true. In many ways he was crazy and in many ways he was a genius. Same thing with Syd."

Who better than to sing "Have a Cigar"?

≡

Both Syd and Harper seemed spurned by the business, and, of course, "Have a Cigar" was based on the rotten, illogical, and corrupt nature of the recording industry. The famous lyric "Oh, by the way, which one's Pink?" was a question that, purportedly, the band was actually asked in prior years.

"When they wanted to say 'hi' to the director of Capitol Records, he said, 'Oh, by the way, which one's Pink?'" Aubrey Powell explains. "They were deeply mortified by the lack of sincerity and knowledge . . . and so it is all about that."

In *Disc and Echo* magazine, Barrett excoriates the business for its ability to suck the soul of artists. Barrett even went as far as to call certain executives and technical people scurrying around the recording studios morally reprehensible. It was a screed against the greed, corruption, and moral bankruptcy of the industry.

This nearly exactly mirrors the level of venom Waters shot at the recording world and its minions in the mid-1970s. From the evidence Waters had discovered, he'd absolutely hated the professional world he had entered, what with circling sharks sent into frenzy when smelling the next hit record.

Aside from the sarcasm of "Money," this sobering view of stardom is something we don't really encounter with *Dark Side*. We don't get a sense of the depth of Waters's bitterness on *Dark Side*, which is a more philosophical, dispassionate record. In comparison to *WYWH*, *Dark Side* is almost "Zen."

Waters's socialist leanings no doubt informed his surgical-strikes on the sociopolitical and capitalist structures of the Western world, and it's likely that the same instincts were stirred in the writing of "Money." Some observers note that "Have a Cigar" is *WYWH*'s answer to "Money," but they may be picking up on the opening riff(s) so central to the feel of both songs. It should be noted that these songs begin in two different keys.

Judy Trim, Waters's then wife, was a Trotskyite by Jenner's estimation, and one who impacted Roger's decisions about helping the less financially fortunate. Practically, and personally, maybe there was some contrition on Roger's part. He was, after all, pressured into returning his E-class/type Jaguar for a Mini—hence the line in the song "Welcome to the Machine."

Socialistic seeds planted during his upbringing clashed with Waters's practical experience as a successful rock star. An oversimplified view of "Have a Cigar" *and* "Welcome to the Machine" would cast them as protest songs against "The Man," putting Floyd in the same company as the most cutting-edge pop music of the era.

Waters's socialist, even communist, views bear some resemblance to the social justice movement and Black Liberation Theology, a philosophy that informed Rastafarianism and was gaining popularity at the time. Many Rastafarians believe that their true place of origin is Africa, a land of which they have been denied full knowledge largely due to the slave trade. Rastafarian faithful revered as a deity the late emperor of Ethiopia Haile Selassie, born Ras Tafari Makonnen and often portrayed as the Lion of Judah. Selassie was supposedly a descendant of King Solomon and the Queen of Sheba and would return to lead his followers—the true descendants of the Israelites—back to the Continent.

The "movement of Jah people," which Bob Marley sings about in "Exodus," refers to this postapocalyptic diaspora from the oppressive grip of Babylon (i.e. Western society's power structures). Marley's 1974 album *Natty Dread*, the following year's *Rastaman Vibration*, and his 1977 global breakthrough album *Exodus* emphasize a mystical connection to Rastafarianism.

Some interpreted the drain that various societal maladies had on our collective psyches and the reversal of fortunes as a sign that Western civilization was crumbling—in fulfillment of prophecy. Bob Marley and the Wailers seemed particularly preoccupied with redemption, earthly salvation, and warning us about political corruption, social injustice, and Babylon's moral impurity. Some Rastafari in Marley's circle even predicted that a great cleansing was imminent and that the Western world was spiraling toward Armageddon.

"[An apocalyptic view] is diametrically opposed to this idea of wealth trickling down to the lower classes," says Michael Goldwasser, producer of *Dub Side of the Moon* and *Dubber Side of the Moon*, reggae interpretations of Floyd's classic album. "As opposed to, 'Now we have to make a change. We have to demand equal rights and justice.' It's how different cultures respond to adversity."

"Babylon" did not crumble around the turn of the twenty-first century, as was foretold. With the death of Selassie in August 1975, Marley, Jamaica's reggae ambassador to the world, wrote "Jah Live," imparting the knowledge that Selassie was not gone forever into the veil but, in a sign of the times, merely *absent*. "He is not dead," Goldwasser says, "he is just not here anymore."

Roger Waters, in his own way, joined the multitudes that pumped their fists in protest. Yet, despite its aura of reflection, "Have a Cigar" seems to wallow in Floyd's woeful lack of self-accountability. It's the song's, and perhaps the entire record's, biggest failing. Floyd discusses the negative aspects of fame without acknowledging their willing participation in the entire charade, if we can rightly call it such. If Waters had pegged Syd a "martyr," then what was Floyd?

We can't lose sight of the fact that Floyd, from its earliest days, benefitted from a certain circumnavigation, if not circumventing, of the system through greasing the wheels. "Welcome to the Machine" and "Have a Cigar" present valid observations, but Faustian dealings have only served to help grow the "monster"—to nourish and feed it.

Waters, despite the success of *Dark Side*, had become increasingly embittered by endless entanglements with soul-sucking recording industry execs. Once enticed by false prophets, musicians are at the mercy of moneymen (i.e. "the suits") and groomed for their own self-destruction—perhaps a subtext to themes throughout *WYWH*, specifically addressed in "Have A Cigar" and revisited with the material appearing on *The Wall*.

So, when Waters uses the line, "Oh, by the way, which one's Pink?" to skewer the object of his ridicule, it may be the manifestation of deeper psychological issues. As others have observed, Waters was morphing into the very embodiment of all the alienation, isolation, regret, and guilt projected upon and attributed to Floyd throughout their history.

Waters steadily assumed the role as the voice, if you will, of the band, but did he actually believe *he* was Pink Floyd? Not in the real sense, of course, but symbolically. If Floyd was faceless, defined more by its stage production than pretty faces on the cover of *Circus* magazine, it should prove prime hunting grounds for a leader to rise.

Still, Waters's lyrical verses and basic music, written before he took it to the band, not only skewers the industry for its dirty practices but seems to be fighting the good fight for musicians who were steamrolled by a Monster Machine selling aspiring artists the formulas for their dreams. The Machine, however, only dilutes their visions and ultimately crushes them through a process of absorption.

$$=$$

The song opens with a scratching and muted guitar chord to which a phase shifter was applied, lending the tone a rounded, almost viscous feel. The guitar is met with bass and electric piano following the opening riff, and a second guitar adds color—a descending line at approximately 0:16 into the song.

The bass, guitar, and keyboards harmonize on, or play off, the song's main riff, starting around 0:24. This kind of simultaneity and harmonizing was part and parcel of the prog rock style of the time, and there appears to be at least four individual recorded tracks working in tandem. At certain moments, a sweeping keyboard sound might pass for a symphonic score to a 1950s Hollywood Western. And for a so-called space or psychedelic or progressive rock band, the Waters-penned song is one of the funkiest and bluesiest tracks on the record.

Few rock bands, let alone a progressive one, could pull off such a schmaltzy, funky blues-rock song, featuring both screaming lead guitar riffs *and* heavy synth lead lines. Then again, and more importantly, few would want to. Add to this directional panning of the guitar tracks, and the mixing session for the record appeared to favor variety and constant flux over uniform consistency.

For all its funk and country-like textures, "Have a Cigar" also nods in the direction of prog rock. Essential instrumentation, from what the author hears, includes first guitar, second guitar, synth, electric piano, and bass. Gilmour interjects lead riffs, rife with string bends, before and during the verses—which might constitute a separate, third guitar performance tracked for the song. In other words, multiple guitar tracks were layered for the song.

Harper is practically breathless in his singing. He plays a fine clueless record company twit, who, despite not really knowing his job, manages to hop onto the gravy train. When Harper asks, 'Oh, by the way, which one's Pink?" he sounds generally sincere in his confusion. The speaker's focus on commercial merits, to the exclusion of all else, is one-dimensional thinking and virtually sickening. The speaker has no understanding of Pink Floyd, why they are signed, who they are, and one gets the sense that this dolt is late to the party, attempting to play catch up with disastrous results. The "Cigar" man will likely, after destroying the profits of a multi-national company, retire with a golden parachute.

There are few people who'd argue that Harper's version of the song is the definitive one. By accepting Harper, the band begrudgingly acknowledged its limitations while also playing to its strengths. This cuts across all musical disciplines involved in constructing the song. For instance, Mason doesn't try to get cute with too many flourishes. Not only would this be unnecessary and inappropriate within context, but one gets the sense that the song benefits from Mason allowing the music to breathe; he either follows the general flow of the piece or adorns it with overdubbed flourishes to help propel the musical momentum.

Mason overdubs sixteenth-note beats on the hi-hats during the guitar solo, keeping the song moving along. It works nicely, and without it Gilmour's spotlight might drag a bit. Mason is a bit busier in the alternate version of the song released on the Experience Edition: he strikes the ride cymbal, but the overdubbed hi-hats still seem to be in there.

The effect is immediate, no matter the version. The rhythm track lulls the listener into thinking this is a toe-tapping common-time offering—and to a degree it is. However, when the verse moves to the refrain, the music switches from 4/4 to a slightly tricky 5/4, helping to further exploit an overall oddness stressed by this strange amalgam of styles.

The added beat of some measures exists to accommodate the canvas-crowding lyrics. If nothing else, this concoction of musical interactions and sonic swooning is a nod to Gilmour's growing interest in certain American music forms—perhaps a subconscious homage to Syd and his falling-off-the-shelf rhythmic feel, exemplified by "Bike" and its jumble of odd tempos.

Gilmour's guitar solo (beginning 3:17), as is the case with "Shine On . . . ," is full of implied notes, finger vibrato, and string bends, but also a mixture of lead notes with muted strumming. It's why and how Gilmour generates two different feels simultaneously: melodic and rhythmic; funk and blues, jazz and rock.

Gilmour injects screaming vibrato notes prior to the introduction of the vocals, but these interjections work perfectly with Harper's voice, as if engaging in a standard blues form call-and-response. Specifically, the bluesy motif of call-and-response was retained from the band's earliest influences and serves them well here. It's likely that Gilmour's interjections were completed after Harper laid down his vocals.

The sonic weep Gilmour generates is indicative of the twang of country and country-rock typically played in the United States at roughly the same time. Gilmour's guitar swells also speak to blues, and Wright's electric piano seems rooted in soul and jazz. The bass is funky and the synth strings are used for an almost faux-rhapsodic effect. It's almost comedic.

The bass track sounds as though it was put through a Binson Echorec. The stuttering effect, the quick repeats, seems to suggest this particular piece of equipment, anyway. Interestingly, Gilmour told *Musician* magazine in 1992 that he tracked many bass parts during the recording sessions for Floyd's classic albums, including the memorable fretless bass riff in "Hey You." Given Gilmour's bass performance in "One of These Days," one has to wonder about "Have a Cigar" . . .

Gilmour admitted in an interview with Gary Cooper to having played the basic guitar track for the song straight through—as well as a *keyboard*. It's unclear when or how, but the keyboard Gilmour likely used was the EMS SynthiA KS to pump up the rhythmic feel of the track with a punchy, repetitive bottom end.

The other prominent keyboard is the Wurlitzer electric piano, which is so funky/jazzy that it's difficult to imagine Gilmour having this feel. Translated to the piano, the first melodic synth line, most likely played on a Minimoog by Wright (rather than a keyboard driven VCS3, for instance), goes something as follows: D-E-F-A#, A#-F-E-D. Those notes are aligned in a mirror image, really. An appropriate configuration for such a reflective album.

Wright undoubtedly embellishes on the notes mentioned but doesn't stray too far from the core pattern. Wright's Clavinet belches sonic beeps as call-and-response patterns emerge between guitar and vocals as well as keys and guitar. Thanks to keyboard drones, sonic interjections from synth and guitar, a lead bass riff or two, the band's music is interactive and teeming with life.

Well, that is until the song closes. With a whirlwind of noise, the audio shrinks, as if being zapped into a transistor radio, the result of the mix being EQ'd and squashing most of the high and low frequencies.

The effect, we've been told, was to mimic some kind of radio reception, as if we were listening to "Have a Cigar" in our automobiles. In a way, we are: Gilmour flipped through the dials on his car radio for the frequency scan and captured it. It's reminiscent of "Revolution 9"—of flipping through radio stations, of scanning frequencies, of a mass of different musical styles colliding.

This is the second time automobiles show up on this album. (The most prominent example being "Welcome to the Machine.") It seems only fitting that the sonic framework shaping band's song about commercialism should be sucked into vortices of a radio transmission.

Radio static is followed by what could be symphonic strings and a faint voice (possibly two) before a clearer verbal dialogue ensues. In attempting to identify this conversation, I initially searched the net for shared wisdom but did not arrive at any concrete conclusions. Some claim the snippet of dialogue was from a radio broadcast of *All Quiet on the Western Front* and others a BBC radio quiz programme with Irene Thomas. I'm unsure if either of these is correct, and as of this writing, anything I could add to this would be speculative.

With more confidence, I know we hear a triumphant snippet of the "Finale: Allegro Con Fuoco," the fourth movement of Tchaikovsky's Symphony No. 4. It's almost fitting that Floyd should choose Symphony No. 4 for *WYWH*. Tchaikovsky was a psychological mess, one could conclude, prior to and during the completion of his fourth symphony—a time in the composer's personal life marred by an unsatisfactory marriage and thoughts of suicide. In addition, Tchaikovsky conducted the symphony in its UK premiere in 1893 at Cambridge University, of all places.

Waters admitted that when members of Floyd had called themselves Sigma 6 they were playing original material, such as "Have You Seen a Morning Rose," that included snippets of Tchaikovsky. It's interesting that it was a Tchaikovsky symphony that emerged on *WYWH*.

From this Tchai-haze we are zapped into a bedroom, where an aspiring musician is listening to the radio and attempting to play along with it—or maybe preening in front of the mirror, prepping for his rock star days. Vanities nurtured by the Machine?

There are those, such as Rick Sanders in his book on Pink Floyd, who remarked that the disembodied spirit playing along with the radio represents Syd. Heck, the rhythm guitar playing may be familiar to those fans of "Jugband Blues," even material appearing on *Opel*.

At the opening of "Wish You Were Here," credited to Gilmour and Waters, we then hear one lone twelve-string acoustic playing. A chortle, a sniff, and heavy breathing, presumably of the aspiring musician. This opening was written by Gilmour in EMI Abbey Road Studio 3 on a twelve-string acoustic guitar. It's believed that Gilmour bought the guitar from a friend or that Harper, having been hanging around EMI, loaned it to him for the session. I was not able to confirm either.

Gilmour wrote the partially strummed opening riff and brought it to Roger and the band. Waters loved it and wanted to develop the idea further, so both he and Gilmour began writing music for the verses.

By 0:58 the song opens in both channels—the right containing a twelve-string acoustic and the left a steel six-string acoustic as accompaniment. As he'd done with electric guitar in other songs on the album, Gilmour slides notes and uses vibrato to great, bluesy effect here.

Gilmour confessed to *Musician* magazine in 1992 that the vocal delivery for the song was based on the rhythmic pacing of the acoustic guitar opening—and then he changed it slightly as the band so desired. Electric slide guitar accents key points in the lyrics.

"Wish You Were Here" features at least three separate guitar tracks: a twelve-string acoustic, a six-string acoustic, and the weeping of an electric played with a slide. Well, although *likely* a six-string electric, the ghostly sonic slur could be steel guitar. Gilmour also performs vocal scatting along with playing Dobro, beginning at approximately 2:40. This Dobro could be the wooden-bodied one guitar tech Phil Taylor talks about in his *Guitar Player* magazine interview from 1984. Around the three-minute mark, what we're hearing is at least three different guitars—the Dobro, the twelve-string, and the steel six-stringed acoustic (possibly a Martin D35). Acoustic piano pokes through a light sonic mist, like Jenner's "Syd" trolley bus.

As they were completing "Wish You Were Here," Gilmour suggested that country fiddle be added to the mix. As chance would have it, French jazz and classical violinist Stéphane Grappelli was in Studio One.

A quick-thinking, lively player with a style the *New York Times* once dubbed "swinging" with an "airy buoyant quality," Grappelli was a master improviser who'd traded musical quips with the best European and American jazzers the first half of the twentieth century had to offer.

Grappelli's personal life has been the subject of rumor and speculation, but no one would deny that the intensity of the elite fiddler's storied past. Grappelli's life was virtually defined and shaped by the two World Wars of the twentieth century. Born in France in 1908, Grappelli was motherless and, for a time, fatherless. He lost his mother when he was just three years old, prompting his father to place him in an orphanage.

After World War I, father and son reunited and bonded over music. The younger Grappelli was later hired to accompany silent films at cinemas and began studying at the Paris Conservatory. In the years leading up to WWII, Grappelli was a member of Quintette du Hot Club de France with legendary Belgium-born Gypsy jazz guitarist Django Reinhardt, whose paralysis in two fingers revolutionized and shifted the course of European jazz. It's interesting that Reinhardt was a favorite of early Floyd collaborator Bob Klose.

Reinhardt was desperate for a violinist and so the fusion of an American artform and more traditional European musical strains generated a buzz, drawing curious musicians far and wide, eager to collaborate with them. Reinhardt and Grappelli were on tour in England when news of WWII broke. Reinhardt fled back to France for safety, but Grappelli decided to stay in Britain and worked with, most notably, English jazz piano man George Shearing.

With the arrival of the 1970s, the violinist made television appearances and began working with then-hip names, such as vibraphonist Gary Burton and fellow French violinist Jean-Luc Ponty, which may have been a deciding factor working in Grappelli's favor.

According to Peter Gammond's original liner notes for the Grappelli and Yehudi Menuhin LP *Fascinatin' Rhythm*, produced by opera house director John Mordler, the two violinists were in Abbey Road Studio One in late May 1975. (Menuhin was one of the few people on earth to have performed with Ravi Shankar *and* be on Carlos the Jackal's hit list.) This would seem to indicate that Floyd was attempting to complete "Wish You Were Here," likely, from middle May onward, until they were on tour in North America in June.

As it happened, Floyd knew Grappelli's handler from their global jaunts. They put in the request: Would Stéphane like to lay down violin for their new song? Grappelli *could*, but for a sizable fee. Once Floyd checked their funds, a deal was struck for £300.

It must have been strange, however, to have been in the room and watched someone like Grappelli listen to the playback of the song and attempt to play to it. As far as I can tell, Grappelli tracked his performance fairly quickly and then went about his business.

The fact is, for all the dealmaking, Grappelli is barely audible on the finished track. There's always been talk that you can just catch the very faint sounds of Grappelli's bow-sawing, but I always believed this to be a myth, something Roger Waters told the press so as not to appear cutthroat in dumping most of Grappelli's performance.

With the volume sufficiently loud, a smidgen below the level of outright discomfort while wearing headphones, one can detect Grappelli's playing at approximately 5:20, near the end of "Wish You Were Here," just as the billowing sound clouds of wind envelop the song and announce the opening of the second half of "Shine On . . . ."

Some have suggested that what Grappelli plays is actually a snippet from the nineteenth-century opera *The Bartered Bride*, by Czech composer Bedřich Smetana. Who could tell?

For years the general public was left with little evidence of this unlikely summit except traces of a once-believed apocryphal studio tale and virtually no audio. However, with the Experience Edition of *WYWH*, fans can officially, and perhaps for the first time, hear Grappelli prominently in an alternate version of the song.

Grappelli's solo takes the place of Gilmour's famous vocal scatting in the original album version. If Gilmour's scatting *had been* added, the Grappelli alternate may today be ranked among some of the most carefree songs in the entire Floyd catalog. Gilmour even lets out a kind of down-home *woot!* at approximately 1:03 into the track, as the lead acoustic guitar joins the opening riff played on twelve-string (panned left channel).

Still, had one not been familiar with the backstory or the later-released Grappelli track, it's likely this high-pitched, squeaky drone might not register at all. So, while Stéphane is on the track, faint as it is, the band decided not to even credit Grappelli for fear of insulting the internationally recognized stringmeister.

No matter how brilliant Stéphane was and no matter how open-minded Floyd had been for encouraging Gilmour, in the final analysis this may prove to be another prudent decision on the band's part.

It may be sacrilege to say, but here goes: Whereas Harper's performance adds to the band's mystique, Grappelli's Appalachian aplomb seems to distract, even detract, from the song. Floyd, like so many British progressive rock bands of that era, excelled when they internalized American influences and spit them out in their own unique, sometimes bizarre, ways. Adding Grappelli's sweet-and-sour violin notes may have been too twangy or country-jazz-y for the reflective track. In the final analysis, "Wish You Were Here" works as a wonderfully droopy, slightly dirgelike piece of self development. Not using the track may be deemed a good call by Floyd.

"'Wish You Were Here' is probably one of the best songs ever written," says Blue October's Justin Furstenfeld. "While it's a step outside of their usual style, this kind of transformation and performance is why Pink Floyd will always be one of the greatest of all time."

"WISH YOU WERE HERE" LYRICS

Waters admitted to friend and journalist Nick Sedgewick that some of the lyrics were penned prior to the tune being composed, a rarity in the Floyd world. It's no surprise that they are so stark and memorable.

The first line is a verbal challenge to the listener: "So you think you can tell." The logical segue would be: If *you can tell* the difference between Heaven and Hell, blue skies from pain, prove it. *How much have you grown as a human being over the years?*

Although many have related the lyrics of "Wish You Were Here" to Barrett, his relationship to the band, or Waters's relationship and possible regret (or guilt?) over Barrett's exit, the song might be about freeing one's mind. The timid and the uncurious gain nothing.

There are issues with this interpretation, however. Singing "We're just two lost souls swimming in a fish bowl" could speak to the level of frustration one has with having wasted his/her life, never taking any chances, and Waters may or may not be addressing a second party or a lover.

Waters hasn't outright rejected this interpretation, only added the caveat that it is a love song in a theoretical and philosophical sense. Perhaps this song is about Waters himself, as he finds it difficult to trust anyone. He had, after all, been experiencing marital issues.

Waters was obviously influenced by John Lennon's post-Beatles confessional, *John Lennon / Plastic Ono Band*. Lennon's primal-scream therapy, supervised by Dr. Arthur Janov, evidently helped give Lennon the courage he needed to write songs such as "God," "Working Class Hero," "Mother," and "Isolation." This radical therapy peeled away years of psychological layers to dispel myths, supposedly, to present unvarnished truths about his celebrity and personal pain he'd harbored since his youth.

Perhaps Waters was going through a more subdued self-realization process. Admittedly, the gospel Waters had written was not as shocking or emotionally raw as *Plastic Ono Band*, but *WYWH* held similar revelations. Rarely had Floyd sounded so intimate.

In 2003, regarding the famous "two lost souls" lyrics, *Rolling Stone* magazine wrote: "[They] would sound natural coming out of the mouth of, say, Willie Nelson. As is, sung by guitarist David Gilmour, they're heartbreaking."

Waters also seems to be calling out phony aspects of life. We accept ghosts in place of true heroes, trade hot ashes for trees, and so on. It's what Plato talked about when he discussed shadows on the cave wall. Specters of life delude us.

The lyrics also dictate that everything has value, even "nothing." For the Floyd, such a mental exercise is par for the course and helps bolster the theme of absence. At the least, standing still is detrimental to one's personal growth. Waters talked about engaging the world in a way his father would have been proud. This song is revelation rather than regret or regression.

Einstein's definition of insanity is performing the same operations, the same way, over and over, and expecting different results. In 1975, anyway, Waters seems to be waking up to the possibility that he was oblivious to the fact that he was "running over the same old ground."

To playing devil's advocate: The song could indeed be about the record business, Barrett, or romantic relationships. As so many have theorized, the "two lost souls" line could refer to the idea of being ogled as an object of fame. Conversely, Waters may be comparing himself to Barrett—or ringing in sympathy with him, arriving at a similar conclusion about life and the recording business.

And more Syd references exist. Barrett talked about (if not *to*) ghosts, steel rails, and a leopard cage in "Long Gone" and other tracks. "Baby Lemonade" sees the narrator beckon the listener to "make your name like a ghost." This kind of apparitional phrasing also manifests in Waters's lyrics for "Wish You Were Here." In addition, lyrical imagery such as "steel breeze" and "steel rail" is similar to the kind Barrett used in "If It's in You" from *The Madcap Laughs*.

"A walk-on part in the war" could easily refer to Barrett, too, but the idea of the "lead role in a cage" might be an acknowledgment of crushing exploitation dealt to musicians and aspiring rock stars. Fittingly, for the performances of *The Wall*, the band were literally put in "cages"—protective covers to keep the members of the band from being pummeled by tumbling bricks in the wall at the end of the show.

I can offer little beyond what has been speculated above. Much like the material on *Dark Side*, "Wish You Were Here" can often be inscrutable and mean different things to various people, and could be interpreted in any number of ways.

SHINE ON, AGAIN

The record closes with the second half of "Shine On You Crazy Diamond," Parts VI–IX, which was most certainly completed, or very nearly so, earlier in the recording process. Atmospheric sound clouds roll in at the opening of the track—a sonic device Waters reprises for "What God Wants (Part III)" on 1992's *Amused to Death*.

Like its sister track, or its other half, this portion of "Shine On . . ." is largely instrumental. Bass notes throb, Gilmour creates rhythmic tension with simmering eighth-notes, a heartbeat kick drum pattern builds, and circling and echoing synth notes assume the sonic foreground.

Slide guitars begin their sonic duel with synth, at approximately 2:27. Wright adds flourishes as Gilmour attacks and grinds his way through a furious run. A second slide joins as Gilmour performs at high octane. What we hear next—wraithlike, whistly tones—appears to be a mixture of synth and perhaps more than one slide. It's a monstrous noise, swirling with slurring notes and dive bombs. Big. Scary.

We are eventually given a respite when we return to some semblance of the original track and hear indications of the band entering a familiar verse. The vocals of Part VII are in a similar mold to those of Part V, taking us back to where it all started.

Waters's vocals are doubled for lines like "how near or how far," and harmonized vocals are likely both Waters, ascending around 5:04. Gilmour's voice and the voices of the Blackberries work perfectly with the song, melding with Waters's double-tracked lead vocals.

Lyrically, Waters appears to indicate that Syd is lost and that Roger will soon reunite with him, symbolically anyway, as he, Waters, continues to absorb psychological attacks from the industry and life in general. The line "and I'll be joining you there," delivered at approximately 5:29, is reminiscent of the "two lost souls" sentiments of "Wish You Were Here."

The second half of "Shine On . . ." presents a classic Floyd paradox: Syd is both winner and loser, a purveyor of "truth" and "delusion," a "boy-child" who basks in the glories of yesteryear yet is urged to continue to shine into the future. In Floyd World, these two opposing tendencies never seem to have any difficulty coexisting.

Waters strains to arrive at a definitive statement about Barrett. With an eye for trends, Syd quickly transcended his surroundings, existing on a different plane from most other LSD enthusiasts in the psychedelic scene. His escapism was truth, and vice versa; his adult fears, creative impulses, and joys were a trolley ride through childhood. Waters attempted to capture these contradictions and impossibilities as economically and precisely as he could at the time.

Once the vocals evaporate and the song breaks down, Hohner Clavinet funks up the proceedings. Bass joins the mix, as does equally funky guitar, (possibly) VCS, Minimoog, and Wurlitzer electric piano. Subtlety is key here. For instance, it's odd where Mason places his hi-hat accents playing off the ride. You can hear him pressing down on the hi-hat pedal when he moves to the toms and plays a pattern (7:39–40 and starting at 7:51), which would be natural for a drummer to do as a timing mechanism. He may be splitting accents—playing ride with one arm and hi-hat with the other—or, as a right-handed player, keeping his hi-hat swishing with his left foot while maintaining an ostinato ride pattern.

Drums announce the opening of the final section of the song, Part IX. After the wraithlike synth wisps pass us by, Gilmour injects a few sonic sighs with pedal steel as the momentum level drops and we arrive at what might be Wright's keyboard centerpiece.

At 11:29, after a slow jazzy section marked by the sad, almost comedic, wispy *womp-womps* of Moog, Wright seamlessly transitions from this section into a homage to the boy-child. Wright's interpretation of what so many have accurately pointed out as an extract of the main melody of "See Emily Play," the band's early single produced by Norman Smith, is tear-inducing, heartbreaking ,and, in typically Floydian paradoxical style, also heartwarming.

The self-referential melody flowing out of Wright's fingertips is similar to the sly maneuver the Beatles accomplished when they slipped in "She Loves You" at the end of "All You Need Is Love," something Syd himself may have appreciated. By reintroducing this relic of a bygone age and completely shifting the momentum of the track, Wright accelerates to the edge of compositional breakdown, twirling on the border between psychedelia, jazz, classical, and prog rock—mining the inescapable truth of what Floyd once was and what they'd become.

This circuitous musical route, looping Floyd back to their primordial beginnings, offers a mirror before which they wave hello and good-bye to all they've known. This musical Möbius strip bends time and space, allowing "Emily" and "Shine On . . ." to interlock, illuminating the band's *raison d'être.*

Caged by their own ambitions and flanked by ghosts, Floyd navigated their life path by visions of their patron saint and guiding light—drifting ever forward through the currents of the past. A paradox? Yes, but it's certainly the reason *WYWH*, perhaps the band's greatest achievement, exists in the first place.

CHAPTER 7

HEROES FOR GHOSTS

After exiting the Senator Hotel in Sacramento, President Gerald Ford walked to the office of California Governor Jerry Brown to discuss offshore drilling and social welfare. A crowd had formed and was cordoned off on a nearby sidewalk. While greeting spectators, Ford caught a glimpse of a woman in a red hooded cape, two or three people-deep inside the crowd, who appeared to be shadowing him. Ford didn't think much of it at the time, and believed she wanted to shake his hand. When he reached into the sea of humanity, the woman burnished a pistol—a .45 caliber automatic handgun and pointed the barrel at Ford. The president ducked, the gun supposedly malfunctioned, and the culprit was subdued and arrested.

No doubt acting on orders from Charles Manson, Lynette Alice "Squeaky" Fromme, a cultist of Charlie's Family, seemed surprised that the plot was foiled so easily by circumstance. This twisted Little Red Riding Hood certainly hit the road--and nearly succeeded in executing a hit ordered on the President.

On September 22, a *second* attempt on Ford's life, this time by Sarah Jane Moore, was also thwarted. Moore was said to be mesmerized by the Patty Hearst case and, apparently, set about raising a little hell, herself. Reportedly, days before her failed attempt at assassinating Ford, an emotionally distraught Moore pleaded with San Francisco police to arrest her and seize her gun, as she feared she would arrive at Stanford University, where Ford was speaking, just to test their security. At the time, Moore's gun was taken and she was questioned by Secret Service, which deduced she was "not of sufficient protective interest to warrant surveillance."

Moore claimed to be a civil-rights advocate, an informant of the FBI and volunteer for the People-In-Need food project enacted by Randolph A. Hearst, established as a term of Patty Hearst's release.

Ford had just given an interview to a San Francisco TV reporter in which a question regarding gun control laws was posed. Ford, again leaving his hotel, was paralyzed when he heard the gunshot ring out near Union Square Park in San Francisco. Moore was a healthy distance away, but she did fire off a shot that passed just off to the left side of Ford, bouncing off the hotel building and veering to the right. Oliver Sipple, a Marine veteran, wrestled with Moore and hampered her ability fire any subsequent shots.

Ford escaped a third assassination attempt in 1975: Gary DeSure and Preston Mayo were indicted in October 1975 for plotting to kill Ford in August of that year, predating both Fromme's and Good's own stunts. The plan was to use a sewer-system bomb as a diversion, possibly leaving Ford vulnerable to sniper fire. Reportedly, prior to the assassination attempt, DeSure had spent time in a mental health facility in Montana for threatening the president. By mid-September, three serious plots to kill Ford were hatched—and two of them nearly succeeded.

This all occurred within a matter of weeks, and *WYWH* was unleashed on September 12 in the United Kingdom and on the 13th in the United States, smack-dab in the middle of it. The world had gone mad, and it seemed no one was at the wheel. Absence was the rule of the day—absent the rule of law, absent clear-headedness, and absent a sense of justice and peace.

The *WYWH* LP was itself a physical reflection of absence. Packaged with black or blue shrinkwrap, *WYWH* was distributed to retail record stores with a hope and a prayer.

Hipgnosis always maintained that EMI hated their design firm and every aspect of their creative process. We could be forgiven for allowing our cynical side to imagine that relinquishing creative control to so-called hippies was only one reason the label had frowned upon the employment of independent illustrators.

"The images were controlled by Storm as the art director, and I was there to do the lighting," explains photographer Howard Bartrop. "It was sort of like how a director of photography works with film. Storm would be the director because he'd know what the content should be and I'd be the person whose responsibility it would be to get it all on film."

Thorgerson was demanding in those days. "Storm was the best of the most difficult [art directors]," says Batrop. "He would give me a brief and I think it was his plan just to annoy me, really. It wasn't really to do with giving me information for photography. His plan was to rile me up and see what happens. . . . I respected him but he was a nightmare to deal with. He had some fantastic ideas. I loved his imagery."

"I think for many of them it was the best time of their lives because we were so out there and had huge amounts of money to spend on these things," says Po. "We were very not corporate, and so it was a proper art studio."

EMI might have offered a differing view. Releasing a record without the band's name or album title was commercial suicide. The label suggested a similar solution to the one that worked for the risqué cover of Roxy Music's 1974 record, *Country Life*. Slapping a George Hardie-designed sticker on the face of the product, identifying the product, was mutually acceptable.

Picking up on the conceptual theme of the LP packaging, four classical elements were represented, and a "wish you were here" postcard was included, an idea courtesy of Hipgnosis.

For a record that partially addresses mental imbalance, it's fairly well rounded musically. The running time of "Shine On You Crazy Diamond (Parts I–V)" is a little over thirteen and a half minutes. "Shine On . . . (Parts IV–IX)," its counterpart, is virtually a minute shorter. Only eight seconds separate "Have a Cigar" (5:25) and the title track (5:17). "Welcome to the Machine" clocks in at 7:33.

The band seemed satisfied. Critics weren't. *Melody Maker*'s Allan Jones panned the record in the September 20 edition of the music-orientated periodical; he wasn't too kind to *The Dark Side of the Moon*, either, saying its "bleak, emotionally barren landscape" left him "equally unmoved."

Jones didn't see—or hear—musical evolution or progress, only a band that appeared to be in "suspended animation" for what may have been more than two years. Jones wrote, "As the world turns in destruction upon itself, the Floyd amble *somnambulantly* along their star-struck avenues, arm-in-arm with some pallid ghost of creativity."

The absence of necessary determination to follow musical ideas to their logical conclusions makes the record something of a lightweight. The title track is "forgettable," and the writer can relate to Floyd's music "running over the same old ground." Floyd was bereft of ideas. "*Wish You Were Here* sucks," Jones wrote. "It's as simple as that."

In the United States, the *Chicago Tribune* gave a generally positive review of *WYWH*, although the critic does say the album can't match *Dark Side*. "For those bent on, uh, escaping their troubles in an artificial fog, Pink Floyd's still the best musical accompaniment." *Cash Box* gave points for Floyd's "funky rocker" "Have a Cigar" and their "unique style," positioning the band "at the top of the rock pile" and later acknowledging that the record shipped Gold.

The *San Diego Union* was awfully nitpicky for a review, rating the record "good, but not great."

Rolling Stone showed no mercy, however. "Talk has it that the waiting period was prolonged by the band's own paranoia," wrote Ben Edmonds. "To release *anything* would commit them to a competition with their own past."

RS went on to say that *WYWH* realized the band's biggest fears, as evidenced by the negative reaction of young fans, who called into a radio program on KWST-FM, Los Angeles, and blasted the new record.

The magazine then began to take the record apart, negatively comparing it to *The Dark Side of the Moon*, and excoriating the band for their lack of technical ability. "The illusion of complexity that caused their drooling legion to make wild claims of high-art accomplishment was actually nothing more than the skillful manipulation of elements so simple—the basic three chords everyone else uses."

Licensing a syndicated article from Newhouse News Service, the *Atlanta Constitution*, bizarrely, compared Floyd with New York-bred singer-songwriter Harry Chapin, who are purportedly linked by their "pretentiousness." *WYWH* is "an obvious attempt to say, 'This is really significant, folks.'" The article does make a valid point, one Floyd themselves no doubt were aware of: "[I]t's hard to sympathize with a rock star who's trying to find himself, or who feels trapped in a gilded cage of his own making."

The *New York Times* was reasonably supportive and judged Floyd a pioneer of electronic rock. John Rockwell indicated that he believed the record's "austere and dreamy" qualities to be "a further extension" of *Dark Side* and noted that the album employs "hypnotic repetition" to create something seamless. "[I]t certainly leaves all the British classical-mythological pretenders gasping in the dust, and most of the German synthesizer bands, as well."

Likewise, the UPI wire services dubbed *WYWH* one of the "new records of interest," even if the review paints a slightly unflattering portrait of the band and its "formula."

Floyd took notice of the editorial commentary but quickly averted their eyes. The worst mud these outlets could sling at the band couldn't match Nick Kent's eye-opening rants. Besides, *WYWH* became No. 1 in the United Kingdom and United States—pissing off critics and forcing them to further sharpen their pencils. For that matter, according to *Rolling Stone* magazine, advanced sales of *WYWH* topped nine hundred thousand units—reportedly the largest pre-sale figures in Columbia history.

If the criticism bothered Waters, he didn't always exhibit disappointment. Rock writers, he mused, seemed to be focused on all the wrong things. "What I object to in rock journalism is this habit of giving things an importance that differs from the amount they really have," Waters was quoted as saying in an article printed in *Street Life* in 1976 and first published in France in the publication *Rock Et Folk*.

But what the critics didn't see, what they could never know, was the creative struggle Floyd waged just to get to this point. Refusing to buckle under pressure, much of it self-imposed, Floyd looked inwardly to produce *Wish You Were Here*, a conceptual, self-referential album that spoke of spiritual depravation, mental absence, and industry corruption while, perhaps inadvertently, reflecting the general madness and societal malaise of the mid-1970s. Created in the spirit of camaraderie, *Wish You Were Here* waged war against the system while paying tribute to a fallen hero and victim of the industry—the creative force fundamental to the band's very existence, Syd Barrett.

Wish You Were Here is, and was, a triumph, whether the naysayers acknowledged it or not.

Soon after the release of *WYWH*, radio had added tracks from the album for airplay or had placed them, by listener request, in heavy rotation in New York City; Rochester, New York; New Haven, Connecticut; Boston; Philadelphia; St. Louis, Missouri; Milwaukee, Wisconsin; Jacksonville, Florida; Denver, Colorado; Los Angeles; and San Jose, California.

By October, stations in Cleveland, Ohio; Eugene, Oregon; Detroit, Michigan; and Toronto were hip to Floyd's sound, and enthusiasm spread through other parts of the North America.

A single for "Have a Cigar" was released, and EMI bought ad space for it in the trades. Although not a chart-topping hit, the song would be played religiously on rock radio for the next two decades, and *WYWH* finished the year within *Record World*'s Top 30. It continued to sell into 1976 and, as of this writing, had topped six million sales in the United States alone.

But Floyd's success was an anomaly of sorts. By mid-year the record industry was on the skids. Sales were on a downward slope and pink slips were regularly being issued, at least according to the October 15, 1975, edition of *Variety*. Overseas markets were relatively unchanged, but domestic US sales were sagging.

Drill down on these figures, however, and you'll find record industry gold. Under the direction of Walter Yetnikoff, who became CBS Record Group's new president in May 1975, the label group experienced what could only be categorized as a financial uptick. Although concerned about the general (or perceived general) downturn in the US economy, which led to a vinyl surplus, the CBS Record Group nonetheless posted strong sales relative to 1974, with the CBS/Columbia division seeing a 20 percent increase in third quarter earnings, year over year. The third quarter, of course, partly included the commercial success of *WYWH*, which was officially available in September.

Other artists such as Bruce Springsteen, Bob Dylan, and Earth, Wind & Fire contributed to the label's success. In fact, the timing of the release of *WYWH* coincided with CBS recording its highest sales ever for the month of September. *Variety*'s Christmas Eve edition reported that *WYWH* was still a top seller in December.

By the mid-1970s, Floyd's music gravitated toward other sectors of industry, enhancing entire parallel commercial enterprises, from touring production to trucking/transport and the visual arts.

Ivan Dryer, founder of Laserium and father of the packaged or planetarium laser show, premiered his laser light entertainment at the Griffith Planetarium in Los Angeles in 1973.

Dryer added classical music and prog rock, including Pink Floyd, to provide a "drugless high," he told the *New York Times*.

At New York City's Hayden Planetarium, at the American Museum of Natural History, laser shows generated such interest that laserists were busy for most of the second half of the 1970s and well into the 1980s. "The spectacle has the effect of sweeping you into the cosmos to be carried weightless through time," read the *New York Times* in 1976.

Laser light shows were enhanced by the growing vinyl LP culture, a widening field of creative designers and engineers, museums/planetariums willing to stage these shows, the use of illicit substances, and the reemergence of sci-fi in the late 1960s and early 1970s—bolstered by the syndication of *Star Trek*, Ancient Astronaut theories achieving peak vogue, and the release of movies *2001: A Space Odyssey* and *The Planet of the Apes* (also a TV series in 1974).

The development of the commercial laser light show occurred in the wake of the counterculture's move toward total liberation, spiritual awakening, and exploration of both the outer and inner cosmos. Anyone who's ever been to any of these shows knows that we experience a sense of weightlessness in a darkened auditorium, looking up at a ceiling or dome-projector screen.

Dryer compared the brain activity fans experience at laser light shows to individuals entering deep meditation. Young hippies couldn't fail to see the significance of this. "Laser shows are very high contrast," says Jay Heck, of Heck Industries, who established the brand Laser Fantasy, which offers several different Laser Pink Floyd shows. "The laser light hits the dome as a small bright line and leaves the rest of the dome dark. Other types of projections light up the theater so you can see around you. I recall the first laser show I saw, after the lights went out and the laser graphic appeared: I couldn't tell where the dome was anymore. It felt like the laser images were floating in space. My brain now understands how it all works, but I frequently think back to my first show experience when designing shows."

Floyd's music complemented and added to the experience. "Pink Floyd's music is creative, has a lot of variety, it's rich with texture, and is what I consider visual music," says Heck. "If you just put on headphones and listen to it with your eyes closed your imagination flows with it. Some types of music are just fun to sing or dance to, but don't conjure up visuals. Our goal is to create visuals that look like the music sounds."

YET ANOTHER MOVIE

Director Alejandro Jodorowsky visited Floyd in the studio to investigate how they worked, and if their music would be appropriate for his new film project. Jodorowsky had released *El Topo* in the spring of 1971, which was an influence not only on Waters but also on Genesis's Peter Gabriel and informed some of his lyrical imagery for 1974's *The Lamb Lies Down on Broadway.*

Talks ensued and Jodorowsky explained that he was hoping to film in the Sahara Desert and wished Floyd would join him and the rest of the cast and crew. Floyd was interested, at least through the late summer of 1975, but composing music on location meant the band had to spend weeks, perhaps even as much as a month, away from London, living in the arid environs of North Africa.

We'll never know if the band was, ultimately, prepared to do so, because the film became unmanageable and lacked funding to proceed. Jodorowsky bowed out of the project and the mantel was eventually passed to David Lynch and Dino de Laurentis in what might be one of the most legendary and protracted and prolonged pre-production film processes in history, frustrating the filmmakers and many sci-fans, in general. Based on the 1960s sci-fi novel by Frank Herbert, *Dune* was released in 1984 but pleased few—it only gained detractors, fan and critic alike.

More directors lined up to work with Floyd. Rumor has it that Italian horror filmmaker Dario Argento reached out to the band in 1975 to cut the soundtrack for the suspense thriller *Profondo Rosso* (translated as *Deep Red*), but evidently nothing ever came of this. Floydless, Argento was forced to look elsewhere for sounds, leading him to commission Italian progressive rockers Goblin for the score. This twist of fate would kick-start a long, prosperous, and mutually beneficial cinematic relationship.

In any case, having just finished *WYWH*, the band was busy trying to finish its own recording studio, the outgrowth of a business partnership that officially formed in November 1975, renting audio and touring gear and equipment.

Floyd was afforded all the time in the world at Abbey Road as long as they gave a certain percentage of the sales revenues of the records back to EMI. The deal had yet to be renewed and Floyd knew that spending as much time in the studio as they did would reap disaster on their bank accounts. The bills would rack up—and for little reason other than they were seeking a new concept or had followed their own artistic path in search of the best sound or composition. Why put money in EMI's pockets when they could spend all the livelong day in their own space?

In 1975 Floyd invested in a recording and rehearsal space at 35 Britannia Row, Islington. Waters had been living in Islington, but his divorce from Judy meant he had to pick up stakes and move to another location in London. The place was still fairly accessible to all Floyds.

Jon Corpe designed the place to be sound proof but also ensured that the walls would absorb sound and not reflect it. When it was completed in the fall of 1975, the band was keen to get started on testing out the premises by working out the kinks in the system.

MASON'S GONG SHOW

The Gilmour-produced Unicorn was one of the first bands that recorded at Britannia Row. "We did the last record at Britannia Row, because, I think, the money was starting to run low," says Unicorn's Pat Martin. "While we were in there the Damned came in, because Nick Mason was producing them. I remember it was quite a comical thing, because they were playing up to their image. I remember walking in there one day and they were just finishing, and they started growling and taking the piss out of everything."

Since Unicorn was one of the early test subjects for Floyd's new studio, some of the technical kinks had yet to be worked out. "[Mason] offered to do the research into what mixing desk and equipment they wanted in there," says Martin. "I think when we first went in there they had a problem getting the room tuned and with the actual acoustics of the room you recorded in. They were experimenting with that a bit."

Of course the band itself, with and without Waters, would record 1977's *Animals*, parts of *The Wall*, and portions of *A Momentary Lapse of Reason* and *The Division Bell* at Britannia Row. "I could never understand why they had a studio on the ground floor and they stored all the equipment up on floors above," says Martin. "Every time they had a massive semitruck full of gear, it had to be hoisted up. I remember saying to one of their guys, 'Why don't you move the studio higher and the have the equipment on the ground floor?' and he gave me a look of 'Fuck off,' basically. 'I agree with you, but I'm not going to tell you I agree with you.'"

Some of the band have better memories of recording *Animals* than *Wish You Were Here*, likely because they were not pressed for time in Britannia Row. The band worked a lot at Britannia, but eventually the rental business idea went bust. Contrary to their initial thoughts, lighting and audio equipment were doing little more than collecting dust. The building at 35 Britannia Row, Islington, was sold in the 1980s, and in the early 1990s the studio moved to a different location.

Back in the mid-1970s, the place was buzzing with activity. Mason was busy there in 1975, as both a performer and a producer, working with Michael Mantler for his *The Hapless Child* album from July 1975 through January 1976.

Mason soon collaborated with, engineered, and/or produced various bands, some from the Canterbury scene branch of the progressive rock evolutionary tree and others of the avant-garde jazz-rock variety, such as Carla Bley. Mason's own 1981 record, *Fictitious Sports*, featuring Bley, bassist Steve Swallow, Mike Mantler, saxophonist Gary Windo, Robert Wyatt, and Chris Spedding was recorded there as well.

Perhaps just as significantly, Mason hooked up with Gong, one of the truly mystifying and technically proficient progressive bands in the English and French rock scenes of the 1970s.

Twist of fate. The late Gong leader Daevid Allen was a Syd Barrett fan, but it was Mason who'd eventually produce the band. This only after Barrett exited Floyd and Allen walked away from Gong.

Allen, an Australian expatriate who co-founded Floyd contemporary Soft Machine, was refused reentry to England due to visa issues and settled in France in the late 1960s. Eventually Gong was signed to Richard Branson's nascent label, Virgin Records. By 1975 Allen had split the band, but he would resurrect various incarnations of Gong in the proceeding years.

That meant bassist Mike Howlett, saxophonist/flutist Didier Malherbe, percussionist Pierre Moerlen, Mireille Bauer (marimba, glockenspiel, xylophone—also Moerlen's girlfriend), and keyboardist Patrice Lemoine inherited the Gong mantel.

The band's previous studio record, 1974's *You*, was (at the time) the last chapter in a conceptual trilogy. As Malherbe says, the *You* theme is "an alchemical fusion between personalities, the idea of the group. It was a schizophrenic attitude and it turned into a mass community anthem."

"The trilogy is a classic form going back to Homer," says Howlett. "*You* was a journey of self-realization, of identity and understanding the vibe of the universe and your place in it. Daevid had this idea of reworking those ancient truths in a modern way. The cartoony stuff was partly to do with breaking down this idea that we are really serious mystical musicians and serious people, and we really like doing serious things. Classic Daevid quote was, 'Gong is far too serious to be serious about . . .'"

In retrospect, Gong experienced a similar transformation to the one Soft Machine went through in the late 1960s and early 1970s as it transitioned from a quirky psychedelic rock band to an avant-fusion, even British jazz-rock outfit. With a decidedly jazz-rock fusion and "World" music bent, Gong's 1976 studio entry, *Shamal*, was infused with ethnic influences, combining African, Indian, and what may be Chinese, with bits of minimalistic patterns played on vibraphones and tubular bells. As much as an Asiatic wind, the album title represents the global sweep of the music.

Tracks such as "Mandrake," "Bambooji" and "Cat in Clark's Shoes" are expansive but not as cosmic or, frankly, loony as the band's earlier material, conducted and coordinated by Allen, the Gong Godhead.

"People enjoy that melody in 'Bambooji,' played with a bamboo flute," says Malherbe. "The track travels, musically, from east to west; it becomes more Arabic and it ends as a South American thing. That piece was meant to show that the bamboo flute is played all around the world and that bamboo is a symbol of the sun. Curiously it coincides with the trip of the sun—the sun rising in the east and setting in the west."

For the sessions, bassist Howlett garnered a greater role in the band than he had previously. "Around this time Daevid, Gilly, and Steve Hillage [guitarist] had left," says Howlett. "[Hillage] did play guitar on some of the tracks, and I ended up being the last man standing, who felt we should keep vocals, because half the band really wanted to go instrumental—completely. I wanted to carry some kind of meaning that related to the whole philosophy of [Gong]. I thought it was a good construct, a modern retelling of eternal truths."

Because Howlett wasn't fully comfortable in a lead role, he valued the atmosphere Nick Mason fostered in the studio during the creation of *Shamal*, recorded at both Basing Street and Olympic studios. (Malherbe seemed to recall recording "Bambooji" at Branson's Manor Studios in Oxfordshire, however.)

"[Mason] was wonderful," says Howlett.

> He was absolutely involved. . . . He created this [atmosphere] of intimate communication between me, out in the [studio], and him up in the control room. When you finish a take and the talk button is activated, you can hear laughter going on in the control room. Basically, it's what bands do: they sit around, getting bored, they joke away without noticing what is happening. Nick immediately saw that. You can't help but feel that as artist that you sung your heart out and . . . you hear big laughs and you immediately get paranoid that [the laughter] is about you. Nick shut them up and said, "We are doing something important, here. If you don't want to listen, go out. Leave the room." It was great. He is a lovely gentleman, Nick, and . . . kept me absolutely focused on what I was doing and always made positive comments. Then he would bring in the critique and say, "I really love when you did that." "I think when you do this you should push more there . . ." Detailed, helpful stuff that I needed as a performer.

"Nick Mason was psychologically skillful and very calm and very understanding," adds Malherbe. "I saw the general vibration he was putting out for us to get a little bit together. It's a very *charmful* album."

No doubt Virgin Records saw the coup they had enacted, enlisting a Floyd to produce one of their records. "Branson's genius is promotion/PR/marketing," says Howlett.

> He would think that, "Let's get a producer, who will give the band some press and perspective," and it worked that way. Nick came out, met the band. We were living in a farmhouse near Oxford and he spent an evening talking about the recording and what we wanted to do with it. I think he was also, being a drummer, particularly impressed with Pierre Moerlen. Pierre was a brilliant drummer; technically amazing, and he studied classical percussion at a conservatory in Strausbourg. He worked with people like Stockhausen. I used to play him Herbie Hancock and the Band . . . He knew his musical shit, but didn't know much about funky rock and roll. He had the techno flash but he didn't have the groove.
>
> But he was focused. Pierre was insanely competent technically. You would wake up in the morning and you could hear in the distance this "thunk, thunk, thunk, thunk . . ." Pierre practiced and you would drift off to sleep, again, and you'd wake up a couple hours later and he is going, "deh-deh-deh-deh-deh-deh . . ." Hours and hours he would play like that, . . . building up the technique and the physical muscles.

Gong's leader in self-appointed exile, Daevid Allen, had always stressed that musicians perform in service to some sort of higher, almost mystical, power. Who better to understand this than Mr. Understated, Nick Mason, who'd always served the song before his ego?

"You don't listen to Nick Mason for higher drum technique, but he always plays the right feel and manages an interesting inversion of things," says Howlett.

> It's never about how clever his playing is. It's about what is right and what works. David Gilmour, he's a wonderful guitarist. You don't listen to him and say, "He is a super shredder" . . . I think he is a beautiful guitarist. Gong was all about making the best music you possibly can, and we are doing this, not to show how clever we are, but to communicate a rich concept. Daevid was very much about the rich storyline and the poetry. He was always pulling us back to that. We were there to serve the music. That's the concept of the "Octave Doctor" in Daevid's mythology. The band are like strings of an instrument played by the Octave Doctor—the collective higher self of the musicians—when you allow music to play you. We achieved that sometimes on recording. . . . Your technique is developed so as to enable things to happen with minimal resistance.

In recalling the *Shamal* sessions, Howlett is struck by how profound that experience was, even as he entered into the producer arena himself. As his song "Wingful of Eyes" suggests, it was an enlightening time. "I see Nick occasionally, and I've always said that I learned a huge amount about production by being an artist produced by Nick," says

Howlett, who had crossed over into academia in the twenty-first century. "I always tell the students I work with that when that person is out there in that [recording] room, they are in the most vulnerable place. They are baring their heart, their life, their soul, their music . . . You're their only link to reality. You have to keep that constant dialogue, constant communication with them. I knew it, because I had been produced and was aware of the importance."

IN THE WIND

Near the end of November 1975, Nick Mason played with Gary Windo at a college gig in Kent. In December 1975, Mason, Waters, and Alan Stiles performed a Christmas tune on John Peel's radio show, to the shock and horror of some music purists. While this was happening, on December 21, 1975, a meeting of Organization of Petroleum Exporting Countries (OPEC) in Austria was stormed by international terrorist Carlos the Jackal (a.k.a. Illych Ramirez Sanchez) and his violent cohorts, resulting in three deaths.

Carlos was wanted in connection to the alleged murder of two French police officers and a Lebanese informant in June of '75. Shockingly, Sanchez, son of a wealthy communist Venezuelan doctor, was once a member of the in-crowd in Swinging London of 1966, who fancied the fashions, the females, and the first-rate, upscale parties.

Carlos was yet another seeming proponent of the hippie generation, having been nurtured by the free spirit of the age yet returning in a different guise to haunt the world nearly a decade later.

Despite an international manhunt, Carlos was in the wind; his whereabouts, said ABC television news correspondent Pierre Salinger, was "one of the world's biggest mysteries."

Capping off a year of absence, fear, and isolation, Cleveland's Eric Carmen scored big with "All by Myself," released in December 1975 on Clive Davis's Arista label and famously covered twenty years later by Celine Dion.

The year 1975 came to a close—a year racked by violence, strange disappearances, cosmic reprisals, incurable madness, murder, attempted murder, radical changes in popular culture, and even the tragic end of a prolonged and costly military engagement. Through it all, Floyd lived to fight (the world and each other) another day.

CHAPTER 8

MADE INTO A MONSTER

Floyd's 1977 studio record, *Animals*, appears on the surface to be inspired by George Orwell's *Animal Farm*, but it's largely a Darwinian affair. Orwell warned of the dangers of a communist economic system and the ease by which it walks hand in hand with, or devolves into, totalitarianism. Waters doesn't offer much hope for the animals in what we can only consider a kind of capitalistic, materialistic societal hierarchy. Each race is doomed in its own way.

Animals does not boast a story line, but it traces Waters's increasing misanthropy and cynical view of modern society and our culture's headlong flight into vapid materialism (i.e., the three variants of "Pigs" represent the rich and greedy; "Dogs" symbolize the aggressive, overachieving alpha dogs; and "Sheep" are the mindless, hapless followers). Band disputes over writing credits and royalties during the sessions for *Animals* only underscored just how wickedly insightful Waters's lyrics were.

Animals is a much darker record than nearly everything that came before it, including *WYWH*. It may be symbolic that the structure of *Animals*—three lengthy tracks sandwiched by two miniscule ones—is the exact opposite, the mirror image, if you will, of *WYWH*. "Pigs on the Wing 1" and "Pigs on the Wing 2"—which run 1:25 and 1:27, respectively—were dedicated to Waters's future wife, Carolyne Christie. Roughly a minute separates "Pigs (Three Different Ones)" (11:28) and "Sheep" (10:21), and "Dogs" runs 17:07.

Mason indicated that *Animals* was a bit more fun to make than *WYWH*, perhaps because of the atmosphere at Britannia Row. He does appear to rise to the challenge of a harder-edged Floyd with the cool metallic timekeeping *thonks* of cowbell ("Pigs (Three Different Ones)") and a menacing, throaty, texturally rich kit sound that would make Bill Cobham proud ("Sheep").

Wright seems to pick the correct sonic timbre to complement Gilmour's electric and acoustic guitar tracks, as he does in the opening of moments of the seventeen-minute-plus "Dogs." The jazzy Fender Rhodes electric piano bleeping at the opening of "Sheep" reaffirms the band's occasional flirtation with jazz-rock fusion, somewhat fashionable in the 1976–1977 time frame. Gilmour simply soars in "Dogs" and imprints his monstrous tones and overdubs in our minds for the later "Sheep."

While the music feels much more aggressive and straightforward, if not claustrophobic at times, there are moments of subtlety. Floyd riffs on Psalm 23 of the King James Bible in "Sheep." Sacrilege? Perhaps this is the case, but the image of lambs lining up for the slaughter works within the context of the song. I once believed that a hybrid sound in "Dogs" (at approximately 9:21) was Vocoder and synth mixed with dog barks from some sound bank, or possibly a field recording, but it isn't. "It is me whistling, my dog, and BBC sound effect records for dog . . . sounds, and no synthesizer involvement during the parts of 'Dogs' you pointed out," *Animals* recording engineer Humphries told me.

Believing the songs were too layered for one guitarist to handle onstage, the band decided to bring in an auxiliary player. Snowy White (Thin Lizzy) got the job, although from most accounts it was not a difficult audition process; he was simply asked a few questions and told to play something. White came aboard for the *Animals* tour and played guitar and even some electric bass. Perhaps without trying, White's stinging lead runs and sliding twang capture the classic Gilmour tone and approach for the track "Summer Elegy," from Rick Wright's 1978 solo album, *Wet Dream*. He was the perfect fit for the Floyd.

White can be heard on bootlegs of Floyd captured in the United States in the South and West (as well as in Europe and at Empire Pool, Wembley). White played the entirety of *WYWH* and *Animals* with Floyd on the 1977 tour. White also appears briefly, ripping a solo near the end of "Pigs (Three Different Ones)" on the eight-track version of *Animals*.

As the record neared completion, all that was left to do was design the packaging. Once again Hipgnosis, and its capable stable of photographers and graphic artists, got the call.

The cover of *Animals* depicts the image of a flying inflatable pig hovering between the giant smokestacks of the Battersea Power Station, an Art Deco structure that had stopped its useful function somewhere in the 1980s. Some sources report that the photo shoot for the cover took place on December 2 and 3, 1976. The shoot may have extended into a third partial day, by some recollections, with a team of photographers on hand and a sharpshooter, at least for one day, in case the inflatable pig escaped.

"We were on top of a five-story block of flats," says photographer Howard Bartrop, who shot the iconic cover image. "I had a really good position, other than it was freezing cold. We were there for two and a half days waiting for the light. It was the only opportunity I think I ever had where I had been asked to wait to get the best light."

The iconic image of clouds gathering, as seen on the wraparound, depicts an ominous sky. "There was one little trick," says Bartrop. "I used a graduated filter for balancing skies with the foreground. I used that to darken the skies to bring all the details out of the sky. So the colors are really strong but there is no real retouching on it."

Timing, says Bartrop, was everything:

We collapsed the tripod and put away the camera, which was quite bulky, and got into the van, and we were about to go home and then I noticed that every day when it is cloudy, there's a point where the sun can get between the lowest cloud and sit on the horizon. Just a tiny little gap, if you're lucky. I noticed the sun starting to go into that spot. The sun is sitting on the horizon. If you look there's this strange shadow on the side of the building, which is a large gas storage cylinder, and it cast this shadow on the side of the building. The sun is just on the point of disappearing below the horizon to the west. In car photography they call that the "Golden Hour." We thought it was a typical cloudy English day. Suddenly the sun came out for just fifteen or even ten minutes. Then it was gone. We just caught it sitting on the horizon. There is not much post production in there. It is pretty much lighting, graduated filter, the fact that I under exposed by accident . . . It has that dramatic landscape look to it.

The official story from the Pink Floyd Web site (www.pinkfloyd.com) maintains that the photographers and the Hipgnosis crew were on hand for three days, with the sharp-shooter only there on the first day. Hipgnosis was able to photograph only the Battersea Power Station because it was taking too much time to inflate the pig. On the second day, the bloated bovine was set to fly, but the errant sow escaped its moorings and no marksman was around to stop runaway oink from floating into airspace. It touched down on a farm in Kent. Stories emerged of air traffic control reporting the Unidentified Flying Pig, but none of these tales have been sufficiently corroborated as far as I am aware. Anyway, would a rifleman be allowed to fire a shot in the middle of London? Probably not, but this makes for a great story, though.

Through a preponderance of the evidence, the image we see on the cover of *Animals* shows a proportionally large inflatable pig overlaid upon Bartrop's nuanced, turbulent sky, hovering over the bleak Battersea building. This was essentially montage, a Hipgnosis signature and specialty.

"The way the building looks, it's almost a bad thing," says Bartrop. "The pig has its obvious connotations, as well. I think this [idea] did come from Roger, but normally Storm would think up the images. I think they will be appreciated more in the future than even now. I've held on to a color Polaroid of the Battersea Power Station—before the pig went up."

Through his association with Hipgnosis, Bartrop gained access to and worked with some of the highest-profile names in rock in the mid-1970s, from Swan Song Records act Bad Company (*Straight Shooter*) to 10cc (*How Dare You!*).

Bartrop shot another iconic album cover for another legendary rock band, the details of which are better left unsaid for legal reasons. "I was told by someone that, if I recounted the real story [of taking the cover photograph], I would never work in the industry again," says Bartrop. "That is my picture but it is credited to [someone else]."

=

A *Melody Maker* article from the January 29, 1977, issue reviewed *Animals*, attaching the headline "Punk Floyd" and saying that the "shocks come as staggeringly as Johnny Rotten gobbing at his audience, an uncomfortable taste of reality in the medium ("progressive" rock)."

While some Britons seemed almost delighted that Floyd revealed their inner punk, others across the Pond were flabbergasted by Floyd's continued success. Wayne Robins, writing for *Newsday*, said that most of the songs appearing on *Animals* "begin with a simple pop or folkish melody and a lyric introduction before evolving into precocious sounding but numbingly dull instrumental jams, dominated by mundane guitar solos that seem to have been conceived by someone on Sominex."

In the early goings on the *Animals* tour (dubbed "In the Flesh" for the North American leg), Floyd performed the entirety of the new record and *WYWH*. Waters used a miked-up transistor radio, secured to a stand, to scroll through stations at the opening of "Wish You Were Here" with surprisingly funny results. As an encore, the band would play "Money" or "Us and Them"—sometimes both, although the former was usually assigned the final slot in Continental Europe.

The *Animals* tour was an even bigger spectacle than *Dark Side* or *WYWH* tours. Toy sheep were hurled through the air via an air canon and the Scarfe film for "Welcome to the Machine" was run. The animation reportedly cost over £100,000.

"Welcome to the Machine" was a great example of Gerald Scarfe's ability to transfer sonic and lyrical ideas to a visual medium. As buzzers go off, a flowerlike shape blossoms and then collapses onto itself and into a sphere. The orb then opens along some sort of center hinge, revealing a window into another world. It's blue skies as a shining four-legged monster crawls across a desolate Mars-esque landscape. Some have identified this sci-fi creature as resembling an armadillo or a metallic Triceratops.

After leaving its desert land, the armadillo encounters various silver geometric shapes, which likely represent a metropolitan skyline, complete with high rises and even, perhaps, a nuclear tower. The tower steadily cracks, exposing a fissure of blood.

Next we are transported to another section of "the machine," where some poor soul, bloodied and dispirited, sits precariously on a metallic beam. Rats race through a maze of metal slats.

A human figure appears front and center. An elastic band stretches from the distant skyline and cuts the man's throat and beheads him. His noggin rolls to a stop. The disembodied head deteriorates and devolves into rather large simian skull. Soon, rolling waves of blood wash the plain and nearly flood the threatening and cold buildings. A sea of "blood arms" sways, like uplifted appendages at a rock concert. Bodies and blood seem to feed the monolithic machine high atop a hill until it escapes the gravity of earth and flies into the clouds and is swallowed up into an entry point of a sphere. A more horrifying picture of Hell could not be illustrated.

The inflatables, as spectacle, were used to bring the show closer to every member of the audience. No fan left behind, so to speak. As such, the *Animals* tour saw an inflatable nuclear family, which was later augmented by household appliances, a big car, and a giant menacing pig set free during, of course, "Pigs (Three Different Ones)." For indoor gigs that big piggy went to market, floating around the entire venue, secured by steel cables. Outdoor piggy was kept on a leash and filled with propane, having been secured to a cord, more or less flapping in place above the stage. (Supposedly the pig caught fire in Miami in April 1977.)

As much excitement was happening onstage, there was plenty of drama off camera. For the last year, the Floyd universe seemed to be wobbling off its axis. On April Fools Day, 1976, Gilmour's home was burglarized and he involuntarily forfeited nearly £7,000 worth of guitars. Then, on August 2, tour manager Pete Watts was found dead by his ex-wife and business partner at a Notting Hill home owned by the members of Floyd. A locked door forced them to use a ladder to enter through the window.

The scene in Notting Hill was disturbing, however; a syringe and traces of heroin were found, indicating overdose.

Throughout his history with the band, Watts struggled with substance abuse. Often it got Watts in trouble, causing the band to give him the boot. Somehow, either out of sympathy or the feeling that no one could quite be the tour manager Watts was, he would find his way back into the Floyd organization. Floyd even footed the bill to help Watts get clean and made sure he had a place to stay.

It was a tough road for Watts: he'd had a spat with the band, taken some time away from them for a year or so, and bought a one-way ticket to the United States, where he succumbed to a heroin addiction. He quit briefly but was hooked again on the junk. He'd returned to England but was alive only a matter of weeks before the drugs claimed his life. Watts had a second wife who remained in America. He hadn't been with the band for their *WYWH* tour.

Aside from all of this tragedy, Waters seemed to be further pulling away from his bandmates. With each passing performance on the *Animals* road jaunt, he'd yell out, while onstage, the number of shows the band had completed, usually while performing "Pigs (Three Different Ones)," as if counting down the days before the tour ended. Roger continued on a kind of self-exiled existence, shuttling to and fro on helicopter and never attending the band's post- and pre-show get-togethers.

The fact is that Waters hated the sporting arenas and auditoriums that were booked for the *Animals* tour. He felt isolated from the fans, and the fans, in turn, were focusing on aspects of the concert experience (or not at all) that had little to do with the music the band was playing onstage.

Waters's growing sense of misanthropy may have led to the infamous spitting incident in Montreal in July 1977 during the final show of the tour before nearly eighty thousand people—what would become the largest paying crowd in Olympic Stadium history. Legend has it that the fan shouted out a request, likely "'Careful with That Axe, Eugene,'" and Waters spat on the fan. Waters seemed to have a somewhat adversarial relationship with fans throughout the mid-1970s, but nothing on this magnitude. It was this incident, and others, that solidified Waters's concept for *The Wall*, which would appear in 1979.

Waters had his own take on the incident: "Toward the end of the tour in July, a few jerks in the audience at Montreal's Olympic Stadium set off fireworks, interrupting the show," Waters said. "It was more than distracting, it was rude, and I told the audience. Things got a bit out of hand when someone tried to scale the barrier at the front of the stage and I spat in his face. The event and my behavior made me think about my relationship with the audience and the obvious wall between some of them and some of us on stage."

Waters wasn't the only member of the band irritated during the tour. Before the encore of the last show, Gilmour walked off the stage, likely in disgust, and manned the mixing console at FOH, leaving Snowy White to handle the electric guitar duties for the remainder of the performance, including a lengthy jam. While still performing, Floyd was slowly undermined by the crew whisking equipment off the stage and out of the venue. Eventually Mason was the only one left onstage playing—with a partial kit even at that. It's surprising that Mason's kit wasn't broken down and carted away while he was still playing it.

"After the tour," Waters said, "when the band had had a chance to rest, I thought about what had happened and developed an idea for a large-scale rock show: A huge theatrical brick wall would be erected between the band and the audience to express the alienation between those in the seats and what we were trying to do."

Waters actually approached the band with two ideas for Floyd's next studio record. One, which the band favored, was *The Wall*. The other developed into Waters's own *Pros and Cons of Hitch Hiking*, which manager Steve O'Rourke liked.

The main character of *The Wall*, a psychologically deteriorating rock star named Pink, was given shape and form based on years of Waters's pains, unresolved issues, and resentments. Pink is the walking dead, pumped full of narcotics and numb with regret, fear, guilt, and personal failure. At one point, while slowly losing his grip on reality, Pink fetishizes violence and fantasizes about persecuting the "riff raff" in his audience.

The bricks in Pink's imaginary though very perceptible "wall" represent all of the incidents—and people—that have dealt vicious cuts to the rock star's mental well being throughout his life. The combat death of his father when he was a child . . . an overprotective and smothering mother . . . sadistic and predatory schoolmasters . . . an unfaithful spouse—all contributed to Pink's growing unease and impending psychotic break.

Because of his growing alienation—the sense of separation he was feeling from Floyd's audience—Waters envisioned a wall existing between himself and his audiences, representing the emotional and psychological barrier artists often construct to shield themselves from criticism. Waters took his idea a step further and wished to construct an actual physical barrier at Floyd's shows, practically enshrining Floyd's 1980 tour in the history books as one of the greatest rock spectacles to ever be staged.

It's difficult not the make a connection between the catatonic Pink as portrayed in the 1982 film *The Wall*, by Bob Geldof, and Syd Barrett and his supposed breakdown.

Although Pink's fascistic tendencies may never even have occurred to Barrett, the character is a gestalt figure who represented Syd but also represented the fire and anger inside Waters, who wished to break free and be left alone to escape from the horrors of everyday life as a performer and recording artist.

Barrett's catatonia was present, but Waters's anger superseded it as the dominant personality trait in Floyd's lyrical narratives. As Kris Di Lorenzo, writing for *Trouser Press*, succinctly expressed in 1978, Floyd had become "less preoccupied with pretty fairytales" and "more concerned with ugly ones perpetuated by society's ruling class and our own blindness."

Focusing on the negative continued to further erode the band's collaborative creative process and wreak havoc on the band dynamics. Most fans know that Floyd was beginning to collapse during the making of *The Wall*. Famously, during the double-LP concept album's making, Waters threatened to withhold his work and his concept if Wright was not fired.

As most people are aware, the sequence of events that led to Wright's demise inside the band goes something like this: Wright was on holiday and the keyboard parts had yet to be recorded. Roger and co-producer Bob Ezrin wanted to hand in the record on schedule and asked Rick to come back. Wright refused to cut his vacation short. Ezrin offered to help Wright and perform some of the parts, but not much progress was made in this direction, and, in fact, Wright wanted to be a producer of the record. Ultimately, without much fanfare, Wright was told he was out and that he would only be a paid member of the touring band.

A lot of speculation has swirled around the band because of this: Was Roger being difficult? Had Wright had enough of the band? Were extenuating circumstances making it difficult for Wright to perform, namely his marriage being on the rocks?

Whatever the reason, much of what Wright did was never up to snuff for Waters. Then again, if someone operates from a position that everything you do is wrong, the probability that you will fuck up is 100 percent.

It'd take him nearly fifteen years to claw his way back to being a member—in the Waters-less Floyd spearheaded by Gilmour. But since the band was in financial straits, being a paid member of the touring band meant Wright didn't have to share the expense of the tour with his onetime bandmates. They had to foot the bill for the entire tour between the three of them. Wright went into the black while the others headed into the red.

"In the welter of arguments about who or what was Pink Floyd," Gilmour wrote of Wright in the *Sunday Times*, upon hearing of his death, "Rick's enormous input was frequently forgotten."

In retrospect, *WYWH* seems like a celebration in light of both *Animals* and *The Wall*. It's an acknowledgment and a sobering view of the evils of the recording industry, yes, but it's also a fairly expansive and, dare I say, joyous by comparison.

WYWH was birthed out of a reckoning of Floyd's collective and personal past transgressions, ambitions, and perhaps materialistic greed. In this sense, *Animals* was the start of a new chapter and less a commentary on the previous ten years—the post-Barrett Floyd period. We can listen to "Pigs on the Wing" (both sections) and understand Waters's message of hope and love. But one would have to concede that, on the whole, *Animals* was far more cynical, and *The Wall* was excessively dark and nearly as depressing. *WYWH* was written by Floyd and perhaps only could have been written by Floyd. It's a personal album—and one that, to its final fade-out, leaves us up a cloud, not obscured by one.

At the Geldof-organized concert Live 8 in Hyde Park, London, in July 2005, Floyd reunited, causing some to speculate if Hell had, indeed, frozen. Just before the band broke into their internationally recognized song "Wish You Were Here," Waters said: "It's actually quite emotional, standing up here with these three guys after all these years, standing to be counted with the rest of you. Anyway, we are doing this for everyone who is not here. Particularly, of course, for Syd."

Syd died of cancer nearly a year to the day, in July 2006, after health concerns regarding a stomach ulcer and years of suffering from diabetes. In life and in death, Barrett remained a mystery to many, even those who had a reasonable assumption to think they knew him.

When Syd left London and returned to Cambridge, at least twice, he settled back in his hometown in 1981, after the release of *The Wall* and the support tour had ended. For most of the rock world, he had assumed the role of a recluse, regardless of whether this was actually true or not, vanishing back into the folds and fabric of his old world.

Julian Palacios, in his book *Lost in the Woods*, described some symptoms of schizophrenia and what he believed Syd Barrett may have been dealing with. Barrett's condition became apparent when talking with interviewers, such as Steve Turner of *Beat International* in 1971. Barrett's speech patterns, Palacios writes, "never conventional or particularly linear, became soliloquies of evasion, paranoia, metaphor and irony." Palacios compared interviews with Syd to attempting to cut through a kind of psychic fog, with someone straining to tune a transistor radio.

"No one that you ever really would have imagined would wind up the way he did wind up," Gilmour told director John Edginton for the 2012 documentary on the making of *Wish You Were Here*.

Perhaps one aspect of madness is an inability to negotiate life's seemingly inherent contradictions. Living in denial of reality's paradoxical nature is not an option for some. What often is labeled madness could simply be a different way of looking at the world.

In the United States, there was a kind of autopsy regarding the release of psychiatric patients from state hospitals, second-guessing the policies enacted by the government and those in the mental health profession, who relied too heavily on community clinics and drugs to address issues facing patients. In addition, the costs involved in running hospitals and caring for those with mental health issues were beginning to reach critical mass.

It all led to a grand reevaluation, championed by the US Congress's Joint Commission on Mental Illness and Health, established in 1955, in which fewer patients were being admitted and, in increasing numbers, more and more patients were being released—in some cases with no place to live but the street.

Squalid living conditions and abusive treatment of patients in state mental institutions had long been the subject of public outcry, and it was time to ease restrictions and guidelines regarding an insanity diagnosis. The Community Mental Health Act, legislation passed in 1963 by the US Congress, only accelerated the problem. Community clinics began administering tranquilizers, keeping those with existing conditions in their chemically imbalanced state—but with the added baggage of suffering side effects as well as being dazed and confused from treatment.

What LSD was to some hippies—a panacea or key to open doors of the mind—tranquilizers were to psychiatrists during roughly the same time frame. LSD had long fell out of favor clinically and recreationally in the mainstream culture.

Certain drugs *did* help individuals stay out of hospitals, but budgets dictated that institutions de-staff and ultimately shutter. This, coupled with the false assumption that local clinics could quite possibly eradicate mental health problems, only doomed the policy shift and fostered chaos.

The United Kingdom had been dealing with this issue of mental illness even earlier. It's true that the mental health sectors in both the US and the UK were in serious need of reform due to patient neglect and abuse. But was the decision to continue deinstitutionalization policies the correct remedy?

When Barrett returned to Cambridge in the late 1970s, or possibly the early 1980s, he supposedly spent some time at Fulbourn mental hospital. He also went for therapy in Essex, at an institution called Greenwoods, and possibly Warley.

Questions still remain: Was Barrett clinically diagnosed as being schizophrenic? Exactly what kind of care did he receive? Was he ever given prescription medication for his alleged mental illness?

The author cannot definitively answer these inquiries. I have not been given access to—and don't expect to be granted such in the future—Barrett's medical history. Some of what has been reported about him may be true. It also may not be.

If Syd did seek therapy in Essex, it was likely not for very long and he may not have been officially diagnosed with anything resembling schizophrenia. (Physical ailments may have been another matter altogether.) Why? How much did deinstitutionalization and the anti-psychiatry creed preached by people like R. D. Laing contribute to this diagnosis?

By the 1980s Barrett had reclaimed his given name, Roger, and his post-Syd life was devoid of most contact with friends and acquaintances from his psychedelic underground glory days.

"It's the same since he left the band back in '68," Wright told the *Boston Globe* in 1997. "Very sad. Now he's in hospital; he's diabetic, sad to say, and possibly going blind slowly. There's not much more I can say. We were asked by his doctors not to be in touch—it reminds him of who he was and puts him in deep depression."

Wright said Syd was doing fairly well. "He's not suffering financially or emotionally," the keyboardist said. "He's generally happy in his own little world."

It was Wright who expressed the most regret that he did not have the opportunity to perform with Syd when the band officially split with Barrett in 1968. In retrospect, Wright mused, if Barrett had been together enough, he, Wright, would have gladly opened a new chapter in his life as a professional musician and stuck by Syd. It was a raw sentiment, no doubt, further aggravated by Wright's own dismissal from Floyd prior to the release of *The Wall.*

In the years from the 1980s until his death, Barrett had been discovered and rediscovered by fans worldwide. Some die-hards, and some who were simply gawkers, flocked to Cambridge, hoping to catch a glimpse of the guy who once led Pink Floyd, the band that would go on to conquer the rock music world.

"From the late '70s until his death, Syd lived in the same small cul-de-sac as my mother," says Kick Horns' Tim Sanders. "She would often see him on his bike pottering off, who knows where, and never making eye contact. From time to time coach parties of dark-clad men of a certain age gather in the road to marvel at the unexceptional semi-detached house that was his last home."

Syd was a free thinker in the purest sense. He had a habit of creating paintings only to destroy them but would keep a record of each one by photographing it. His sister Rosemary claimed he may have done so for her benefit—so she could enjoy his work. For years he was reportedly writing a book on the history of art, but, as far as I know, he never meant to publish it. He occasionally (read: rarely) picked up the guitar.

For the past several decades, there has been talk of a Syd Barrett biopic, but it doesn't ever seem to come to fruition. Many creative projects involving Syd's life and music, especially film productions, have been halted full-stop. Through the course of my research for this book, one source told me that a documentary, perhaps even a feature-length film, might be in the works, but as of this writing, no detailed cinematic treatment had surfaced, to my knowledge.

Stephen Pyle, onetime bandmate of Syd back in Cambridge (now an internationally known sculptor and scenic designer), said he was raising funds for a garden at Addenbroke's Hospital, the same health facility at which Dr. Arthur Max Bennett practiced medicine, and where Syd spent his final days.

"The garden will be in celebration of [Syd]," Pyle says. "It will include sculpture, created by me, of the young man I used to know very briefly in the early 1960s. By the mid-1970s he and the Pink Floyd had gone their separate ways, but the ghosts of Cambridge continued to haunt them."

What would *Dark Side*, *WYWH*, and *The Wall*—the band's most successful albums—be if not for Syd? We can debate whether these records—without Syd's presence—would exist in the form that they do today. Would they exist at all?

And what of *The Division Bell* from 1994? Stuart Shea, in *Pink Floyd FAQ*, identifies the two main personalities of the song "Poles Apart" as Syd Barrett and Roger Waters.

The organ grinding noises, bell ringing, and other audio snippets are not only self-referential audio cues of the band's music, but its roots in Cambridge. Its genre mash-up might also be a nod to the circus-like atmosphere of Barrett's "Jugband Blues" and the annual carnival Jenny Spires talked to us about, which sweeps through Cambridge at regular intervals.

The record is full of self-referential tidbits, from the heartbeat rhythmic pattern in Rick Wright's "Wearing the Inside Out," featuring lyrics by Anthony Moore, to the church bell rings cycling through "High Hopes," the final song on the record. A reflective track, with lyrics o-written by soon-to-be Gilmour spouse, Polly Samson, "High Hopes" is largely the work of a songwriter in middle age, painting imagery that radiates concepts that resonate throughout the Floyd catalog.

By contrast, Waters has been touring the globe with an updated, high-tech version of *The Wall* and cleaning up. Ironic, since Floyd in the latter half of the 1980s and throughout the 1990s seemed to be a much bigger business concern. Reversal of fortunes, really, as Floyd became largely dormant and Waters rose to commercial ascendancy. According to figures compiled by tour trackers Pollstar, Waters was in the Top 10 concert earners in the world for 2018—and he owes it all to *The Wall* and the very Syd-like characteristics of Pink.

But *WYWH* remains the most honest and honorable example of Floyd memorializing their onetime limitless leader. It's certainly the greatest and most conscious one.

The benevolent spirit Barrett, an Angel of Mercy, who embodied the Zeitgeist of the era, motivated the surviving members of Floyd to unify in their time of need. This may sound overly dramatic, but it's essentially true: *WYWH*, the most consistent and personal of the Floyd records of the 1970s, would not exist without Barrett. Paradoxically, as the band moved further away from the Prince of British Pop-Psychedelia in time, space, and musical direction, Syd was physically and increasingly absent but never truly departed from them.

EPILOGUE

FLOYD SAVED MY LIFE

To say that Pink Floyd's music has had a major impact on the global community is putting it mildly. Professional artists from David Bowie and Marc Bolan to Muse, Porcupine Tree, and the Ghost of Paul Revere to Sigur Ros and Radiohead have likely worn out their vinyl copies of *The Dark Side of the Moon*, *Wish You Were Here*, and *Animals*.

"I see Pink Floyd as being one of the first bands to capture pure darkness and the beauty of embracing it through truth," says Justin Furstenfeld of Blue October.

Equally impressive is the diverse list of artists, spanning several decades, who've been known to cover Floyd either in concert or on record. Phish, Velvet Revolver, Guns N' Roses, David Bowie, Milk Carton Kids, Dream Theater, Italian jazz singer Boris Savoldelli, cellist Maya Beiser, Widespread Panic, Korn, Limp Bizkit, Foo Fighters, Government Mule, Easy Star All-Stars, Les Claypool . . . just to name quite a few.

An infinite number of tribute acts have sprung up, as well, in just the last twenty or thirty years, all over the world. Consider: Celtic Pink Floyd (an international cast), El Monstero (US), Big One Project (Italy), Think Pink Floyd (US), Eclysse (Italy), Brit Floyd (UK), Australian Pink Floyd (Down Under), Pink Droyd (US), the Machine (US), Paranoid Eyes (Egypt), Pigs (Canada), Shine On (Sweden), the Other Side (Spain), and— How can we forget?—Wish You Were Here (US).

"The band and the music have become a part of my life," says Eric "Eroc" Sosinski of Wish You Were Here, who were planning to do a fortieth-anniversary show celebrating *The Wall*. "I never thought in the 1980s or 1990s . . . that I would be doing it for twenty-three years."

"Every single song of the band becomes new at every listening, and every time you listen to it, it reveals some new sounds and details," says keyboardist/vocalist Marco Bellone of Italy's Eclysse. "There's a big paradox in Pink Floyd music: it's so easy technically to play and yet difficult emotionally."

Members of Floyd seem to realize the importance of keeping the music alive. We hear echoes of "Shine On . . ." in the glacial pacing and heartbeat-like rhythmic pulse of "It's What We Do," the second track on the largely instrumental 2014 Floyd odds-and-ends studio release *The Endless River*, a tribute of sorts to the late Rick Wright.

Aside from the cinematic, widescreen, *WYWH*-esque atmosphere of some of the band's more modern tracks, Floyd have passed the baton on to a younger generation of tribute band players, who continue to deliver Floyd's music on a nightly basis. "In the past I played at David Gilmour's fiftieth birthday party," says Damian Darlington of Brit Floyd. "He's now in his early seventies. On that occasion I got to play with Rick Wright on 'Comfortably Numb,' with David Gilmour and Nick Mason watching in the audience."

Russian glass player Igor Sklyarov performed "Shine On . . ." with Gilmour when the guitarist toured Italy as a solo artist. Earlier in his career, Sklyarov had traveled through Central Europe, busking and picking up the language, until he settled in Italy, where, on one fateful day in 2006, he happened to be performing on the street.

"Gilmour saw me and decided to play together [in Venice]," says Sklyarov. "Venice is, after all, the city of Murano glass. And it became a feature of the concert. My task was to play an exact copy of the sound on the original recording. On my glasses I can sing several sounds at once—together in a chord."

Sklyarov rehearsed with Gilmour prior to the show, and Gilmour "pointed out some features in harmony," says Sklyarov. "This further eliminated some errors in my performance. We played a few more times."

"I played the composition in G-minor," Sklyarov continues. "I tried to play close to the original. What changed? The nature of the sound. It's no longer electronic [sound], but natural. I was told by my friends that the composition with the glasses was the best in the concert."

Icelandic classical musician and composer Hafliði Hallgrímsson, cellist for the *Atom Heart Mother* sessions, said: "[O]ur two younger sons, Andri and Sölvi, complained about the children at school teasing them, because I was a classical musician. I told them about my encounter with Pink Floyd, and few days later they came home from school beaming, as the children completely changed their attitude, and all was well. For that alone it was worth playing that short tune for the Pink Floyd."

Floyd's music is so universal that people from all walks of life have kept this music sacred. Likely, in more than a few cases, Floyd's music provided a lifeline for those in distress.

"I had this shitty little amp in this apartment . . . in San Antonio [Texas] and was learning *Animals*," says Warr guitarist and Stick player Trey Gunn (Security Project, King Crimson). "There was a lot of druggie folks coming through the place, because of roommates, and I remember being hassled by these two drug dealer-type guys. It kind of got a little scary. One of my friends sent me away and I started playing along with that *Animals* record with the bass in my room. Those guys were so impressed it kind of defused the whole atmosphere. Pink Floyd maybe saved my life."

The ultimate measure of Floyd's dominance is provided by the enemy itself. Leafing through the pages of a single publication and tracking its reviews of Floyd, from the 1970s through the 1990s, is a good lesson in how Floyd had worn down the press.

In March 1977, for Floyd's *Animals* tour, *Financial Times* flat-out stated that "it gets easier and easier to review a Pink Floyd concert without mentioning the music." The writer seemed genuinely confounded by Floyd's success and admitted he'd never witnessed so many ticketless fans loitering outside a concert arena, all in the hopes of catching sounds wafting out of the auditorium.

In 1988, *FT* was at Wembley to cover a reconstituted Waters-less Floyd, but was no less kind. "The package—the sounds, the lights—is the thing." The band's music hasn't really progressed, or so the newspaper said, although Floyd had certainly kept up with cutting-edge developments in lighting technology. Without the spectacular light show, the concert would be "rather less than the sum of its parts." It all, said the writer, "seems now woefully dated."

By 1994, *FT* had resigned itself to concluding that Floyd's lyrics are "often heavy with revolutionary fervor" despite the band's members being part of the ultra rich. In addition, the band is stuck in a time warp; fans will continue to pay to see them no matter what. If Floyd can remain on the tour circuit, there's something dreadfully wrong with the current state of the pop music scene. The enemy concedes, however, that "Floyd's success drives critics mad."

APPENDIX

For most of the decade of the 1970s, Floyd took financial advice from Norton Warburg Management. Official agreements with clients were signed in 1975—the same year Norton Warburg was awarded a license as a securities dealer. Deposits totaled three-quarters of a million pounds. Floyd, the firm's largest account in the early and mid-1970s, was a former client of insurance brokers Scott Warburg and Partners. By spring 1976 Norton Warburg held a controlling interest in T.F.A. Electrosound Ltd., supplying audio gear to rock bands.

In the late 1970s, something went horribly awry. At the end of 1979, seven directors resigned from Norton Warburg Holdings. By winter 1981, the firm's UK assets had been frozen by court order, claiming a £2.5 million deficiency in their UK accounts.

Several months later, in September, the investment management company was in the crosshairs of a Fraud Squad investigation. By the early 1980s, Norton Warburg was in the process of liquidation, and Floyd reportedly sued the group for £1 million.

Norton Warburg were thoroughly embroiled in the shit, but the firm's problems started well before the early 1980s. By 1978, NW was said to be insolvent and, at the time of their financial collapse in the early 1980s, four hundred people had invested with the group.

Norton Warburg bet and lost bigly, squandering clients' money on speculative financial ventures. Norton was in the hole for £4.7 million and coming up short on their clients' accounts to the tune over £2.5 million. The *Times*, on July 4, 1987, reported that one victim, the mother of a blind and deaf child, lost £10,000.

However, a June 1987 article in the *Financial Times* revealed that in 1978 Floyd withdrew £860,000 from the investment house, leaving the company in the lurch and in desperate need of an infusion of cash. In the wake of Floyd's large withdrawal, quarterly reports to investors continued to be sent out but did not indicate any of the financial troubles behind the scenes. The company even presented a fraudulent balance sheet to the Bank of England, a major client, which convinced honest, hard-working people and retirees to invest with Norton Warburg.

Andrew Warburg eventually admitted guilt in participating in fraudulent accounting and trading schemes from 1978 through 1981 and was sentenced to three years in prison for his part in the financial scheme. Warburg, however, explained that he did not pocket cash in any of these misdealings.

The Norton Warburg scandal and others led to the establishment of the Securities and Investment Board (SIB), which was tasked with overseeing and regulating the investment industry. Legislation introduced in the wake of the scandals, namely the Financial Services Act of 1986, was intended to further protect investors' money by ensuring clients won't get wiped out if an investment house goes belly up. Also, if a client invests with a financial services group, the investment company must open up at least one separate bank account to reflect this; withdrawals and deposits from those accounts would need to comply with new regulations.

The Financial Services Act—in essence, a combination of self-regulation and government oversight—was repealed in 2001, and the SIB was absorbed into a new regulation board, the Financial Services Authority (FSA).

Mason has said that the firm looked to take the band's money and scatter it to a series of investments, perhaps as a tax shelter. One of these investments involved a pizza company, if one can believe it.

The problem was that each individual member of the band, at least according to Mason, was keen on having his own venture capital company. This kind of spreading of the wealth may not have been wise and could have led to financial ruin.

England's economic paper of record, the *Financial Times* (*FT*), believed that Floyd may have unknowingly forfeited £500,000 in the Norton Warburg Group's venture capitalist investments during this time frame. Other estimates put that figure at being much higher.

However, in February 1981, *FT* further speculated that the Floyd raked in £2 million to £3 million per year, taking into account live performances and record royalties. The band was given a big fat check for £5 million for *The Wall*, an album that earned the band something on the order of £10 million. But back in the late 1970s, before the balloon had burst, it was recommended, more like demanded, that Floyd leave the United Kingdom and become, more or less, tax exiles while the financial types advising them could sort out the mess from the fallout of Norton Warburg's financial malfeasance and dodgy investments.

Keeping as much of the money as they'd earned was key: Continuing to work at Britannia Row was out of the question. Floyd would have to find a new temporary base, and they decided to record part of *The Wall* at Super Bear Studios, in France, where both Gilmour and Wright had recorded their recent solo albums. Gilmour, Waters, and Ezrin stayed nearby as tracks were recorded, while Mason and Wright took advantage of the considerable amenities the studio environment offered.

The Wall was eventually finished by employing the technology and equipment of various studios in America and Europe. History shows that each of the Floyd members had at least one home in the United Kingdom.

WISH YOU WERE HERE
TOUR DATES, 1975

The band's set list, for most nights, was composed of the entirety of *The Dark Side of the Moon*, half of *Meddle*, "Shine On You Crazy Diamond," "Have a Cigar," "You Gotta Be Crazy," and "Raving and Drooling."

FIRST LEG OF NORTH AMERICAN TOUR 1975

Date	Venue	City
April 8	Pacific Coliseum	Vancouver, Canada
April 10	Center Coliseum	Seattle, Washington
April 12–13	Cow Palace	Daly City, California
April 17	Denver Coliseum	Denver, Colorado
April 19	Community Center	Tucson, Arizona
April 20	Arizona State University	Tempe, Arizona
April 21	Sports Arena	San Diego, California
April 23–27	Sports Arena	Los Angeles, California

SECOND LEG OF NORTH AMERICA TOUR 1975

June 7	Atlanta Stadium	Atlanta, Georgia
June 9–10	Capital Centre	Landover, Maryland
June 12–13	Spectrum	Philadelphia, Pennsylvania
June 15	Roosevelt Stadium	Jersey City, New Jersey
June 16–17	Nassau Coliseum	Uniondale, New York
June 18	Boston Garden	Boston, Massachusetts
June 20	Three Rivers Stadium	Pittsburgh, Pennsylvania
June 22	County Stadium	Milwaukee, Wisconsin
June 23–24	Olympia Stadium	Detroit, Michigan
June 26	Autostade	Montreal, Canada
June 28	Ivor Wynne Stadium	Hamilton, Canada
July 5 (U.K. date)	Knebworth Festival	Knebworth, England

BIBLIOGRAPHY

BOOKS, LITERATURE

Blake, Mark. *Comfortably Numb: The Inside Story of Pink Floyd*. Cambridge,
 MA: Da Capo Press, 2008.

Boyd, Joe. *White Bicycles: Making Music in the 1960s*. London: Serpent's Tail, 2006.

Bright, Kimberly J. *Chris Spedding: Reluctant Guitar Hero*. United States: independent,
 2016, e-book format.

Brinkley, Douglas. *Gerald R. Ford*. New York: Times Books, 2007.

Buckley, David. *The Thrill of It All: The Story of Bryan Ferry & Roxy Music*. Chicago:
 A Cappella Books, 2005.

Burrows, John, ed. *Visual Reference Guides: Classical Music*. New York: Metro Books, 2010.

Case, George. *Jimmy Page: Magus, Musician, Man (An Unauthorized Biography)*.
 Milwaukee, WI: Backbeat Books, 2009.

Case, George. *Led Zeppelin FAQ: All That's Left to Know About the Greatest Hard Rock
 Band of All Time*. Milwaukee, WI: Backbeat Books, 2011.

Cavanagh, John. *33 1/3: The Piper at the Gates of Dawn*. New York: Continuum, 2004.

Coleman, Ray, ed. *Today's Sound*. London: Hamlin Publishing Group, 1974.

Cott, Jonathan. *Stockhausen: Conversations with the Composer*. London: Picador, 1974.

Dallas, Karl. *Pink Floyd: Bricks in the Wall*. New York: Shapolsky, 1987.

Dannen, Fredric. *Hit Men: Power Brokers and Fast Money Inside the Music Business*.
 New York: Vantage Books, 1991.

Davis, Clive. *Clive: Inside the Record Business*. With contributions by James Willwerth.
 New York: Ballantine Books, 1976.

Ford, Gerald R. *A Time to Heal: The Autobiography of Gerald R. Ford*. New York:
 Harper & Row / Reader's Digest Association, 1979.

Forrester, George, Martyn Hanson, and Frank Askew. *Emerson, Lake & Palmer:
 The Show That Never Ends . . . Encore*. London: Foruli Classics, 2013.

Gablik, Suzi. *Magritte*. New York: Thames and Hudson, 1985.

Garnett, Mark. *From Anger to Apathy: The Story of Politics, Society and Popular Culture in Britain since 1975*. London: Vintage Books, 2007.

Geesin, Ron. *The Flaming Cow: The Making of Pink Floyd's Atom Heart Mother*. Gloucestershire, UK: History Press, 2013.

Grahame, Kenneth. *The Wind in the Willows*. Ashland, OH: Bendon, 2014.

Harris, John. *The Dark Side of the Moon: The Making of the Pink Floyd Masterpiece*. Cambridge, MA: Da Capo Press, 2005.

Henrit, Bob. *Banging On*. New Romney, UK: Bank House Books, 2013.

Heylin, Clinton. *Bootleg!: The Rise & Fall of the Secret Recording Industry*. London: Omnibus Press, 2003.

Hipgnosis, George Hardie, and Storm Thorgerson. *An ABC of the Work of Hipgnosis: 'Walk Away Rene.'* Limpsfield, UK: Paper Tiger (A Dragon's World Book), 1978.

Kurtz, Michael. *Stockhausen: A Biography*. Translated by Richard Toop. London: Faber and Faber, 1994.

Laing, R. D. *The Politics of Experience*. New York: Ballantine Books, 1978. First published 1967 by Penguin.

Lesmoir-Gordon, Nigel. *Life Is Just . . . .* Bedfordshire, UK: Eventispress, 2015.

Lydon, John. *Rotten: No Irish—No Blacks—No Dogs*. With contributions by Keith and Kent Zimmerman. New York: St. Martin's Press, 1994.

Mabbett, Andy. *Pink Floyd: The Music and the Mystery*. London: Omnibus Press, 2010.

MacDonald, Bruno, ed. *Pink Floyd: Through the Eyes of . . . the Band, Its Fans, Friends, and Foes*. New York: Da Capo Press, 1997.

Manning, Toby. *The Rough Guide to Pink Floyd*. London: Rough Guides, 2006.

Mason, Nick. *Inside Out: A Personal History of Pink Floyd*. Edited by Philip Dodd. London: Phoenix, 2005.

Michell, John. *The View over Atlantis*. Falmouth, UK: Abacus/Sphere Books, 1975. First published in 1969 by Sago Press.

Miles. *Pink Floyd: A Visual Documentary by Miles*. New York: Putnam Publishing Group (A Delilah/Putnam Book), 1982.

Miles, Barry. *Pink Floyd: The Early Years*. London: Omnibus Press, 2006.

Norman, Philip. *John Lennon: The Life*. New York: Ecco, 2008.

O'Dair, Marcus. *Different Every Time: The Authorized Biography of Robert Wyatt*. Berkeley, CA: Soft Skull Press, 2015.

Palacios, Julian. *Lost in the Woods: Syd Barrett and the Pink Floyd*. London: Boxtree / Macmillan, 1998.

Pink Floyd Anthology. Milwaukee, WI: Hal Leonard, 1986.

Pink Floyd: Dark Side of the Moon. Milwaukee, WI: Hal Leonard, 2000.

Pink Floyd: Piano Sheet Music Anthology. Van Nuys, CA: Alfred Music, 2011.

Pink Floyd: Wish You Were Here. Guitar tablature edition. New York: Music Sales, 1992.

Povey, Glenn, and Ian Russell. *Pink Floyd: In the Flesh (The Complete Performance History)*. New York: St. Martin's Griffin, 1997.

Reisch, George A., ed. *Pink Floyd and Philosophy: Careful with That Axiom, Eugene!* Chicago: Open Court, 2007.

Revill, David. *The Roaring Silence: John Cage: A Life.* New York: Arcade, 1992.

Roberts, Andy. *Albion Dreaming: A Popular History of LSD in Britain.* Singapore: Marshall Cavendish Editions, 2012.

Sandbrook, Dominic. *Seasons in the Sun: The Battle for Britain, 1974–1979.* London: Penguin Books, 2013.

Sanders, Rick. *The Pink Floyd.* London: Futura (A Contact Book), 1976.

Scarfe, Gerald. *Scarfeland: A Lost World of Fabulous Beasts and Monsters.* London: Penguin Group, 1989.

Scarfe, Gerald. *The Making of Pink Floyd: The Wall.* Cambridge, MA: Da Capo Press, 2010.

Schaffner, Nicholas. *Saucerful of Secrets: The Pink Floyd Odyssey.* New York: Dell (A Delta Book), 1991.

Scoates, Christopher. *Bullet Proof . . . I Wish I Was: The Lighting & Stage Design of Andi Watson.* San Francisco: Chronicle Books, 2011.

Shea, Stuart. *Pink Floyd FAQ: Everything Left to Know . . . and More!* New York: Backbeat Books, 2009.

Shepherd, Janet, and John Shepherd. *1970s Britain.* Oxford: Shire Publications, 2016.

Southall, Brian. *Dark Side of the Moon Revealed: The Real Story of Pink Floyd's Landmark Album.* Huntingdon, UK: Clarksdale Books, 2013.

Thomson, Graeme. *Under the Ivy: The Life & Music of Kate Bush.* London: Omnibus Press, 2012.

Unterberger, Richie. *Won't Get Fooled Again: The Who from "Lifehouse" to "Quadrophenia."* London: Jawbone Press, 2011.

Warwick, Neil, Jon Kutner, and Tony Brown. *The Complete Book of the British Charts: Singles and Albums.* 3rd ed. London: Omnibus Press, 2004.

Watkinson, Mike, and Pete Anderson. *Crazy Diamond: Syd Barrett & the Dawn of Pink Floyd.* London: Omnibus Press, 2006.

Wheen, Francis. *Strange Days Indeed: The 1970s: The Golden Age of Paranoia.* Philadelphia: PublicAffairs, 2010.

Whitburn, Joel. *The Billboard Book of Top 40 Hits.* 4th ed. New York: Billboard Publications, 1989.

Whitburn, Joel. *The Billboard Book of Top 40 Hits.* 9th ed. New York: Billboard Books, 2010.

Willis, Tim. *Madcap: The Half-Life of Syd Barrett, Pink Floyd's Lost Genius.* London: Short Books, 2002.

DVDS AND VIDEOS

John Lennon: Plastic Ono Band: The Definitive Authorized Story of the Album (DVD). Isis Productions / Eagle Rock Entertainment, 2008.

Monty Python and the Holy Grail (DVD). Columbia TriStar Home Entertainment, 2001.

One Flew Over the Cuckoo's Nest (VHS). Republic Pictures, 1993.

Pink Floyd in Concert: Delicate Sound of Thunder (VHS). CBS Music Video Enterprises, 1989.

Pink Floyd: Live at Pompeii: The Director's Cut (DVD). Universal Pictures Visual Programming, 2003.

Pink Floyd: The Dark Side of The Moon (DVD). Eagle Rock Entertainment, 2003.

Pink Floyd: The Story of Wish You Were Here (DVD). Eagle Rock Entertainment, 2012.

MAGAZINES AND PERIODICALS

"A $2-Bil Biz in Search of a Trend." *Variety*, January 8, 1975, page 1.

Adels, Robert. "Talent on Stage: Pink Floyd." *Cash Box*, May 13, 1972, page 26.

"Album Preview: Pink Floyd—*Wish You Were Here*." *Cash Box*, September 13, 1975, page 10.

"Album Reviews: Pop Picks: *Wish You Were Here*." *Cash Box*, September 20, 1975, page 32.

"Allman Bros. Band Cracking Up Over Drug Testimony." *Variety*, August 18, 1976, page 55.

Alperin, David M. "New York's Last Gasp?" With Phyllis Malamud and Barbara L. Davidson. *Newsweek*, August 4, 1975, page 18.

Alperin, David M. "Where's Jimmy Hoffa?" With James C. Jones and Jon Lowell. *Newsweek*, August 18, 1975, page 14.

Alperin, David M. "The Story of Patty Hearst." With Gerald C. Lubenow, William J. Cook, Mary Alice Kellogg, and Peter S. Greenberg. *Newsweek*, September 29, 1975, page 20.

Associated Press. "In the News: Pink Floyd Wins Legal Battle with EMI over Online Sales." *Goldmine*, April 9, 2010, page 8.

"Auditorium-Arena: Cleveland's Top." *Variety*, July 18, 1973, page 40.

"Auditorium-Arena: D.C. Capital Centre's Box Score (July 1, 1974–June 30, 1975)." *Variety*, July 16, 1973, page 54.

Betrock, Alan. "Pink Floyd: More Gritty, Less Giddy." *Circus*, October 1975, page 45.

Billboard charts: various "Top 200 Albums," "Hot 100" from November 1971 through March 1977.

Blackwell, Mark. "*Out of This World* Production Set for Pink Floyd." *Amusement Business*, January 31, 1994, page 3.

Blake, Mark. "Classic Rock Presents Pink Floyd." With Hugh Fielder, Polly Glass, Rob Hughes, Dave Ling, and Henry Yates. *Classic Rock*, December 2016, page 33.

Boucher, Caroline. "A Touring Circus—That's What Floyd Want Next." *Disc and Music Echo*, November 14, 1970, page 9.

Brown, Jimmy. "Learning to Fly: In This Exclusive Lesson, David Gilmour Reveals the Secrets Behind His Larger-Than-Life Sound." *Guitar World*, February 1993, page 60.

Buskin, Richard. "Pink Floyd's 'Shine On You Crazy Diamond.'" *Sound on Sound*, December 2014.

Charlesworth, Chris. "Caught in the Act." *Melody Maker*, October 28, 1972.

"Chatter: Alucard Sues Cap for $40,000 over Giant LP." *Variety*, September 24, 1975, page 85.

"Columbia Ships Pink Floyd Gold." *Cash Box*, September 20, 1975, page 16.

Constantin, Philippe. "Really Wish You Were Here: The Politics of Absence." *Street Life*, January 24–February 6, 1976. Page 24.

Cowley, Jason. "The Wow Factor." *New Statesman*, February 7, 2005.

"Daydream Productions Ad: Thank You! Pink Floyd . . ." *Performance*, July 25, 1975.

Di Lorenzo, Kris. "But Is It Art?: Staunch Floyd Fan Tries to Explain . . ." *Trouser Press*, May 1978, page 15.

Di Perna, Alan. "Careful with That Axe: Pink Floyd Guitarist David Gilmour Reflects on 25 Years of 'Eclipse.'" *Cash Box*, April 7, 1973, photo and caption on page 16.

"Exploring the Outer Limits of Music with One of Rock's Most Innovative and Experimental Bands." *Guitar World*, February 1993, page 52.

Di Perna, Alan. "Mysterious Ways: Mind-Bending Psychedelia. Breathtaking Light Shows. Million-Selling Albums. This Is the Inside Story of Pink Floyd, Rock's Most Cosmic Entity." *Guitar World*, December 2001, page 68.

Edmonds, Ben. "The Coast." *Record World*, March 1, 1975, page 21.

Edmonds, Ben. "The Coast." *Record World*, September 20, 1975, page 14.

Edmonds, Ben. "Records: The Trippers Trapped: Pink Floyd in a Hum Bag." *Rolling Stone*, November 6, 1975, page 63.

Edwards, Gavin. "The Rolling Stone Hall of Fame: Pink Floyd, *Wish You Were Here*." *Rolling Stone* magazine, July 24, 2003.

Erskine, Pete. "Dirty Hair Denied." *New Musical Express*, January 11, 1975, page 5.

Erskine, Pete, and Nick Kent. "Floyd Juggernaut . . . the Road to 1984?" *New Musical Express*, November 23, 1974.

"FCC's Ray Hints Possible Public Hearings on Payola." *Billboard*, September 2, 1972, page 3.

Feiden, Robert. "Pink Floyd Stunning at Radio City." *Record World*, April 7, 1973, page 29.

Flippo, Chet. "After a Record-Breaking Decade on the Charts, Pink Floyd's David Gilmour Tries a Solo Tour." *People Weekly*, March 12, 1984, page 103.

"FM Action." *Billboard*, October 26, 1974, page 22.

Fong-Torres, Ben. "Clive Davis Ousted; Payola Coverup Charged." *Rolling Stone*, July 5, 1973, page 1.

Fricke, David. "Pink Floyd: The Inside Story." *Rolling Stone*, November 19, 1987, page 44.

Garcia, Guy. "Waters Still Runs Deep." *People Weekly*, October 26, 1992, page 166.

Garcia, Guy. "The Division Bell." *Time*, May 30, 1994, page 61.

Gilmore, Mikal. "The Madness & Majesty of Pink Floyd." *Rolling Stone*, April 5, 2007, page 55.

Goddard, Lon. "Could Too Much Work Be Suicide for the Floyd?" *Record Mirror*, February 20, 1971.

Goldman, Peter. "The Bronfman Drama." With Stephan Lester, Anthony Marro, Barbara Davidson, Stephen Michaud, and Holly Camp. *Newsweek*, August 25, 1975, page 14.

"Gold Records of 1974: *Ummagumma*, February 28." *Variety*, January 8, 1975, page 127.

Hackett, Vernell. "Touring Records Are Broken: Gross Beats 1988 By $45 Mil." *Amusement Business*, December 30, 1989, page 3.

"Have a Cigar" full-page ad. *Record World*, November 15, 1975, page 19.

Hayman, Martin. "Dark Moon Eclipses Rainbow." *Sounds*, November 10, 1973, page 34.

Hogan, Richard. "Pink Floyd's Zoo Story: When Pigs Have Wings *Animals* Will Rule the Top Ten." *Circus*, April 28, 1977, page 26.

Humphries, Jamie. "Jewel in Their Crown—Pink Floyd: 'Shine On You Crazy Diamond.'" *Guitar Techniques*, Spring 2007, page 22.

Ingham, John. "Stormcock in Heat, That's Roy Harper." *Rolling Stone* (UK), December 7, 1972, page 21.

Ingham, John. "Floyd Wows 'Em at Knebworth." *Circus*, October 1975, page 61.

"James Mangold to Direct Patty Hearst Drama, Elle Fanning in Talks." *Variety*, December 6, 2017.

Jones, Allan. "Uncut Speaks to Roy Harper About Tales of Escapes from Psychiatric Hospitals, Tempestuous Dealings with the Music Business, and the Sinister Connection Between Tony Blair and Cliff . . ." *Uncut*, September 28, 2013.

Kaus, Bob. "For the Record." *Cash Box*, October 18, 1975, page 20.

Kesey, Ken. "The Loss of Innocence." *Newsweek*, November 28, 1983, page 78.

LaFong, Carl. "Notes from the Underground." *Record World*, May 16, 1970, page 50.

Lang, Brent. "Milos Forman, *One Flew Over the Cuckoo's Nest* Director, Celebrated Non-Conformists." *Variety*, April 15, 2018.

Lang, Brent. "*A Star Is Born* CinemaCon Trailer Shows Lady Gaga, Bradley Cooper Singing Live." *Variety*, April 24, 2018.

"Last Chopper out of Saigon." *Time*, May 12, 1975, page 11.

"Lawyers Ask $117G in Pink Floyd Fees." *Variety*, February 18, 1976, page 111.

"Led Zeppelin." *Classic Rock*, September 2010.

Logan, Nick. "Rex on the Road—From Manchester: A Ringside and Backstage Report." *New Musical Express*, June 24, 1972, page 5.

"London." *Record World*, March 24, 1973, page 53.

MacDonald, Ian. "The First In-Depth Examination of the Strangest Rock Scene in the World." *New Musical Express*, December 9, 1972, page 26.

MacDonald, Ian. "Boom Blasts and the Beat." *New Musical Express*, December 16, 1972, page 34.

MacDonald, Ian. "From Amon Duul to Faust's New Sound-World." *New Musical Express*, December 23, 1972.

Mark, Matthew. "Pink Floyd: Consistent Magnificence." *Record World*, July 5, 1975, page 45.

Markey, Sanford. "Fireworks, Real and Political, Light Up Cleve. Concert Scene."
    Variety, July 20, 1977, page 58.

Meltzer, R. "Between the Planets Electronic Birds Pipe at the Gates of Dawn, Heralding
    the Interstellar Thunder of Pink Floyd." *Circus*, October 1971, page 20.

Meyer, Frank. "CBS Disk Sales Surge Upwards; Yetnikoff to Expand Roster." *Variety*,
    October 15, 1975, page 59.

"Milwaukee Judge Drops Drug Rap; Calls Bust Illegal." *Variety*, August 6, 1975,
    page 51.

Mulhern, Tom. "David Gilmour: Pink Floyd and Beyond." *Guitar Player*, November
    1984, pages 92

"Music-Records: Idle Pic Studios as Rock Echo Chambers." *Variety*, July 23, 1975,
    page 100.

"Nick Mason: Delicate Thunder." *Modern Drummer*, November 2011, page 38.

Paytress, Mark, and Mark Blake. "Blow Up." *Mojo '60s*, Pink Floyd Special, page 78.

Peacock, Steve. "Robert Wyatt Backs Away from a *Strange Alien World*." *Sounds*,
    May 31, 1975, page 14.

Perrin, Jeff. "Transcriptions: Pink Floyd's One of These Days." *Guitar World*, February
    2012, page 138.

"Pianist Byron Janis Makes Film on Chopin." *Variety*, September 17, 1975, page 1.

"Pink Floyd French Tour." *Billboard*, September 30, 1972, page 54.

"Pink Floyd into Westbury Prior to East Coast Tour." *Variety*, March 19, 1975, page 65.

"Pink Floyd Pulls 225G Advance SRO for a N.J. Concert." *Variety*, June 11, 1975,
    page 57.

"Pink Floyd Pulls 825G in Cleveland Show." *Variety*, June 29, 1977, page 51.

"Pink Floyd: Trouble?" *Performance*, May 30, 1975, page 1.

"Pink Floyd: Untold! Unseen! Unearthly! . . . The Whole Crazy Trip." *Q*,
    Pink Floyd Special Edition.

Povey, Glenn. "Diamond in the Rough." *Guitar World*, February 2012, page 60.

Rathbone, Oregano. "Things Cannot Be Destroyed Once and for All." *Record Collector*,
    November 2016, page 78.

Resincoff, Matt. "Careful with That Axe: David Gilmour Chops Through Pink Floyd's
    Past to Build a New Future." *Musician*, August 1992, page 54.

"Rock 'n' Roll News." *Creem*, October 1976, page 15.

Rudman, Kal. "Money Music." *Record World*, March 17, 1973, page 14.

Rudman, Kal. "Money Music." *Record World*, June 9, 1973, page 24.

Saxby, Mark. "It's That Man Again." *The Amazing Pudding: Pink Floyd & Syd Barrett
    Magazine*, issue 47, page 12.

Schaffner, Nicholas. "Repent, Pink Floyd Idolators: British Hordes Invade American
    Heartland." *Musician*, August 1988, page 70.

Stewart, Tony. "Electric Chaos, but Just Great." *New Musical Express*, January 29, 1972.

Stump, Paul, and David Stubbs. "The Incredible Journey." *Uncut*, November 2001, page 40.

Sutcliffe, Phil, and Peter Henderson. "The First Men on the Moon." *Mojo*, March 1998, page 66.

"Talent in Action: Pink Floyd: Radio City Music Hall." *Billboard*, April 21, 1973, page 20.

"The Album Chart." *Record World*, December 20, 1975, page 48.

"The Album Chart." *Record World*, January 3, 1976, page 24.

"The FM Airplay Report." *Record World*, September 20, 1975, page 32.

"The FM Airplay Report." *Record World*, October 25, 1975, page 30.

"The FM Airplay Report." *Record World*, December 6, 1975, page 32.

The History Of Rock: 1974, issue 10.

The History Of Rock: 1975, issue 11.

"The Last Grim Goodbye." *Time*, May 12, 1975, page 6.

"The Star Shakes Up the Party." *Time*, November 24, 1975, page 16–19.

Thompson, Dave. "Pink Floyd: The Near Side of the Moon." *Goldmine*, December 8, 2006, page 14.

Thompson, Dave. "See You on *The Dark Side of the Moon*: Uncovering the History Behind the Pink Floyd Classic That Became One of the Biggest-Selling Records Ever." *Goldmine*, August 29, 2008, page 34.

Hollywood Reporter Staff. "Former *NYPD Blue* Writer Arrested After Fatally Punching Dog in Face." *Hollywood Reporter*, June 17, 2012.

Touzeau, Jeff. "Shine On You Crazy Diamond: The Early Studio Sessions of Syd Barrett and Pink Floyd Explored." *EQ*, December 2007, page 14.

Udo, Tommy. "The Ripple Effect." *Guitar World*, February 2012, page 68.

"*Variety* Top 20 Air Plays This Week." *Variety*, June 21, 1972, page 57.

Watt, Mike. "Syd Barrett." *Melody Maker*, March 27, 1971.

Williams, Richard. "CAN DO: Don't Take Pop Rituals Too Seriously." *Melody Maker*, January 27, 1973.

NEWSPAPERS AND NEWSLETTERS

"104 More Arrested at Rock Concert in L.A. Sports Arena." *Los Angeles Times*, April 27, 1975, page 4.

"1976: When National Happiness Peaked." *Independent*, March 17, 2004.

"2 Indicted in Plot to Assassinate Ford." *Newsday*, October 21, 1975, page 3.

"2500 Ball at IT-Launch." *International Times*, October 31, 1966, page 14.

"60 Arrested at Coliseum Rock Concerts." *Newsday*, June 19, 1975, page 31.

"A Body Identified in London Bombing." *New York Times*, September 7, 1975, page 9.

Apple, R. W., Jr. "Margaret Thatcher Assumes Her Office as Prime Minister." *New York Times*, May 5, 1979

"Arab Investment Showing a Shift." *New York Times*, September 19, 1975, page 49.

Atkinson, Rick. "Alice's Show Must Go On." *The Record*, July 6, 1975, page 40.

Bacon, Dick. "No Time to Talk About Selling, Says Alouettes' Berger." *Montreal Gazette*, May 30, 1975, page 21.

"Bad Scene," *Jersey Journal and Jersey Observer*, June 20, 1973, page 1.

Barnes, Clive. "Montreal Ballet: The Problem of Petit." *Financial Times*, November 28, 1967, page 28.

"Big Blowout in Hamilton." *Ottawa Journal*, June 30, 1975, page 16.

"Britain Averts Rail Strike, but Disputes Plague Chrysler Unit, Courtlauds' Plant." *Wall Street Journal*, June 23, 1975, page 8.

"Black Outs in Britain: British Economy Gripped by Crisis as Coal Strike Cuts Power Supply." *Wall Street Journal*, February 14, 1972, page 2.

"British Conservatives Re-Elect Mrs. Thatcher." *New York Times*, December 5, 1975.

Borders, William. "A Killer Terrorizes Yorkshire and Taunts the Police." *New York Times*, September 9, 1979, page 5.

Brown, Christine. "Olympia's Heat Didn't Wilt the Jazzy Sounds of Pink Floyd." *Detroit Free Press*, June 25, 1975, page 10-C.

Brown, Jonathan. "R. D. Laing: The Celebrity Shrink Who Put the Psychedelia into Psychiatry." *Independent*, December 29, 2008.

Burr, Rosemary. "A Cautionary Tale for Investors." *Financial Times*, March 14, 1981, page 17.

"Businessman Jailed for Fraud on Small Investors." *Financial Times*, June 30, 1987, page 9.

Cain, Scott. "Ten Years After, Turk Murphy Play." *Atlanta Constitution*, April 16, 1972.

Cain, Scott. "Alice Cooper, Engelbert, Pink Floyd Are Scheduled." *Atlanta Journal and Constitution*, March 18, 1973, page 14-F.

Cain, Scott. "Pink Floyd, Mac Davis and Tina Turner Due." *Atlanta Journal and Constitution*, June 1, 1975, page 7-F.

Canby, Vincent. "Film: *Tommy*, the Who's Rock Saga." *New York Times*, March 20, 1975, page 48.

Christgau, Robert. "So Payola Isn't Good, But It Isn't Such a Bad Thing Either." *New York Times*, June 17, 1973, page A18.

Classified ad. "Desperation!!" *Green Bay Press-Gazette*, May 29, 1975, page 44.

Clements, Andrew. "Pink Floyd: Wembley Stadium." *Financial Times*, August 8, 1980, page 13.

Cohn, Nik. "*Tommy*, the Who's Pinball Opera." *New York Times*, May 18, 1969, page D36.

"Coliseum to Tighten Up Security After Incident." *Newsday*, February 26, 1980, page 18.

"Concert Aftermath." *Montreal Gazette*, July 2, 1975, page 29.

"Conviction Brings a Suicide in Court." *New York Times*, June 19, 1975, page 38.

"Cooper Concert Tickets Will Go on Sale Tuesday." *Jersey Journal and Jersey Observer*, May 24, 1975, page 1.

Cromelin, Richard. "At the Sports Arena." *Los Angeles Times*, April 25, 1975, page G25.

"Curtain Descends in Algiers on OPEC Terrorists' Fate." *New York Times*, December 24, 1975, page 4.

Damsker, Matt. "Pink Floyd Even Has Big Piggy." *Evening Bulletin*, June 29, 1977, page 56.

Dickson, Tim. "Filling a Gap in the Market." *Financial Times*, March 21, 1981, page 7.

Dickson, Tim. "New Owners for Chicago Pizza Pie Factory." *Financial Times*, August 27, 1982, page 6.

Doran, Dennis. "Concert Score: 1 Dead, 15 Arrested, 2 in Hospital." *Jersey Journal and Jersey Observer*, June 16, 1975, page 1.

Edwards, Henry. "There's Art in the Led Zep's Heavy-Metal Hullabaloo." *New York Times*, February 2, 1975, page 20.

"English Pop Group Plays Roosevelt Stadium." *Jersey Journal*, June 12, 1973, page 26.

Evans, Rob. "The Past Porton Down Can't Hide." *Guardian*, May 6, 2004.

Evans, Norman. "The Pink Floyd: London Free School Sound/Light Workshop." *International Times*, December 12–25, 1966, page 10.

"Family in LSD Case Gets Ford Apology." *New York Times*, July 22, 1975, page 63.

Farnsworth, Clyde H. "Terrorist Raid OPEC Oil Parley in Vienna, Kill 3." *New York Times*, December 22, 1975, page 1.

Ferretti, Fred. "Witness Details Workings of the Record Industry." *New York Times*, June 8, 1973, page 24.

Fish, Tom. "LSD Making Comeback as Professionals Drop Acid Before Work." *Daily Star UK*, April 9, 2018.

Fitzpatrick, Rob. "And for Our Next Brick: Interview; Gerald Scarfe Drew It While Roger Waters Played It. Now You Can Catch Pink Floyd's *The Wall* Again on Stage and Page." *Sunday Times*, October 24, 2010, page 22.

"Free School: First Meeting: Success." *The Gate: Notting Hill Gate Neighborhood Newsletter*, April 4, 1966, page 1.

Gale, David, and Mick Rock. "An Eternal Summer with Syd." *Guardian*, July 15, 2006.

Gartland, Peter. "Family Monday: A City Failure and His Victims." *Times*, July 4, 1987.

Goodman, Walter. "A 'Prime Time' Journey on the Trail of Carlos." *New York Times*, January 3, 1991.

Heckman, Don. "Rock Aura Frames Show by Pink Floyd." *New York Times*, May 3, 1972, page 38.

Heckman, Don. "Volume Goes Up and Up at Pink Floyd's Concert." *New York Times*, November 17, 1971, page 42.

Hersh, Seymour M. "Family Plans to Sue C.I.A. over Suicide in Drug Test." *New York Times*, July 10, 1975, page 61.

Hinckley, David. "Frankie Crocker Dies: Deejay Helped Create Urban Contemporary." *New York Daily News*, October 23, 2000.

"Hot Notes." *Montreal Gazette*, March 17, 1973, page 50.

"Hudson Youths in for Rock." *Jersey Journal and Jersey Observer*, April 24, 1975, page 29.

Grover, Rob. "Pink Floyd's Music Was Fine, But . . ." *Baltimore Sun*, June 22, 1975, page B1.

Hazlett, Bill. "Davis Hits Arena Manager as 'Cry Baby' over Festival." *Los Angeles Times*, April 29, 1975, page 3.

Horrock, Nicholas M. "C.I.A. Views on Use of Poison Reported." *New York Times*, September 11, 1975, page 1.

Horrock, Nicholas M. "Senate Intelligence Panel to Investigate Why C.I.A. Failed to Destroy Poisons." *New York Times*, September 10, 1975, page 23.

Howard, William. "Pink Floyd at Boston Garden." *Boston Globe*, June 20, 1975, page 38.

Hunter, Marjorie. "A Plea to Bind Up Watergate Wounds." *New York Times*, August 10, 1974, page 1.

Ingham, Jonh. "To Celebrate England's Opening Victory at the Ashes, We Revisit Roy Harper's Track 'When An Old Cricketer Leaves the Crease,' with a Piece Published in 1975 from Rock's Backpages." *Guardian*, July 17, 2013.

"Interview: Pink Floyd Legend Roger Waters." *Mirror*, May 15, 2008.

"Is L.A. Changing Rock Bust Policy?" *San Francisco Chronicle*, October 29, 1975, page 46.

Johnston, Laurie. "Ford Signs $750,000 Grant in LSD Death in C.I.A. Test." *New York Times*, October 14, 1976, page 42.

Kalina, Mike, and Regis Stefanik. "Three Rivers Concerts Rocked by 45,000 Fans." *Pittsburgh Post-Gazette*, June 21, 1975, page 1.

Kalodner, John David. "Pink Floyd Has Turned Pale." *Philadelphia Inquirer*, June 14, 1975, page 4-C.

Kanzer, George, Jr. "Chapin, Floyd—Pretentious." *Atlanta Constitution*, October 9, 1975, page 33.

Kendall, John. "Arena Manager Accuses Chief Davis of Harassing Rock Fans, Hits 511." *Los Angeles Times*, April 29, 1975, page 1.

Kendall, John. "Davis Rock Show Report Ordered by Police Board." *Los Angeles Times*, May 2, 1975, page D1.

Kilborn, Peter T. "British Inflation Rate up to Record 26.1% in June." *New York Times*, July 19, 1975, page 45.

Kilborn, Peter T. "As Britain Tackles Inflation, Jobless Soar." *New York Times*, July 26, 1975, page 37.

Kisselgoff, Anna. "Roland Petit, Choreographer, Dies at 87: Conquered Ballet Taboos and Hollywood." *New York Times*, July 10, 2011.

Knippenberg, Jim. "Pink Floyd More Rock Than Movie." *Cincinnati Enquirer*, April 26, 1974, page 45.

Kornheiser, Tony. "Lost in Space." *Newsday*, June 18, 1975, page 8A.

Laurence, Robert P. "Pop Records: Count Basie's Band Is Back on Track." *San Diego Union*, December 14, 1975, page E-8.

"Led Zeppelin Tour Put Off." *New York Times*, August 10, 1975, page 39.

"Letters to the *Times*." *Los Angeles Times*, May 6, 1975, page C6.

Lewis, Anthony. "The Chronic Crisis: II." *New York Times*, June 30, 1975, page 29.

Lichtenstein, Grace. "C.B.S. Limits Help in a Payola Study." *New York Times*, July 14, 1973, page 55.

"Liner Notes." *Arizona Republic*, March 17, 1975, page 24.

Linquist, Gary. "Records." *Boston Globe*, February 1, 1974, page 21.

Lloyd, Jack. "Pink Floyd Trip: Lights Fantastic." *Philadelphia Inquirer*, June 29, 1977, page 4.

Mann, Bill. "Let's Face It—Quebec Has Strange Taste." *Montreal Gazette*, April 5, 1975, page 43.

Mann, Bill. "Rock & Pop." *Montreal Gazette*, December 7, 1974, page 16.

Marsh, David. "Quadrophonic Nothing." *Newsday*, August 22, 1974, page 8A.

McFadden, Robert D. "Suspect Was Defender of Manson 'Family.'" *New York Times*, September 6, 1975, page 1.

McGrath, Tom. "The Editor Flips Out." *The International Times*, January 16–29, 1967, page 1.

Meyer, Bruce. "Rock Music Record Review." *Greeley Daily Tribune*, October 22, 1975, page 41.

Miles, Barry. "*Pink Floyd—A Saucerful of Secrets*—Columbia SCX 6258" album review. *International Times*, July 26–August 8, 1968, page 16.

"Miss Fromme Indicted Under Law of Presidents' Assassination." *New York Times*, September 11, 1975, page 28.

Nicholson, Michael. "Pink Floyd Brings Cosmos Indoors at Music Hall." *Boston Globe*, November 12, 1971.

Ochs, Mark. "10,000 Fans Roar Approval of Pink Floyd." *Tucson Daily Citizen*, April 21, 1975, page 9.

"Oil Exporters on Alert for Terrorist." *Newsday*, December 14, 1976, page 11.

Paglia, Camille. "Endangered Rock." *New York Times*, April 16, 1992.

Palmer, Robert. "The Pop Life: Early Shades of New Age from Tangerine Dream." *New York Times*, June 25, 1986, page C25.

"Pickets Let Rock Show Go On." *Vancouver Sun*, April 8, 1975, page 38.

"Pink Floyd Dazzles Fans in Grand Style." *Montreal Gazette*, June 28, 1975, page 57.

"Pink Floyd Packs Stadium." *Fond Du Lac Commonwealth Reporter*, June 23, 1975, page 15.

"Police Arrest 332 During Rock Concert." *Montreal Gazette*, May 8, 1975, page 28.

"Police Make 125 Arrests at Arena Rock Concert." *Los Angeles Times*, April 26, 1975, page 1.

"Pop Battles with Theatrical Rock for London Audiences." *Montreal Gazette*, June 3, 1975, page 19.

Popham, Peter. "Nightmare of Kidnapping Returns to Italy as Millionaire's Wife Is Held." *Independent*, June 22, 2004. https://www.independent.co.uk/news/world/europe/nightmare-of-kidnapping-returns-to-italy-as-millionaires-wife-is-held-733071.html

Price, Hardy. "Agenda: Panovs Plan Visit?" *Arizona Republic*, April, 17, 1975, page 97.

Price, Hardy. "Pink Floyd Rescheduled." *Arizona Republic*, April 16, 1975, page 18.

Provick, Bill. "New Sound, Fewer Gimmicks—40,000 Cheer Pink Floyd." *Ottawa Citizen*, June 27, 1975, page 58.

Reich, Kenneth. "Coliseum's Hardy Retires After Vote by Supervisors." *Los Angeles Times*, September 5, 1986.

Richard, Ray. "Official Who Killed Himself Might Not Have Gone to Jail." *Boston Globe*, June 19, 1975, page 3.

Riley, Barry. "SIB Issues Draft Protection Rules." *Financial Times*, May 23, 1986, page 8.

Robards, Terry. "260,000 Miners Strike in Britain." *New York Times*, February 11, 1974, page 1.

"Rock Concert Leaves Brewers Field Scarred." *Leader-Telegram*, June 25, 1975, page 25.

"Rock Concerts Will Roll for Summer." *Jersey Journal and Jersey Observer*, June 17, 1975, page 13E.

"Rock Orgy Stirs Row." *Hudson Dispatch*, June 20, 1973, page 1.

Rockwell, John. "Townshend, One of the Who, Faces a Creative How." *New York Times*, June 13, 1974, page 53.

Rockwell, John. "Led Zeppelin Excites Crowd at Garden but Somehow Delirium Wasn't There." *New York Times*, February 4, 1975, page 26.

Rockwell, John. "Who's Sick? Not the Who in the Eyes of Rock Fans." *New York Times*, May 13, 1976, page 13.

Rockwell, John. "Pink Floyd: Dreamy Rock and Nightmare Words." *New York Times*, July 3, 1977, page 31.

Rockwell, John. "The Pop Life." *New York Times*, December 14, 1979, page C15.

Rockwell, John. "A Pink Floyd Album Marks 10 Years as a Best Seller." *New York Times*, May 6, 1984, page 108.

Rohter, Larry. "The Pink Floyd Experience." *Washington Post*, June 10, 1975, page B7.

Ross, Bob. "Pink Floyd Rises Above Audience." *St. Petersburg Times*, July 2, 1973, page 2-D.

Saffire, Wiliam. "Mrs. Thatcher's Soliloquy." *New York Times*, July 25, 1976, page 24.

Sampson, Anthony. "Viewpoints: America's Year of Trauma." *Newsday*, December 31, 1974, page 29.

Sandall, Robert. "The Dark Side of Pink Floyd: It's Rock Music's Most Complicated Saga, Involving Ego Wars, Madness and Death." *Sunday Times*, March 22, 2009, page 12.

Santosuosso, Ernie. "Pink Floyd Rock Feature a Hallmark of Determination." *Boston Globe*, August 24, 1974, page 9.

Seligsohn, Leo. "High on Light." *Newsday*, November 20, 1975, page 1A.

Selvin, Joel. "Tedium from Pink Floyd." *San Francisco Chronicle*, April 15, 1975, page 36.

Shabecoff, Philip. "2D Coast Episode: The Suspect Had Been Queried but Freed by Secret Service." *New York Times*, September 23, 1975, page 1.

Shuster, Alvin. "Britain Will Ban I.R.A. and Impose Curbs on Travel."
    New York Times, November 26, 1974, page 1.

Shuster, Alvin. "Italians' Apathy over Kidnappings Is Shaken by Girl's Murder."
    New York Times, September 12, 1975, page 2.

Siskel, Gene. "The Movies: Pink Floyd and Pompeii." *Chicago Tribune*, August 8, 1974,
    page B6.

Smith, Andrew Phillip. "John Esam Obituary." *Guardian*, September 11, 2013.

Smith, Bob. "Pink Floyd: Full House, Good Humor." *Vancouver Sun*, October 2, 1972,
    page 35.

"Special Stage Will Be Used by Pink Floyd." *Arizona Daily Star*, April 17, 1975, page 5,
    Section B.

"Stadium Authority Is Silent on Safety." *Pittsburgh Post-Gazette*, April 21, 1972.

Stanley, Don. "Pink Floyd: Like Technicians from the Land of Gadgetry." *Vancouver
    Sun*, April 9, 1975, page 47.

"Statement by the President in Connection with His Proclamation Pardoning Nixon."
    New York Times, September 9, 1974, page 24.

"Storm Slugs Area, Knocks Out Power." *Green Bay Press-Gazette*, June 23, 1975, page 1.

"Strikers Halt Preparation for Rock Show." *Vancouver Sun*, April 7, 1975, page 8.

Sullivan, Jim. "The Dark Side of Pink Floyd's Rick Wright." *Boston Globe*, January 3,
    1997, page D13.

Sweeting, Adam. "Monster Sound—Pink Floyd's Latest Mega-Tour Is in Town: The
    Music May Be Terrible but It Goes On, and On." *Guardian*, October 10, 1994,
    page 8.

"The Madness: This Time the Gun Is Fired at the President." *New York Times*,
    September 28, 1975.

"The Nation: Even Nixon's Mail Was Read by the C.I.A." *New York Times*, September
    28, 1975, page 4.

Thorncroft, Antony. "Earls Court: The Pink Floyd." *Financial Times*, May 21, 1973,
    page 3.

Thorncroft, Antony. "Earls Court: Pink Floyd." *Financial Times*, August 6, 1980, page 11.

Thorncroft, Antony. "Elizabeth Hall: The Pink Floyd." *Financial Times*, May 13, 1967,
    page 7.

Thorncroft, Antony. "Empire Pool, Wembley: Pink Floyd." *Financial Times*, March 22,
    1977, page 3.

Thorncroft, Antony. "Pink Floyd in Docklands." *Financial Times*, July 8, 1989.

Thorncroft, Antony. "Planetarium: The Pink Floyd." *Financial Times*, March 2, 1973.

Thorncroft, Antony. "Pop: Pink Floyd." *Financial Times*, October 19, 1994, page 21.

Thorncroft, Antony. "Rainbow: Pink Floyd." *Financial Times*, February 22, 1972, page 3.

"Three Teams Protest Shape of Stadium." *Waukesha Daily Freeman*, July 9, 1975, page 14.

Treaster, Joseph B. "Army Nerve Experiments as Late as 1974 Reported." *New York
    Times*, September 13, 1975, page 53.

Treaster, Joseph B. "Detective Said Scientist Had 'Severe Psychosis.'" *New York Times*, July 11, 1975, page 34.

Treaster, Joseph B. "Senate Hearing Is Told that Pentagon Conducted Drug Tests with Virtually No Outside Supervision." *New York Times*, September 11, 1975, page 22.

Van Haintze, Bill. "5 Coliseum OD Cases Released by Hospital." *Newsday*, June 21, 1975, page 16.

Van Matre, Lynn. "A Sound Lineup of New Albums." *Chicago Tribune*, October 12, 1975, page E6.

Van Matre, Lynn. "Ethereal and Good." *Chicago Tribune*, October 28, 1971, page B16.

Van Matre, Lynn. "Pink Floyd's Musicality Transcends Gimmickry." *Chicago Tribune*, March 8, 1973, page B5.

Van Matre, Lynn. "Plug in Kraftwerk; There's No Pain." *Chicago Tribune*, April 13, 1975, page E7.

Van Matre, Lynn. "Solo, but Gilmour Is Still in the Pink." *Chicago Tribune*, July 9, 1978, page E2.

Van Matre, Lynn. "The Relics of Syd and Mull." *Chicago Tribune*, August 18, 1974, page E12.

Vena, Michael. "Pink Floyd Clouds Coliseum with Haze of Space Sound." *Wisconsin State Journal*, March 5, 1973, page 10, section 1.

Vitale, Neal. "Pink Floyd Group Switches On Flash and Thunder." *Boston Globe*, March 16, 1973, page 28.

Watrous, Peter. "Stephane Grappelli, 89, Jazz Violinist and Master at Improvisation, Is Dead." *New York Times*, December 2, 1997, page B7.

Weber, Bruce. "Harvey Schein, Promoter of Betamax Sony, Dies at 80." *New York Times*, May 15, 2008, page C12.

Weiner, Tim. "Obituaries: Sidney Gottlieb, 80, Dies; Took LSD to C.I.A." *New York Times*, March 10, 1999, page C22.

Weinraub, Bernard. "Elusive Figure Hunted in Europe as Terrorist Key." *New York Times*, July 14, 1975, page 6.

Weisman, John. "Flashpot Goes Berserk; So Do Pink Floyd Fans." *Detroit Free Press*, March 7, 1973.

Williams, Jonathan. "Stadium Death Inquest Slated." *Pittsburgh Post-Gazette*, April 22, 1972, page 1.

Willis, Thomas. "Floyd's Midnight Raga." *Chicago Tribune*, April 13, 1970, page D6.

Wilson, John S. "Old-Time Jazz Violinist Plays Smoothly." *New York Times*, October 1, 1974, page 35.

Wilson, John S. "Stephane Grappelli Has Fiddle Power at Reno Sweeney." *New York Times*, June 10, 1976.

Wyles, John. "Red Faces in Venice over Pink Floyd." *Financial Times*, July 19, 1989, page 2.

Young, Cy. "Obituary: Derek Meddings." *Independent*, September 13, 1995.

WEBSITES

Ali, Tariq, and Robin Blackburn. "Interview w/ John Lennon About Primal Therapy." The Primal Center: Official Site of Primal Therapy (primaltherapy.com).

AmericanRadioHistory.com

BBC News (bbc.com/news/magazine)

Brain-Damage.co.uk (Pink Floyd News Resource)

Cannane, Steve. "Brexit Vote: All Too Similar to UK's 1975 Referendum." ABC News (abc.net.au/news), June 16, 2016.

Carter, Jimmy. "Address to the Nation on Energy and National Goals: *The Malaise Speech*." The American Presidency Project (presidency.ucsb.edu), July 15, 1979.

ChrisSpedding.com

DavidGilmourBlog.co.uk

Davies, Joe. "Waiting for Summer to Start? It Was Much Worse in 1975." ITV.com, June 2, 2015.

"Facts About Strychnine." CDC.gov.

Gallup.com

Herman, George. "Gerald Ford: Interview on CBS News' *Face the Nation*." The American Presidency Project (presidency.ucsb.edu), June 5, 1976.

Hipgnosis Album Art. "Pink Floyd *Wish You Were Here* 1975." RichardManning.co.uk.

History.com Staff. "September 05, 1975: President Ford Survives Second Assassination Attempt." History.com, 2009.

History.com Staff. "September 12, 1974: Violence in Boston over Racial Busing." History.com, 2010.

Hollis (hollis.harvard.edu)

Imperial College London (imperial.ac.uk)

I-SpySydInCambridge.com

"John Lennon and Primal Therapy." The Primal Center: Official Site of Primal Therapy (primaltherapy.com).

Longman, Phil. "Was 1976 All It's Cracked Up to Be?" BBC.co.uk, March 17, 2004.

Maps.org

Masri, Allan. "Goodbye Mr. Rose." Masri Zone (masrizone.blogspot.com), May 10, 2009.

MayoClinic.org

Myers, Marc. "Roger Waters on 'Another Brick in the Wall.'" *Wall Street Journal*, September 21, 2015. (retrieved online)

PinkFloyd.com

"Rastafarian Beliefs: Original and Modern Beliefs." BBC.co.uk, October 9, 2009.

RIAA.com

RoyHarper.co.uk

Russ, Hilary (editing by John Quinn). "IRS Wins $3.2M from Estate of Long-Dead Music Lawyer." Law360.com, Aug. 11, 2011.

Shah, Anisha. "The Drought of 1976." BBC.co.uk, August 4, 2006.

Turner, Steve. "A New Book on the Beatles and Primal Therapy." The Primal Center: Official Site of Primal Therapy (primaltherapy.com).

The Guardian Blog: https://www.theguardian.com/news/datablog/2010/jan/28/divorce-rates-marriage-ons

UPI.com

DOCUMENTS & OTHER SOURCES

Capital Radio interviews, December 17, 1976–January 21, 1977.

CNN broadcast miniseries, *The Seventies*, 2015.

Dayal, Geeta. "Harmonia—Complete Works Vinyl Box Out October 23, 2018." *Gronland*, 2015.

Smith, Sid. Liner notes: Robert Wyatt's 1970 solo debut, *The End of an Ear* (Esoteric Recordings, ECEC 2324, 2012).

Swedish Film Institute file on Michael Meschke movie (1974).

US Department of Health, Education and Welfare, *Monthly Vital Statistics Report: Advance Report: Final Divorce Statistics, 1975*. From the National Center for Health Statistics.

ORIGINAL PERSONAL INTERVIEWS

Howard Bartrop

Jeff Baugh

Chris Joe Beard

Marco Bellone

Steve "Boltz" Bolton

Joe Boyd

Root Cartwright

Michael Chaves (e-mail)

Simon Clarke

Peter Clifton

David Courtney

Damian Darlington

Arya Degenhardt

Venetta Fields

Simon Francis (e-mail)

Justin Furstenfeld

Ron Geesin

Michael Goldwasser

Parker Griggs

Trey Gunn

Hafliði Hallgrimsson

Donny Hartman

Jay Heck

Mike Howlett

Brian Humphries (via e-mail)

Peter Jenner

Nigel Lesmoir-Gordon

Didier Malherbe

Richard Manning

Pearce Marchbank

Pat Martin

Durga McBroom

Mike McInnerney

Michael Meschke

George Dennis O'Brien

Alan Parsons

Joe Petagno

Aubrey Powell ("Po")

Eddie Prévost

Stephen Pyle

Tim Sanders

Neil Rice

Igor Sklyarov
Eric "Eroc" Sosinski
Jenny Spires
Shel Talmy

Cyrille Verdeaux
Martyn Ware
Stuart Watson
Joshua White

ARCHIVED ORIGINAL INTERVIEWS

John "Twink" Alder
Jody Ashworth
Mike Butcher
Gary Duncan
Richard Evans

John Helliwell
Hugh Hopper
Anthony Stern
Eric Woolfson

SELECTED DISCOGRAPHY

WYWH AND RELATED RELEASES

Wish You Were Here (Columbia vinyl, PC 33453, 1975)

Wish You Were Here (Columbia vinyl, white cover DJ version, PC 33453, 1975)

Wish You Were Here (Harvest cassette, TC-SHVL 814, 1975)

Wish You Were Here (Columbia eight-track, CAQ 33453, 1975)

Wish You Were Here (Columbia CD, CK 33453, 1975)

Wish You Were Here (CBS green vinyl, CBS 80955, 1975)

Wish You Were Here (Columbia vinyl, half-speed mastered, HC 33453, 1981)

Wish You Were Here (Minidisc, Columbia, CM 33453, 1994)

Wish You Were Here (CBS|Sony yellow vinyl, 30AP 1875-01, 2003)

Wish You Were Here Discovery Edition (B004ZN9T00, 2011)

Wish You Were Here (Thirty-Fifth Anniversary Edition, Analogue Productions, SACD, CAPP 33453 SA, 2011)

Wish You Were Here (Limited edition picture disc, date unknown)

Wish You Were Here (180 gram vinyl, APFLR 42618, 2011)

Wish You Were Here: Experience Edition (EMI CD, 4607|47909508 30274, 2011)

Wish You Were Here: Immersion Box Set (EMI CD, 5099 029435 2 7, 2011)

Wish You Were Here (Sony CD, PFR9 88875170922, 2016)

PINK FLOYD ALBUMS: COMPILATIONS, STUDIO, AND LIVE RELEASES

The Piper at the Gates of Dawn (1967)

A Saucerful of Secrets (1968)

More (1969)

Ummagumma (1969)

The Best of the Pink Floyd (1970; later released as *Masters of Rock*, 1974)

Atom Heart Mother (1970)

Meddle (1971)

Relics (1971)

Obscured by Clouds (1972)

The Dark Side of the Moon (1973)

A Nice Pair: The Piper at the Gates of Dawn / A Saucerful of Secrets (1973)

Wish You Were Here (1975)

Tour '75 (1975)

Animals (1977)

The Wall (1979)

The First XI (EMI boxed set, 1979)

A Collection of Great Dance Songs (1981)

The Final Cut (1983)

Works (1983)

A Momentary Lapse of Reason (1987)

Delicate Sound of Thunder (1988)

Tonite Let's All Make Love in London . . . Plus (1991)

Shine On Boxed Set (1992)

The Division Bell (1994)

Pink Floyd: London '66–'67 (1995)

P.U.L.S.E. (1995)

Is There Anybody Out There: The Wall Live 1980–81 (2000)

Echoes: The Best of Pink Floyd (2001)

Oh, By the Way (2007)

Discovery: Pink Floyd Boxed Set (remastered studio albums, 2011)

Pink Floyd Sampler (part of the *Why Pink Floyd . . . ?* series, 2011)

The Best of Pink Floyd: A Foot in the Door (2011)

The Endless River (2014)

1965: Their First Recordings (2015)

The Early Years 1965–1972 (2016)

Cre/ation: The Early Years 1967-1972 (2016)

London 1966/1967 (2017, CD/DVD/LP vinyl reissued by Snapper Music)

Cambridge St/ation: The Early Years 1965–1967 (2017)

Dramatis/ation: The Early Years 1969 (2017)

Devi/ation: The Early Years 1970 (2017)

Germin/ation: The Early Years 1968 (2017)

Obfusc/ation: The Early Years 1972 (2017)

Reverber/ation: The Early Years 1971 (2017)

The Later Years 1987–2019 (2019)

SELECTED PINK FLOYD SINGLES

"Have a Cigar"/"Shine On You Crazy Diamond Part 1" (France, 2C 010-97-357)

"Have a Cigar"/"Shine On You Crazy Diamond Part 1" (France JB HAR 600.190, DJ/Jukebox)

"Have a Cigar"/"Shine On You Crazy Diamond Part 1" (Italy, 3C 006-97357)

"Have a Cigar"/"Welcome to the Machine" (US, 3-10248)

"Have a Cigar"/"Welcome to the Machine" (Japan, SOPB 347)

"Have a Cigar"/"Welcome to the Machine" (Australia, BA 222183)

Wish You Were Here, three-track CD single (UK, LC 0542)

SELECTED OTHER FLOYD SINGLES

"Lucy Leave"/"King Bee" (1965, EMIdisk, under The Pink Floyd)

"Arnold Layne"/"Candy and a Currant Bun" (1967, Columbia DB 8156, mono)

"Arnold Layne"/"Candy and a Currant Bun" (1967, Tower Records)

"See Emily Play"/"Scarecrow" (1967, Columbia DB 8214)

"See Emily Play"/"The Scarecrow" (1967, Tower Records 356)

"See Emily Play"/"The Last Thing on my Mind" by the Seekers (1967, Columbia 8214, 8134 respectively)

"See Emily Play"/"Scarecrow"/"Arnold Layne"/"Candy and a Currant Bun" (1967, Spain, four-track 45 rpm, Compañia Del Gramofono-Odeon/La Voz De Su Amo EPL 14.377)

"Apples and Oranges"/"Paintbox" (1967, UK, Columbia DB 8310)

"Flaming"/"The Gnome" (1967, US only, Tower Records 378)

"Let There Be More Light"/"Remember a Day" (1968, US, Tower Records 440)

"It Would Be So Nice"/"Julia Dream" (1968, UK, Columbia DB 8401)

"Point Me at the Sky"/"Careful with That Axe, Eugene" (1968, UK, Columbia DB 8511)

"The Nile Song"/"Ibiza Bar" (1969, France, Columbia 2C 006-04506M)

"One of These Days"/"Fearless" (1971, US, Capitol Records PRO-6378 mono promo)

"One of These Days"/"Fearless" (1971, US, Capitol Records 3240)

"Free Four"/"Stay" (1972, US, Capitol 3391)

"Money"/"Any Colour You Like" (1973, US, Harvest 3609)

"Time"/"Us and Them" (1974, US, Harvest 3832)

"Another Brick in the Wall, Part 2"/"One of My Turns" (1979, UK, Harvest HAR 5194)

"Another Brick in the Wall, Part 2"/"Another Brick in the Wall, Part 2" (1979, US promo, Columbia 1-11187)

"Another Brick in the Wall, Part 2"/"One of My Turns" (1980, US reissue, Columbia 1-11187)

"Run Like Hell"/"Don't Leave Me Now" (1980, US, Columbia 1-11265)

"Comfortably Numb"/"Comfortably Numb" (1980, US promo Columbia 1-11311)

"When the Tigers Broke Free"/"Bring the Boys Back Home" (1982, *The Wall—Music from the Film*, UK, Harvest 5222)

"When the Tigers Broke Free"/"Bring the Boys Back Home" (1982, *The Wall—Music from the Film*, US, Columbia X18 03142)

"Not Now John"/"The Hero's Return, Parts I and II" (1983, US, Columbia 38-03905)

"Learning to Fly"/"Terminal Frost" (1987, US, Columbia 38-07363)

"One Slip"/"Terminal Frost" (1987, UK, limited edition EMI EMG 52)

"On the Turning Away"/"Run Like Hell" live (recorded in Atlanta, 1987) (1987, US, Columbia 38 07660)

"Take it Back"/"Astronomy Domine" live (recorded at Joe Robbie Stadium, Miami, Florida) (1994, US, Columbia 38-77493)

"High Hopes"/"Keep Talking"/"One of These Days" (live) (1994, CD single EMI CDEMS 342)

"Interstellar Overdrive" (2017, believed to have been recorded in 1966, one-sided twelve-inch, Pink Floyd Records PFR12S6-A)

SELECTED PINK FLOYD APPEARANCES AND SAMPLERS

Various, *Progressive Story* (four-LP set, EMI Italy, 1968)

Various, *Underground* (Tower Records compilation, 1969)

Zabriskie Point soundtrack (1970)

Picnic—A Breath of Fresh Air (1970)

The Heavyweights (double LP, featuring "Have a Cigar," 1975)

A Harvest Sampler (featuring "Point Me at the Sky") (1978)

The Harvest Story, Vol. 1: Art School Dancing (1984)

Live8 (2005)

A Breath of Fresh Air—A Harvest Records Anthology 1969–1974 (2007)

DAVID GILMOUR

David Gilmour (1978)

About Face (1984)

David Gilmour in Concert (2002)

On an Island (2006)

Remember That Night: Live at the Royal Albert Hall (2007)

Live in Gdańsk (2008)

Rattle That Lock (2015)

Live at Pompeii (2017)

DAVID GILMOUR (PRODUCER)

Unicorn, *Blue Pine Trees* (1974)

Unicorn, *Too Many Crooks* (1976)

Unicorn, *One More Tomorrow* (1978)

Kate Bush, *The Kick Inside* (co-producer, 1978)

Kate Bush, *Army Dreamers* (seven-inch, co-produced "Passing Through Air," 1980)

The Dream Academy, s/t (co-producer, performer, 1985)

The Dream Academy, *A Different Kind of Weather* (co-producer, performer, 1990)

DAVID GILMOUR (APPEARANCES)

Jokers Wild (five-song, one-sided 33 1/3 LP, 1965, limited release;
    later appeared in 1997)

Roy Harper, *HQ* (1975)

David Courtney, *First Day* (1975)

Roy Harper, *The Unknown Soldier* (1980)

Kate Bush, *Passing Through Air* (1980)

Kate Bush, *The Dreaming* (1982)

Paul McCartney, *Give My Regards to Broad Street* (1984)

Bryan Ferry, *Boys and Girls* (1985)

Pete Townsend, *White City: A Novel* (1985)

Supertramp, *Brother, Where You Bound?* (1985)

Pete Townshend, *Deep End Live!* (1986)

Various Artists, *The Secret Policemen's Third Ball: The Music*
    (1987)

Kate Bush, *The Sensual World* (1989)

Blue Pearl, *Naked* (1990)

B. B. King, *Deuces Wild* (1997)

Jools Holland, *Jools Holland, His Rhythm & Blues Orchestra and Friends*
    (Warner Music, 2001)

Alan Parsons, *A Valid Path* (2004)

Bryan Ferry, *Olympia* (2010)

The Orb featuring David Gilmour, *Metallic Spheres* (2010)

NICK MASON

Fictitious Sports (1981)

Profiles (1985)

White of the Eye (1987)

Unattended Luggage: Boxed Set (2018)

NICK MASON (PRODUCER)

Principal Edwards Magic Theatre, *The Asmoto Running Band* (1971)

Principal Edwards, *Round One* (1974)

Robert Wyatt, *Rock Bottom* (1974)

Robert Wyatt, *Ruth Is Stranger Than Richard* (1975)

Gong, *Shamal* (1975)

The Damned, *Music for Pleasure* (1977)

Steve Hillage, *Green* (1978, credited as producer and performer)

Steve Hillage, *Aura* (1979; Mason appears as producer and performer for single
    "Getting Better"/"Palm Trees (Love Guitar)")

Gong, *Wingful of Eyes: A Retrospective—'75—'78* (1986)

NICK MASON (OTHER APPEARANCES)

Various, *V.* Virgin compilation (with Robert Wyatt on "Yesterday Man," 1975)

Michael Mantler, *The Hapless Child: And Other Inscrutable Stories* (also co-engineered, 1976)

Michael Mantler, Live (1987)

Robert Wyatt & Friends, *In Concert: Theatre Royal Drury Lane, 8th September 1974* (2005)

RICK WRIGHT

Wet Dream (1978)

Broken China (1996)

RICK WRIGHT (APPEARANCES)

Zee, *Identity* (1984)

Blue Pearl, *Naked* (1990)

Snowy White, *Goldtop: Groups & Sessions 1974–1994* (1995)

The Orb, *The Orb Remix Project: Auntie Aubrey's Excursions Beyond the Call of Duty Part 2* (remix of "Runaway," 2001)

Wright, Gilmour, and David Bowie, "Arnold Layne" (single, 2006)

ROGER WATERS

Music from the Body (with Ron Geesin, special Pink Floyd appearance on "Birth of a Smile," 1970)

The Pros and Cons of Hitch Hiking (1984)

Radio K.A.O.S. (1987)

The Wall Live in Berlin (1990)

Amused to Death (1992)

In the Flesh (2000)

Flickering Flame: The Solo Years, Vol. 1 (limited edition, 2002)

Ca Ira (2005)

The Wall (2015)

Is This the Life We Really Want? (2017)

ROGER WATERS (APPEARANCES)

When the Wind Blows Original Motion Picture Soundtrack (with the Bleeding Heart Band, 1986)

The Legend of 1900: Original Motion Picture Soundtrack (music by Ennio Morricone)

Marianne Faithful, *Vagabond Ways* (songwriter, 1999)

The Last Mimzy: Original Motion Picture Soundtrack (music by Howard Shore, 2007, co-produced "Hello (I Love You)")

12-12-12: The Concert for Sandy Relief (To Benefit the Robin Hood Relief Fund) (2013)

SYD BARRETT

The Madcap Laughs (1970)

Barrett (1970)

The Madcap Laughs/Barrett (includes *The Madcap Laughs* and *Barrett*, 1974)

The Peel Session (1987)

Opel (1988)

Wouldn't You Miss Me (Dark Globe) (1988, Capitol Records LP promo)

Octopus: The Best Of (1992)

Crazy Diamond Box Set (1993)

Crazy Diamond four-track EP (1993, limited edition via Capitol Records)

The Best of Syd Barrett: Wouldn't You Miss Me? (2001)

The Radio One Sessions (2004)

An Introduction to Syd Barrett (2010)

SYD BARRETT (APPEARANCES)

Last Minute Put Together Boogie Band, *Six Hour Technicolour Dream* (2014)

DVD/VIDEO/FILM (LIST INCLUDES CONCERTS, CONCERT FOOTAGE, AND DOCUMENTARIES, EXCEPT WHERE INDICATED)

Tonite Let's All Make Love in London (Peter Whitehead doc, 1967)

San Francisco (music only, directed by Anthony Stern, 1968)

More (music only, 1969)

Stamping Ground (1971)

La Vallée (The Valley, a.k.a. *Obscured by Clouds)* (music only, 1972)

Rock City (1973)

Crystal Voyager (music only, 1973)

Pink Floyd Live at Pompeii (VHS, 1984)

The Wall (VHS, 1989; DVD, 2005)

Delicate Sound of Thunder (VHS, 1989)

Le Carrera Panamericana (old, edited, and new Floyd material used for soundtrack, VHS, 1992)

Pink Floyd: London '66–'67 (filmed by Peter Whitehead at Sound Techniques, released 1994)

The Pink Floyd and Syd Barrett Story (NBD, Voiceprint, 2001)

Live at Knebworth (2002, recorded 1990)

Pink Floyd: The Dark Side of the Moon (Classic Albums, Eagle Rock Entertainment, 2003)

Pink Floyd Live at Pompeii: The Director's Cut (DVD, 2003)

P.U.L.S.E. (Columbia, 2005)

Pink Floyd: Behind the Wall (2011)

Pink Floyd: The Story of Wish You Were Here (Eagle Rock Entertainment, 2012)

P.U.L.S.E. (Parlophone, 2014)

ADDITIONAL DVD/VIDEO/FILM SOLO & APPEARANCES

David Gilmour

Solo:

David Gilmour (1984, recorded live at the Hammersmith Odeon)

In Concert (2002)

Live and in Session (2006)

Remember That Night: Live at the Royal Albert Hall (2007)

At Hammersmith Odeon (DVD, 2008)

London 1984 (2011)

Appearances:

Pete Townshend's Deep End: *The Brixton, England Concert* (1986)

Les Paul & Friends: *He Changed the Music: LIVE at the Brooklyn Academy of Music in New York* (1991)

Colours of Infinity, presented by Arthur C. Clarke (directed/co-written/produced by Nigel Lesmoir-Gordon; Gilmour provides music, 1994)

Paul McCartney: *Live at the Tavern Club (2001)*

Roger Waters

Radio K.A.O.S. (1988)

The Wall: Live in Berlin (2003)

In the Flesh: Live (2000)

The Wall (2015)

SELECTED UNOFFICIAL PINK FLOYD RELEASES

BBC Archives (1967–1969)

Amazing Pudding in Bath 1970 (Floyd scheduled to appear June 27; recording made June 28, 1970)

The Masked Gadgets & Hercules (1970–1974)

Black Holes in the Sky (recorded at Empire Pool, Wembley, London, November 15, 1974)

BBC Archives 1974 (recorded at Empire Pool, Wembley, London, November 16, 1974)

British Winter Tour '74 (recorded at Trentham Gardens, Stoke on Trent, November 19, 1974)

Riding the Cow (recorded at Cow Palace, San Francisco, April 13, 1975)

Cruel but Fair (recorded at Los Angeles Memorial Sports Arena, April 26, 1975)

Pink Millard (recorded at Los Angeles Memorial Sports Arena, April 26, 1975)

Dragged Down by the Stone (recorded at Nassau Coliseum, Uniondale, New York, June 7, 1975)

Exposed in the Light of Landover (recorded at Capital Centre, Landover, Maryland, June 9, 1975)

Havin' a Cigar (recorded at Capital Centre, Landover, Maryland, June 10, 1975)

Rave Master (recorded Boston Garden, June 18, 1975)

All Due Respect (recorded at Olympia Stadium, Detroit, Michigan, June 24, 1975)

Hamilton '75 (recorded at Ivor Wynne Stadium, Hamilton, Canada, June 28, 1975)

Yesterday's Triumph (recorded at Knebworth, United Kingdom, July 5, 1975)

A Great Live Set (1977)

Animals at the Omni (recorded in Atlanta, Georgia, April 26, 1977)

Live at the Oakland Coliseum, billed as the Abdabs (recorded May 9, 1977)

Caught in the Crossfire (recorded at Madison Square Garden, New York City, July 2, 1977, and BBC, London, 1971)

Live in NYC: 1977 (recorded 1977)

Welcome to the Machine (recorded in Frankfurt, Germany, January 27, 1977)

The Committee and Other Stories (includes soundtrack to film, 1985)

The Man (recorded at Concertgebouw in Amsterdam, September 17, 1969, released 1985)

The Dark Side of the Moo (1967–1971, released 1986)

The Calhoun Tapes (recorded in Atlanta, Georgia, 1987)

Tongue Tied & Twisted (recorded in Los Angeles, November 26, 1987)

Rhapsody in Pink: The Psychedelic Years, billed as the Screaming Abdabs (1990)

Paris 1977 (recorded February 25, 1977, released 1991)

Wish You Were Here Trance Remixes (1994, limited edition, unofficial)

Jurassic Sparks (recorded in Pasadena, April 17, 1994, released 1994)

Echoes from Osaka (recorded in Osaka, Japan, March 9, 1972, released 1995)

Psychedelic Games for May (1996)

Amsterdam 1969 (see *The Man* for details, 1999)

Respect for These Knights (The Copenhagen Secret Gig) (credited to the Fishermen, recorded at the Annabels Disco and Night Club, Copenhagen, August 1, 1988, released 2009)

Ceci N'est Pas Une Version Officielle (unknown)

INDEX